The
Indian Way

INDIANS AND THE NORTH AMERICAN FUR TRADE

Neil Van Sickle and Evelyn Rodewald

ISBN: 1-4662-6202-8
ISBN-13: 978-1-4662-6202-7
LCCN: 2011915257
CreateSpace, North Charleston, SC

DEDICATION

This book is dedicated to my wife Faye Van Sickle,
who was my constant companion in research.

Take the best of the white man's road, pick it up and take it with you. That which is bad leave alone, cast it away. Take the best of the old Indian ways, always keep them, do not let them die.[1] *Sitting Bull*

CONTENTS

ILLUSTRATIONS AND MAPS

ACKNOWLEDGMENTS

Jennifer S. H. Brown, professor of history at the University of Winnipeg and former director of the Centre for Rupert's Land Studies, crystallized our theme by her belief in the importance of the Indian role in the fur trade. Though we have visited many fur trade sites and appreciate the help of the site managers, our principal reliance has been on state historical societies, as well as public and university libraries and archives in Canada and the United States, Hudson's Bay Company Archives, and the Missouri Historical Society at St. Louis. In every place, we found enthusiastic and understanding help. The reference staff of the Flathead County Library borrowed many books at our request. We are greatly obligated to Timothy J. Kent for his generous canoe expertise; William R. Swagerty for his broad appreciation of western history and friendly advice; Anne Morton, reference chief at the Hudson's Bay Company Archives, and her helpful staff; Martha Clevenger, former director of Collections and Conservation at the Missouri Historical Society; Elizabeth Vibert, Department of History, University of Victoria; Anne Acco of Cumberland House; anthropologist James A. Clifton, University of Wisconsin; Sylvia Van Kirk, professor emeritus of the University of Toronto; and the Canadian Departments of Parks and Tourism—to name only a few who filled our notebooks over the years. Historian Anne Millbrooke's comprehensive editing made a significant contribution. The essential brevity of this acknowledgment neglects many whose names appear in the bibliography. In addition, my coauthor, Evelyn Rodewald; the support of her husband, Gordon; and the companionship, research help, and patience of my late wife, Faye, made the work possible.

INTRODUCTION

The creation of *The Indian Way: The North American Fur Trade* was inspired by our realization that works about the fur trade in both Canada and the United States were written from the European viewpoint. Fur-trade history has been largely a portrayal of the courageous, persevering penetration of the new North American continent by European explorers and entrepreneurs, extending from the early sixteenth to the mid-nineteenth centuries. Their motivation has been correctly portrayed as a fascination with vast lands, empire expansion, and profit from North America's apparently unlimited fur-bearing resources.

To describe this endeavor, most works about the fur trade view the aboriginal as a hindrance to be managed, overcome, or exploited. While the collection of pelts, primarily of beaver, might have occurred in a new land devoid of any native human presence, the entire style and sequence of events relied upon, and exploited, aboriginal lifestyles, knowledge, wilderness skills in living and travel, and also the incessant labor of Indian women.

We actively conducted research over a period of at least fifteen years, probing and expanding as the critical role of aboriginal people was appreciated. Admittedly, we had a tourist-like desire to see the places known from aboriginal living and legend, as well as those resulting from the white man's exploration and building. From this exploration, the concept of a book began to materialize. During these travels, many archivists and librarians gave their unstinting support.

We have used, as far as possible, aboriginal oral history, and have relied upon recognized ethnological expertise to portray aboriginal participation. The broad, general aspects of aboriginal cultures were always present, and the white man, at his cost and peril, often failed to see and learn this pervasive reality.

To successfully manage such a broad subject, we have centered our work around 1833, a year of substantial maturity of the fur trade.

CHAPTER 1:

INDIAN CULTURE

The white man, coming to North America in the early seventeenth century, believed he was bringing a method of trapping, traveling, and trading that would exploit the wilderness to great profit in furs, principally beaver. Instead the North American fur trade rested in the cradle of the Indian culture and a European had much to learn if he were to make a profit. The trader was ignorant of the nature and extent of North America and its people. Neither his rural nor his urban habits and skills enabled him to travel, trap, trade, command aboriginal cooperation and respect, or even survive in the new land. In addition, the European was saddled with a strict class-consciousness and an inbred sense of superiority that could not accept the native as a partner. He had to learn to respect the Indians' ways and values.

The culture widely found among Indians across North America—and which had a direct impact on the fur trade—included, perhaps first of all, hospitality; but other aspects were the provision of food, means of travel, the role of trade middlemen, land ownership, the importance of ceremonies, gift giving, language skills, family life, transportation, war, and revenge. While focusing on the indigenous culture of the fur-trade story, we can only flash spots of light on this rich, varied, fascinating lifestyle that became part of the very nature of the fur trade.

Aboriginals had adapted to their environment, living in settled villages, raising crops, hunting, and fishing; or if the environment was not amenable to crops, they were nomadic hunters and gatherers. Maize, beans, and squash, developed in the Americas, had, over the centuries, been adapted to diverse climate and agricultural conditions and were staples of local diet. Cornfields were found by European settlers in Virginia and Massachusetts, by Champlain with the Huron, along the Missouri river, and south to the Pueblo villages. In 1826 the Paiutes showed Jedediah Smith their irrigated corn, growing out of the red soil of the Great Basin. The Mescalero Apache planted corn on the plains of New Mexico, and the Mohave irrigated their corn, squash, and bean fields from the Colorado River. These and other vegetables were widely traded. For meat, the Europeans—both traders and colonists—depended on native hunters for fresh buffalo, elk, deer, geese, and fish. Pemmican, which was made from bison or salmon, was produced in lodges across the continent and made possible the fur trade in the Far North.

Indian people have always traded. From northern British Columbia, southern California, eastern Oregon, and Wyoming, a series of middlemen brought obsidian for arrowheads and spearheads. Amber moved southward from the Arctic, and marine shells and diverse dentalia decorated necks, ears, and clothing far from the source.

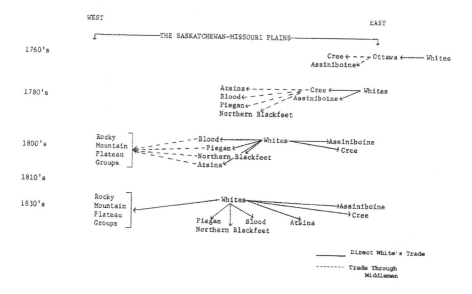

Fig. 1.1 Middleman Trade Patterns, "The Middleman Role in the Fur Trade," S. Giannettino, *Western Canadian Journal of Anthropology*, vol vii, No 4 (1977) p. 26, Fig. 3. By permission.

Native travel depended on memorizing the terrain as they moved through forests or along rivers and lakes.[2] They shared information using linear sketches in the sand that emphasized the trail through hills, bends, rapids, or mountain passes. Indians measured distance by "sleeps" rather than space. In the winter of 1823, when Americans wintered with the Crow in present Wyoming, long discussions around the fire resulted in them copying into their journals the maps that would lead them to beaver streams.[3]

On the plains, well-known trade centers included the Dakota Rendezvous at the mouth of the James River, where the Dakota bands Yanktonai, Sisseton, Yankton, and Teton came to trade. In the south, the permanent Pecos and Zuni pueblos along the Rio Grande welcomed Plains tribes such as the Apache, Kiowa, and Comanche to their trading fairs, where they traded their corn, squash, and beans for buffalo meat and animal hides.

The agricultural villages of the Arikara and Mandan on the upper Missouri River were both important sources of horses and food for early traders. The Cheyenne and Crow brought horses from the south and traded them for vegetables. Na-Kwoel of the Stuart Lake Carrier band in British Columbia acquired an iron ax in about 1730 while trading on the Skeena River, where no European or Asian traders had ever appeared.[4]

Historian Arthur Ray, discussing the seventeenth-century trade on Hudson's Bay, pointed out that Indian middleman really controlled the fur trade from the beginning. As fur-trading posts appeared, the Cree became brokers between Canadian traders and other tribes, such as the Chipewyan, Blackfoot, Assiniboin, and Mandan. Their middlemen reached from the Mackenzie River basin to the Missouri, trading with the Dene in the Far North and the Assiniboin to their southwest. They acquired trade guns and ammunition from the French, the North West Company, and later the Hudson's Bay Company, and the superior armament enabled the Cree, and their alliance with the Assiniboin, to gain a firm foothold on the plains.[5] They traded not only for furs and robes, but also horses, pemmican, and slaves.

The concept of land ownership created friction among groups. Europeans believed that "new" land, and the New World, belonged to them by right of conquest. But this belief was not limited to whites. The Iroquois, the Cree, and the Sioux also displayed this mentality in their westward progression. To them "ownership" was defined as controlling access to preferred hunting, fishing, water, and camps. Warring over hunting grounds went on for years, and examples reach throughout North America.

In the early eighteenth century, the Chippewa had attacked the Dakota villages at Mille Lacs and pushed the Dakota Sioux beyond the Mississippi River, out of their historical hunting grounds and the wild-rice area. The Cheyenne, who had been farmers in that region, were then forced south and west, changing from an agricultural society to one of buffalo hunting on the plains, and they became the prosperous middlemen of the plains' horse trade.

The Osage middlemen on the Mississippi River received trade goods— and passed them on to other agricultural tribes. As the Osage moved west toward the Missouri River, where they were dominant traders and warriors, a powerful tribe and widely feared on the central prairie, the Kiowa, Comanche and later the Cherokee became their enemies in the rivalry over horses and hunting grounds.[6]

The practice of giving gifts also had a deep significance. A trader established his trustworthiness by giving gifts. "Gifts were part of the very thread that bound the Ojibwa into a society; the organizing principle of their economy and culture: kinship," according to historian Bruce White. "If you wished to seek to establish with someone a relationship that had all the rights and obligations that were found in the family... you gave gifts."[7]

Gifts could provide reparation for an inflicted injury, even murder, and appease the characteristic passion for revenge. The manner of giving, the role and status of the participants, the words spoken, and the attendant ceremony all indicated the value the gifts represented. Gifts from Europeans were at times considered a payment for the use of land for trading posts or freedom of travel. Beads, rum, tobacco, and clothing were given by trading companies to secure trading loyalty.

Ceremonies established the atmosphere for trade and could not be aborted or hurried, but respected and observed by traders. Ceremonies were usually identified with nature, respect for animals, and personal power, or "medicine." Individual dignity and fortitude, eloquence, love of posing and drama, and the mystery assigned to tobacco and the pipe, or "calumet," governed all. Most Native Americans made use of some

form of pipe ceremony, using native tobacco or bark as smoking material and pipes of various sizes, decoration, and materials. The smoke of
the pipes carried prayers to the sky, and could establish a bond between
groups or gain protection from enemies.

Smoking a pipe with your host as you moved through native home-
lands was a simple courtesy and established trust. In 1822, as fur traders
William Ashley and Jedediah Smith stopped at the Mandan village, a
trip described in Chapter 13, they spent a day in council smoking with
tribal leaders and discussing their plans for building a trading post and
for trapping.

Trading itself was no less stylized and just as obviously rooted in
ancient trading practices. The native approach to the trading post involved certain parade-like courtesies that required appropriate flour-
ish and precision in both the offering and the reception, including, at
times, cannon salutes and flag displays. A trading chief initiated the
trade, but only after a ceremonious exchange of gifts and compliments,
and often a pipe ceremony. The native gift might be dried meat, wild
rice, or other food item; the trader would respond with rum, knives,
flint, powder, shot, beads, or ribbons.

As Rocky Mountain fur trader Jedediah Smith traveled with his party
of trappers to the Southwest in the fall of 1826, a Ute approached him
with a gift of corn as a symbol of peace, and he returned the compliment
with the usual twists of tobacco and other trade goods. A form of tobacco
grew in many areas of North America, but when in the seventeenth century Hudson's Bay Company (HBC) traders introduced Brazilian tobacco
as a trade item, the Indians preferred it above all others.

The multiplicity of language was a problem for native and newcomer
alike. Though many tribes were part of the same linguistic family, each
language had many local dialects. Women who married into the band

and slaves from other tribes were often used as interpreters within the villages. As the numbers of multilingual fur traders and employees expanded and spoke English, French, Spanish, Iroquois, or Cree, they also acted as interpreters. Sign language was in its most developed form on the plains and was used widely from Mexico to Canada.

Trade jargon developed at coastal trade sites on the Atlantic, Gulf of Mexico, and in the Arctic. Within our time frame of the early nineteenth century, the Chinook Jargon expanded up the Columbia River from the Pacific. The speech was based on the Chinook, Nootka, and Shahaptin languages of the coastal tribes and expanded by the various languages spoken by visiting sailors. The additional impetus of the English and French used at Astoria and Fort Vancouver resulted in a useful jargon that became the most widely used lingua franca throughout the Columbia Plateau.

The structure of the family, although at first seemingly irrelevant to the fur-trading Europeans, came to broadly affect the trading environment. As Europeans married native women, the new family relationships strengthened the position of the fur trader. Throughout native family life, there was strict protocol, and respect for elders was automatic. Marriage, generally arranged by the parents, was formalized by gift giving, a simple ceremony, and usually a post-nuptial celebration.

The role of native women was often more complex than superficial observation indicated, and it varied from nation to nation. In nomadic hunter-gatherer tribes, a woman's strength and skills were essential in camp and to survival on the trail, and she owned the camp, from utensils to shelter. She captured small game and harvested roots and berries. Earlier, women on the plains had directly participated in the bison hunt, but with the advent of the horse, their role devolved into taking care of the meat and cleaning and scraping the hides.

Fig. 1.2 The Ojibway girls, a trader said, 'have pretty black eyes, which they know
well how to humor in a languishing and engaging manner.'
Painted by Eastman Johnson, courtesy of the St. Louis County Historical Society,
Duluth, Minn.

In aboriginal agrarian mythology, women were regarded as the source of life. The land and produce belonged to them, and they planted and harvested the crops. In many, if not most, tribes, women occupied a subordinate role in decision making and were even considered as chattels for barter or diplomacy. But there were also tribes where women expressed opinions in tribal or band council and where their views were often considered significant.

The role of the fur-trader's wife varied by location, whether in a village, a camp, or at a post. Among some tribes, having a native wife allowed an independent trader to benefit from the same use of the land as other band members. In New Mexico, a native wife legalized his trapping and trading.

The acquisition of fur pelts, deerskins, and buffalo robes; the purchase and positioning of trade goods; and the providing of provisions all depended on long-range transportation. Natives developed a variety of watercraft, including dugouts and rafts of logs, kayaks, umiaks (wooden boats covered with skins), the Aleut baidarkas developed for ocean hunting, and the famous birchbark canoe. Of all the aboriginal contributions to the North American fur trade, the birchbark canoe was unique in its almost universal utility and adaptability. It permitted the penetration of the water courses extending from the St. Lawrence and Hudson's Bay, the subarctic, and the Great Lakes/Mississippi valley into remote but profitable trapping and trading areas.

Another practical form of water transportation was the bullboat. Hudson's Bay Company traders saw bullboats used by the Mandan on the Missouri River in the late eighteenth century. They were a useful conveyance for people who lived on the plains, where green, untreated bison hides were plentiful and the rivers were bordered by willows. Used often by women, bullboats were easily constructed with branches for the framework and covered with a bison hide, which, as it dried, shrank tightly around the framework. The circular tubs transported meat, firewood, furs, and children across rivers and lakes.

As the fur traders stood on the edge of the prairie and faced westward toward the mountains, they needed to go where canoes could not take them. This environment required walking hundreds, even thousands, of miles over sometimes obscure and dangerous trails. The native construction and use of snowshoes for winter travel quickly spread among Europeans. The toboggan was also developed to carry large loads of meat and other provisions, and was pulled by both humans and dogs.

The domestication of dogs was first practiced in North America. On the plains, dogs were trained and harnessed to pull a travois, particularly in moving villages from place to place. When the plains people first saw the horse, they identified it as a big dog and developed a larger travois, often using the lodge poles, to carry larger loads. In addition to the utility of dogs for pulling and carrying, their ubiquitous presence allowed dogs to be used as food, either as a delicacy or necessity. As horses became more widely available, they replaced pack dogs.

The Apache, living on the borders of the Spanish settlements, may have been the first aboriginals to ride horses. The widespread adoption of horses permitted heavier loads, greater speeds, and more direct trails to water sources, and facilitated the bison hunt. Demand for horses among Indians became and remained strong, and they were a principal trade item. In less than one hundred years, the horse spread from the Rio Grande to the Saskatchewan River, numbering, by estimates of various observers, from nearly eighteen thousand by 1835 to more than half a million by 1875.[8] The demand for horses for the fur trade accentuated this movement. Pack trains that moved large amounts of goods, particularly on the brigade trails to the Snake River plain and California, helped make the years after 1830 the most productive for both the American and Canadian fur companies.

The Shoshone, or Snakes, terrorized the northern plains from horse-back, using as weapons bows and arrows and stone clubs until they were challenged by the Blackfoot equipped with guns. The Blackfoot apparently were the first of the northern tribes to have both horses and guns.[9] Just as southwestern natives acquired status through the horse trade, in the north, the Cree, Assiniboin, and Blackfoot acquired power through the trade of new and used firearms.

The Blackfoot made strenuous efforts to prevent the movement of guns and ammunition west of the Rockies to keep them out of the hands of their enemies, the Kutenai and the Salish. So intense was this effort, they blocked the passes across the southern Canadian Rockies, forcing the HBC to use the more northern Athabasca Pass to reach the furs of the Columbia plain and New Caledonia.

Between whites and natives, cultural misunderstandings about theft and murder led to the most serious difficulties. To the native, theft was merely taking what you needed; if someone had a surplus, it was acceptable to take some of it, particularly horses, guns, or knives. If necessary, the only punishment would be to return the item. The Crow were outstanding horse thieves, but if confronted they would either return them or sell them back. Stealing horses was a widespread tribal activity. To the white fur traders, horses were personal possessions needed to carry loads or provide transportation, and they might kill someone who stole them.

Some murders were acceptable, according to Edwin Thompson Denig, an American Fur Company trader who compiled an extensive report on the Assiniboin and other nations of the northern plains. He found that it was considered acceptable to kill white intruders if they interfered with Indian activities or provided guns to their enemies. They did not kill without provocation, unless the opponent was an enemy. Killing an enemy was considered a good thing, an act of self-preservation to remove any danger in the way.[10]

Murder could also start a revenge reaction that could go on for years or generations. Even a fancied slight could precipitate a long-enduring, revengeful, war-seeking passion. The need for revenge could be locked up, only to erupt years later. Revenge could be extracted from a perceived offender or from any of his relatives or friends. When Jedediah Smith and his party returned to the Southwest in 1828, as described in Chapter 17, and attempted to cross the Colorado River at the Mojave villages, they were attacked. Ten of Smith's parties were killed and the women with them were captured. Unknown to them, about a year earlier, trapper Ewing Young and others from Santa Fe had visited the Mojave, and there had been a scrimmage resulting in a number of Mojave killed.

War was constantly in the native mind. "Indians to be Indians must have war," historian Alvin M. Josephy wrote, "Without it the young men have no occupation, no ambition, even if so disposed can do nothing to render their names and characters conspicuous."[11] Killing an enemy, or "counting coup" by touching rather than killing an enemy, taking a scalp, or stealing horses brought distinction, which was necessary for a young warrior to earn a respected place in aboriginal society. Certainly without a creditable record in war, the young man could not expect the hand of a respectable young woman.

War and revenge interfered with the flow of commerce, either through the middlemen or at the trading posts. The fur traders recognized that they must work within that system and actively support peace treaties.

The fur trade prospered only as it adapted to the culture of Native Americans. Yet European goods and mores were the weft, and Native American culture was the warp that formed the tapestry of the fur trade. Inevitably, both native and white learned from each other.

CHAPTER 2:

BEGINNINGS ON THE ST. LAWRENCE

For three hundred years, there were North American fur-trade efforts, from the Mississippi Delta to the Arctic, and from New England to the Pacific. But the fur trade of the greatest significance, and the trade with which this book deals, was in Canada, from the mouth of the St. Lawrence River and James Bay to Victoria Island and northward to the Arctic, and in the United States, from Lake of the Woods to Santa Fe and from Ohio to the Pacific.

First there were the Algonquian-speaking Micmac of Nova Scotia. Jacques Cartier, a trained navigator from St. Malo in Brittany, serving King Francis I of France and seeking a Northwest Passage to the Orient, met the Micmac in 1534. They had been trading with European fishermen for twenty years. Cartier obtained pelts of walrus, bear, fox, wolf, and deer; they received axes, knives, and trinkets. Sailing upriver on successive voyages, Cartier met the Montagnais from the boreal forest north of the St. Lawrence River and a group believed to be Laurentian Iroquois, who lived in agricultural villages on the St. Lawrence near today's Quebec.

In 1603, Samuel de Champlain arrived and sealed a friendship pact with the Montagnais. Sailing on the St. Lawrence in 1608, he found that all traces of the villagers reported by Cartier had disappeared. Instead he encountered the Huron, who with the Ottawa and Nipissing, were part of the Ojibwa tribe living north of the Great Lakes. He also found the Algonquin and Montagnais, who had developed an alliance and trade system that extended from the Great Lakes to Quebec and Montreal.

The Huron, who were accomplished middlemen, lived in what was called Huronia—twenty-five villages located closely together and surrounded by cornfields. Situated on the southern end of Georgian Bay, Huronia dominated the trade routes that crossed North America.[12] They traded Indian hunter's agricultural products for furs which they then traded to the French. "By the 1620s the Huron supplied from one-half to two-thirds of all furs obtained by the French."[13]

Meanwhile, the League of Five Nations of the Iroquois—from west to east, the Seneca, Cayuga, Onondaga, Oneida, and Mohawk—seeking to control the fur trade, had long been harassing tribes along the St. Lawrence. In 1609, to affirm his alliance with them, Champlain marched with French guns against the Iroquois Confederation and defeated them at Lake Champlain. The Iroquois then closed all southbound trade routes to the French and moved their trade to the Dutch at Albany. Champlain had earned Iroquois enmity for 150 years.

These exploits in exploration and trade were guided by Indian trails and carried out with the Indian canoe. The canoe was an Indian invention, made with stone tools using wilderness materials. It was the only means of travel through the St. Lawrence-Great Lakes waterways, and later found importance as far as the subarctic.

The Algonquin-Franco alliance gave the French an early advantage in the North American trade. Their trade routes opened before them as they moved up the St. Lawrence River. Trade goods arrived from Europe aboard the ships that unloaded at Quebec or seventy-five miles upstream at Trois Rivierés. Barges or canoes carried the goods farther upriver to the Lachine rapids; by frequent portaging, goods were sent westward beyond the many rapids. As the fur trade developed, French traders routinely traveled along the St. Lawrence fur-trade route to Lake Superior, although between Lake Huron's Georgian Bay and Trois Rivierés, Jesuit Father Isaac Jogues counted forty portages.[14]

Before the seventeenth century passed, the Iroquois had also established trading relationships with the English, which provided them with strong individual roles throughout fur trading's history. In the mid-seventeenth century, the Iroquois moved to control the fur trade of the St. Lawrence by blockading the canoe routes and attacking villages. In 1649 the Iroquois attacked the Huron and Algonquin, driving them westward, where they dispersed.

The French encouraged colonization, chartered private fur-trade companies and gave them governing authority, and established the colony of New France. Jesuit missionaries exerted considerable influence. The fur trade superseded the earlier Jesuits as the dominant force in French progress. Settlers, known as "habitants," could have all the land they could till, in secure title and free from the burden of seigniorial dues customary in northern France. Among these colonists were enterprising young men who aspired to the fur trade. In the 1670s, Louis de Buade, count de Palluau et de Frontenac and governor of New France, tried to control the flow of furs to protect the colony's market economy by forbidding habitants from absenting themselves from the settlements without licenses.[15] Many departed surreptitiously, going as far as Lake Superior, and independently brought furs back to the colonial market. Thus in Frontenac's eyes, they became outlaws. They became known as *couriers de bois* (wood runners), and became a principal factor in French wilderness operations.

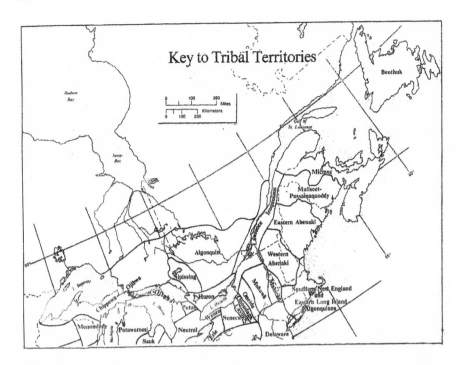

Fig. 2.1 Northeastern cultural area

Handbook of North American Indians, vol.15. Courtesy Smithsonian Institution,

The British, in 1668, were the first to exploit Hudson's Bay, establishing their headquarters at York Factory about halfway up the west coast of Hudson's Bay. The British called their primary trading posts "factories." York Factory began a vast trade network. On May 2, 1670, King Charles II chartered and incorporated the Hudson's Bay Company (HBC) and named his cousin Prince Rupert as its head. The Hudson's Bay Company charter granted it "the sole trade and commerce" of what was, in essence, all lands draining into Hudson's Bay. It was the whole of the Precambrian, or Canadian, Shield, later called "Rupert's Land." This charter, along with the French trade as far as the Great Lakes, marked the beginning of the Anglo-French struggle for control of the continent. Eventually, the British charter was extended to the Arctic and Pacific oceans, and for two centuries, the

"Honourable Company," as the Hudson's Bay Company was known, was the longest-lasting British monopoly.

York Factory was built on the west side of Hudson's Bay at the mouth of the Hayes River. The term factory meant that trading would take place at that location instead of on board ship. The title Chief Factor went to the person in charge of the posts, under his direction might be a chief trader, traders, and other employees. The governance of the company was a governor and seven committeemen in London, frequently referred to as the G & C. Almost all of their trade goods and furs came and went through York Factory for more than two hundred years. Generally unaware of the location, strength, and trading capabilities of the indigenous people with whom they would trade, the company's first policy was to establish trading posts close to Hudson's Bay, expecting to entice Indians to come to them. As expert middlemen, the Cree, Chippewa, and Montagnais soon controlled the trade available to the British.

During the half century ending with the Treaty of Utrecht in 1713, New France struggled economically and fought wars against the British operations at Hudson's Bay for control in North America. The cost of shipping goods from England to the Bay's posts was far less than shipping from France to Quebec. In the end, France's Louis XIV had to make concessions for peace in the European War of the Spanish Succession, and he made them in New France. He surrendered French claims to Rupert's Land, Hudson's Bay, Acadia "with ancient boundaries," and Newfoundland, recognizing British suzerainty over the Iroquois Confederacy and admitting that commerce with western native nations would be open to English, as well as French, traders. France retained Newfoundland fishing rights and kept the Acadian tribes—the Abenaquis, Malecites, and Micmacs—in their old hunting grounds. Though the British gained commercial privileges in the interior, the French merely tightened their hold on the Great Lakes basin.

French control of the Great Lakes began when Champlain sent explorer Jean Nicollet west in 1634. Nicollet traded with the Nipissing and discovered what is now known as the Straits of Mackinac, between Lake Huron and Lake Michigan. He also found the important aboriginal trading center located at present Sault Ste. Marie. The first French presence was Father Marquette's Jesuit mission at Saint Ignace on today's Michigan Upper Peninsula. The French augmented the mission in 1683 as Fort de Buade, they abandoned it in 1698.

Later, in 1715, the French reestablished it as Fort Michilimackinac, and it became a great fur-trade center. From there, traders could reach the tribes that would be trading partners for both the French and English for the next hundred years, including the Huron and Ottawa, who had escaped westward from the Iroquois and settled around the Great Lakes.[16] Fort Michilimackinac fell alternately under British and French control until the French and Indian War (1754–1763). British General James Wolf defeated French General Louis-Joseph Montcalm at Quebec in 1759.[17] Although continuing to fight, France gradually lost Indian battles, and thereby lost both New France and the North American fur trade.

Both the forts and the communities around them remained and grew as fur-trade centers. Fearing an attack by rebels of the American Revolution, the British moved the fort and community to Mackinac Island in 1781. Although boundary disputes had remained after the Treaty of 1783, the Jay Treaty of 1794 established a boundary commission that resolved many of them and prompted the British to withdraw totally from the area south of the Great Lakes that the Americans called the Northwest Territory. However, the Indian traders remained.

In the Treaty of Paris, which ended the French and Indian War in 1763, France had ceded to Great Britain Upper and Lower Canada (now the provinces of Ontario and Quebec) and all possessions east of the Mississippi. But French traders continued to compete both in the fur trade and for Indian loyalties. The Iroquois, for example, swung back and forth between the French and English traders for another half century. The French presence was evident in their skills, names, diffusion of blood as the Métis voyageurs, and camp employees known as *engagés*. They left an indelible mark on the culture of Canada. The Métis, mixed-descent people, primarily French and native, played a critical role throughout the British and later the American fur trade and in frontier life. They worked as voyageurs, engagés, middlemen, interpreters, and trapping and trading freemen.

The scene was further entangled by native tribal wars, and loyalties were complicated. The British were determined to retain and exploit lands south of the Great Lakes, despite the American presence, fluctuating fur markets, and the strains of European wars. The new American government was determined to establish its authority and destiny.

As competition between the French St. Lawrence-based trade and the British Hudson's Bay trade increasingly strengthened, it became apparent that Hudson's Bay Company's policy of counting on native traders to come to posts, rather than going after furs in the field—as did the French and the independent Scottish traders from Montreal, whom the British called "pedlars"—was no longer working.

First at Grand Portage, and after 1805, forty miles north at Fort William on Lake Superior at the mouth of the Kaministikwai River, the loaded canoes from Montreal, manned by the "porkeaters" (those who only brought supplies westward), met the incoming "winterers" (fur traders who had spent the winter beyond Fort William, likely in Indian villages). The winterers traded pelts for staples: wild rice, corn, maple sugar, ammunition, tobacco, liquor, and a few personal items. By tradition, only the winterers could become members of the famous and exclusive "Beaver Club" in Montreal.

The Hudson's Bay Company, seeing the need to trade westward from the posts, Andrew Graham Chief Factor at York, sent Anthony Henday westward into unknown country in 1680. In the Hudson's Bay Company, the term Chief Factor was not only a much sought title of commander of the important posts, having the best pay, but was the senior rank so important the term was customarily capitalized. Henday's mission was to estimate French influence and to induce natives to continue to trade at Hudson's Bay. Henday's journal indicated that he reached the Calgary area, encountering both the Assiniboin and Blackfoot on the upper South Saskatchewan River. Responding to an invitation to bring his furs to York Factory, "the Blackfoot Chief made little answer, only said that it was far off, and they could not paddle, and that many starved on the way."[18] From their lodges to Hudson's Bay and return was about 2,232 kilometers or 1,387 miles.

Although he made inroads with the Assiniboin, Henday's report was discouraging. "The French talk several languages to perfection, they have the advantage of us in every shape; and if they had a Brazil tobacco, which they have not, they would entirely cut off our trade."[19] The HBC's London governing committee rewarded Henday "with a 20£ bonus, and promptly went back to sleep."[20]

The posts at Albany and Severn on Hudson's Bay were also receiving fewer furs, and news spread that pedlars were building trading posts between the bay and Lake Winnipeg and intercepting middlemen coming from the west.

In 1777, HBC Chief Factor Thomas Hutchins of Albany sent John Kipling and David Sanderson to build a temporary trading house away from Hudson's Bay. Traveling with native women as guides, they established a post with provisions supplied by friendly Cree families. When the tribes moved away to winter hunting grounds, they urged the white men to return to the bay for the winter, since it was obvious they couldn't survive alone in the forest.

Hutchins also sent George Sutherland west with a native trader, Caupermertissnewinnekee. Sutherland accompanied the band during their summer hunting and fishing and was introduced to wild rice. They occasionally encountered English or French independent traders and went as far as Lake Winnipeg, eight hundred miles from Albany. The Indians explained that many pedlars crossed the lake going west, and they again refused to take their furs all the way to the Bay when there were trading posts near them. [21] But the decade that followed saw the development of HBC inland posts.

The move to the far north beyond Lake Winnipeg required even stronger motivation. Only when Moses Norton, governor at Prince of Wales Fort near Fort Churchill, then visiting London, dropped a chunk of rich copper ore from the Coppermine River on the conference table of the HBC's governing committee in London and reported that two Chipewyans—Matonabee and Dholaize—also reported streams thick with beaver, did the committee order Norton to launch an expedition to the Far North. Norton selected Samuel Hearne, trained in navigation in the Royal Navy, for the expedition.

Hearne made three expeditions, wisely ceding leadership to Matonabee. He reached the mouth of the Coppermine, found no ship access for taking out the ore, found extensive beaver, and learned from Matonabee that taking native women on expeditions was vitally important. Women made new moccasins, wove snowshoes, carried heavy packs, snared rabbits and other small game, and had the skills necessary to live mainly off the country. In September 1774, Hearne was sent to establish a post at Pine Island, later known as Cumberland House, near the mouth of the Saskatchewan River. According to historian E. E. (Edwin Ernest) Rich, the "origin of Cumberland House and the choice of the site, made clear a breakthrough in HBC policy and created a threat to the Pedlars."[22]

In addition to French competition, the Hudson's Bay Company also faced the aggressive Scottish independent traders. In 1777, independent trader Thomas Frobisher wintered at Isle à la Crosse Lake, and in 1778, Peter Pond, a Vermonter, crossed what became the Methye Portage to the Clearwater River, returning in 1779 with about eight thousand prime furs.

Beginning in 1779, Montreal businessmen and fur traders Benjamin and Joseph Frobisher, William Holmes, Robert Grant, John Ross, Stephen Waden, and Peter Pond joined into what, in 1783, would formally become the North West Company (NWC). Historian Paul C. Phillips explains the importance of Montreal to the fur trade:

> The Montreal merchants were the mainstay of the Canadian trade. They furnished goods to the traders in the interior and gave them credit. They fixed the prices of furs and explained the demands and market prospects. They divided the country among traders and tried to keep down rivalry in the fur country. They arranged for the transport of furs to Montreal and provided storage. They shipped the furs to England and brought back the goods used in the Indian trade.[23]

Alexander Mackenzie, an employee of the North West Company, who had reached the Pacific at Bella Coola on July 22, 1793, also saw great profits in expanding trade to the Pacific. He was knighted for his trip and for writing the book describing it. Bitter disagreement developed in 1799 between Mackenzie and Simon McTavish, known in Montreal as the Marquis of the Fur Trade, over several issues: lack of recognition of younger partners of the North West Company, competition with Americans in the Great Lakes, and the possibility of developing a northwestern trade route ending at the mouth of the Columbia River. Mackenzie and Peter Pond, having opposed the old-timers, finally joined other

Montreal merchants in 1800 to form their own short-lived New North West Company. It was known as the XY Company, XY being the partnership's mark on its packs of furs. Mackenzie's arguments were far-sighted; he desired to wrest the Pacific Coast trade from the Americans, whose Boston ships were capturing that trade. He also deplored unnecessary competition between factions of the North West Company, believing that limits on their capital would force the two firms to combine.[24] With the death of McTavish in 1804, the two companies rejoined.

In 1808, in the United States, a powerful newcomer entered the North American fur trade. John Jacob Astor of New York obtained from the governor of New York State a charter for the American Fur Company (AFC). As will be seen later, the AFC gathered much of the American fur trade, became the most powerful of American fur companies, and throughout its life was a competent competitor to the great Canadian companies.

During the early nineteenth century, when the competition between Hudson's Bay Company and North West Company was at its height, a new development arose, which, though virtually spinning in its own orbit, made a lasting impact on all fur-trade operations. It became known as "Red River," lying in the drainage basin of Lake Winnipeg.

Red River began as a colonizing effort by a Scottish peer, the wealthy, idealistic, but tubercular Thomas Douglas, fifth Earl of Selkirk. He had acquired a large holding of HBC stock during a bear market in 1809. Using his power on the HBC's governing committee and supported by members Andrew Wedderburn (later Colvile) and John Halkett, Selkirk obtained from Hudson's Bay Company a grant of over 116,000 square miles drained primarily by the Red River and its tributaries. The charter of the company did not include a colonization requirement, but the area could become a place of refuge for the thousands of Scottish shepherds and farmers (crofters) driven from their small acreages in Scotland to permit the landholding nobility there to increase the grazing needed to feed wool to the growing British woolen mills.

Selkirk's first Scottish refugees left Stornoway in the Western Isles of the United Kingdom in August 1811. By late September, they had landed at York Factory on the western shore of Hudson's Bay. Twenty were hired by the Hudson's Bay Company. There they camped through the winter, disease and malnutrition reduced the number of the remainder from seventy to about twenty. On July 6, 1812, Miles McDonnell, a strict disciplinarian, led them from York Factory. By the end of August, they had survived the rough waters of Lake Winnipeg and reached Red River. There they found a small Hudson's Bay Company post and the North West Company's Fort Gibraltar. Unfortunately, the Selkirk Grant, which Lord Selkirk envisioned as unoccupied virgin land, was already in use by the Assiniboin, who lived off the buffalo, and as an important North West Company fur trade area, and later became a Métis locale. From their semiannual buffalo hunts, the Métis provided the tons of pemmican by which the "Northwesters" and later the HBC traders were able to conduct their fur-trade travels throughout the prairie, into the subarctic, and west across the Rockies. When the bulk of the colonists arrived at Red River in October 1812, they faced starvation. Buffalo was the only solution. Poor crops made their 1813 winter provisions further dependent on buffalo and pemmican.

The North West Company agents became convinced that this Hudson's Bay Company colony must be destroyed because the Selkirk colonists were taking the pemmican needed for North West Company's northern brigades. A dismal, tedious, costly, and legalistic running battle followed between Selkirk and Hudson's Bay Company against the North West Company. In the end, Selkirk found defeat at court in Montreal, and back in Britain, impoverishment and death in 1820. The Métis community and the Red River colony continued to grow. There the Hudson's

Bay Company located its headquarters. Eventually it became the city of Winnipeg.

The vicious competition between Hudson's Bay and North West companies was costly for both. Independent fur traders who lived in closer contact with native trappers and middlemen took advantage of the competition. A degree of financial distress made it clear to the HBC stockholders, partners, and governing committee members that it was time for the self-destructive competition to end. Moreover, the HBC Governor and Committee (G and C), which directed all HBC activities in North America, had observed that the deep divisions between the agents and the winterers weakened the North West Company. The result was the July 1821 merger of the two companies.

An 1821 act of Parliament known as the Deed Poll preserved the rights of the expanded Hudson's Bay Company over Rupert's Land and extended its trade rights to Athabasca River, Peace River, the Rockies, New Caledonia, Mackenzie River, and the Pacific Coast. Although the Canadian-U.S border west of the Rockies to the Pacific lacked clear definition until 1846, the 1821 act specified that Hudson's Bay Company personnel "were not to trade in the specified territory of the United States, and their grant was not to exclude American citizens from the trade on the north-west coast westwards of the Rockies, since the two countries, by the Convention of 1818 had agreed on joint access to that area for a period of ten years."[25]

The Deed Poll required that Hudson's Bay Company improve the condition of the natives and prohibited the trade in spirits with them. Successful relations with the aborigines were the key to success. Hudson's Bay Company effectively ruled the lands where it conducted business. Company officials were required to "bring justice to any criminal offense, and were to enter into securities for the due execution of all criminal processes and of all civil suits in which more than £200 was involved."[26]

Hudson's Bay Company acquired the North West Company posts, whose value, like those of the HBC's, had been unspecified in the Deed Poll. To the new company went many North West Company personnel, their trading skills, and their talented and experienced leaders. Andrew Colvile, HBC deputy governor and a director of the company, as one of the seven members of the Governing Committee who had participated in initial correspondence with the NWC, was farsighted enough—and displayed prescience and a breadth of vision that would become foundations of the company's greatness—to avoid prejudice against newly acquired North West Company men who had been vigorous contestants during the competition. However, he did temporarily exclude the more combative Northwesters, such as Alexander MacDonnell, Peter Skene Ogden, and Samuel Black, all of whom later entered the Hudson's Bay Company and became Chief Factors. But Colvile's view, according to historian Rich, was fundamental to the company's greatness in the next half century.[27]

Of paramount importance, in 1820 the HBC sent thirty-five-year old George Simpson to Rupert's Land, where in 1821, he became governor of the company's Northern Department. Simpson was a sociable young man with an accounting and mathematical background. Though he had only two years' experience in the London headquarters and was a novice in the fur trade, he "soon displayed those qualities of administrative ability, resourcefulness and toughness that were to stamp themselves on the operations of the Company during the next forty years." [28]

As governor, Simpson adopted the practice of meeting and acknowledging native leaders. In an 1822 letter to London, Simpson expressed his early Indian policy: "I have made it my study to examine the nature and character of the Indians and however repugnant it may be to our feelings, I am convinced that they must be ruled with a rod of iron, to bring and to keep them in a proper state of subordination, and the most certain way to effect this is by letting them feel their dependence upon us."[29] He later saw the need and profitability of treating them humanely and in a friendly manner. He and the Hudson's Bay Company and its factors in general developed awareness and understanding in native communities.

When Simpson went to Norway House, a post on Little Playgreen Lake just north of Lake Winnipeg, for the first Northern Department Council meeting, he had already made a fifteen-hundred-mile circuit of the general area, including Red River and Pembina. He faced the Sioux through mixed-descent Joseph Renville, who earlier had agreed to lead the company's trade south from Pembina. Governor Simpson used flattering tactics in dealing with the Sioux. As a result, Simpson gained a long immunity from Sioux threats.[30] Thus, when he went to his first council meeting, he was well aware of the problems of the settlers, supply needs, complications arising from nearness to the American border, trade matters, and tribal relations. The governor and the several department councils managed policy, personnel assignments, and operations, subject to the overall authority of the Governor and Committee in London. Simpson had great latitude, but was careful to keep the committee in London as well informed as sailing ships permitted.

Simpson was a great and fast traveler, who set a killing pace; desiring to impress natives and Hudson's Bay Company people alike with the power and majesty of the "Honourable Company," he always made a point to arrive at way points and destinations with a spectacular entry. For example, Chief Trader Archibald McDonald, accompanying Simpson to inspect the Columbia Department in 1828, described a typical arrival:

> As we wafted along under easy sail, the men with a clean change and mounting new feathers, the Highland bagpipes in the Governor's canoe, was echoed by the bugle in mine; then these were laid aside on nearer approach to port, to give free scope to the vocal organs of about eighteen Canadians to chant one of those voyageur airs peculiar to them, and always so per-

fectly rendered....On the signal hill of rock, from a tall Norway Pine shaft, floated the 'grand old Flag'...then the grand thunder–skirrl of 'the bag pipes,' with their 'Campbell's are coming, hourray! hourray!' Or some such 'music of our mountain land,' loud droned out to the very vault of heaven. And then—as a cadenza of soothing, gladdening, exquisite charm—the deep and soft and so joyously toned voices of those full throated voyageurs, timed with a stroke—so quick—of glittering paddle blade, singing with such heart their 'La Claire Fontaine,' or some such loved air of their native land—our own land, let us say....when the Governor's canoe, with its grand high prow rounded, and brightly painted, flashed out of the dark 'rock' at the 'point' into our full view, and gracefully turned into the little 'port' at our feet, the heart seemed to swell with admiration and delight at the sight. Never; never, had anything so grand and splendid, and delightful withal, been seen in those primitive wilds!31

A year after Simpson arrived at Hudson's Bay, the Governor and Committee in 1821 divided its endeavors into the regions named Northern, Southern, Montreal, and Columbia departments, based primarily on accessibility by water and ease of control. These were subdivided into districts for accounting and logistics purposes. The Northern Department was the most important and reflected the merger of the major trading areas of the North West and Hudson's Bay companies. It extended from the Lake Winnipeg drainage to the Continental Divide, and from the United States to the Arctic Ocean. York Factory was its headquarters.

The Southern Department, trading with the Cree and Naskapi, represented the first efforts from Hudson's Bay. The area grouped roughly around the southern part of Hudson's Bay, with headquarters and depot at Moose Factory, where ships had first landed in the seventeenth century. As trade moved away from Hudson's Bay, the Southern Department lost much of its influence. The department's boundaries extended generally along a line from the Severn and Ashweig rivers, southwest to Lac Seul, then southeast to Lake Superior and west to Fort William. Outposts were at Albany, Moose, and Eastmain, each of which served rivers emptying into the bay. In 1826, Governor Simpson took control of the Southern Department, as well, heading its council and making its separate identity moot.

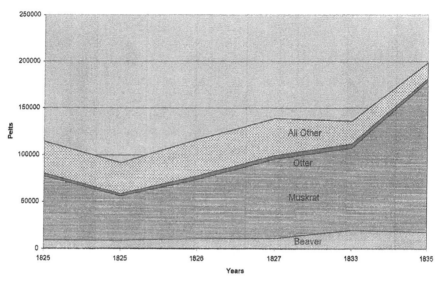

Fig. 2.2 Southern Department returns, 1825–1835

The Montreal Department consisted of Upper and Lower Canada (now Ontario and Quebec), and the "King's Posts," formerly old French posts strung on rivers eastward along the north shore of the St. Lawrence between Isle aux Coudres and Sept-Isles and northward to the river's headwaters.[32]

Labrador alone, presented a unique but intriguing problem. The Governor and Committee believed that Labrador could be a source of furs that would offset reduced returns due to overhunting in other areas. They saw great potential there: whale oil, minerals, furs, and Eskimo trade. Unlike natives in the other departments, the few Naskapi were indifferent to Hudson's Bay Company trade requirements, and their lifestyle was far different from those in other departments. They hunted primarily to survive.

The Columbia Department, which extended Hudson's Bay Company authority to the Pacific, was not so designated until 1825, and included New Caledonia, the Columbia Plateau, and the Northwest Coast up to the Russian-American Company in Alaska.

In 1826, the Governing Committee expanded Simpson's authority beyond the Northern Department, designating him "Governor-in-Chief" of the whole of Hudson's Bay Company operations. Over a century and a half, due in large measure to Simpson's management and using its monopoly to cut costs, HBC employed both fixed official and varying unofficial standards for trade. In those developmental years, Hudson's Bay Company established certain principles guiding its operations. They explored new regions in search of furs, while restricting overhunted areas, subject to the dictates of competition, both economic and political. At remote posts, they encouraged traders' self-reliance and initiative, and wherever possible used Indian or Métis labor. They devised new ways, such as the York boat, to facilitate transportation in subarctic areas and on waterways. They reduced costs by using locally made tools and equipment—"country-made goods." They learned the necessity of searching for and relying upon aboriginal help in obtaining provisions. And as time passed, they were alert to the possibilities of exporting commodities other than furs. With Simpson's management genius, the company's profits by 1833 were unmatched in the fur trade.[33]

Simpson developed effective aboriginal policies, borrowing freely from Indian culture and adopting their methods. Though he often disparaged Indian capabilities, he and his people relied heavily on them. He insisted the company use aspects of Indian culture, including relying on native or natural provisions and acquiring skill in Indian subarctic travel techniques, such as dogsleds, toboggans, and snowshoes.

In two hundred years, the fur trade in today's Canada had expanded from the eastern coastal fishing to the Pacific Coast. The following chapters describe in more detail the American Indian role in this remarkable and successful expansion.

The fur trade in the United States during the same time, beginning with the eastern colonies, developed in a similar manner under John Jacob Astor's American Fur Company. Unrestrained by a government-supported monopoly, from the Mississippi River to the mouth of the Columbia River, the American Fur Company, smaller St. Louis-based companies, and independents all conducted a different trade. But Americans, from the United States Congress to the mountain men, were always alert to British aspirations of territorial expansion.

CHAPTER 3:

THE CANOE AND THE VOYAGEURS

"**M**ay 2nd. Left La Chine at 4 am in two Canoes, manned by 15 hands each; all strong, active, fine looking Canadians. The passengers consisting of Mr. & Mrs. [J. G.] McTavish and Maid Servant in the one, and Mr. Simpson, Myself & Servant in the other....Our canoe, a most beautiful craft, airy and elegant beyond description, was 35 feet in length."[34]

So wrote Frances, Governor Simpson's new bride, fresh from England in 1830, en route to Fort Garry—Winnipeg—and York Factory.

Fig. 3.1 Canoe and voyageurs passing a waterfall. Painting by Frances Hopkins, Courtesy of the Library and Archives of Canada, access no. 1989-401-1.

Frances Simpson's beautiful, airy, and elegant craft came after at least 230 years of European experience with the Indian birchbark canoe, which fur traders relied upon from the seventeenth to the twentieth centuries. The Indian birchbark canoe was unique in its almost universal utility and adaptability, permitting traders and trappers to penetrate the water courses extending from the St. Lawrence River and Hudson's Bay into profitable trapping and trading areas.

East of the Continental Divide, the birchbark canoe's areas were the Canadian Precambrian Shield, the subarctic, and the Great Lakes/Mississippi valley region. In these areas, ancient travel routes followed the waterways, rather than the less-penetrable forests and the windswept, arid plains.

In typical native fashion, Indians mapped only by showing successive landmarks and measuring distance by "sleeps"—how far one could travel in one day. The concept of space that the white man described by latitude and longitude did not exist. No doubt the ancient trails and portages were the subject of campfire legends and experience passed from father to son. In historic times, the explorers and traders followed these routes. In prehistoric trading voyages, the Ottawa traveled by canoe at least as far as northwestern Lake Superior and western Lake Michigan. As trade grew when the French traveled the prehistoric routes, the Algonquin and Great Lakes natives, including the Ojibwa, continued to play significant roles in trade as Cree and Athabaskan canoes took them to the far north and northwest and into the subarctic.

In Canada, east of the Rockies, south of the subarctic drainage, and extending south into northeastern North Dakota and northwestern Minnesota, lies the Precambrian Shield, known to the Hudson's Bay Company as "Rupert's Land." This vast, glacier-scraped, shallow bowl with an irregular surface filled with myriad lakes, swamps, and streams, all drained into Hudson's Bay. The soil overlaying the bedrock is shallow, and the lakes and swamps that dot the surface provide a home for beaver, muskrat, otter, and other marketable furbearers living near the ancient water highways. This was the environment of the canoe.

The French appreciated and exploited the ancient trade routes, resulting in a uniquely intimate relationship between the French and the Indians, all of whom relied on the canoe for transportation. Later the British and Americans learned the importance of the canoe and of the relationships formed around it.

The birchbark canoe, in various sizes, was the only means of travel on the rivers and lakes, and often the only profitable craft on smaller waters after the introduction of the York boat on large rivers As good and versatile as the canoe was, fur companies developed boats to carry some loads. Two primary factors motivated Hudson's Bay Company to develop the York boat to displace the canoe on rivers large enough for the boats to operate. With the passage of time, HBC found it difficult to obtain the large numbers of canoe men able and willing to handle the freight and express canoes properly and efficiently. More importantly, canoes required a large number, a brigade, of expert watermen and laborers, and the company wanted to reduce its payroll. George Sutherland, HBC trader at Cumberland House, experimented with boats on the Saskatchewan in 1795. The result was the York boat, named after York Factory. Men from the Orkney Islands accustomed to boats were naturally adept at handling the York boat, and Canadian voyageurs easily learned to handle it as well.

Fig. 3.2 York Boat at Rocky Mountain House

A typical York boat was twenty-eight feet long, with a broad, shallow, lapstrake, double-ended design. Fully loaded, it drew no more than three feet of water. York boats were manned by eight, ten, or twelve men. At a portage, thirty men were needed to carry one, though fewer men often portaged by drawing the boat over log rollers. In 1833 Hudson's Bay Company regulations required that each boat going from York Factory to Norway House be loaded with eighty pieces upward and seventy pieces downward. This was exclusive of ten pieces for "Commissioned Gentlemen," five pieces for senior clerks, and three pieces for junior clerks and postmasters. In addition, the load could include the small packs of the voyageurs, camp items, arms, and provisions.[35] While the York boat made its contribution to the fur trade, the canoe remained the staple.

Eventually, barges came to the Great Lakes, keelboats to the Missouri, and bateaux (flat-bottomed boats) to the Columbia River. In the more accessible areas, such as the Mississippi, Missouri, and Saskatchewan rivers, and the more prominent subarctic waters, such as the Athabasca, Churchill, Peace, and Mackenzie rivers, trappers and traders used a combination of birchbark canoes and larger craft well into the twentieth century.

The number of birchbark canoes in the early years certainly astonished the Europeans. "In 1633…140 to 150 canoes with 500 to 700 Hurons traveled to the St. Lawrence to trade….These voyaging craft were built by both the Algonkins [*sic*] and the Hurons."[36]

For fur trading, birchbark canoes characteristically featured the high, narrow, upswept bow and stern, with the bow somewhat higher than the stern. Many had a slight rocker, or upward taper of the keel, extending back and forward somewhat from the canoe's ends. This rocker feature had the effect of lessening the straight-tacking characteristic of the canoe and made it easier to turn, a feature important in rough or shallow water and shifting currents. The high bow and stern not only split waves in rough water, but served to prop the overturned canoe in such a way that it provided night shelter for its crew. The load-carrying body of the voyageur's canoe had a nearly flat or moderately rounded bottom, and the bilge areas—the curved area between bottom and lower side—rose from the bottom in a moderate curve. The straight upper sides angled slightly outward (as do the sides of the much smaller modern "cruising model" canoes).

The basic elements of the birchbark canoe were: the ribs, which defined the cross-section; the inside sheathing, which provided strength and support to the skin; the thwarts, which determined the lateral shape; the inner and outer gunwales, which defined the top curve of the edges and to which the ribs were secured; and the gunwale cap, which protected the lashings that secured the skin. Most distinctive were the birchbark panels, which, sewed and caulked, created the waterproof skin. The caulking, made of pine or spruce gum mixed with fat and sometimes charcoal, made the structure waterproof.

The Huron, Ottawa, Ojibwa, and Potawatomi were the early canoe makers. While there were many native canoe builders of varying skills in the St. Lawrence valley, the most famous was Louis de Maître of Trois Rivieres. From his canoe design and production center came the *Canot du Maître*, a freight canoe.

Summer was canoe-making time. From the surrounding forests, cedar trees provided wood for frames and sheathing; birch trees, the bark for skin; and spruce trees, the roots and gum for tying the parts together and waterproofing seams. Men peeled and shaped the birchbark, formed ribs, thwarts, gunwales, and bow and stern from spruce. They applied the bark to the frame with the bark's inside facing outward. Women stitched the bark and tied framing together with watap, which they made by stripping the bark off the roots of spruce trees and splitting the bare roots into threads; they gummed the seams with an amber-colored spruce gum softened with lard and heat. The tools they used until the advent of the white man's tools were made of sharpened bone and stone and required a high degree of skill.

Canoe makers, Indian and white, preferred cedar for the wooden frame. In the nineteenth century, white pine was commonly used for sheathing, and ash for ribs and gunwales. The birchbark came from white birch, preferably from trees with relatively large pieces to reduce the number of seams. The bark peeler, upon approaching the tree, would split the bark longitudinally, cut horizontal girdles, and pry the bark free. Bark separated from the tree easily in midsummer. It could be stored for years, and then soaked to prepare it for use.

For those who wish to know more about the construction of these canoes, volume two of Timothy Kent's *Birchbark Canoes of the Fur Trade* is essential and comprehensive, John Jennings' *The Canoe: A Living Tradition* is informative, and a 1753 master's thesis provides an excellent description of building expedition canoes in the St. Lawrence River valley.[37] (See the bibliography.) Anders Chydenius, a Swedish student, wrote the 1753 thesis, and Kent provides an English-language summary, paraphrased here: The longest possible pieces of birchbark are obtained, though for larger canoes, the bark must be pieced, overlapped, and sealed with gum. The bark needed for a particular canoe is placed on the ground, with the inside of the bark forming the outside of the canoe. A jig or frame is placed on it to form the symmetrical bottom shape and is weighted with stones. Following this, the bark edges are lifted to make the canoe sides, and posts are set on the sides to retain the shape.[38]

The whites observed and learned Indian skills. In 1721, French military inspector Charlevois at Detroit and Michilimackinac (later Mackinac Island), observed: "Of all the Indians, the most expert builders are the Outawais [Ottawas] and in general the Algonkin [sic] nations excel the Huron Indians in the trade. There are few Frenchmen who can make a canoe even so much as tolerably well."[39] Other tribes also made good quality canoes. As white contact with Indians spread, it became evident to North West Company and Hudson's Bay Company traders alike that the Cree and the Athabaskan tribes were also expert at making canoes.

Amid the keen competition of the late eighteenth and early nineteenth centuries, both North West Company and Hudson's Bay Company established and maintained canoe-building yards. In these yards and at remote posts, company canoe builders gathered materials and produced company canoes. Hudson's Bay Company's "Minutes in Council of 1832" records "that Chief Factor Bethune be directed to provide and keep up a stock of 12 new and efficient North Canoes at Fort William with as much Canoe Bark, Gum, Watape as can be conveniently collected."[40] At Fort William on Lake Superior, the company established a canoe yard, probably around 1821, and continued making canoes there until the fort closed in 1881. Its last white builder, there when the fort closed, was Michael Collins, who had made canoes for seventy-five years.

A standard set of equipment for a traveling canoe included paddles, "setting" poles, for pushing on the stream bottom, mast, sail and lines, towing line, and a set of poles on the interior canoe bottom to distribute the weight of the load. In addition, there would be repair tools, powder, lead, cook kettles, and fishing equipment. Sails were important. The mast was stepped through a hole in a wide thwart just aft of the front paddler. The sail was suspended from a yard fastened to the top of the mast in such a way that it could be lowered to reef the sail. The sail was secured at the bottom corners by sheets that fastened to points on the gunwales. If there was a lower yard, it was fastened to the mast just above the gunwales.

The important towing line, usually about sixty yards long, was in all canoes. Called a cordelle, it was used to tow upstream when paddling or poling were ineffective, or for letting partly loaded or empty canoes down rapids to avoid portaging. The cordelle and the Canadians to man it were important parts of Lewis and Clark's struggles against the currents of the Missouri and the Columbia.

Each voyageur's personal kit was quite uniform, except for intimate treasures. It would consist mainly of a knife, eating utensils, pipe and tobacco bag, spare clothing, guns, perhaps a compass, maps, and, rarely, writing materials.

The voyageurs loaded the canoe by wading into the water to place or remove the loads. Passengers waded, too; or if they were ladies or sufficiently distinguished, they were carried between canoe and shore. Voyageurs tied the loads in place and often covered them with rain protection. In general, cargo was loaded to obtain the lowest possible center of gravity and to facilitate its removal for portaging or camping at day's end. The canoe was not beached before unloading. Canoes were always carried out of the water to permit drying and, if necessary, repairing, and to provide shelter for crew members.

Canoe sizes changed to meet the demand as the fur trade expanded and increased. French canoe licenses indicate that four-man canoes began to appear in 1720. Five-man canoes started appearing in 1723, eight-man canoes in about 1730, and ten-man canoes around 1749. Both this latter canoe and the smaller eight-man canoe were known as the "Canot du Maître." The six-man canoes were the most popular in the mid-eighteenth century and were known as North Canoes. The five-man canoes were second in popularity.

Political and economic factors affected canoe sizes. In the late seventh century the governor-general of New France, Louis de Baude, Comte de Frontenac, relied upon licenses to control the trade of the *coureur du bois* ("wood runners," considered to be illicit traders) and to protect his income. Fewer licenses also meant fewer traders and smaller canoes. Larger canoes were built as the fur companies began transporting larger loads. Larger canoes meant fewer canoes, making more economical transport. When military deployments appeared, they required larger canoes. Inland depots such as Mackinac, Rainy Lake, Cumberland House, and Fort Chipewyan needed large-capacity canoes solely for provisions for brigades coming from eastern posts, though many smaller brigades planned to live off wild game.

The ten-man canoes were thirty-two to thirty-six feet long and weighed six hundred pounds. These were the largest until the end of the French regime, about 1760. The ten-man was called the Montreal canoe, because it carried provisions from and furs to Montreal. They were also called great canoes because they were the largest in general use. Ten-man canoes could carry a crew of fourteen to sixteen voyageurs, plus passengers. They were typically used for carrying important passengers from Lachine to Lake Superior, at considerably higher speeds.

There was an economic need for large canoes that were not as big as the "Great," or Montreal, canoes. Hudson's Bay Company, for example, sent traffic from York Factory to Cumberland House and from there on north to Fort Chipewyan and west to Fort Edmonton. The eight-man "bastard" filled the need for these kinds of routes. The canoe was about twenty-nine to thirty-two feet long, also informally called the called the Montreal. With varying loads, the bastards were sufficiently versatile to be used over a number of waterways, including the rivers from Montreal to Lake Winnipeg. They could be heavily loaded with cargo, or lightly loaded for passenger runs.

During the 1740s, the use of large eight-man canoes increased, with a consequent increase in the reputation of the canoe builder, Louis de Maître of Trois Rivierés. A ten-man Canot du Maître leaving Lachine for Lake Superior in the 1740s had a cargo capacity of sixty to sixty-five "pieces" of merchandise, each weighing eighty to ninety pounds, plus twelve pieces of provisions, personal baggage, and canoe equipment. Including the crew, the load was 6,500–7,000 pounds.

As the fur trade penetrated western waterways that were narrower and brush filled, portages became more frequent and more difficult. Voyageurs met these problems by unloading the Montreal canoes into smaller, more versatile canoes at depots like Fort William and Mackinac Island. Explorers such as Sieur de la Verendrye, and Alexander Mackenzie followed this practice. The canoes they used were the famous North canoe, twenty-four to twenty-eight feet long, weighing about three hundred pounds, and manned by four to six voyageurs. The North canoe could carry thirty to thirty-five pieces of cargo, usually consisting of twenty to twenty-five pieces of merchandise, plus provisions for the men, for a total carrying capacity of three thousand pounds. The Fort William post inventory, shows about 95 percent were North canoes in 1821.[41]

Canot du Maitre or Montreal canoe, 10-place model c. 37-40 feet. 14-16 paddlers. Capacity: passengers & provisions. plus baggage, equipment. and crew.
Canot du Maitre or Montreal canoe, standard 8-place model c. 33-36 feet. 8-10 paddlers. Capacity: 70-75 pieces cargo (60-65pcs. merchandise. plus pro- visions), plus baggage, equipment, and crew. <u>Grand total</u> capac- ity 7,000-9,000 pounds (3--½ to 4-½ tons), including the crew.
Bastard canoe c. 29-33 feet. 6-8 paddlers. Capacity: 35-50 pieces cargo (25-40 pcs. merchandise, plus pro- visions). plus baggage, equipment, and crew.
Canot du Nord or North canoe c. 24-28 feet. 4-6 paddlers. Capacity: 30-35 pieces cargo (20-25 pcs. merchandise, plus provisions), plus baggage, pes equipment, and crew. <u>Grand total</u> capacity 3,000 pounds (1-1/2 tons), including the crew.
Bastard 16-Piece canoe or Half-size canoe c. 18-24.fcet. 3-4 paddlers. Capacity: 16 pieces cargo (merchandise and provisions), plus baggage, equipment, and crew.
Fishing canoe c. 15-18 feet (?), 2 paddlers. Capacity: 10(?) pieces cargo (merchandise and provisions), plus baggage. equipment, and crew.
Indian canoes c. 13-16 feet, 2 paddlers.

Fig. 3.3 Table of Canoe Types from Kent, *Birchbark Canoes of the Fur Trade,* 1:101. Reprinted by permission

Indian canoe builders favored the highly competitive North West Company. Northwesters had traveled the remote routes to obtain furs. Samuel Hearne, at Cumberland House in 1775, indicated that Hudson's Bay Company had great difficulty in getting Indians—probably Cree—to make the large freight canoes used by the North West Company, which were needed for smaller, more economical fleets. Similarly, in 1779, Philip Turnor, HBC's first full-time surveyor, wrote from Cumberland House:

> The Canadians have greatly the advantage of the Honourable Company
> in getting goods inland as five of their men with one Canoe will carry

as much goods as ten of the Honourable Company's Servants can with 5 canoes, the Canadian's canoes being from 24 feet long, 4 feet 8 inches wide and 21 inches deep to 27 feet long five feet wide & 2 feet deep."[42]

Though HBC, at various posts, did develop canoe builders among its employees—or "servants," as they were called—such as Robert Longmore, who spent forty years as HBC's prime canoe builder, the company still relied primarily on Indian skills, but at a price. In 1797, the Hudson's Bay Company trader at Rainy Lake paid eighty "made beaver" to have the local Indians make one canoe. A made beaver was a dressed beaver skin of good quality and was, for many years, the "coin" of trade. The equivalent value of the eighty beaver was "2 blankets, 2½ point, 4 yd cloth, one camp Kettle No 6, Powder 6 lb, shot 10 lb, tobacco 3 lb, and 53 quarts brandy."[43]

Edward Smith, Chief Factor at Fort Chipewyan in 1821, described the canoes that made the run to Fort Chipewyan: "Those for the Trade measure about thirty-two feet from stem to stern, width four feet, five inches, and two feet deep at amidships, carry twenty five pieces [of merchandise], five men, not including provisions, and men's baggage. Thus Equipped they come in fifty six days from York Factory to Athabasca Lake."[44] Measured as the crow flies, this route was more than a thousand miles; via Lake Winnipeg, the Churchill River, Methye Portage, and the Clearwater and Athabasca rivers, the actual route was much longer and included numerous portages. The canoes on that journey traveled at least nineteen miles a day.

Alexander Henry the elder, one of early British explorers/traders, noted at Cumberland House, "On the 10th day of June, 1775, I left the Sault [Ste. Marie] with goods and provisions to the value of three thousand pounds sterling, on board twelve small canoes and four larger ones. The provisions made the chief bulk of the cargo, no further supply being obtainable till we should have advanced far into the country. Each small canoe was navigated by three men, and each larger one by four."[45]

Referring to the difference in performance of different canoes, Canadian Postmaster General and painter George Heriot wrote in 1808:

> In traveling to the north-west by the Outaouais [Ottawa] river, the distance from Montreal to the upper end of Lake Huron is nine hundred miles; the journey may be performed in a light canoe in the space of about twelve days; and heavy canoes, in less than three weeks, which is astonishingly quick, when we reflect on the number of portages and powerful currents to be passed.[46]

Skilled men manning express canoes were paid higher wages. This was particularly true of the *boutes*, the French term describing the *avant* (leader) in the bow who selected the course to avoid obstacles, and the *gouvernail* (the steersman at the stern). The avant might also be the brigade guide, the most experienced and responsible member of the brigade crew. He determined when, where, and how the canoes moved, and was responsible for the care of the loads. The canoes traveled five or six miles per hour in calm water or seven or eight miles per hour under sail. Overall, it required incredible work to maintain a high speed for a given trip in fur-trade canoes. That toil was in addition to the labor of carrying canoes and loads over rough, brushy, steep, or otherwise difficult portages; dragging canoes upstream while wading in cold water from knees to waist; and poling upstream over shallow, rough bottoms. U.S. Treaty Commissioner Thomas McKenney described a trip along the southern shore of Lake Superior. The crew consisted of eight paddlers in a thirty-foot bastard canoe and about eight paddlers in a thirty-six foot Montreal canoe. McKenney wrote:

> Left at…half past three [a.m.]….At seven 'clock [p.m.] and while the voyageurs were resting on their paddles, I inquired if they did not wish to go ashore for the night—they answered, they were fresh yet. They had

been almost constantly paddling since three o'clock this morning. They make sixty strokes a minute. This, for one hour, is three thousand six hundred; and for sixteen hours, fifty-seven thousand six hundred strokes with paddle and 'fresh yet'! No human beings, except the Canadian French, could stand this. Encamped...at half past nine o'clock; have come today seventy-nine miles.[47]

The paddles used were quite different from modern wide-bladed canoe paddles. The voyagers paddle was long with a narrow blade. His strokes, rather than the gracious, languid paddling of today, were short and hard, and not allowed to drag through the water. He could do 60 strokes a minute, and keep up with the tempo of voyageur songs.

The real test of speed was: how long does it take to accomplish a purposeful mission? Was the estimate sufficiently reliable to use as a basis of planning, given the dominating constraints of climate? Could the canoes from Fort Simpson make timely contact at the Methye Portage with the canoes carrying goods from York Factory? And could the canoes get back to Fort Simpson in time for the goods to be sent to the outlying posts, such as Fort Liard and Fort Good Hope, before ice closed the rivers?

Birchbark west of the Rockies was inferior, so Indian canoe makers there used bark from other trees, such as spruce, fir, white pine, or balsam. Canoe historian Jennings also noted their "striking similarity to the Manchurian birchbark canoes of the Amur Valley, one of the few bark canoes found outside North America." Jennings also believed that "they generally stood up better in the canoe-building process than the paper-thin birchbark of the British Columbia interior."[48] Birch bark was usually used only for the side panels.

American Fur Company trapper Warren A. Ferris described in his journal on December 13, 1833, the many canoes used by the Flathead and Kutenai Indians on the Clark Fork River at Flathead Post near present-day Thompson Falls, Montana. Ferris considered the canoes fast but unstable, and confined to the interior Salish–Flathead–Kutenai region. He observed that whole families traveled in the bark canoes, carrying them and their baggage downstream "with surprising velocity." He noted that they were "managed by squaws, who, with paddles, direct their course with great steadiness, astonishing rapidity, and apparent ease and dexterity."[49]Manpower for canoe travel was always a serious consideration. By custom on Great Lakes trade-route waters, two sets of men were employed. Half of them—eight to ten men—brought the large canoes and goods from Montreal to the Grand Portage and returned to Montreal. The other half changed the loads into the smaller North canoes to distribute the trade goods to the more remote posts.

This split defined the famous proud distinction that voyageurs made between the porkeaters (newcomers to the trade), who merely brought canoes as far as the interior depots, and the winterers, who took the North and the Half Canoes from the depots into the more restricted wilderness and remained at their destinations, often in Indian camps, throughout the winter. When they were back in Montreal, only the winterers were qualified to join the Montreal Beaver Club. So important was this distinction that it was reflected in the attitudes of company lords and traders as well.

While the voyageurs' lifestyle was developed under the French on the routes from Lachine to the Great Lakes, the North West Company also depended on voyageurs, employing more than eleven hundred, half of them on the shuttle run between Lachine and the head of the Great Lakes. Their role is well described by Peter C. Newman in *Caesars of the Wilderness*. They agreed to a severe contract, often for three years. "A typical winterer might be given two blankets, two shirts, two pairs of trousers, two handkerchiefs, and fourteen pounds of tobacco." With longer service, they might get thirty British pounds a year and "two rods of trade cloth, a three-point blanket, three ells [distance between the point of the middle finger and the elbow] of cotton, a pair of shoes, one towline, two pounds of soap and three pounds of tobacco." They also agreed to specific demands of loyalty to his bourgeois, the French a term used to identify the "gentleman" manager of any post. It was vicious, "but once inland, voyageurs were encouraged to go into debt to company stores" at high markups, and then to work out their debts through further service.[50] This stabilized the work force.

Voyageur food was an expansion of the diet to which the poorer French Canadians were accustomed. When they left Lachine, they lived on "peas or beans, sea bisquit and salt pork, considered a lush diet." Moving westward, they received maize as hominy, with suet, bacon fat, or bear grease, and wild rice and maple sugar, though the rice was insufficiently sustaining. Pemmican was available on more remote legs. Fish often supplemented or constituted the whole diet west of the Continental Divide.[51]

In time, Hudson's Bay Company developed among its white employees highly skilled watermen, but the Métis voyageurs were always held in high regard. In addition, Iroquois, whose own lands had been stripped of beaver, headed westward. They were found in the western subarctic and as far west as the Columbia River. They were well-known, brought a strong Catholic influence, and were in demand as expert trail guides on both waterways and trails, and as voyageurs, hunters, and trappers.

The Métis voyageurs left other tracks in American and Canadian culture. Fur-trade history is full of the wilderness skills, hardiness, and joie de vivre of the voyageurs, principally the Métis. Many are the familiar words they have left to describe the terrain: coulee (from *coule*), for a deep gulch or ravine; butte for a flat-topped hill; and prairie, from *pre*, or meadow.

Sharing the hardships and lifestyle were native and Métis women who traveled in the canoes to do their trip chores. It was they who had to pitch camp, dry meat, collect berries, dress skins, carry burdens, sew skin clothing, and make net snowshoes. They were no less remarkable. The strenuous life in canoes and boats continued until the appearance of the outboard motor and the airplane. Just how strenuous it was is described by Elizabeth Taylor as late as 1892, for life in the wilderness remained hard throughout the long fur-trade era:

> The life of the [Athabasca] river is much as it used to be in the old voyageur days, except that the hours are short and the stops longer. One is awakened at about half-past four o'clock by the cry from the head guide, Ho Leve! Leve! Leve! and then comes the sleepy stirring of the men and the fragrant smoke of the balsam poplar, telling that the fires have been lighted; and in less than an hour we have taken a hasty cup of tea, tents are taken down, bedding packed away, and our voyage is resumed. We stop for breakfast at half-past seven or eight o'clock and again at noon, at four o'clock and at camping time....The same sturgeon-head boats of the downward trip were in readiness, loaded with bales of furs. The boats seemed roomy and comfortable without the oarsmen, having one man only at the sweep and one at the prow, with a large pole to keep the boat off the rocks.
>
> Six men in harness drew the boat along, a stout leather band passing around the chest and being. The latter was about two hundred feet long and the boat was drawn along in the stream at quite a distance from the shore...it seemed unkind to feel so comfortable when the men in harness were toiling so hard to pull our craft along. And painful work it was, climbing over the rocks, plunging into water to the waist, scrambling over fallen trees, sometimes climbing over the sloping hillsides high above the rapids, and sometimes forced by the power of the rushing waters to give up foot and foot of ground....Sometimes two crews had to combine....The men have kept little of the picturesque

costume of the voyageur of the old days, only the bright handkerchief on the head, the moccasins, and an occasional fine bag and L'Assumption sash.[52]

Elizabeth Taylor's relatively late but vivid description, including L'Assumption sash, a characteristic feature of Métis dress, does not adequately cover the struggles to pull the boats over a portage, or to carry the canoe or drag the boat and carry up to two hundred pounds of baggage with a "tumpline"—a broad weight-bearing strap extending from the sides of the pack across the forehead—over the rough portage trails. But she captured the essence of the trader's life on the river.

CHAPTER 4:

THE OLD NORTHWEST

On an August day in 1833, three Dakota hunters—Iron Shirt, Red Boy, and Walker in the Pines—beached their canoe at the junction of the St. Peter's (now the Minnesota) and Mississippi rivers.[53] Alexis Bailly of the American Fur Company greeted them. The St. Peter's trading post had the powder and shot, blankets, and possibly the traps they needed for the winter hunt. From Bailly or other traders at the post, the tribe had heard rumors forecasting a change in the way the Dakota lived. President Jackson was moving Indians west across the Mississippi River to open land for white settlers. Like a chilling breeze or a shadow across the moon, the rumors reminded them of the stories of the past, told around campfires. In the past twenty years, they had seen the arrival of U.S. Army troops, Indian agents, and white settlers in the Old Northwest. All had threatened the Indian life they knew.

Generally, the Old Northwest included the valleys of the Ohio, Illinois, and Mississippi rivers. The territories of this very productive area would eventually become the states of Ohio, Indiana, Illinois, Michigan, and Wisconsin.

The Jay Treaty of 1794, which ended the Revolutionary War, gave the Americans nominal sovereignty, but not actual control, over the Old Northwest. British fur traders refused to give up their profitable trade in the Ohio River valley and along the Mississippi River, and their alliances with the Indians. British troops continued to occupy lands along the Great Lakes that the treaty had ceded to the United States. Hudson's Bay Company, as a British-supported monopoly, ignored the international boundaries.

The War of 1812 revealed not only British violation of the boundary in fur trade, but also brought to light the role of the great Tecumseh, who fought to restore Indian rights. Tecumseh and his brother Tenskwautawa (the Prophet) attempted to organize the tribes from Alabama to Mackinac to resist white settlement. When war broke out, he led his Indian force with the British in the capture of Michilimackinac on July 17, 1812. Tribes now flocked to the British flag. Tecumseh was killed in southern Ontario on October 5, 1813. His death destroyed the coalition he had created.

Eventually British efforts waned, as European preoccupation with Napoleon governed their priorities. Americans brought the Indians to their side. Many of the tribal leaders of the 1830s in the Old Northwest had lived through the War of 1812, which lasted into 1815. During the war, their loyalties had been divided between the British and Americans. For example, Dakota Chief Red Thunder, or Wanaton, had sided with the British and led the Dakota against the Americans. Red Thunder's brother-in-law was a British agent and trader named Robert Dickson, who by his concern for the welfare of the Dakota, had endeared himself to them.[54] Waneta, chief of all the Dakotas, was a War of 1812 hero fighting for the British. He led an attack on Fort Snelling, was betrayed and captured, and watched American soldiers destroy his British medals. He later became an admired, loyal U.S. supporter and helped maintain peace between the races.

In contrast, Red Wing, Mdewakanton Sioux chief, initially fought with the British in 1812, but he had a vision that the British would be defeated, so he then proclaimed his neutrality. A Seneca leader, Red

Jacket, led American Iroquois against British Iroquois at the Battle of Chippewa on July 5, 1814. This, among other skirmishes, brought about the Treaty of Ghent in 1814, ending the war, though it did not settle conflicting claims. In that treaty, the British attempted to establish an "American Indian Territory," but failed.[55]

Subsequently, Hudson's Bay Company moved its trading posts north across the border. In the United States, John Jacob Astor's American Fur Company and competing firms attempted to replace the British with posts and traders of their own.

Red Wing and other leaders discovered that winning battles did not win the war; after the war, the Dakota people found themselves clearly in the United States.

Although various tribes had been active participants in the war that determined fur trade partners, their survival lay in the control of their customary hunting areas. Tribes with agricultural backgrounds, who had been pushed west out of their lands in the late eighteenth and nineteenth centuries by white settlement or by other tribes, drifted first toward productive land and a more favorable climate in Illinois and the Ohio River valley. Those more inclined to hunting and gathering remained in the north for game, fish, and rice. All were involved in the fur trade.

The Chippewa, known in Canada as Ojibwa, lived near Lake Superior. The Menominee, Potawatomi, and Winnebago were grouped closer to Lake Michigan. South of them were the Sauk and Fox. In the eighteenth century, the Chippewa had pushed the Santee Sioux out of their excellent hunting grounds south of Lake Superior, and they continued to press them along their shared borders. Leading the Santee raiders were such Dakota chiefs as Wabash, Little Crow, French Crow, and Shakope, and the Sisseton's Sleepy Eyes and Red Wing.

The Sioux "Seven Council Fires" now lived in central and southern present-day Minnesota, the Dakotas, and eastern Wyoming. The Seven

Council Fires consisted of seven separate Sioux nations. They were the Mdewakanton, Wahpekute, Sisseton, Yanktonai, Yankton, and Teton. The villages of Mdewakanton, Wahpekute, Sisseton, and Yanktonai, were generally known as the Santee. The Teton in the Missouri breaks also had seven branches; The Two Kettles, Sans Arcs, Oglala, Brulé, Sihasapa, Minniconjou, and Hunkpapa all of the prairie.

The Mdewakanton lived along the Minnesota and Des Moines rivers near Alexis Bailly's post, and the Sisseton camped near Big Stone and Traverse lakes. The Teton horsemen lived from the James River to the Missouri.

Each Sioux division, or band, lived in a village or area bearing the name of the band, though each band actually went by various names. The bands spoke different Sioux dialects, but in the Sioux mind, they were seven parts of the one Great Sioux Nation. The number seven, like the number four, was sacred to the Sioux. The historian Royal B. Hassrick noted that the Sioux believed that "this was the pattern of nature and logically the ideal and proper pattern for a nation."[56]

The relationship of the Dakota to northwest fur traders was an intimate one, bonded by kinship through marriages. Fourth-generation Little Crow, born in 1815, grew up fully aware that white traders such as Jean Baptiste Faribault, Louis Provencalle, Joseph Renville, and the three Campbell brothers—Scott, Duncan, and Colin—were part of his extended family."[57] Renville was married to Little Crow's niece Mary. Alexis Bailly was himself the son of a French trader and his part-Ottawa wife. He was married to Lucy, the part-Santee daughter of Jean Baptiste Faribault.

Fur traders established long-term relationships with the various bands, as did Joseph Rolette at Prairie du Chien, first as a British trader and then for the American Fur Company. Joseph Renville was a Dakota trader for many years on Lake Traverse, source of the Red River on the border between North Dakota and Minnesota, and he had a post on Lac Qui Parle and Big Stone Lake. The Wahpeton and Sisseton bands hunted along the upper Minnesota River and traded with Louis Provencalle at the Traverse Des Sioux post, about fifteen miles downstream from the junction of the Red and Blue Earth rivers. They also went to John Baptiste Faribault's post thirty miles downstream. Although the Dakota were Alexis Bailly's most frequent customers at the St. Peter's post, the Menominee, Winnebago, and Chippewa also came there on occasion.

The western band of the Chippewa numbering about 836 people, were centered at Leech Lake. The band was led by Chief Aysh ke bah ke ko zhay (meaning Flat Mouth) also called Guelle Plat. Flat Mouth, by then a famous war leader who had fought against the Sioux, had been loyal to the United States in the War of 1812. His diplomacy had enabled the Chippewa to retain most of their lands. (Later Flat Mouth was memorialized with a marble bust in the U.S. Capitol building.)

In this remote region along the border with British North America, the Chippewa traded for the best prices and at the most convenient locations, which meant a choice between either British or American traders. William Aitkin was the American Fur Company trader in charge of the Fond du Lac Outfit among the western Chippewa, with outlying posts managed by experienced traders William Morrison, Lyman Warren, and John Holliday. This remote region bordering on Hudson's Bay Company territory to the north and the Dakota to the south was the scene of attacks and retaliation between the Chippewa and Sioux tribes. It was also the scene of keen competition between the American Fur Company posts at Sandy Lake, Leech Lake, and Cass Lake, and the Hudson's Bay Company posts along the undefined border at Lake of the Woods and Rainy Lake.

The American government had appointed Indian agents to regulate and supervise native/fur trader relationships. The governor of a territory, in this case Governor Lewis Cass of Michigan, acted as an ex-officio superintendent of Indian affairs. He supervised Michigan Territory, which in the 1820s, included Wisconsin and parts of Minnesota. General William Clark served as superintendent for the Louisiana Territory.[58] The area west of the Mississippi River was under his jurisdiction. When Missouri became a state, he continued to serve as both governor and superintendent of Indian affairs in St. Louis.

Agents who served under the superintendents were assigned to a location at or near an Army post and worked with the tribes in that area, issuing trading licenses and trying to enforce treaties. The French, British, and American governments all had used the issuance of licenses to prevent exploitation of the natives and control the activities of the fur trader. A typical license was intended to somewhat control the trader's destination, inventory of goods, and amount of liquor carried. In June 1824, traders had been prohibited by law from living with the natives in their winter camps, a practice called trading *en derouine*; they were also required to trade from a particular post designated by the Indian agent, who kept extensive records.

Indian Agent Henry Rowe Schoolcraft, born in Albany, New York, in 1793, was a geologist who became known as the foremost pioneer of Indian ethnology. He was appointed Indian agent at Sault Ste. Marie, Michigan, for the Chippewa, or Ojibwa, people. In 1823 he married Jane Johnson, a half-Ojibwa daughter of a fur trader and the granddaughter of Wawbogeeg, a famous warrior and tribal leader.

Schoolcraft commented that abundance of fish and furred animals made this one of the most valuable areas for American trade. He reported that nearly $7,000 worth of furs was traded annually, and that "great quantities were sold to the British trader at Fort Frances, Rainy Lake, for whiskey and British goods." He explained that "these Indians have a partiality for the British, which they take no pains to conceal, and as far as is in their power, they obtain their supplies from the British Traders. Mr. Aitkin, the American Fur Company trader, is of the opinion that this band annually trades four or five thousand dollars' worth of furs across the lines to the Hudson's Bay Company."[59]

Finally, in 1833 Hudson's Bay Company Governor Simpson agreed to pay £300 per year to the American Fur Company if it would not inter-fere— particularly not trade—to the north or west of Lake Superior for the next ten years.[60]

Schoolcraft further reported that Chippewa remoteness from the white settlers permitted them to retain much of their native character. He described them as having fine appearance: proud, haughty, strong, ath-letic, muscular men, who were independent, fearless, and demonstrated no respect for the power of the United States government. Clark Wissler noted the skills and industry of Chippewa women.[61] The Leech Lake band of about two hundred Chippewa warriors was nearest the Sioux, and fought constantly with them. Leech Lake's hatred for their Dakota Sioux enemy, according to Schoolcraft, was "perhaps the strongest feeling of their nature."[62]

The Chippewa had captured the best of the Santee wild-rice fields. Chippewa and Menominee women in their canoes harvested the rice in the lakes south of Lake Superior. Rice stored easily and was an impor-tant supplement to fish and game in winter. Natives throughout the border region encompassing the northern United States and south-ern Canada harvested wild rice, which grew in shallow lakes across the prairies created by the actions of glaciers more than ten thousand years earlier.

Fig. 4.1 Gathering wild rice. Engraving by Seth Eastman, published as plate 68 in *Indian tribes of the United States*, Vol 1. Henry Schoolcraft. Courtesy Wisconsin Historical Society, WHI-9023

The Menominee occupied the land just east of the Chippewa and Sioux. Indians and whites, whether American, French, or British, had traded with the Menominee at the important trade center of Green Bay for 150 years. From Green Bay, the Fox River flowed near the Wisconsin River. A short portage, now at Portage, Wisconsin, connected the Fox to the Wisconsin and thus to the Mississippi. Their Green Bay location had put the Menominee in what had been the heart of the fur trade since the French under La Salle first went down the Mississippi River in 1682. Grizzly Bear, Kaush-kaw-no-naïve, was the orator of the Menominee nation and represented them at treaty negotiations on the land divisions. Chief Oshkosh, meaning "The Brave," signed on behalf of the Menominee.

There were other pressures, even from East Coast bands, locally called "New York Indians." Among them were the Oneida, led by a Stockbridge Indian named John W. Quincy. The Oneida bought land from the

Menominee at Green Bay, and by 1833 they had replicated their New England villages and farms on the east side of Lake Winnebago.

The warlike Winnebago, living south of the Menominee, were surrounded by the Potawatomi, Sauk, Fox, Santee, and Chippewa. In their midst, in a triangle bordered by the Wisconsin and Mississippi rivers, lay ancient lead mines, now, in 1833, teeming with white settlers who worked the mines and shipped the lead downriver.

When the British moved across Lake Huron, in the eighteenth century, the Michigan peninsula tribes—once fur trappers themselves—had become fur-trade middlemen. Chippewa bands lived on the east side of the peninsula; the well-known and politically astute Ottawa middlemen lived on the western shore. In the south-central region of the peninsula, some remnants of the Potawatomi remained, benefiting from the Mackinac Island/Lake Huron barge traffic and the increasing number of steamships.

While the Chippewa, Sauk, Fox, and Sioux have been much written about, there is no tribe's history that is more illustrative of the long-term influence of the fur trade and the subsequent fading of traditional life in the Old Northwest than that of the Potawatomi. For our understanding of this reality, we are indebted primarily to James Clifton,[63] a professional anthropologist who spent three years with the Potawatomi in Kansas in 1962–65, and maintained contact until his death in 2002. In 1653, the Potawatomi and their allies had successfully met and defeated the Iroquois, thus ending forever the Iroquois's broad western pressures. Five years later, moving westward, the Potawatomi were established at Green Bay, on Rock Island and the Door Peninsula between Green Bay and Lake Michigan. Here they controlled access from the Great Lakes to the rivers leading into the Mississippi.[64]

Between 1768 and about 1837, the fur trade was the dominant economic and nonnative cultural influence on the lives of the Potawatomi people. It influenced and to a degree sustained them during their forced displacement westward. Their villages and hunting lands extended in the form of a thick "L." By 1833, Potawatomi boundaries had remained much the same, embracing what later became a center of American commerce and industry.[65]

As Clifton described, each village proper was at root a clan group—that is, a corporate, patrilineal, exogamous, totemic descent group. The term "totem" here is used in the technical English sense; the word, in fact, derives from a corrupted form of a Potawatomi expression, "ototeman," which means "those who are related (to him) as brothers and sisters," that is, those who are actually or putatively descended from the same male parent. Thus Potawatomi clans were in fact villages.[66]

A chief or *Okama* presided in each village as "an agent and a creature of the clan villages, selected by the elders, closely supervised by many "[a]...relatively powerless figure." Whites, however, had not recognized the powerlessness of the Okama. As Clifton explained, the French had identified, rewarded, and supported the chief. This support as an economic channel to the village gave the chief great prestige as a trade middleman, an "intercultural go-between."[67]

This relationship later became the style of colonial management involving "the use of existing, traditional, political roles to further the interests of the colonial power. Here lay the difference between European and native understanding of politics. Europeans eventually thought in terms of obedience and discipline; Indians thought of relationships not involving coercion."[68]

Chilgabe, a Saulteur chief...told Governor Frontenac: "Father, it is not the same with us as with you. When you command, all the French obey and go to war. But I shall not be heeded and obeyed by my nation in a like manner. Therefore, I cannot answer except for myself and for those immediately allied or related to me.[69]

When British power replaced the French after the Treaty of Paris in 1763, British imperial policy sought economy in administration, ascendance in the fur trade, a strong market for British industry, and limits to western expansion of American colonies.[70] American aims, which the weak new American government was unable to enforce, "were to achieve peaceful relations through negotiation and to reduce tensions on the frontier through control of frontier expansion and effective management of the fur trade."[71] These policies affected both the fur trade and the development of land-cession treaties. Between the Treaty of Paris in 1763 and 1837, the Potawatomi agreed to thirty-four different treaties, first with the British and later the American government, becoming increasingly dependent upon American goods, annuities, and lifestyle.

Beginning in about 1750, horses became generally important, primarily for packing, giving Indian traders easier access to a wider variety of trade routes, and lessening the burden on women. As the trading predominance of the fur trade declined, the natives began to expend their lands as capital, leasing or ceding them for annuities. Either furs or cash were essential to obtain the widening variety of Euro-American products, which over a century and a half had become integral to their daily needs. The Potawatomi were, in the summer of 1833, anticipating a further move west of the Mississippi River, since through land-cession treaties, they had lost their land on the west side of Lake Michigan and northern Illinois.

In 1833, three treaties were drawn up by commissioners appointed by the War Department; Jonathan Jennings, John W. Davis, and Marks Crume. Various segments of the Potawatomi were awarded staggering cash settlements. "Term annuities running from twelve to twenty years were awarded, with a total of value of $800,000....Many Potawatomi were now living with some fair degree of comfort on credit," settling debts to traders amounting to $111,879. In these three treaties, about

$1,374,279 was transferred.[72] (The treaties included goods and services, in addition to specie.) It was not surprising that more and more people identified themselves as "Indian by blood." Native Americans were at the same time marrying whites, thus disappearing as natives and avoiding the tribal movements westward by "hiding in plain view" as whites. This identification also made them eligible to retain ceded lands, just as white settlers could. The increase in trading posts, the decrease in furbearing animals, the reduction in their trade value, and the prospect of losing their land to whites all made for a gloomy future.

Events leading up to 1833 drastically changed life for some around the Great Lakes. Indian agents had appeared. New military forts brought American soldiers. Missionaries and educators became a regular feature at the agencies and trading posts. The U.S. Army, which arrived in 1815, was a new element in the region. French, British, and Métis were all considered security threats. The recent war exposed the need to defend the international border. Fort Crawford at Prairie du Chien and Fort Howard at Green Bay were built on land purchased from local tribes. At Rock Island, the Army built Fort Armstrong to protect incoming settlers and mediate intertribal warfare.

The various Indian clans and the American frontier settlers had much in common. They both used guns and iron tools. Both depended on distant markets. They were organized on kinship ties and had little regard for institutions imposed from outside their kinship circle. Both groups lived from day to day killing and eating whatever animals they could find, until seasonal food gathering or agriculture taught the need for storage.

Though they maintained peace in their villages or community, they were outwardly aggressive. They were hard drinkers, given to violence and brawling. While the natives used gifts to settle disputes, the frontier communities did not understand the gift philosophy. Both relied on force to settle disputes and obtain revenge. Indian preparation for war was complicated and mystical; the settlers were guided by a mixture of anger, fear, individual wilderness skills or lack of them, and limited pragmatic military experience. Both relied on volatile, temporarily committed forces, and both suffered.

The native population was small compared to the vast land and its animal and wildfowl population. The fancies of the 1970s writers applauding the conservationist or ecologist nature of the Indian have disappeared into later realistic appraisals. The Indians came to recognize that both fire and overhunting of buffalo, beaver, and deer brought game to near extinction. American governmental conservation policy did not yet exist.

Settlers from the eastern states followed the erection of the forts, particularly at Green Bay after Fort Howard was built. A number of French, American Fur Company, and independent traders had been at Green Bay for years and had purchased land from the Menominee for homesites, trading posts, gristmills, and sawmills. Territorial Governor Cass established a court with general, civil, and criminal jurisdiction at Green Bay in the 1820s, and the territory's first lawyer, Henry Baird, arrived.

The Selkirk Red River Colony occupied lands to the northwest. When Swiss farmers newly recruited for the colony arrived in the 1820s, they found food shortages, lack of tools, and the best land already gone. The colonists knew the route to the Mississippi River and had occasionally sent buyers to Prairie du Chien for grain when drought or grasshoppers killed their crops. With such a route to the south known and available, destitute colonists left the Red River Colony in steady numbers after a devastating flood in 1826. They were able to travel the three hundred miles along aboriginal trails to the headwaters of the Red River, portaging to the Minnesota River and floating down the Minnesota to Fort Snelling. Some found transportation on down the Mississippi River to more favorable agricultural prospects in Illinois and Missouri.

As many as 157 civilians remained around Fort Snelling and were living on the military reservation, in addition to the assigned troops. Their small farms provided food supplies and a workforce for the garrison, but their grog shops contributed to the alcohol problem. The Army and the Indian agent struggled to keep the peace.[73]

Lawrence Taliaferro, a Virginian, resigned his major's commission in the Army to be appointed in 1820 as the first Indian agent at Fort Snelling. His dedication and influence quickly became evident. With Army support, his role involved securing payment of annuities promised for land purchased fifteen years earlier for fort construction. Payment was delayed by an already unresponsive federal bureaucracy. He was to keep peace among 6,700 natives and regulate the fur trade at thirteen trading posts that employed more than a hundred men. Taliaferro served at this agency for twenty years, until 1840. His reputation for fairness and honesty and his disgust with the fur traders in general and the American Fur Company in particular was well-known. He wrote detailed and extensive journals.

The Office of Indian Affairs in the War Department in Washington often made the agents' tasks extremely difficult and no doubt frustrating. Washington policy decisions were based on the politics of land for settlers and protection of American agriculture and commerce at the expense of Indian welfare. In 1819, Congress authorized teachers and missionaries to live among the tribes, and later appropriated funds for missions. The agents believed that the survival of native people rested in agriculture. Agent Taliaferro established a farm for the Santee called "Eatonville." He brought in missionaries, teachers, and farming instructors. It was only partly successful. Warriors considered tilling the soil to be demeaning and quickly discovered that the instructors themselves would plough the fields if they did not.

An act of Congress on May 5, 1832, gave agents a small budget to vaccinate tribes against smallpox. Schoolcraft reported that at his agency in 1832, 2,070 people were vaccinated; Taliaferro reported 600–700. Large numbers of Ottawa, Miami, and Potawatomi in Michigan were also vaccinated.[74]

As the white population increased, both boarding and day schools slowly appeared, first for children of military families. "Teachers…were well qualified to give instruction in reading, writing, arithmetic, English grammar and geography," the only branches introduced. An ability to teach English grammar and geography was considered a high attainment; up to that time, the only qualifications required of common-school teachers were to read, write, and "cipher to the rule of three." Educated persons who were available to teach were often clergy, or persons connected to a missionary society, and their first objective was the education and conversion of Native American children.[75] Although boarding schools were organized for Indian children, the families did not like having their children living away from them, and many closed. Catholic missionaries, first withdrawn after the British-French treaty of 1763, began returning in the mid-1830s. Rev. Samuel Mazzuehelli opened a Catholic mission school in Green Bay in 1830, and Rev. Frederic Baraga arrived at La Pointe in 1835. At Lac Qui Parle, fur trader Joseph Renville encouraged the establishment of a Catholic mission, which provided school and agricultural training to the Sioux. He also translated the Bible into the Dakota language. American Fur Company trader Joseph Rolette was one of the first to hire a teacher for his children at Prairie du Chien.[76]

Liquor was always a major problem. The agents and the Army tried to enforce laws enacted to keep alcohol out of the hands of Indians. The binge nature of alcohol consumption among most tribes and their physical vulnerability to alcohol were widely regarded as destructive to their culture, although the consumption per capita was probably no more than in the white population.

Alexis Bailly, as the trader living nearest Agent Taliaferro among the Santee, and as an employee of Joseph Rolette, took the brunt of much of Taliaferro's antagonism toward fur traders. Rolette had a reputation as a trader who would stoop to any means to obtain his furs, and Taliaferro assumed that Bailly would also. In May 1830, Taliaferro wrote to Bailly that the welfare of the Indians demanded that they not be given whiskey, and implored his help: "It is now time that they should be planting and looking out for the means of subsistence or starve during the greater part of the year. Humanity calls for the present prohibition on the subject of whiskey to Indians and I hope you will attend to it."[77] Someone burned the Taliaferro council house in the summer of 1830. He reported it as an act of drunken Indians, but he suspected that the traders were somehow responsible. Taliaferro's further strenuous efforts proved to be ineffectual.

The 1783 Treaty of Paris established the northern border between the United States and Canada as west to the most northwestern point of Lake of the Woods and on to the Mississippi River, although the headwaters of the Mississippi are actually to the east and south. Boundary commissions were established in the Jay Treaty of 1794 to resolve disputed borders all across the region but were not completely solved until 1842.

The multiple lakes and irregular shorelines created an uncertainty from which traders on both sides sought to profit. It was here that the liquor problem was the hardest to control. Both companies, Hudson's Bay and American Fur, protested to their respective governments that alcohol had to be used to trade, or profits would be lost to the other side of the border. John J. Astor and his principal agent, Ramsay Crooks, used their influence with Congress and the U.S. secretary of war to assert that if Hudson's Bay Company would refrain from using "spirits," they would also, but as it stood, competition demanded its use.

Schoolcraft learned from clerks at northern American Fur Company posts that while HBC traders at Fort Frances on Rainy Lake did not send employees south to trade, they did keep high wine on hand to encourage those who might be inclined to come north across the border.

Schoolcraft noted that the tribes were not universally happy with the result of the 1832 congressional act that prohibited the introduction of liquor into the country for any reason. In 1833, General Clark wrote to Secretary of Indian Affairs Herring that the law is "hard to enforce in the remote areas....I am disposed to believe that most of them [the traders] secretly manage to convey quantities of liquor into the Indian country. It is evident that the use of it among them is very limited. If it is too much the Indians would complain....Could punishment of death be inflicted, and the Indians speak up at the trials, it might be stopped."[78]

War such as that between the Chippewa and the Santee was an ancient condition, intensified by the fur trade and encroaching white settlement. But war restricted trade. In 1825, Agents Schoolcraft and Taliaferro had organized a large intertribal council at Prairie du Chien designed to settle territorial disputes between the Chippewa and Santee. General Clark and Michigan Governor Lewis Cass expanded it to include other tribes. Their objective was to relieve problems generated by the white settlers' westward advance.

Clark and Cass presided. Representatives of the Chippewa, Santee, Iowa, Menominee, Ottawa, Sauk and Fox, Potawatomi, and Winnebago tribes gave orations. The resulting treaty was designed to define tribal boundaries between the Santee and Chippewa, and between the Winnebago and their neighbors, the Ottawa, Chippewa, and Potawatomi. Lines were drawn on existing maps defining the Chippewa, Santee, and Sauk and Fox hunting areas. There was general agreement, but Congress did not approve it until 1831, and not until 1833 did appropriated funds become available for a variety of promised goods. Finally, a blacksmith

was hired and installed, agricultural tools and implements were purchased from the lowest bidder, and distribution of the goods began. But
the line, unsurveyed and unmarked until 1835, was ignored.[79]

While the conflict between the Santee and the Sauk and Fox on their
southern border diminished, that between the Santee and the Chippewa
on the northern boundary did not. Schoolcraft was dismayed to hear of
the murder of a Chippewa girl at Fort Pembina, close to the international
boundary. A war party, one hundred strong, had left Leech Lake to avenge
her death upon the Yanktonai band. Schoolcraft spoke to the Chippewa
in 1832, reminding them of the advantages they gained through peaceful hunting and trade, and listened to their worries about the Santee.
Guelle Plat or Flat Mouth (Aysh-ke-bah-ke-ko-zhoy) responded: he had
attended the Prairie du Chien 1825 council, but every year since, the
Sioux had attacked them, killing forty-three since they had "touched the
quill." He implied that, lacking American defense, they would ask the
British for help.

The tribes in council had experienced the presence of agents, the
Army, and settlers on their land. They may have known that not far to
the east, the Winnebago had recently ceded land to the whites for mining
lead, that many whites were there and more seemed to be coming every
year. The Potawatomi, Ottawa, Kickapoo, and Miami in Ohio, Indiana,
southern Michigan, and Illinois had already signed treaties giving up
large tracts of their lands to advancing settlement and were either living
on reservations or moving westward. The continuing encroachment of
white settlers angered the Indians, already upset by the loss of their hunting territory to other tribes.

Lead, used widely for shot, was found in abundance in the heart of
the agricultural and hunting ground of the Sauk, Fox, and Winnebago.
Shipped by water transport to New Orleans, production, and the subsequent immigration of whites, increased slowly until in 1829 the total

production on the upper Mississippi reached 13,343,150 tons. The population of white miners and their families ballooned to 10,000 in 1829, increasing the opportunities for friction between Indian and settler.[80]

Settlers were already clearing the fertile lands of western Illinois, which became a state in 1818. They raised corn and wheat and provided food supplies to the miners. The Winnebago did not take this incursion lightly. Scattered attacks on the trespassing miners alarmed the settlers, and they prepared to defend themselves. A militia was called up and some Indians arrested. To avoid future conflict, the Indian agents worked frantically to obtain cession of aboriginal lands and to enforce the cession when established. A provisional treaty in 1829 moved the Indians out of the mining area, and provided payment to the Winnebago for the trespass on their mines.

Specie promised in treaties was paid to heads of families based on the number of people in each family. The two thousand dollars promised to these Santee bands amounted to about one dollar per person. Taliaferro found it so difficult to find all the heads of families, he decided he would in the future give the money to the chiefs and let them distribute it. He also accused the fur traders of taking advantage of their customers, claiming reimbursement against the annuities for unpaid credits previously extended for the purchase of tools, clothing, and hunting supplies.

Filling government contracts for treaty goods and transporting them to villages became a major source of considerable revenue for the fur-trade industry, and since further treaties required compensation, they were often used to clear Indian credits. To ease the process, agents used the traders as compensation-disbursing agents, delivering both goods and specie.

Treaties were signed, land was ceded, and the settlers, lead miners, Indian agents, and traders hoped for peace, but the traditional intertribal animosity continued. The Indian Removal Act, passed in 1830 at the urging of President Andrew Jackson, provided for the cession, by treaty, of all Indian lands east of the Mississippi River and the removal of the tribes to areas west of the river. All tribes had reason to fear removal. Although primarily directed at the Choctaw, Cherokee, and Creeks of the southern states, the U.S. government used the act to remove the northern people as well.

The Black Hawk War, "the last in the numerous wars for the Old Northwest," lasted fifteen weeks in 1832.[81] It was led by Ma-Ka-Tai-Me-She-Kia-Kiak, Black Sparrow Hawk, who was born in 1767 of Montreal Sac (Sauk) parents in Saukenuk, a large and permanent village on the Rock River above its confluence with the Mississippi. From youth, he was a warrior, and during his life, resolved many inter-tribal quarrels by war. His successes made him a war chief among the Sauk.

The Sauk had been ordered to move across the Rock River, abandoning their ancient tribal agricultural lands. Black Hawk decided to fight. Keokuk, a famous Sauk chief, advocated following the orders and moving, though he was accused of seeking favor in Washington. A series of ineffective and even contemptible militia skirmishes followed. Finally, regulars under General Henry Atkinson defeated Black Hawk in the Battle of Bad Axe, in which twenty whites and three hundred Indians were killed. This indicated the futility of the effort. As a result, Black Hawk's people abandoned their lands and moved across the Mississippi to join Keokuk.

Black Hawk surrendered, was imprisoned at Fort Jefferson, and on April 25, 1833, stood before President Jackson in Washington. At the recommendation of Generals Atkinson and Clark, and through the slow bureaucratic process, Black Hawk and two companions, briefly restrained comfortably at Fortress Monroe, Virginia, were paraded along the East Coast to impress them with the power of the whites. They were treated with respect and kindness. By late summer they were back at Fort Armstrong on Rock Island.

In 1838, Black Hawk and his family moved to a new home along the Des Moines River. When he was honored at an Independence Day celebration in Fort Madison that year, he could not resist one last complaint against Keokuk. "I was once a great warrior," he said. "I am now poor, Keokuk has been the cause of my present situation." Black Hawk died on October 3, 1838. After his grave was robbed, his remains were eventually deposited in the Burlington, Iowa, Geological and Historical Museum, which burned in 1855. The remains were destroyed.[82]

Under the Treaty of 1828, in which the Potawatomi ceded land in northern Illinois and Wisconsin, the Potawatomi agreed to pay $10,895 to settle claims made by fur traders for merchandise loss and unredeemed credit. After the Black Hawk War, as part of the treaty of cession to the United States, the Sauk and Fox agreed to pay $40,000 to their traditional trading partners, American Fur Company traders Davenport and Farnham at Rock Island, to settle claims. This type of action would benefit and even sustain the fur trade for years to come.[83]

During the 1830s, the combined distractions among the Native Americans caused by encroaching white settlers and perennial revenge against their native enemies had a disastrous effect on the fur trade. With the over-trapping of beaver, muskrats became the staple pelt traded along the upper lakes. But hunting parties, fearful of attack, were uneasy about leaving women and children in camp while they were away.

In 1827, to the extent that data was available, 356,749 muskrats, the most important fur of that period, were reported taken. In 1828 the number dropped to 99,661, the year of the "Winnebago War" and their attacks against the miners at the lead mines. After the Treaty of 1829, which established boundaries between the Winnebago and their neighbors, the number rose to near 250,000. But in 1832, the year of the

Black Hawk War, the total number of muskrats taken was 12,590. The numbers rose slowly for the next few years as Native Americans moved across the Mississippi into new grounds and white settlers replaced them. By 1834, the total number of muskrats taken in the United States was 487,010, reflecting the additional trapping done by settlers.[84]

The rolling hills of the Northern Department of the American Fur Company in 1833 were still covered with untouched forests, and wild game could still be found. The Black Hawk War brought public notice of the new availability of agricultural lands in northern Illinois, southern Wisconsin, Iowa, and Missouri. The number of white settlers increased.

The Indians who did not cross the Mississippi River moved northward, seeking protection among the myriad rivers, streams, lakes, and forests that had first lured the fur traders. They, as did many other tribes in North America, watched the meteor shower on a cold, clear night in November 1833 and called it in Chippewa "Jebiug nemeiddewaud," or "dancing spirits," and wondered what it portended for their future.[85]

CHAPTER 5:

INDIAN TRADE WITH JOHN JACOB ASTOR

John Jacob Astor arrived in New York City in 1784, a 21-year-old immigrant from Waldorf, Germany. He opened a shop to sell musical instruments, but quickly observed the profit to be made in buying and selling furs. He soon began trading with the Iroquois Confederation in the upper New York area and developed relationships with American and British traders. Inspired by the U.S. purchase of the Louisiana Territory in 1803 and the news of the Lewis and Clark expedition through that territory to the Pacific Ocean, Astor saw possibilities for developing the fur trade throughout the western territories.

Astor lobbied for a corporate charter that would grant him a monopoly. He finally convinced his Masonic brother, De Witt Clinton, a former a state legislator and then mayor of New York, to help the bill through the New York legislature. Astor argued that his company would prevent traders from allegedly cheating the natives and would stop the flow of furs to British North America (Canada). He asked for a full monopoly "in the Lusuanas & Missouri."[86] The bill passed the New York legislature without debate, and the new company, the American Fur Company, with Astor as president, received its charter on April 8, 1808. With New York being the largest fur market in the country, the New York charter gave Astor an advantage that allowed him to develop the biggest fur trading and marketing company in the country and the monopoly he wanted.

After the 1783 Treaty of Paris ended the Revolutionary War, the tribes around the Great Lakes involved in the colonial British fur trade had, for the most part, allied themselves with the British. The treaty allowed the British to remain in what were referred to as Indian lands until the United States resolved the land issue. President Washington sought to secure peaceful trade with the Indians. They were frustrated by the machinations of Canadian traders. Washington tried a succession of expeditions, which succeeded finally with General Anthony Wayne's victory at the Battle of Fallen Timbers.

The decisive battle took place amid a field of fallen trees on the Maumee River south of Lake Erie on August 20, 1794. An ambush initiated this Battle of Fallen Timbers, but General Anthony Wayne led the U.S. troops to victory. Defeated, the tribes had no recourse but to sign the Treaty of Greenville in 1795, which opened their lands west and north of the Ohio to white settlement. With that land no longer a legal issue, American diplomat John Jay, in London, negotiated the Jay Treaty with the British in 1796. Under the terms of this treaty, the British surrendered all their forts south of the border between British North America (Canada) and the United States. But, ignoring the treaty the British traders continued their exploitation of Indian trade south of the border. Their trade was aggressive and profitable.

Article III of the Jay Treaty, paraphrased, provided that British and U.S. subjects and Indians dwelling on either side of the boundary line could cross the land freely and navigate all the lakes, rivers, and waters; and carry on trade and commerce with each other at will, except in those lands controlled by the Hudson's Bay Company. The Mississippi River was available to all. Along the Great Lakes, the North West Company and the XY Company, an offshoot of the North West Company, competed aggressively.

President George Washington proposed and Congress passed legislation which appropriated $50,000 to enable the U.S. government to open and operate trading "factories" in the southern states. These were intended to ensure that Indians got a fair trade. These government trading posts proved to be inefficient, managed by salaried political appointees with no profit motive. Astor argued that government was stifling private enterprise.

American fur traders also complained when Congress established tariffs to protect American manufacturers. Popular trade goods, such as British woolens and British-made guns, became more expensive, but only these goods were acceptable to the Indians in trade. To compete successfully, American traders had to buy the desired British goods and pay the duty. In turn, the British had to pay a duty on American goods; but since they did not need them, tariffs hurt only American traders.

As Astor's American Fur Company began operation in 1808, Astor had more than twenty years of experience in the business, and he had a plan. He envisioned trading on the Pacific Coast and in the Northwest Territory and squeezing out all competitors in between. He was financially astute, quickly grasping the ways of international fur markets, and had an understanding of system organization. He used political influence, obtaining early support from Thomas Jefferson and later help from men such as Missouri Senator Thomas Hart Benton.

In his American Fur Company, Astor demanded and obtained compliance with strict accounting practices by the most remote traders. He attended to detail down to and including packaging and loading furs and supplies for transport in a manner that would facilitate the insurance claims he anticipated. He exploited every possible source of profit-producing income in business, and regulated financing, fur sales, procurement and provision of trade goods, and transport from trading post to American and European markets.

The principal European fur markets from about 1750 to 1850 were the Easter and Michaelmas fairs in Leipzig. To those markets went pelts from the U.S. and British North American prairies and forests, as well as from European and Siberian lands. Although Russians and those along the Northwest Coast were already trading in Canton through Boston ship captains, and Russians were trading through Irkutsk to the Chinese mart of Fortress Mai-mai-cheng and to St. Petersburg, the American and British companies sought Indian trade for the European trade alone. Nevertheless, Astor was aware of the Canton trade of Boston shippers, and he foresaw an oriental trade should he succeed in a West Coast effort.

To Astor, the Indians were an important consideration in the American Fur Company's consistently far-sighted, shrewd, ruthless, sometimes law-skirting scheme for dominating the North American trade. Astor was a wise trader. Hercules L. Dousman, at the American Fur Company post at Prairie du Chien, declared, "If by accident a gun, a blanket, or any other article sold to an Indian was not up to standard, the policy, regardless of trouble or expense, was to replace it with a perfect article as soon as possible." This was a strict rule in Astor's dealings with the Indians, and it is undoubtedly responsible for much of the success that rewarded his enterprise in the wilderness.[87]

Astor's reason for this apparent fair-mindedness was simply that it was good business. Astor needed to compete with Hudson's Bay Company, which, "however else they might have [in places] mistreated and debouched the Indians, never failed to supply them with superior and dependable merchandise."[88]

In October 1810, Astor was relaxing at the Beaver Club in Montreal. Both Astor and his British North American counterparts were concerned about an increasingly probable war between the United States and Great Britain. They pondered how to continue to trade should war come. Months later, North West Company and its subsidiary, Michilimackinac

Company, operating in the Great Lakes area, sent William McGillivray to New York City to negotiate a partnership agreement. The Dakota, Chippewa, Ottawa, Potawatomi, Winnebago, Menominee, Sauk, and Fox, all or partly on U.S. soil, were trading with Forsyth, Richardson and Company and McTavish, McGillivray and Company, both partners in the North West Company, which owned the Michilimackinac Company.

McGillivray and Astor agreed on January 28, 1811, to form a Canadian-American company to be known as the South West Company, which, as a subsidiary of North West Company, would replace Michilimackinac Company for five years. North West Company agreed to "abandon every post and surrender every interest it held" in the United States after 1811.[89] The new South West Company would not trade in the Lake Huron area, which was not part of the area served by North West Company trading posts. The territorial restrictions upon the companies, according to the agreement, "did not extend to any Countries beyond the Rockey Mountains nor the River Missouri nor the North West Coast of the Pacific Ocean."[90] The North West Company was enabled to acquire a substantial interest in the South West Company. Astor had brought a very desirable peace in Indian trade to the Old Northwest Territory.[91]

Astor became aware that North West Company partners claimed ownership of all lands west of the Rockies based on the explorations of Alexander Mackenzie and Simon Fraser. Having observed that Boston ship owners had created a triangular trade, buying sea-otter skins along the north Pacific Coast, selling them in Canton, and returning home with unique Chinese tea, silk, and chinaware, Astor cast his eyes on the Pacific. In 1810, he planned a trade primarily with coastal tribes and a supply depot at the mouth of the Columbia, using both overland and sea expeditions.

Ramsay Crooks, a Scot who would become Astor's most trusted executive, had come to Montreal with his mother in April 1803 at age sixteen.

He immediately secured employment in the fur trade, and at twenty, after holding various fur-trade jobs, primarily of a clerical nature, he arrived in St. Louis. There he joined Robert McClellan and Joseph Miller in a brief partnership with the intent to trap the Missouri River. They followed Manuel Lisa of the Missouri Fur Company as far north as present-day South Dakota, where the Sioux threatened and discouraged them, and then retreated to St. Louis. Crooks, who had learned from this experience that a relatively small party was inadequate to confront the Sioux, blamed Manuel Lisa for putting the Sioux on their trail.

In April 1809, in St. Louis, Wilson Price Hunt, a partner in Hunt and Hankinson's retail store, invited Ramsay Crooks, Robert McClellan, and Joseph Miller to join an expedition to the Pacific for the American Fur Company. All would be partners in Astor's new project, the Pacific Fur Company, incorporated on June 23, 1810, with Astor holding the majority of the shares. In Montreal, Astor hired a number of experienced Northwesters, including Alexander McKay, Donald McKenzie, Duncan McDougal, David and Robert Stuart—all North West Company partners—to lend their Indian trading experience to the project. Astor gave five shares each in his Pacific Fur Company to McKay, McKenzie, McDougal, David Stuart, Hunt, and Crooks; two and a half shares went to McClellan and Miller.

Then Astor made two mistakes: trusting in Hunt as a businessman, he made him the overall commander, as well as commander of the overland expedition. Hunt was loyal and determined, but completely inexperienced as a wilderness traveler and trader, and indecisive. McKenzie, who was experienced in the wilderness and Hunt's co-captain, was much disgusted but followed the best he could.

An even worse mistake, Astor, in New York, hired Jonathan Thorn, a former U.S. Navy lieutenant, to command the sea expedition as captain of Astor's ship *Tonquin*. Thorn was an arrogant, malicious disciplinarian and aboard ship contemptuous of his passengers, even though they were his employers.

The land expedition finally headed west from the Missouri-Nodaway River junction on July 18, 1811, but its members became lost and scattered. It wasn't until February 11, 1812, that the first survivors dribbled in small groups into the new post, called Astoria, at the mouth of the Columbia River. They had traveled 3,500 miles to cover the 1,800 miles from St. Louis.

Aboard the ship were company owners Alexander McKay, Duncan McDougal, and David and Robert Stuart and eleven clerks, including Gabriel Franchère and Alexander Ross, and thirteen voyageurs, four technicians, and a boy. A total of thirty-three left New York on September 6, 1810, aboard the *Tonquin*. Thorn's malicious arrogance soon became apparent to both crew members and passengers. Thorn showed his nature when he tried to abandon McKay, McDougal, and David Stuart on a Falkland island after they didn't hear his signal to return to the ship. Only when Robert Stuart placed a pistol to Thorn's head did he wait for them to row back to the ship.

The *Tonquin* arrived at the Columbia's mouth on March 23, 1811. In high seas, the captain sent two boats in succession to reconnoiter the Columbia's channel. Eight men died in the attempts. When they finally reached the Astoria site, extensive supplies and twenty-five men remained to be unloaded.

On June 1, 1811, while the post at Astoria was still under construction and many supplies were still on the ship, Thorn, eager to head north along the coast to trade, insisted on departing. Finally, he dropped anchor in Clayoquot Sound. Thorn would accept advice from no one, failed to rig boarding nets, as done by all ships trading on the coast, and displayed his hot-headed nature. Indians were permitted to flood onto the ship, and in anger, killed all but one sailor, who hid below and blew up the ship. An

Indian from Gray's Harbor did escape and returned in October 1813 to describe the disaster.[92]

After the land expedition dribbled in, McDougal, who was in charge, sent off various trade trips. Clarke, David Stuart, and McKenzie went to Okanagan and Spokane. They acquired 140 packets of furs and returned to Astoria on May 25, 1812.[93]

Norwester trader and explorer David Thompson arrived by canoe from his upper Columbia River explorations on July 15, 1811, believing that the North West Company owned one-third of the Pacific Fur Company. He had posted a sign at the confluence of the Columbia and Snake on July 9, proclaiming British ownership of the territory. Later, North West Company people from Fort William arrived, reporting British success in the War of 1812.[94]

On June 29, 1812, Robert Stuart and a small party were sent back overland to deliver messages to Astor. With him were Ramsay Crooks and Robert McClellan, both of whom who had resigned. Following an unknown trail, and under extreme hardship, they crossed South Pass, though then unaware of its importance, and arrived in St. Louis on April 30, 1813.[95]

Meanwhile, Astor's supply ship, the *Beaver,* arrived on May 9, 1812, at the Astoria post. Hunt used it to explore the coast northward and to contact the Russians at Sitka. A diversion to Hawaii and a six-month delay kept him away until October 13, 1813, when he returned on the *Pedler,* which he had chartered in Hawaii. On April 11, 1813, J. G. McTavish, Joseph LaRoque, and nineteen voyageurs, flying the British flag, arrived at Astoria. They were awaiting the *Isaac Todd,* with cargo for the North West Company. With the *Isaac Todd* was the British ship *Phoebe,* whose captain was instructed "to protect and render every assistance in your power to the British traders from Canada, and to destroy and if possible totally annihilate any settlements which the Americans may have formed either on the Columbia River or on the neighboring Coasts."[96]

Before Hunt's return, the remaining partners, facing these inescapable realities, agreed to sell the assets of the Pacific Fur Company to the North West Company. When apprised of the situation, Hunt agreed with McDougal's action, and the agreement was signed on October 16, 1813.[97]

Hunt and several clerks then embarked on the *Pedler*. With him were with those who preferred returning home by sea. Most employees of the Pacific Fur Company joined the North West Company at Astoria, now named Fort George and flying the British flag. An additional eighteen people, including those who did not wish to serve the North West Company, departed for Montreal via Athabasca Pass, the Saskatchewan, and Lake Winnipeg. They reached Montreal on September 1, 1814. In November, 1814, New York City papers announced, "The Firm of the Pacific Fur Company is Dissolved." Astoria was restored to America after the War of 1812.

Partly as a result of the Astoria experience, Astor came to trust Ramsay Crooks, who, on returning from the Pacific Coast saw how the War of 1812 had affected the fur trade in the Great Lakes and the upper Mississippi valley. The Treaty of Ghent, ratified by the U.S. Congress on February 18, 1815, provided that boundary lines should remain as they had been at the outset of the war.[98] The British had to withdraw from the Northwest Territory of the United States, dissolving long-term Indian loyalty to the British.

Crooks got the postwar job of turning native loyalty and trade to Astor's American Fur Company. It was not an easy job. Despite the treaty, the British continued trade operations south of the border and eroded American fur trade. Other factors included the efficiency of British and French

Canadian traders, restrictive licensing rules, politics, tariffs, and the weakness of the still-young American government in dealing with either Indians or British companies.

Astor sent Crooks to Mackinac to recover furs stored there from previous Indian trading conducted by the South West Company. He also continued operations of the South West Company, which were scheduled to end in 1815. The North West Company again sent William McGillivray to New York City to negotiate with Astor. Astor agreed to extend the charter of the South West Company for another five years provided that the U.S. government did not prohibit the presence of British traders in the United States. On April 29, 1816, Congress approved legislation that forbade granting licenses to trade with the Indians to any but citizens of the United States. The government mandated severe penalties for violators. The North West Company had to deal again with Astor.

Astor bought out the Indian trade of the Canadian partners in the South West Company for about $100,000. The name of the South West Company disappeared. In its stead, Astor organized the Northern Department of the American Fur Company. Departmental headquarters were at Mackinac, and Robert Stuart was put in charge of Mackinac operations. On March 17, 1817, Crooks accepted Astor's offer to be his agent at Montreal, New York, and Michilimackinac for a salary of $2,000 per year and a one-twentieth interest in the American Fur Company.

Crook's experience as clerk and trader and his rapport with the various tribes he had encountered made him the logical choice to head Astor's Northern Department. While in Mackinac, Crooks fathered a daughter by a Chippewa Métis, named her Hester Crooks, and took responsibility for her. He saw to Hestor's education, and after she married, visited her and her family.

The prohibition of trading by foreigners created a problem for the American Fur Company. As the companies north of border did, it employed French-Canadian and Métis camp workers and boatmen. They were called *engagés*, though that term originally described imported indentured French workers. Lewis Cass, governor of the Michigan Territory responded to the American Fur Company's concern by authorizing the employment of Canadian boatmen. But the ban on other foreign participation in the fur trade did enable the American Fur Company to acquire control of the trade throughout the Old Northwest.

Government trading posts provided the principal competition and only temporarily. Crooks led the task of lobbying Congress to put an end to the factory system, contributing to Congress's abolishment on May 6, 1822, of the "United States Trading Establishments with the Indian Tribes."[99] Astor then had a clear path to monopoly. Stuart managed Mackinac Island with great success and secured the Great Lakes trade with the Indian tribes.

Under Crooks and Stuart, the Northern Department created a network of supply centers fed by Mackinac Island. Each center was called an "Outfit,"[100] and the network included trading posts throughout the Great Lakes region and the rivers draining into the upper Mississippi. A year's supply of trade goods also was called an "outfit." From an Outfit, the principal traders sent goods to remote trading posts. The Upper Mississippi Outfit, for example, was based at Prairie du Chien, where traffic from Lake Superior via the Fox and Wisconsin rivers met the Mississippi. Prairie du Chien became an American Fur Company center under the direction of semi-independent trader Joseph Rolette and sent supplies to outposts like St. Peter's. It remained an important secondary supply point for Astor's fur trade on the upper Mississippi River into the 1830s.

Rolette had arrived at Prairie du Chien in 1804. James Lockwood, a Prairie du Chien attorney in the early nineteenth century, noted that the city was "considered by the Indians as a neutral ground, where different tribes, although at war, might visit in safety; but if hostile, they had to beware of being caught in the neighborhood, going or returning."[101] From 1820, Rolette was the bourgeois for the American Fur Company's trade out of Prairie du Chien under contract as a semi-independent trader. In 1826, the American Fur Company brought in Hercules Dousman to work with Rolette in the company's large regional Indian trading post.

Astor varied the company's contracts with traders, depending on the situation. The Northern Department usually hired traders on a salary. Many contracts included profit sharing as an inducement to effort, an inducement in part because the clause also included sharing any loss. For example, Joseph Rolette's contract stipulated that, in addition to salary, he would receive one-third of any profit and bear one-third of any loss. With few exceptions, traders were required to buy and sell their wares through the company, and the company prices thereby ensured a profit. The arrangement allowed Rolette to live as the "gentleman trader" on the upper Mississippi for many years. Though primarily a fiercely competitive fur trader, Rolette obtained permission of the Chippewa to build a sawmill on the Chippewa River. He raised cattle, sheep, and grain, and had contracts to supply tallow and flour to the Army at Fort Snelling

Crooks maintained oversight of the Northern Department and the American Fur Company's new Western Department from company headquarters in New York City. In 1825, he married Emilie Pratte, daughter of Bernard Pratte of St. Louis, who was prominent in the fur trade and a cousin of trader Pierre Chouteau Jr. This marriage brought Crooks into the rarified business and social atmosphere of St. Louis. It also extended his influence in the fur trade. He and Emilie had nine children.

Astor made all the major policy decisions for the American Fur Company, including a firm policy of underselling and thus crushing competition and expanding company territory. The company's financial strength provided force and stability that no other American company at that time possessed. When son William joined the firm in 1818, the separate supply company of John Jacob Astor became John J. Astor and Son The firm supplied goods for trade, sold furs, owned ships for international trade, and accumulated very profitable real estate.

To compete with independent traders, the company raised the prices of goods in Indian trade, and reduced the prices traders paid for trade goods when needed. During the 1820s and 1830s, most of the American Fur Company's competition slowly disappeared. As competition declined, the company stabilized prices in a given area.

For sale to individuals, traders marked up goods 100–150 percent above their cost at Mackinac. As reported by Indian Agent Thomas Forsyth of Rock Island, in 1831 a trader could buy a gun at Mackinac for $12 and sell it for $25, the markup covering profit, transportation costs, wages for employees, and the risk involved in providing credit.[102] When Dakota hunter Red Boy from chapter 4, bought a gun with muskrat skins at 24 cents a skin, he owed 100 skins or $24 for the gun.[103]

Indian Agent Henry Schoolcraft provided specific information to the War Department's Office of Indian Affairs on the number of furs needed to buy common goods at the trading post at Sault Ste. Marie. For two hundred years, beaver had been the skin most prized by Europeans and had become the medium of exchange. Only in the 1820s had muskrat replaced the increasingly scarce beaver as a product.[104] In contrast to a regional Outfit base such as Mackinac, trading posts throughout the British and American trade areas varied in size from a small, dark, bark-covered shelter to a large group of buildings. Whatever the size or location, a clerk or two, and often a few engagés, sold goods and collected furs from the local tribesmen. A larger post had one building that served as the trader's office and home. Boatmen, interpreters, and hunters lived in smaller barrack-like rooms or huts. Trade centers such as St. Peter's, Prairie du Chien, Chicago, and Green Bay might have a separate Indian trading room, storerooms, workshops, a smithy, and a shed to shelter canoe making and repair.

The principal variations were determined by the amount of trade transacted and the area served, and by the need to build the post as a fort, particularly in the western frontier areas. A fort usually had strong palisades and bastions on at least two corners. Sometimes armament included small cannon. Posts in the Great Lakes area by the 1830s were not all bleak. Small, happy, domestic communities were often present.

Although the trader bought many of the provisions for his Outfit at Mackinac, employees often raised potatoes and some garden vegetables at the trading posts. They regularly traded with Indian women for corn, pumpkins, and beans grown in clearings around their villages, and for the wild rice harvested from northern lakes. The traders did some hunting or fishing for subsistence. White hunters were commonly employed both on expeditions and at posts, but provisioning was generally the prerogative of the Indian people, so resident traders traded for game, too, or hired an Indian hunter to supply them with meat.

The inventory of a trading post reflected the needs of its customers. Indian women continued to make baskets—makuks—used to hold berries, roots, and nuts, but they welcomed brass or copper kettles for cooking, and knives and scrapers for butchering and dressing skins. In the maple-sugar country of northeastern United States and southeastern Canada, large iron kettles made easy the work of boiling down the syrup. Similarly, fishing nets made fishing less work, and buying the twine to make or repair the nets was easier than the time-consuming tasks of gathering and softening the plant fibers traditionally used.

Fabrics such as wool, cotton, flannel, and the early English fabrics melton and stroud, along with thread for sewing these into breech cloths, leggings, shirts, and dresses, were also in demand. When trade fabrics replaced deerskins for clothing, the Indians had more skins to trade.

Traders displayed superior wool blankets of British manufacture in large stacks. The northern tribes found these blankets essential.

From his New York office, Crooks corresponded extensively on the subject of woolen blankets, which were essential to maintaining good trade relations. Trade blankets had become critically important in Indian life. Although they could not replace fur robes for winter warmth, the blankets and other woolens were lighter, dried more easily, and were readily fashioned into leggings, capots, hooded coats, or shawls. The most highly prized blankets were the large, colorful three- and four-point Hudson's Bay Company wool blankets. The points, or marks, on the blanket had originally indicated the price, with each point equal to one made beaver. The blankets with two and a half, two, and one points were progressively smaller and lighter. Blankets reached every corner of the trade in North America and remained popular into the twentieth century for making colorful jackets. In the 1830s, the new American mills at Lowell and Buffalo became serious competitors of the foreign mills.[105]

Decorative items were important. Glass beads made as early as 1620 in Murano, Italy, were always in demand. Indians used ribbons and braid to decorate sashes and leggings. They desired silver bracelets, German silver brooches, and ivory combs for wear by both men and women. Foxtails and cock feathers decorated hair among many tribes. Vermilion for face paint was imported from China and replaced ocher. Iron tomahawks, guns, powder, lead, steel traps, and knives met more essential Indian needs. These were major supply items and prominently displayed. The trapper could rent beaver and muskrat traps, payable when the trapper returned with furs. The trader used small items, such as gunflints, needles, thread, and tobacco, as gifts to visiting Indians. Spirits were always a prime gift, despite various company and governmental efforts to control alcohol throughout the history of the fur trade.

Table 5.1 Prices paid by Indians in furs

Items Purchased	Muskrats	Beaver
3 point blanket	50	2
Cloth for capote	50	2
2 1/2 blanket	40	1 1/2
Montreal gun	100	4
Gill of Powder	10	1
25 bullets	10	1
Beaver trap	30	2
Muskrat trap	15	1
Bag of flour	25	2

Source: Henry Schoolcraft, U.S. Congress, Sen. Doc. 90, 22 Congress, 1st Session Report No. 6.

The American Fur Company became expert in selecting and providing the traders' and trappers' supplies that were critically important. Traders wanted such luxuries as coffee, sugar, whiskey, and tobacco, but also they needed oilcloth, tents, and rain hats (called "duck-hats"). Stockings, shoes, and ready-made clothing allowed for a change from the skins and moccasins worn every day; though readily available, buckskin when wet was miserably cold and hard to dry, and it could be expected to shrink. The French engagés loved simple clay pipes, easily broken, but cheap to replace, which the chief trader purchased by the gross. The trader also had to have food supplies for himself and his employees, including pork and flour, lard tallow for candles, and tools to maintain the buildings and watercraft.In late winter, after assessing the needs of the traders in the field, including special requests, the trader at the post placed his order for the next year's supplies and Indian trade goods. A courier traveling on snowshoes or by dogsled delivered the order to the principal trader, and from there it was sent to Robert Stuart at Mackinac or possibly direct to John J. Astor and Son in New York City. Stuart, chief factor of Mackinac

Island, oversaw all transactions with traders, assembling goods for their posts, and keeping the detailed accounts that the Astor system required.

When spring arrived and the streams opened, Indian and white trappers brought furs to nearby posts, where furs were pressed and packed into ninety-pound "pieces." The post trader then sent the pieces by canoe or boat to the principal trader for the respective Outfit. That trader consolidated the furs into a large load, which was placed on barges for the trip on Lake Superior, Lake Michigan, or Lake Huron to the Northern Department's headquarters on Mackinac Island. There loads were again consolidated for shipping eastward through the Great Lakes and beyond.

Also each spring, freight canoes, and by the 1830s also steamboats and schooners, arrived at Mackinac with the year's supply of trade goods from New York or Montreal. Their arrival always prompted celebration. Dormitories accommodating a hundred voyageurs and warehouses large enough for a year's supply of goods dominated the waterfront. The clerks in the warehouses efficiently sorted and counted the furs and pelts from each winterer's "pieces."

According to Schoolcraft, the clerks sorted and priced the furs as "prime," "out of season," or "bad." Furs of poor quality were sharply discounted, reducing the price by one-half to two-thirds, something the field and post traders would have already considered when buying the furs. After sorting the furs and paying the respective traders, the American Fur Company repacked the furs for shipment to New York, for the markets there and also to be sent to the European markets. The prices the Indian trader got for furs changed each year depending on the demand for each type of fur in New York, London, Leipzig, and even Canton, where the Chinese demand for furs was famous. Hard bargaining by the trader at Mackinac or one in New York, and hard bargaining by Astor's agent in London, Curtis Lampson, could also influence the trader's income.

Table 5.2 Prices received for furs in Mackinac

First Lot Furs (highest quality)	1831	1832	1833
Beaver	$4.50	$3.50	$5.00
Bears	$9.00	$7.00	$9.00
Muskrat	$0.25	$0.24	$0.22
Martens	$1.25	$1.00	$1.25
Mink	$0.46	$0.40	$0.40

a.Henry Schoolcraft, U.S. Congress, Sen. Doc. 90. 22nd Congress. 1st Session.

American Fur Company ledgers illustrate Joseph Rolette's success as the trader at Prairie du Chien. In the summer of 1830, he brought in furs, mostly from Indian hunters, worth $43,000. After subtracting the cost of his goods, a profit of $7,416.81 remained. Under his agreement with the American Fur Company, he received one-third of that, or $2,472.27, which he accepted as a share of the furs. Rolette then sent his share of the furs to New York to be sold by the company. He estimated that revenue from the sale of his furs would be $14,333.33.[106]

Company profits, Astor's personal profit, and the profits earned by individual traders are difficult to determine because the American Fur Company records were burned in fires in both Mackinac and New York. However, Indian agents were required to record the value of goods sent to the trading posts. Those records were retained at first by the War Department and later by the Office of Indian Affairs, and they provide some information.

Not all trade goods came to Mackinac as finished products. Blacksmiths on the island forged iron and brass into axes, traps, and other metal goods. The American Fur Company sometimes employed silversmiths to create the bracelets and brooches the Indians admired. Post carpenters manufactured boats, wagon wheels, or furniture all ordered by—and charged to—the traders.

After returning from Astoria in 1814, Gabriel Franchère, the American Fur agent in Montreal for the next twenty years, hired replacement voyageurs who traveled westward from Mackinac.[107] The American Fur Company charged the Northern Department $25 for each Frenchman or Métis delivered at Mackinac, and provided each recruit a credit of $100 per year. From that amount, the American Fur Company deducted the cost of at least two cotton shirts, one three-point blanket, a tumpline, and a pair of "beef," or leather, shoes. Given the supplies and expenses necessary to go into the field, voyageurs often ended a year of work in debt to the American Fur Company.

This indebting policy was standard procedure for the American Fur Company and often adopted by independent traders because voyageurs or engagés in debt literally could not leave. There was no way for them to buy passage on a company vessel. The policy provided stability in the workforce of voyageurs and engagés. Other than when live game was available, these lowly employees lived a life and upon the diet described below.

> All this to an American was a novel way of living, and appeared to be hard fare; but to a person acquainted with the habits of life of the Canadian peasantry, it would not look so much out of the way, as they live mostly on pea soup, seasoned with a piece of pork boiled down to grease;...with this soup, and a piece of coarse bread, their meals were made....These people in the Indian country...prided themselves upon the distance they could travel per day, and the small quantity of provisions they could subsist on while traveling, and the number of days they could go without food.... [Engagés] were easily managed by a person who understands something of their nature and disposition, but their bourgeois must be what they consider a gentleman or superior to themselves.[108]

Indian Agent William Johnson offered a similar assessment: "The engagés...perform all the menial services...their labour is very hard for in a few years they are completely broken down....[They are] exposed constantly to change of heat and cold; which soon brings them to an untimely grave."[109] The turnover was high. Joseph Rolette requested ten to twelve new engagés annually. They were, likely as not, Métis voyageurs skilled in camp and in handling watercraft, and willing to endure severe labor and hardship.

The fur traders did not create the portages. They were the result of game trails and Indian travel over thousands of years, and many today are challenges to the modern canoeist. The brutal work of carrying ninety-pound "pieces" over portages or moving a loaded barge upstream demanded strong men who were accustomed to severe work. Before 1833, there were various examples of ways to reduce the labor, such as the Fox-Wisconsin River portage at present-day Portage, Wisconsin. There two men helped transport loads across the eleven-mile portage by wagon. They charged $.40 per hundred pounds of freight, and $10.00 for the barge. Thus for about $140, four thirty-four-foot boats and twelve or so tons of freight could be moved across the two-mile portage with relative ease.[110]

Crooks took advantage of Astor's 1834 retirement to buy the American Fur Company. The final papers were signed in April 1834. That same year, Crooks terminated the Company contract with the Western Department in St. Louis, run by the Chouteaus. Robert Stuart left Mackinac for Detroit, where he became active in real estate and in 1840, and superintendent of Michigan Indian Affairs.

Crooks replaced older traders with younger men. He realigned Outfits and the Northern Department. Prairie du Chien became the departmental headquarters of a new Western Outfit no longer associated with the Western Department on the Missouri River. Mackinac remained the headquarters and principal supply depot for the Northern Department.

Detroit also remained a supply post, as well as the scene of extensive Indian–white trade. With the addition of new Outfits around Lake Superior, Crooks maintained the existing trading posts and sub posts.

The future for the new American Fur Company looked promising. The opening of the Erie Canal reduced the cost of shipping merchandise. The market for furs remained strong. As historian David Lavender summarized, "During the latter part of the 1830s, more fur left the United States than ever before. Crooks' company exported nearly 600,000 small skins and sold another 170,000 abroad for Chouteau."[111] But as the Indians were moved west across the Mississippi River, north to Canada, or blended into the white population, the fur trade was no longer an interaction between whites and Indians but a source of income for new settlers.

Crooks continued in the fur business for the rest of his life. He lived in New York, but traveled extensively, preferring always to travel by canoe. He was known as honest, and socially urbane and smooth, but tough minded and incisive in business matters. He died in New York on June 6, 1859.

By the time Astor retired in 1834, he had established the richest, most far-flung fur-trading company in America. He had dominated the Old Northwest, worked inside the Canadian North West Company to his advantage and their discomfort, and shaped American Indian policy. He had attempted to fling his efforts across the continent, though he failed in that adventure. Yet the company's momentum and name was moving westward to dominate the upper Missouri and eventually the trapping and trade in the Rockies in the fur trade's fading years. As a far-sighted American entrepreneur of his time, he had no peer, and the fur trade was his medium.

CHAPTER 6:

ACROSS THE METHYE PORTAGE

*M*ake friends of your dogs and think of them first. They will pay you; when you spell, always give your dogs a little bit, even a mouthful. It puts heart into them; feed them well and be careful not to burn the fish at the fire when you thaw it, the burn hurts them inside; always try to cut a little brush for them to lie on at night, they rest better; look well to their feet when the snow is like coarse salt. How far have you come today? That's good, watch your dogs and keep them happy and they won't tire. Ah, I wish I could travel again! It's long, sitting here.

Attributed to Joseph Bouvier, aged musher and boatman at HBC's Fort Providence at the mouth of Yellowknife Bay on Great Slave Lake. Bouvier lived to an old age and yearned for his long-past trail days. His sled dogs were to winter travel what the voyageurs' canoes were to summer journeys. In the fur trade, dogsleds were the usual means of transport over the winter snows of North America. The dog team was important wherever winters were long and lakes and streams were locked in ice and snow. In the Canadian barren lands, the Inuit hitched dogs into a fan-shaped arrangement. Mushers in forested areas used the more familiar single line. Snow covered this subarctic terrain from 140 to 200 days a year, though occasional mild winters in some localities were not unusual. The presence or absence of snow and its density and hardness determined the rate of freezing, the thawing of lakes and rivers, the ease and even possibility of longer-range travel, trapping for furbearers, and big-game hunting. Much of the quality of life depended on the condition of the snow.

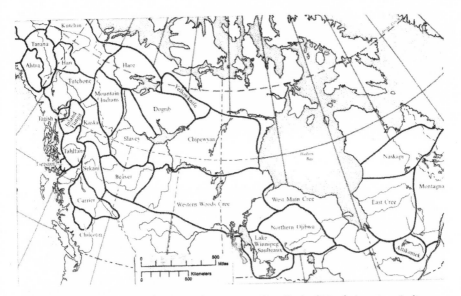

Fig. 6.1 Northern and subarctic culture areas. *Handbook of North American Indians,* vol. 6. Courtesy Smithsonian Institution.

North of the Saskatchewan River, the plains of Canada give way to a boreal forest that extends to the barren lands. The cultural, physical, and societal existence of the hunting peoples of the subarctic expanse is sharply and immediately keyed to the terrain and its subsistence resources.[112]

On these forest lands grow primarily white spruce, with black spruce, balsam fir, jack pine, aspen, some birch, and willow. Extensive, poorly drained areas are filled with sphagnum moss, cranberries, blueberries, and other water plants, forming muskeg—a bog or marsh containing thick layers of decaying vegetable matter and often overgrown with moss. As the forests gradually become thinner, they are known as "the land of little sticks," transitional areas of muskeg and open woodland with scattered trees of stunted growth, lichen, and shrubs. Permafrost— permanently frozen subsoil—is continuous and extends through the transitional shrub land. In more southerly regions, the soil might melt twenty to thirty inches deep each year, making travel extremely difficult. The "tree line" at the highly diffused northern edge of this transitional shrub land and into the boreal forest marks the southern edge of Arctic barren lands. North is the tundra, with its lichens, moss, sedges, and other low-growing plants.

Permafrost in the barren lands was continuous, though it might melt deeply each year. The result was high, treacherous hummocks, which made summer land travel virtually impossible, even more so than the muskeg areas to the south. But the barren land was truly barren. It is the land of the Inuit. A people known in Alaska as Eskimos live on the Arctic prairies, but they are distinct from the Inuit by race, language, and culture.

Anthropologist June Helm wrote that aborigines of the northwest may be collectively termed "Dené," which denotes "people," and the speaker's own kind of people. She believed that the identification and demarcation of "tribes" is in most cases a matter of judgment, and that establishing "boundaries" to tribal territories is especially arbitrary

Variations of language generally determined the diffused and some-what mobile boundaries between the groups. Some tribes (the common term used in the United States) or nations (the common term used in Canada) were bound together by dialect, social contact, amity, and mutu-ally available hunting areas, such as for caribou. The Chipewyan, for example, occupied country that extended six hundred miles east–west across northern Canada. They objected to white men coming into their territory. Fur trader Daniel Williams Harmon, a Vermonter employed by the North West Company and trading on the upper Peace River system, commented in his journal on September 1, 1817: "Those Chipewyans are a savage people; and they have as I believe, killed more white men than any other tribe in the North West Company."[113]

Harmon had no difficulty distinguishing between the Chipewyans and nearby nations of Yellowknife, Dogrib, and other Indians, nor the mixed-descent Métis of the subarctic: "The Subarctic Métis live in community association with Indian neighbors and kinsmen throughout the western prairie provinces and north to the MacKenzie delta, but they are perceived, and perceive themselves, as having a distinctive ethnic heritage and identity."

The Métis, with their native relatives, contributed materially to making the subarctic fur trade successful. They provided a bridge between the Dené subsistence economy and the European fur-and-trade-goods market systems. Trade wars between the Yellowknife and the Dogrib made the Dené hesitant to travel with expeditions outside their own territories. The result was that the extensive Métis population of that area was more familiar with trade routes than were the local Indians. The strong Métis population in the subarctic excelled as interpreters, and many became permanent HBC "servants," or employees.

The Algonquian-speaking Cree initially lived in the woodlands near Hudson's Bay and established themselves as the dominant middlemen between York Factory, the western subarctic nations, and other independent fur traders. Archeological evidence confirms historical evidence that Cree populations prehistorically exploited the Churchill River drainage, as well as lands south of that drainage. They kept the Chipewyan from coming to Hudson's Bay themselves, and as the Cree expanded westward with the fur trade, they pushed the Chipewyan north toward Lake Athabasca.[114]

At the center of the developing fur trade in this vast region was the Athabasca River basin. In the latter part of the eighteenth century, North West Company and Hudson's Bay Company located trading posts there, where various tribes could come to trade for the precious European goods.

Indians on Peace River and around Athabasca, Great Slave, and Great Bear lakes had acquired goods at high prices through the Cree middlemen. The Cree had also pushed the Beaver from along the Peace River. The Beaver in turn forced the Rocky Mountain Indians west and north. By the late eighteenth century, the Beaver occupied an area south and west of the Slave River, bounded on the west by the mountains, and on the south and east by the Peace and Hay rivers, an area of roughly 138,000 square kilometers (one-fifth the area of Alberta). The Slavey left their area along the Slave River and moved into territory north of Great Slave Lake.

The Dogrib's home territory lay in a broad strip from Great Bear Lake southeast to Great Slave Lake. Northeast of the Dogrib lived the Yellowknife, whose country extended to the barren lands. The Hare were north of Great Bear Lake and the Dogrib, whose chief, English Chief, had even traded at Hudson's Bay and acted as middleman for his and other tribes. West of the Mackenzie River and into the eastern slopes of the mountains were the Mountain bands. This term included the Dahotinne and Umbahotinne, who traded at Fort Simpson. North of the Mountain Indians, in the Pelly River country, lived the Tuchones, who did not enter the fur trade until 1841. Though the home-area boundaries of the various tribes were diffused and sometimes overlapping, hunting rights were generally respected, although at times they were changed or violated because of weather, availability, or hunting pressure by neighboring nations.

The Nahanni, or Kaska, named from the Nahanni River, lived in the cordillera that extended southward to the Sekani on the upper reaches of the Liard River and down the Peace River as far as the modern town of Peace River. Helm defines the nebulous, oft-mentioned Nahanni in this manner: "In…ethnic classifications the so-called 'Nahannis' became a mélange of ambiguous identities and cannot be treated as or assigned to a single societal-tribal entity."[115]

Of the Sekani, fur trader Harmon wrote in his journal on October 17, 1810:

> The Sicannies are a quiet, inoffensive people, whose situation exposes them to peculiar difficulties and distresses. When [on] the west side of the mountains, the natives of that region…attack and kill many of them. And when they are on this side, the Beaver Indians and Cree are continually making war upon them. Being…too feeble successfully to contend, they suffer frequently from want of food; for when on the west side, they dare not fish, and when on the east side, they are frequently afraid…where animals abound. They are compelled, therefore…to subsist upon roots…and their emaciated bodies frequently bear witness to the scantiness of their fare.[116]

The weak Sekani were an exception; they were a nation that had lost its hunting rights. They were primarily hunters, with no permanent villages. They lived in bark-covered pole structures.[117]

Anthropologist Cornelius Osgood, in his discussion of the subarctic Athabaskan, or Na-Dene, concluded that "the natural geographical distribution of the Na-Dene speaking peoples proves extremely significant in that almost all the Indians are directly associated with rivers or lakes which serve as routes of travel and from which fish, so important in their food supply, are obtained."[118] He further noted that the various peoples were dispersed into small kinship groups. They traveled as needed for subsistence hunting and fishing and for obtaining furs or provisions for trade.

The Dené people ate lots of fish: white sucker, lake herring, broad whitefish, northern pike, goldeye, burbot (inland cod), round whitefish, Arctic char, Dolly Varden, brook trout, Arctic grayling (bluefish), American smelt, and Atlantic salmon. The fur traders, when they came, adopted the Indian fish diet. In season, waterfowl were also important. The fisheries at the large and small lakes and rivers in the region provided food for themselves, for their sled dogs, and for trading at the fur posts.

The Dené got not only food, but also skins for clothing and shelter from land mammals: moose, elk, barren ground and woodland caribou, beaver, and the Arctic hare. Hare availability varied in a ten-year cycle, based on the presence of wolves. Their absence could mean human starvation. Caribou were similarly crucial in some areas. To a great extent, the annual caribou migrations southward governed the hunting of the Yellowknife, Chipewyan, and Dogrib nations. In the winters of 1833–34 and 1835–36, the caribou failed to migrate to the Martin Lakes region, the result being starvation and death among the people living there.[119]

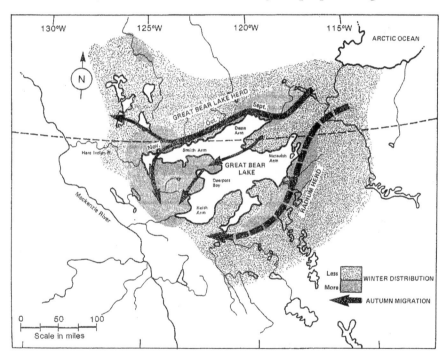

Fig. 6.2 Fall and winter caribou distribution. *The Subarctic Indians and the Fur Trade, 1680-1860. J.C. Yerbury, p. 142, Fig. 17. Reproduced by permission.*

The human body cannot properly assimilate the protein in the lean meats of such animals as caribou and moose when that protein alone comprises the entire diet. The Dené often ate up to eight pounds of meat a day, with no carbohydrates from fruits or vegetables—except during the short summer season. The types of meat combined in the diet affected health.

Fish provided some fatty acids. Beaver were another important source of fats, especially during the spring and winter, when other mammals were particularly lean. Beaver flesh provides approximately three times the caloric value of other red meats. People understood the effects, if not the science, of their diet choices. These factors alone made beaver an important game animal to natives long before traders sought the pelts and castoreum.

The Northern Woods Cree had prevented the Chipewyan from trading at Fort Churchill on Hudson's Bay during the late seventeenth and early eighteenth centuries. In 1714, HBC Governor James Knight recognized that a bright, strong young Chipewyan woman Thanadelthur, "the Slave Woman," whom the Cree had captured and who had escaped to Fort York, was the key. Thanadelthur knew the traders were supplying guns to the Cree, and she was motivated to strengthen her people with arms and household trade goods. She persuaded Knight to send an expedition to her people, and she, in effect, led the expedition, accompanied by William Stuart.

Though the expedition included 150 Cree, the need to hunt forced it to break up into smaller units to avoid starvation. Many of the dispersed groups turned back to Hudson's Bay. Thanadelthur and William Stuart, accompanied by a small group, continued. When they, too, could go no further, she went on to the Chipewyan and returned with more than one hundred tribal members to council with the Cree. Thanadelthur, by the force of her oratory and will, was able to bring about a temporary peace. She later returned to York Factory. In Governor Knight's journal, he described Thanadelthur: "She was one of the Very High Spirit and of the Firmest Resolution that ever I see any Body in my Days." Thanadelthur died at York in 1717. "Before she died she trained a young company servant to be an emissary to her people by instructing him in their customs and telling him how to trade with them."[121]

The Chipewyan slowly expanded their trade at Hudson's Bay during peaceful interludes and also obtained guns. In the following years, the

Chipewyan were able, eventually, to drive the Cree to the south and, as middlemen, controlled their own trade network until posts were established in the Athabasca and Mackenzie basins. Then they also were able to venture southward into the boreal forest to trap for furs to trade. However, the Chipewyan did not extend their peace with the Cree to fur traders who interfered with their hunting or trading rights.

Expansion of the fur trade into the subarctic is a complicated history involving bitter competition between white traders and some bloodshed. Relying heavily on information from E. E. Rich's *Hudson's Bay Company, 1763–1870*, and John K. Stager's "Fur Trading Posts in the Mackenzie Region up to 1850," his Occasional Paper for the Canadian Association of Geographers, we present an abbreviated history, leaving out many important players in the interest of brevity.

This expansion was the result of a concerted effort to overcome great distances by organized and aggressive means of transportation. In the late eighteenth century, Peter Pond, a Connecticut Yankee, in partnership with a group of Montreal traders, or "pedlars," cooperated to get the rich furs of the subarctic northwest, which a number of small independents had revealed. Pond's partners in trade were at one time Alexander Henry (the elder), Joseph and Thomas Frobisher, and Charles Patterson.

Assembling at Cumberland House and The Pas in 1775, the partners split up and traveled in different directions to interdict HBC traders who also were seeking profits from the interior. Pond, a visionary and the most aggressive, had two canoes; Henry had eight, Patterson fourteen, and the Frobisher's twenty. By 1779, they had become the North West Company.

In 1775, Pond's associate, George McBeath, promising to meet him with supplies at Grand Portage off Lake Superior instead of returning to Montreal, allowed him to explore. Pond headed northwest, and in 1778 crossed the northern Continental Divide known later as Methye Portage and established himself on the Athabasca River. For more than a hundred years, the Methye Portage was a critical point in northern fur-trade travel. Equally important, the impossible round trip from the Mackenzie River to York Factory or Grand Portage in one summer season was avoided by having inbound and outbound brigades meet at Methye Portage to exchange loads. In two seasons, despite the opposition of the Cree middlemen who took furs from Athabasca to Hudson's Bay, Pond returned to Grand Portage with a large pack of superior furs, having left an equal amount on the Athabasca.

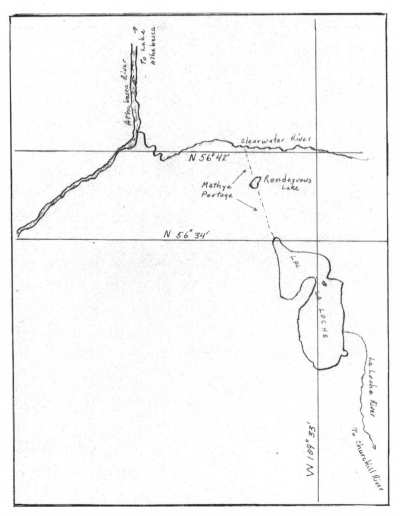

Fig. 6.3 Methye portage. The portage which connects the Churchill River water route to Lake Athabasca and the far north.

In 1786, Pond built Fort Providence at the mouth of Yellowknife Bay on Great Slave Lake. As a partner in the North West Company, he had explored and mapped western and northern Canada. That same year, North West Company sent Laurent Leroux, with John Ross, to compete with Cuthbert Grant of Gregory, McLeod, and Company on the south shore of Great Slave Lake. On June 3, 1789, Leroux and Alexander Mackenzie left Fort Chipewyan en route to the Mackenzie River. Mackenzie's party consisted of four Canadian men, two with wives; a German, John Steinbruck; and a canoe headed by English Chief, or Nestabeck, who had traveled to and from Hudson's Bay, along with other aboriginal hunters, to explore the river to its mouth.

On Great Slave Lake, Leroux, with his own canoe and trade goods, diverted to Le Martre Lake to trade. He was to meet Mackenzie in late summer when the explorers returned. He then wintered at the old Fort Providence and was the first white man to explore Great Slave Lake.[122]

Despite local guides, Mackenzie's party became confused in a group of islands. The Indians wanted to return to Fort Chipewyan, but Mackenzie insisted they push on. They finally found and descended the Mackenzie River, and became lost in a maze of channels at its delta. On July 12, they reached an island that was obviously on the Arctic Ocean; the sight of beluga whales convinced Mackenzie.[123] In August, they headed back upriver. On August 24, he and Leroux were reunited on Great Slave Lake. By September 12, Mackenzie and his party were back at Fort Chipewyan. In 105 days, they had traveled 3,000 miles without a material accident.

Fort Providence supplied outposts farther into the wilderness. When North West Company and Hudson's Bay Company merged in 1821, the fort became a Hudson's Bay Company supply center until it was closed in 1823. The North West Company, stimulated by Pond's success and by the rebellion of Alexander Mackenzie's XY Company, excelled and trumped the Hudson's Bay Company in the far northwest until the merger of 1821.

The Mackenzie River system is the largest in the subarctic. It has a mean annual flow at its mouth of 400,000 cubic feet per second, comparable to the Columbia and St. Lawrence rivers. Mackenzie River tributaries, the Liard, Slave, Peace, and Athabasca, are significant rivers in their own right. Permanent posts appeared on the Mackenzie River. The North West Company built Fort of the Forks on an island at the mouth of the Liard River in 1803 and operated it until 1811. Hudson's Bay Company built Fort Norman and Fort Good Hope in 1810. They constructed Fort Simpson (named for Governor Simpson) near the mouth of the Liard River in 1820, and it became the Mackenzie Basin trade center, the company's depot, and headquarters of the Mackenzie River District. In about 1825, HBC moved Fort Good Hope about a hundred miles upstream to Manitou Island near the Ramparts.[124]

On Lake Athabasca, the North West Company built Fort Chipewyan in 1788. It benefitted from abundant fisheries, which were a prime factor in the diet. The post became a focal point of Northwest fur trade. The Chipewyan people no longer had to face the danger of Cree opposition and starvation as they traveled to the far-away Hudson's Bay posts. Fort Chipewyan was known as the "Emporium of the North" and was "more than a trading post; it was the important regional depot for receiving and transferring goods and men...transferred to the Hudson's Bay Company in 1821."[125] John McLean, visiting in 1833, "found that the trade of this district, although it bears no comparison to that of former times, is still very extensive....Trade is carried on in this quarter solely by barter, which secures the Company from loss....The people at this post subsist entirely on the produce of the country, fish, flesh, and fowl, of which there is the greatest abundance."[126]

The fur trade developed and changed through the years after the arrival of traders in the Far Northwest. Posts were built where there was a likelihood of trade and remained only as long as profitable. In 1829, for example, Edward Smith, chief factor of Hudson's Bay Company's Mackenzie District, sent young clerk John Hutchinson up the Liard to follow its "East Branch" (later renamed Fort Nelson River) to its confluence with the Prophet and Muskwa rivers. There he built Fort Halkett, which succeeded in attracting the trade of the Sekani and Beaver nations. Four years later, in 1833, John M. McLeod moved Fort Halkett to the confluence of the Liard and Smith rivers.[127]

The trading forts in the district, small outposts, and white traders in general relied upon the labor, furs, and aid of subarctic tribes. The trader had to anticipate his trade needs usually two years in advance, and error could mean a substantial reduction in fur and provision returns.

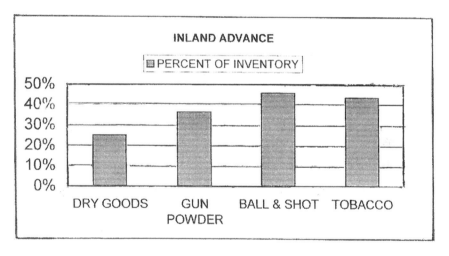

Fig. 6.4 Athabasca District Outfit: Inland advance of inventory
Dry goods: cloth, clothing, files, garters, guns, gun flints, wire, kettles, needles, pans, pins, ribbons, mirrors, steel, awls

Fur-trade historian Theodore Karamanski has argued, "By 1833 in the subarctic, there was substantial post dependency related to the direct provision of subsistence to the fort, and subsistence from the fort to nearby Indian tribes in times of hunting or fishing deficiency, which could, and did, lead to starvation."[128] However, the very term "dependency" arouses much argument among historians and ethnologists. It is important because the nature and degree of dependency influenced greatly the native-trader relationship, and the still maturing relationship between American, Canadian, and native nations—and not only in the subarctic.

Shepard Krech[129] identified two forms: "dependence" was reliance on others, as when "the fur trader needs nothing from the Indian while the Indian relies on the trader for the fulfillment of all his needs. The greater the magnitude of the interest of the Indian in goods provided by the trader," and the greater control the trader has over his available goods "and the less able the Indian is to substitute for what the trader offers, the greater the degree of dependence." Krech's second form of dependence was that "people who are dependent lack political as well as economic autonomy." He noted that "the two are by no means mutually exclusive."

John Stuart was an example of a successful trader in the Mackenzie River District. In 1796, at the age of sixteen and with some education, he left his home in Scotland, bound for North America. He took a job with the North West Company, which promptly sent him to Fort Chipewyan. He served eight years in the Athabasca River basin, at various trading forts and outposts. He went to New Caledonia (later British Columbia) with the explorer Simon Fraser in 1805, traveling down the Fraser River with him. He stayed there for the North West Company until 1817. He then served three years back in the Athabasca River basin, part of the time harassing Hudson's Bay Company traders at Lake Athabasca. He returned to New Caledonia in charge of North West Company operations there. At the 1821 merger, he was appointed a chief factor for Hudson's Bay Company.

Stuart was in charge of the Saskatchewan District in 1824–26, and the Winnipeg District in 1826–32. In 1832, he was moved to the Mackenzie River District, apparently a punitive act. He had sharply criticized

Governor Simpson and John G. McTavish for abandoning their country wives and children in order to return to Britain to marry and bring out English wives. One result was that in his famous "Character Book," Simpson severely criticized Stuart, despite having written of him earlier, "the Father...of New Caledonia; where for 20 years of his Life, he was doomed to all the misery and privation...who with a degree of exertion, of which few men were capable, overcame difficulties, to which the business of no other part of the country was exposed...which will long reflect the highest credit on his name and character, as an Indian Trader." In 1833 Stuart was still chief factor at Fort Simpson. He was fifty-three and a crusty veteran whose toughness and skills had been tested many times in his thirty-seven years in the fur trade.

Stuart's third and then current wife, Mary Taylor, was a sister to Governor Simpson's country wife, Margaret Taylor. Stuart described his tumultuous love affair with Mary in his Fort Simpson post journal. She was much younger than he, and she attracted younger suitors. The resulting scandal prompted Stuart to abandon Mary in 1839 when he retired to Scotland. But loving her, he later sent for her and promised marriage. She came, but he did not marry her, and she returned to her family. Stuart died in Scotland in 1847. Afterward, his surviving sisters, through litigation, reduced Stuart's legacy to Mary from £500 to £300.[130]

As chief factor, Stuart maintained the "Fort Simpson Journal of Occurrences, Outfit 1833." This journal provides an excellent and intimate view of the degree to which the fur trade and post life depended on area natives for both furs and provisions. The year 1833 was successful for the Mackenzie River District, which produced 4,968 beaver, the third-highest number during the fourteen years from 1821 to 1835.[131] It was also a year during which, in some parts of the district, the people suffered despair and starvation because the winter was warm with little snow, resulting in hunting failures. Many of them starved to death or died from malnutrition-related disease. Fort Simpson provided some aid to natives in distress. According to the post's journal, "Indians taking fish to reduce starvation." [132]

Although there were times of emergency or heightened activity at Fort Simpson, the post's journal reveals a pattern of frequent and utter boredom, represented by simple and brief entries like "people at usual tasks." The 1833 Fort Simpson journal was evidently written partly by the post clerk and partly by Chief Factor Stuart. For Governor Simpson and members of the council supervising and analyzing fur-trading activity, a consistent pattern of any information was of considerable value.

The Fort Simpson journal has carefully recorded entries about the coming and going of the Indians and hired hunters—alas not in much detail. Entries make evident the division of effort between subsistence for survival and the acquisition of furs. Between May 1833 and March 1834, the fort received 7,385 pounds of various meats, 1,962 fish, and 3,774 pelts of various kinds. Also recorded in the journal were building and equipment maintenance; fabrication of snowshoes, boats, and sleighs; and firewood cutting. All of these activities took time away from actual trade. Historian Arthur Ray estimated that only about 6 percent of employee time at the fort was devoted directly to the fur trade, and that occurred mostly in October, when the annual outfit arrived. Obtaining the provisions needed to survive took the most time.

Excerpts from the Fort Simpson journal for 1833–34 reveal the Indian-dominated white man's life, isolated in the northland, in detail usually read only by curious scholars at the Hudson's Bay Company Archives in Winnipeg. Historian Elizabeth Vibert observed that a journal writer could be affected by "time limits, and by his perception of the audience, such as the Governor and Committee in London. Much may have been left unsaid." [133] Quoting the journal:

May: Monday, 27th [1833] Stuart leaves for lower posts with 11 men; now rations at this post limited to 1½ lbs pounded meat and 1 pint barley daily. Planting potatoes in AM.

Thurs 30th: Ice was flowing in the river in the forenoon. In evening Boistert and Johnson arrived from Fort de Liard, 1 bale leather, 3 bales dried meat, 65 lbs each. For want of proper craft McPherson could not send more. [Then clerk Murdoch McPherson, made chief trader in 1834 and chief factor in 1847.] No news from Fort Halkett. Weather fine, men in gardens.

Fri. 31st: So short of provisions, am sending the 2 men on with a few night's provisions—leaving tomorrow for Fort de Liard, also 2 Indians I supplied with ammunition, and a fishnet by which means they can reach their destination. Weather fine, river ice free.

June: Sat, 1st: The Liard men left. The state of the river is such that they must leave canoes below rapids and make bark canoes above. Gardens finished, water rising, ice not drifting so much.

Mon 3rd: Received the first furs brought by Cactins [an unidentified Indian] 17 beavers, 1 bear, 22 muskrat and 2 Moose. Cactins left toward evening. From the quantity of ice they declined going upstream with their canoes, preferring to go across land from Big Island to Liard River [225 miles]. Eschalais and his few followers plan to pass the summer in upper McKenzie River. Water seldom as high as now.

Thurs 6th: Furs brought yesterday: 99 beaver, 9 martens, 5 lynx, 6 bears, 3 otters, 2 wolverines and 112 muskrats. Hunters departed. Carpenter making oars for outgoing brigade. Only 7 fish netted. Weather fine.

Mon 10th: 2 Dahotinne Indians arrived, 93 beaver, 2 martens, 7 deer skins. Later others brought from Upper Mackenzie River 16 beaver, 640 muskrat, 5 lynx, 1 wolf, 12 marten, 7 wolverine, 7 bear, 1 moose. Thunderstorm in PM Hail and rain.

Tues 11th: Indians arriving yesterday left today.

Thurs 13th: Packing [and pressing] furs into 87 lb packs.

Fri 14th: Boat to be finished tomorrow. Fur packs (31) made up. Turnips from the garden, twice as many as formerly 50 to 60 kegs.

Sun 23rd: Cargoes given out and stowed. Light rain.

Busy preparing to embark for Portage la Lochs [Methye Portage]. Chief Factor Stuart, Chief Trader [John Jr.] Macleod, and Mr. Brisbois[134] left in 4 boats with returns of '32. 135 packs of furs, 4 kegs castoreum, leaving at this place Pierre St. Germain[135] and Father Armand [Catholic missionary], for the summer. With Stuart are 3 men intended for W. Branch [later called the upper Liard River], expected to go the length of the little lake to meet men from Athabasca. One, Douglas McDougal is required as a boute [front canoe paddler whose expertise permits taking routes through rapids] for the West Branch. Weather fine.

August Mon 26th: [Two months later, after a boat trip of more than 650 miles each way] John Stuart arrived with outfit from Portage la Loche [Methye Portage]. 4 boats, 6 men each. Though fewer men made the trip, it was faster than ever before. Left here 24 June, Portage La Loche 27 July, delayed 2 days at Portage Labonne making arrangements with Capt Back RN [Royal Navy][136] now on his 3rd voyage on land to the Arctic Sea. NOTE: When Chief Factor Stuart left Fort Simpson on June 24, 1833, he was taking the returns of the Outfit for 1832. His party traveled in four York boats, with 135 ninety-pound packs of furs and four kegs of castoreum. The outbound trip required 650 miles of travel upstream: up the Mackenzie River, along Great Slave Lake, to Fort Resolution, up the Slave River to the Athabasca River, up the Athabasca to the Clearwater River, and up the Clearwater to Methye Portage. There beside the Clearwater, Stuart transferred the furs and castoreum to Hudson's Bay Company voyageurs that would actually make the portage and take the goods eastward. Stuart received from the voyageurs westbound mail and trade goods. The trip back to Fort Simpson was downstream. He reached home on August 26, 1833. It had taken two months and two days for the round trip, averaging 20.6 miles per day, the days at Methye Portage excluded.

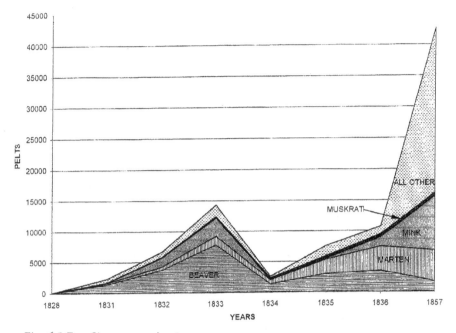

Fig. 6.5 Fort Simpson production

Continuing the September 1833 journal:

Mon [September] 9th: This day some of the men came from the fisheries in two boats and collect Provisions....We can depend but little on the supplies from the Indians and more on the fisheries to keep us from starving this winter. Beaulieu also went off. He is to pass the autumn with his Beau Frere St. Germain and I [Stuart] have forbid the people from having any dealing whatsoever with him, and him from dealing with the Indians either. The penalty is forfeiting what little money he has in the Company Hands. I now remain here with but three men and am not sorry the bustle is over.

NOTE: To understand fully the trading problems that post traders faced, it is necessary to leave the journal briefly to describe fully the
independent trader Beaulieu. Stuart scorned Beaulieu. He was a Métis
of considerable significance in the Mackenzie District. Stuart's apparent
dislike and mistrust of Beaulieu may well have arisen from Beaulieu's
independent trading capabilities, which were always fought by the "Honourable Company" and its traders, since independent traders either cut
into the company's take of furs, or took a middleman's profit.

Free traders took advantage of competition between Hudson's Bay
Company traders, and could exploit the differences in transportation
costs in the Far North. For example, if Francois Beaulieu were to offer
prices slightly less when trading with the Dené at Lac La Martre, he
would take trade from a post like Fort Norman. Beaulieu, in possession
of cheaper furs, could then trade profitably by going to Fort Chipewyan
or Fort Simpson, where he could get the standard better prices.

Francois Beaulieu, then fifty-two, was the son of Jacques Beaulieu and
a Montagnais woman. The Montagnais were among the earliest Indians
the French encountered along the north shore of the St. Lawrence River.
Francois Beaulieu "had three wives and other casual relationships." In
later years, he lived on the Salt River and developed a profitable trade in
salt. Beaulieu was known also as Francois II, Le Patriarch, or Old Man
Beaulieu. The company, with whom he enjoyed great prestige, granted
him a monopoly in the salt trade.

Father Emile Petitot wrote of Beaulieu:

He was one of the oldest witnesses of events that have taken place in the

north. His father, a Frenchman, was a trader in the service of the Cam-

pagnie des Sioux. He settled in this distant wilderness, without anyone in

Canada suspecting it. His son, our hero, whom he had with a Chipewyan

woman. He saw the arrival, in 1780, of the first fur trade explorer of

Great Slave Lake, Peter Pond; then, in 1789, of Sir Alexander Mackenzie. His uncle, Jacques Beaulieu, served as interpreter to the first of these officers of the North West Company.[137]

The Dené credited Francois Beaulieu with strong medicine—the ability to hunt as well as to heal, characteristics he is said to have passed down to his descendants. He was able to broker truces between the Dogrib and Yellowknife in 1829 and 1831, and very likely including a famous peace established by Yellowknife Chief Akaitcho and the Dogrib chief Edzo. His diplomacy impressed the wary Hudson's Bay Company so much that they hired Beaulieu to run their post at Fort Resolution.[138]

Illustrative of the patriarch's power, "W. L. Hardisty was taking a fur brigade up the river to Portage la Loche when, near Francois Beaulieu II's place on the Salt River, the boat crew rebelled. Hardisty sent for Beaulieu. The old dictator came, pulled his long knife and pretended to shave his tobacco plug. 'Get back to your boat and give no more trouble to your Chiefs.' he told the rebels, who took to their boats. Hardisty gave the old rascal a suitable present for his trouble."[139]

In 1848, at age 77, Beaulieu was baptized a Catholic, set aside two wives and lived faithfully to one. An active communicant, he precisely followed religious observances and "exerted himself to open the eyes of those Indians who had been led astray by the Protestant minister." He was an active hunter to age 85, and died at just over 100, in November 1872, at Salt River.

Continuing the Fort Simpson Journal:

Sun [September] 29th Weather same. Akathlak brought 719 lbs fresh meat. Killed 3 moose, Indians starving, so they ate one. 3 Mountain Indians arrived, brought only 15 beaver, 2 small bear, 2 wolverines, 2 Martens, a few reindeer skins and 50 lbs dry meat. I paid them and they left. Never have I [apparently Stuart] seen [furs] so badly arranged, and they have been frequenting the Establishment for 30 years. Claimed not their fault, and

now that I have told them, no one would find fault again. Michael Villa-
neuve arrived with 4 servants and 5 Indians, 2 boats, from Upper Mackenzie
River. Has been to the Big Island, [a famous fishery at the point where the
Mackenzie River leaves the western end of Great Slave Lake] where he built
a house for people who are to winter there. Left Felix and LeFeure there with
400 fish. Fishing has not been good but they neglected nets. Brought 600
fish, all rotten. At the same time [another] brought 800 taken at the same
time, not so bad. If cold weather comes, may be eatable. Indians I sent to
Hay River have had a good hunt and St. Germain[140] has collected it.
October Sat 5th: 3 Indians brought 12 beaver, 80 muskrat, 200 lb half dried
meat. Traded and departed.

Stuart used the journal for occasional philosophical comments on the
nature of trade and on the company policies with which he apparently
disagreed:

Gave a few iron works on debt. Regret stopping debt giving on the Mackenzie River. Stopping debt does more to reduce returns than all other
factors together. Anyone conversant with trade knows that Indian trade
never was and cannot be carried on to advantage when no debts given.
They are naturally improvident and supplies given in fall enable them to
hunt in winter. How much debt is a matter of judgment. Too many debts
or none at all are equally bad. No better criterion for evaluating a trader
than how he settles Indians beginning winter. Any blockhead can trade
skins, but not every literate man of education and sense can do justice
to an Establishment. Experience needed. Before long HBC will again be
taught by experience what they have forgotten....
Fri 22nd: Clear and cold. Indians have never seen weather so mild or river so
low.
Tues 24th: Weather same. Christmas eve. Gave double rations of fresh
meat to all hands, also flour, potatoes, turnips.

Thurs 26th Sent off hunters. Letter from McPherson at Fort de Liard, all well there. There is little doubt they can maintain the Establishment through the winter. [Obviously, survival was a continuing issue at remote posts.]

Tues 31st: This being the last day of the year, I issued extra rations for the commencement of another. Consisting of Fresh Meat, Back Fat, grease, flour, potatoes, turnips and cabbage more than enough for one day. Three Indians arrived from the Liard River and surprising to relate they brought a loaded sleigh.

January 1834: Wed 1st: This being the commencement of a new year the People are coming today the compliments of the new year fired a salute at the door. Then they were ushered into the Hall and after the Bon Jours was over each of them was treated to a couple of glasses of wine the only Liquor we have. An abundance of cakes, some raisins, also a fathom of Tobacco, and Pipes. After chatting some time the men returned, firing a salute as when they came. After which the Guide and the Interpreter returned and assisted my servant to lay the table in the Hall and all hands invited to a Plentiful Breakfast.

February: Wed 5th[:] Calm, mild. Same tasks. In evening St. Armand and Wells arrived from Fort de Liard, taking 6 days, brought letter from McLeod at Fort Halkett and McPherson at de Liard. Conditions couldn't be better. McPherson estimates from word already heard from Indians considerable increases in returns from Ft. Liard. At Halkett appearances favorable beyond expectations. Before close of navigation the people had caught 3000 excellent fish and 30 reindeer [evidently at Fort Simpson]. This will last all hands till March. Things appear favorable, but in the Rockies, as the season advances, difficulties arise. Am apprehensive of want in the summer. My experience is if the people could find subsistence the fur returns would be good as a matter of course. Fiddle arrived with 22 hares.[141]

And so the yearly routine continued. The chief factor, or the chief trader, or the clerk in charge at Hudson's Bay Company posts faced similar problems, time and time again. Provisions controlled all. If the Indians were "starving"—well-known as a term natives sometimes used in trading—they devoted their time to getting sustenance, not furs. If fort provisions were short, natives had to be persuaded to bring provisions rather than furs to trade. Peace had to be maintained between all—among whites, among natives, among mixed-descent people, and between the races. Boats had to be built, buildings constantly repaired to resist the weather, firewood had to be cut and hauled, injury and illness doctored, and communications had to be maintained with other posts.

The bourgeois in charge of a post had considerable latitude in managing affairs, providing discipline, and administering justice, so long as accounts were meticulously kept. The profit to the "Honourable Company" was the prime consideration, and company trading policies were scrupulously followed. On August 30, 1833, Chief Factor Stuart wrote to all the posts in the Mackenzie District. Based on his long experience in the fur trade, he provided definite ideas about trading. His trader philosophy about native relations, expressed in that letter, differed from company policy as defined by Governor Simpson and the Northern Department Council. Stuart reflected on his extensive trading experience throughout the Far Northwest, including British Columbia. Anticipating approval of the council, he ordered changes in the district because, he wrote, "We are selling property for less than at Norway House [HBC supply depot on northeast end of Lake Winnipeg, and advance depot from York Factory], regardless of the increased cost of transport."

He ordered that prices paid in made beaver be raised for bear, otter, muskrat, foxes, lynches, martens, and swans, and restricted purchase of reindeer (caribou) hide leather for servants' use. He listed trade goods in detail, specifying prices. He prohibited barter accounts. Believing that provisions were priced too high, he said that the natives would exploit the higher prices, "and if they could get their wants for nothing they would loiter their time in perfect idleness." Stuart added to these instructions other pricing and administrative details.[142]

Stuart's letter backfired. Instead of getting company approval, he upset the chain of command. Governor Simpson reported critically to the Governor and Committee in London:

> He [Stuart] was repeatedly instructed to follow up the policies and measures of his predecessor—One change, in particular,—that of raising prices of goods to the natives which—is unjust, oppressive, and highly irregular and improper—instead of increasing it, we had it in contemplation to reduce it, as a measure both of humanity and of policy, as it is but proper that a fair price should be afforded for their skins, and as that is the most effectual means of bringing them into habits of industry.[143]

Simpson apparently never did understand that his idea of native indolence or lack of industry was really a difference in priorities. Simpson solved the problem by placing Chief Factor Edward Smith, who had been at Fort Chipewyan since 1833, in charge of both. Simpson wrote Smith, "It is with much concern we learn that Mr. Stuart has altered the Tariff of Mckenzie's [sic] River, as regards the Indian Trade, which we consider to have been injudicious and improper, as the prices usually charged during your administration were sufficiently high; you will therefore be pleased to revert to former prices."[144] Stuart was again demoted. During the mess, he went to Scotland on furlough.

Due to poor health Stuart extended his furlough, left Hudson's Bay Company in 1839, and died in 1847. Although Simpson had regarded Stuart highly, he was very spiteful in his "Character Book" when Stuart retired.

CHAPTER 7:

NEW CALEDONIA

Na-Kwoel was an aged nobleman of the Athapaskan-speaking Stuart Lake Carrier band. About 1730, while trading on the Skeena River near present-day Hazelton, present British Columbia, he acquired an iron ax or adze. The arrival of an iron tool through the ancient coastal-river middleman system was a significant event. It forecast the importance of Indian trade on British Columbia rivers and, later, on the Northwest Coast fur trade.[145]

Indian middlemen had brought the cutting tool from seashore flotsam, and then, probably by successive trades, 225 miles up the Skeena River. To the Carrier, the iron tool must have meant an unknown or perhaps legendary—and still remote—people who were capable of making such a tool. Not until Vitus Bering landed his ship the *St. Peter* near Mount St. Elias in June 1741 did another white trade source arrive. It is possible that from that landing, coastal Indian trading saw a trickle of white man's products brought south along the coast by Indian craft. More regular trade for furs and Indian artifacts began in 1774, when Juan Perez, commanding the Spanish ship *Santiago*, put in at Nootka Sound on the west coast of Vancouver Island. From that time, white men appeared in ocean-going ships and continued to be the coastal sources of interior trade.

New Caledonia was the name early fur traders gave to the northern and central part of British Columbia. In time, the geography of New Caledonia and the diverse trade capabilities of the Indian people would determine New Caledonia's profit-producing value. Within New Caledonia, support of trade from the east, whether from Montreal or Hudson's Bay, was a more difficult matter. Exploration was needed.

Alexander Mackenzie, after his 1789 exploration to the mouth of the Mackenzie River, was determined to find a way to the Pacific. Having discovered on his Arctic expedition that he could not fix positions accurately, he traveled to London to remedy his lack of celestial navigation skill. In 1793, he crossed New Caledonia, and reached the sea. Advised by Carrier Indians not to attempt the river later called the Fraser, he headed westward to present Bella Coola, and its steep, deep canyon.

Mackenzie found the hospitable Bella Coola Indians. In an Indian canoe, he traveled down a fjord called the Bentinck Arm of the Pacific and back to the head of nearby Dean Channel. There he printed on a rock cliff, "Alexander Mackenzie, from Canada, by land, the twenty second of July, one thousand seven hundred and ninety-three."[146] He was first across the continent and had experienced Pacific coastal trade. By Saturday, August 24, his whole party was back at Fort Fork near present-day Peace River villages.

Bringing the resources of the North West Company to the Pacific required actions Mackenzie recommended in his far-sighted plan for trade to be opened on the Pacific Ocean. His popular book, *Voyages from Montreal,* brought him needed publicity, secured a knighthood, opened the ears of Cabinet ministers in London, and made him a fur-trade statesman. He continued to pursue his plan.

But Napoleon was then a threat in Europe and to England, and his plan lay ignored in the "slumbering" foreign office. As historian Barry Gough wrote, "Mackenzie...understood the potential American threat as evidenced by Lewis and Clark's discoveries and by the U.S. acquisition of Louisiana in 1803. [He was] the first to raise the alarm about possible loss of the Oregon country through British indifference."[147] Fur-trading companies in London and fur-trading interests in Montreal were unresponsive or opposed. Mackenzie's reputation as an explorer, aggressive personality, determination, and popularity as a Montreal business and social celebrity were ineffective.

Frustrated from lack of North West Company action, he formed a New North West Company, known as the XY Company because of the marks on its fur packs. Severe competition ensued between NWC and XY Company traders, reaching as far as to the Peace River country. Indians were persuaded to pillage canoes, retaliation was expected, and arms and liquor were brought in. This bitter and costly competition ended only when the "fur trade premier" Simon McTavish of the North West Company died in 1804. Mackenzie then brought his company back into the North West Company fold.

In 1805, the North West Company sought to develop Mackenzie's new discovery by expanding the lower Peace River trade. They first sent Simon Fraser across the Canadian Rockies in 1805 to build Fort McLeod on McLeod Lake. He helped build forts on Stuart Lake and Fraser Lake in 1806, and Fort George at the junction of the Nechako and Fraser rivers in 1807. Fraser named the country New Caledonia in memory of his Scottish Highlands.

Seeking a route to the sea, he descended the Fraser River, later named for him, but when he viewed its violent surges between vertical cliffs and crawled along sheer walls, he and his partner James Stuart, found the Fraser too dangerous to be a practicable route. Yet these actions allowed the North West Company to establish their prior claim to the New Caledonia fur trade. North West Company control would last until the merger with Hudson's Bay Company in 1821, when the British government extended the Hudson's Bay Company monopoly and civil authority from Rupert's Land to the Pacific.

While Fraser and Stuart were building forts in northern New Caledonia, David Thompson was making a completely different, and even more important, exploration. His task was to find a route to the mouth of the Columbia River.

David Thompson ranks today as North America's premier surveyor, whose greatest achievement was his 1814 map of British America, now resting in the Library and Archives of Canada. The map stretched from the Fraser River to Lake Superior, so accurate that it still is a basic reference.

In 1800, the North West Company partners had been alert to fur-trade possibilities beyond the Rockies. Duncan McGillivray, Simon McTavish's nephew, was sent west and reached Rocky Mountain House, west of present Red Deer, Alberta, on October 23. There he met David Thompson, who had been trading with both the Kutenai and Piegan. In November, Thompson returned to the Piegan on the Bow River. McGillivray went to Athabasca Pass, but was unable to cross it due to poor health. He returned to Rocky Mountain House and thence to Fort William, suffering from rheumatism. Before leaving, McGillivray charged Thompson, then a full partner, with "discovering" the Columbia River. Thompson then left to trade at Peace River.

Lewis and Clark's expedition so intrigued North West Company partners that Thompson was recalled to Rocky Mountain House in 1806 to explore across the Rockies. In June 1807, with thirteen men and women, including his wife, Charlotte, and six children—among them his six-year-old Fanny, three-year-old Samuel, and thirteen-month-old Emmy. Thompson headed up the Saskatchewan. Struggling through deep snow, they crossed the Howse Pass. On a high plain above Upper Columbia Lake, he built Fort Kutenai, where the party wintered.

In 1808 and 1809, Thompson explored the Kutenai and Clark Fork rivers, building Fort Kullyspell on Lake Pend Oreille and Saleesh House—later Flathead Post—near present-day Thompson Falls, Montana, where he spent the winter. In 1810 he crossed the mountains eastward and returned to Rainy Lake with furs.

News of Astor's plan for the mouth of the Columbia sent Thompson immediately back to Rocky Mountain House with the mission of exploring the Columbia and building a post to compete with the Americans. But by 1810, the Piegan would not allow use of Howse Pass, fearing that white trade in guns would arm their enemies, the Kutenai. So Thompson had to travel more than a hundred miles north to Athabasca Pass.

He and his party crossed the pass and wintered on the Canoe River, where they spent the winter building boats to navigate the Columbia River. Lacking birchbark pieces large enough for a canoe, Thompson invented and built cedar-plank canoes, using thin cedar planks, using a clinker design, fastening the planks only at the bow and stern, and gumming the joints. They were light and strong, forty feet long, and could carry heavy loads. This craft later developed into the Columbia River bateaux, which was a prime mover during fur-trade years. The party christened the camp the "Boat Encampment."[148]

Understanding the Columbia's circuitous route, Thompson headed north and downstream. On July 15, he arrived at Astoria. He had explored the Columbia from its source to the sea. At its juncture with the Snake River, he had placed a sign, claiming what was then known as the Oregon country for the British Empire.

Meanwhile, in New Caledonia, Fraser, Stuart, and their traders faced the problems of a country vast with forests, plains, and the rapids of many critical rivers. All geographical aspects affected the fur trade and the transportation routes. From north to south, the Stikine, Nass, Skeena, Bella Coola, and Fraser rivers, which cut through the Coast Range to the sea, were prominent keys to interior trade and subsistence. The Coast Range impedes the flow of ocean storms, making the interior warm and dry in summer. Winters are generally cold and wet. Fall freeze-up and spring breakup provided the most difficult travel conditions.[149]

The extremes of the mountains and rivers demanded that fur traders find new ways to deliver furs. On May 13, 1813, John Stuart led a party of nine men in two canoes from Fort St. James down the Fraser for eight days; leaving the river, they took horses to Fort Okanagan to meet John McTavish. The two led seventy-five men with ten canoes down a section of the Columbia needed to reach the Pacific. They arrived in time to participate in the purchase of the Pacific Fur Company's assets. With this purchase, the North West Company controlled the fur trade of New Caledonia and the Columbia.

From Fort George (previously Astoria), the North West Company tried shipping furs to Canton. Fees assessed by Britain's East India Company's monopoly and Chinese custom regulations made it impossible to barter, and trade was unprofitable. Because of the shipping hazard of the Columbia River bar, the North West Company built Fort Nez Perces in 1818 as a depot to accept and store "outfits" of trade goods. The company shipped £71,000 of trade goods to the Columbia between 1815 and 1818.[150]

As elsewhere, exploration and fur trade by the NWC—and after 1821, the HBC—depended on the Indian people. The basic culture described in chapter 1 generally applied to Indian life in New Caledonia. In matters such as kinship, mysticism, war, and child care; finding subsistence, clothing, and shelter; and family and tribal cultural relations, there were distinct and essential qualities of their lives that had a direct bearing on the HBC fur trade in that area.

Except for the impact of European trade goods, upon which different tribes came to be more or less dependent, and the effect of missionaries somewhat later than 1833, there was, by 1833, no great change in Indian trade priorities from the time of Mackenzie's 1793 exploration. The inland tribes—Carrier, Tahltan, Inland Tlingit, Tagish, and Chilcotin—were all dependent on salmon runs, and their life revolved around successful fishing. When annual salmon runs sometimes failed to materialize, survival required much trading among tribes. All the tribes made rectangular bark-covered structures at summer fish camps for fish drying and for shelter.

The tribal name Carrier comes from the Carrier custom of requiring widows to carry their deceased husband's cremated bones in a bag fastened to the neck for one year after the husband's death. The Carrier, who fished the headwaters of the Nass and Skeena rivers, along with others nearby, had good salmon runs most years. The upper Fraser, where the runs were not so reliable, forced the Chilcotin and the Stuart Lake Carrier to rely on trading, depending heavily on the coastal tribes, the Shuswap and Bella Coola, for subsistence items. All tribes, dependent on fishing, hunting, and gathering, were forced to be mobile. The Sekani were more so than others, since they had come from a hunting culture east of the Rockies before being driven west by the Beaver Indians.

Annual salmon runs were crucial events for the white traders also, determining nutrition and even survival. Fish were always a principal part of survival, and large game was generally scarce, as Simpson reported to the HBC governor and committee in London in 1832; he said he considered New Caledonia the poorest district of any, from the standpoint of subsistence, with agriculture ineffective because of early and late frosts. There were few large animals, and the natives depended solely on fish.[151] It was not surprising that desertions at the posts resulted. Eventually HBC paid a small bonus to those serving in New Caledonia.

Fig.7.1 Dried salmon cache at Fort St. James Photo by author, 1999

Historian James R. Gibson wrote in *The Lifeline of the Oregon Country*, "In 1836 the two officers, seven clerks, and fifty-two men at the seven posts of New Caledonia consumed an astonishing total of 67,318 dried and 30 fresh salmon, 781 sturgeon, 346 trout, and 11,940 other fish, plus 2,166 rabbits, 1534 ducks, and 58 geese, as well as 226 kegs of potatoes and 153 kegs of turnips."[152]

The fur traders carefully observed how Indian character and lifestyle affected the fur trade. Both Indians and whites traded because they considered it mutually beneficial. Interior tribes had many common cultural characteristics, though competition for white trade goods brought hostility and even intertribal war. Indian bands traveled incessantly. Through trade, interior tribes enjoyed the benefits of the bountiful coastal environment and contact with the coast's dense, sophisticated, and relatively stable Indian population.

Because of the mobility of hunting, fishing, and gathering, any classification of aboriginal people shown on a map, and any arbitrary selection of terms such as tribe, band, and so forth, raises the question: What sort of group is a tribe? Tribe and band have been given conflicting meanings. A band is a small group of people, usually kinfolk, who live together through the seasons of the year. When these small groups at times join other similar small groups for visits, battle, or other reasons, they may be termed a tribe. The dictates of cordilleran weather, terrain, and subsistence sources forced people into villages for mutual support, which, in essence, determined how they became known and grouped.

Mackenzie first encountered the Sekani in 1793 on the upper Peace River. The Athapaskan-speaking Sekani inhabited the mountainous areas drained by the Finlay and Parsnip rivers and the Peace River above Fort Dunvegan. The Cree and Beaver had forced them westward near the beginning of the nineteenth century. The name Sekani, according to Fort St. James missionary Adrian Morice, means "people on the rocks" or "people on the mountains." Sekani are entirely nomadic, and their social structure permitted wide dispersion and mobility to exploit the natural environment.[153]

Before the arrival of the white man's guns and traps, they used efficient aboriginal systems for hunting. As anthropologist Robin Ridington commented, "The essence of this [native] technology was the possession of knowledge, not the possession of artifacts, [for] with knowledge they could produce whatever artifacts necessary."[154] They used deadfalls, snares, brush fences, and other traps that were ingeniously contrived and effective for the wide variety of prey.In hunting, dreams were important. "Hunters dreamed [of] their kills and used instructions received in their dreams. Dreams…provided maps as real to them as paper maps are to the cartographer." In Beaver and Sekani mythology, a Swan dreamer named Makenunatane prophesied the coming of the European and the fur trade of the eighteenth century.[155]

Regarding the Sekani, Richard Mackie wrote, "Kinship was reckoned bilaterally (traced through both father's and mother's families), and this expanded the network to its fullest extent."[156] With a population of about a hundred, a band required at least 1,400 pounds of meat per week.

Hunting areas were clearly recognized as the communal property of every member of the band and available to all. Despite intermarriage and a common language, there were interband feuds.

The Sekani wore clothing made of skins, until fabrics became available. Their decorations were dentalium, shells, bracelets of horn or bone, and necklaces of bear claws. They made cooking vessels of spruce bark or woven roots, and utensils of wood, bone, and horn. They cached excess food in trees, removing the lower bark as a protection from a persistent and ingenious thief, the wolverine. Being mobile hunters, their shelters were conical lodges made of poles and spruce bark. Spruce bark also formed the shell of their canoes. The Sekani periodically lived on lake fish in summer. They traded hunting products to the Carrier, their middlemen for the coast trade.

Because of the long-standing coastal Indian trade, the coastal tribes cannot be entirely separated from interior Indian activity. The coastal tribes were the Tlingit, Haida, Tsimshian, Kwakuitl, Nootka, Bella Coola, and Coast Salish. A major trade route went from the Tsimshian up the Skeena to the Gitskan to the Bulkley River Carrier, thence to the Sekani. The Gitskan were an upper Skeena Tsimshian coastal people who spoke the Tsimshian dialect, hunted land animals, and exploited the vast flow of Skeena River salmon.

Anthropologist Glenda Denniston describes how the Sekani also affiliated with coastal Indians; their social alignments had been marked variously by movement, splitting, amalgamation, and regroupings, as well as by intermarriage with other tribes; the Sekani traded at all of the northern posts on the Peace, Skeena, Stikine, and Fraser rivers during the first half of the nineteenth century.[157] In 1833, these posts would become Forts Connolly, Babine, McLeod, Fraser, and St. James.

At Fort McLeod, Simon Fraser noted that the bands divided into smaller groups, each with a headman and a second in command. When the HBC took over in 1821, traders tried to break up this free movement. It seriously complicated their planning for procurement of trade goods. Failure to have a proper inventory at the proper time could adversely affect returns and, inevitably, promotion.

The Carrier lived in a relatively cohesive social unit consisting of a group of male siblings, their wives, children, and married sons' wives and children. This exogamous group recognized the firstborn male among siblings as a headman. Anthropologist Osgood divided the Carrier into seven distinct groups that lived from the upper end of Stuart Lake to Fort Alexandria. They were known by their location, although all occupied the central part of New Caledonia's fur-production area. Band members identified as nobles controlled fishing, gathering, and hunting areas. This control permitted them to accumulate surpluses, which made potlatches possible, and ensured noble rank. A potlatch was a community party staged by a noble to demonstrate his wealth and power. Attendance in a community was mandatory. The host could destroy his property, or even kill slaves, to show his indifference to wealth. The Indian philosophy of reciprocity and communal support required sharing of resources when a village, or a trading post, for that matter, was distressed by the failure of the salmon run.

Hudson's Bay Company reports indicate that more provisions from outside sources were consumed at Stuart Lake than anywhere else in New Caledonia. In 1823, people at the fort consumed 1,000 fresh and 6,500 dried salmon, 2,800 whitefish, 2,000 fresh and 3,000 dried carp, 7 sturgeon, and 4 kegs of roe. In addition, 8,600 salmon were eaten by winter travelers. Fort Fraser was built in 1806 as an additional source of fish. The fur traders attempted to run their own fisheries, but quit, having quickly discovered Carrier resistance and their own lack of skill. One journal writer concluded: "It were much better we should stop all idea of fishing for ourselves."[158]

Whites introduced fish hooks, fishnet twine, and gill nets, but with the salmon at least, Indian fishing methods endured well into the twentieth century.

Fort Babine (Fort Kilmaurs) was built by Chief Trader William Brown for the HBC in 1822 at the north end of Lake Babine. It proved to have unanticipated importance. In 1825 the post produced 44,000 salmon, and sent 18,000 to other posts. The Fort Kilmaurs production of sockeye salmon made it a superb asset to the people at Forts St. James and St. George, who virtually lived on salmon.[159] In addition, Babine Lake waters flowed into the Skeena River, which enters the Pacific at present-day Prince Rupert. This permitted travel for annual meetings between interior Indians and the Indian coastal traders, who brought guns and hatchets to exchange for beaver pelts.

The European items found at or retrieved from the coast represented a long-established coastal trade. Ethnologist Catharine McClellan wrote that the coastal Indians were always feuding over guns and access to new trade goods. "The Carrier feared the Shuswap, and farther north, the Kaska and Tsetsaut were raiding the Thaltan nearest to the coast. All feared, but traded with, the Tlingit and Gitskan, who traded directly with American, British, and Russian ship captains. Coastal Indians were consistent in preventing interior Indians from going to the coast to trade directly with sea captains."[160]

The Carrier evidently adapted their lifestyle to that of surrounding people, including their use of tools and weapons. In the south, their partly underground housing copied that of the Chilcotin and Shuswap. Northward, they built "A-frame" type structures roofed with spruce bark. In summer, their shelter was the same, but elevated with low plank walls, similar to those of the Tsimshian and Bella Coola. They might use a simple lean-to in fishing and hunting camps.

Canadian Indian historian Diamond Jenness generalized that the coastal culture of nobles, commoners, slaves, and the potlatch leavened Carrier life. Clan chiefs jealously guarded every district and fishing place, tolerating no poaching without prior agreement and requiring compensation. Various phratries (two or more clans descended from a common ancestor) in a village were led by the leading nobleman of the largest phratrie. The benefits of wealth passed in the patrilineal.[161]

The Carrier annual cycle which lasted well into the nineteenth century described their lives. The annual migration cycle began with the ice breakup by mid-April. They moved to small lakes for ice and open-water fishing. Getting adequate trout, whitefish, and carp was critical. Later in summer, they subsisted on dried fish, if available. In addition, they ate berries, lichen, plant stalks, and the inner bark of the cypress and jack pine. This menu lasted until the salmon returned. As the winter became severe, families gathered near food storage.

This cycle eventually changed to trapping for winter and summer furs to accommodate traders' needs. In mid-August, people gathered at weirs to intercept migrating salmon. Here they potlatched, visited, feasted, gambled, and traded. Before the snow fell, individual families dispersed to winter hunting areas and to beaver trapping. The nobles did not permit all commoners to trap beaver, but they could trap marten, which the traders encouraged.

Individual Indians were seldom well-known or described in HBC journals. The Carrier chief Kwah, or Qua, is an exception. A study of his life illustrates many of the Indian and trader customs that governed mutual understanding and support.

In 1840, Kwah, the most prominent and famous of Carrier Indian chiefs recognized as nobles, died at Stuart Lake at the age of about 85. Charles Bishop, in his detailed biography of Kwah, cautioned of error that might exist between Indian views reported by Fort St. James missionary Morice in 1904, and the views found in the HBC Fort of St. James journals. "For the European trader and other Carrier Indians he was probably the most important Indian in New Caledonia."[162]

Frieda Klippenstein, Parks Canada Historian, reported, "The traders recognized him [Kwah] as a man of great influence and worked to build an alliance with him."[163] By this they won his significant subsistence support and cooperation, and that of his extensive family as well. Kwah sustained Fort St. James with fish.

After bridging the difference between Kwah's and the traders' ideas of trade and reciprocity, and after making clear to him, as Chief Trader Daniel W. Harmon and trader McDougall did, that they would brook no cheating, a mutually beneficial system was built, designating Kwah as "fur trade chief." The traders dressed him and awarded him a capote, handkerchief, dressed moose skin, and gifts for his small sons, hoping for his preferential treatment.

They considered him "independent" because the Carrier got many of their necessities from their neighboring middlemen in the coastal trade. For provisions alone, the traders had to trade a disproportionate amount of goods. At times, furs became a second priority. The traders also expected Kwah and other chiefs to settle arguments between traders and Indians, to coordinate post provisioning, and to encourage Indian trading.[164]

At Fort St. James, after the future British Columbia governor Sir James Douglas had apprehended and hanged an Indian murderer, Kwah returned from a hunt and with a war party, pinned Douglas to a table with a knife at his throat. His wife, Amelia, hiding above, began throwing down tobacco and other trade goods, and begged for his life. Kwah consented and retreated from the post.[165] He was in every way a leader. Today, his progeny among Stuart Lake Indians use his third son's name, "Prince."

South of the Carrier and between the Bella Coola and the Shuswap, lived the Chilcotin. Their minimal group was the nuclear family, which acted independently, though their culture was an absorption of neighboring cultures. The missionary Morice found Chilcotin men to be shorter and with broader shoulders than the Carrier.[166] Unlike the Carrier, the Chilcotin virtually opted out of the fur trade. David Thompson thought them bolder than the Carrier and Shuswap, and famous for quarrelling.[167] The Chilcotin envied the traditional role of the Carrier Indians as middlemen for coastal trade. They sought to bypass the Carrier trade by dealing directly with the Bella Coola. They were continually at war with the Carrier, and attacked them at Fort Alexandria in 1826. Morice considered the Chilcotin violent and not so very scrupulous. They were capable of making a concerted attack on an enemy, and when doing so, attacked at dawn and continued until the enemy was destroyed.

The Interior Salish fell into five well-known divisions, all of which differed in customs, dialects, and even physical appearance from the Coastal Salish. The Interior Salish Shuswap controlled "the Fraser valley from Lilloet to Alexandria, and all the country eastward to the summits" of the Rockies.[168] They were known to be easy to get along with, honest, strict and demanding, but kind to their children.

The Bonepart, Fraser, and Thompson River Shuswap were considered the most typical Shuswap. They were bold but not rash, manly and proud, good horsemen, aggressive, independent, cruel, and vain.

The other divisions of the Shuswap nation varied according to the terrain they occupied. The canyon and lake divisions were the most expert salmon fishermen. The canyon divisions were the bon vivants and the most cunning traders, but traveled little, while the lake division was more composed, but good hunters and trappers. Anthropologist Teit[169] considered the North Thompson division to be the greatest travelers and hunters. Otherwise quiet, the Shuswap lake division was similar, but they were better at fishing and canoeing. Teit also noted the presence of an Iroquois community near Tete Jeunne Cache. The Thompson Indians lived along the lower Fraser and the Thompson River up as far as Ashcroft.

The Lilloet bands, Shuswap who lived in the Lilloet River valley, were the most prominent middlemen in trading with coastal people. Influenced by the coastal people with whom they traded, the Lilloet adopted their exogamous clan system. The western bands near the Chilcotin and Carrier adopted their organization of nobles, commoners, and slaves.[170]

Travel, when canoes could not be used, was by foot using pack dogs, backpacks, and the famously fine snowshoes of the Shuswap. When horses arrived during the eighteenth century, the horsemen made their own packsaddles out of carved wood and leather.

The Interior Salish depended on the salmon and on lake fish in spring. Game hunters shared their take. The gathering by women of the many available berries and roots was very important. Plant foods were dried for winter consumption.

The Shuswap were famous for the quality of their birchbark baskets, distinguished by the cornered squareness of design, a design used also for woven baskets made with split spruce roots. The Thompson Indian women produced more fine baskets than any other people, usable even for boiling. Interior Salish tools were representative of the stone materials at hand, from hide scrapers to arrowheads.

Despite the difficult life at Fort McLeod, the post was the terminus for shipments of furs or freight to and from York Factory via the Peace River route. Eastbound, after the very dangerous fourteen-mile Rocky Mountain Portage of the Peace River Canyon, the route included Fort Chipewyan, Methye Portage, and Norway House. Chief Factor William Connolly, who succeeded John Stuart as the New Caledonia District boss in 1824, moved the depot and headquarters from Fort McLeod to Fort St. James, which was more accessible. The Hudson's Bay Company finally took over in New Caledonia and in Columbia when the HBC and NWC merged in 1821, but the change was really not effective until 1824–25, when Governor Simpson made his record trip to Fort George—formerly Astoria. It took him six days to cross Athabasca Pass from Jasper House to Boat Encampment on the north Columbia, and a total of eighty-four days from York Factory. Simpson promptly instituted policies that brought efficiency and increased profit.

Simpson worked under the assumption that the Americans would probably make good their claims to control the mouth of the Columbia and access the interior by the river route.[171] Therefore, he planned that HBC trade to the West Coast would be built around the Fraser River, rather than around the Columbia and its territory. He did not change his mind until he descended the Fraser River himself in 1828 and found that Simon Fraser's appraisal of it as too dangerous and unusable was correct.

Hudson's Bay Company expanded the Brigade Trail instituted by the North West Company to carry freight. The trail used canoes and bateaux where possible and switched to pack horses to leave the most dangerous section of the Columbia River and go overland to upper Columbia posts. In 1825, HBC decided to transport goods around Cape Horn to Fort Vancouver and send fur packs to London on the return trip. This ended the transport of goods and furs across country from Columbia and New Caledonia to York Factory, though the Brigade Trail was still used to move personnel and mail.

The Brigade Trail had five segments. The first segment was by canoe from Fort St. James down the Stuart River and the Nechako River to the Fraser at Fort St. George. The second segment involved using canoes and bateaux to go down the Fraser from Fort St. George to Fort Alexandria. The third segment, at Alexandria, was to organize, outfit, and load a packhorse train. At Alexandria, the large game of the Peace River became important. Moose, deer, elk, and bison hides were the source of leather that was essential to horseback packing. In 1829, the Northern Department council ordered Chief Factor William McIntosh, then in charge at Dunvegan, to deliver to New Caledonia the following items during 1830: "500 dressed moose, 18 parchment skins, 100 pounds of leather thong for snares and nets, 2000 fathoms—12,000 feet—of pack cord, 30 pounds of sinews, and 30 pieces—kegs—of grease. This was in addition to the large quantity of meat that was already going over the mountains, and increased the strain on local resources even further."[172] Twelve years later, moose were rare, and buffalo had all but disappeared.

By 1830, brigade travel was generally along the upper Fraser, cross-country to the San Jose River, up that valley to the Beaver River, across the Thompson plateau to the North Thompson, and along that valley to Fort Kamloops. Thus the fourth segment was from Fort Kamloops, along the South Thompson, then across to the Salmon River, to the west shore of Lake Okanagan, along the Okanagan Lake and River, and finally to Fort Okanagan at the Columbia.

Fort Okanagan, on the right side of the Columbia River at the mouth of the Okanagan River was a stockaded fort, built in 1811. Though it produced a few furs, its primary role was as the transition point from horse packs to canoes and bateaux on the Columbia, and the reverse for outfits headed north. On the fifth segment of the Brigade Trail, the traders traveled by bateaux and canoe on the Columbia from Fort Okanagan to Fort Vancouver, on the north shore of the Columbia.

One result of this shift to packhorse transport was a great increase in the demand for horses. At the same time, the company had embarked on a plan to turn the Columbia and Snake river basins into a "fur desert" (detailed in chapter 14) in opposition to the Americans. These expeditions also called for many horses. The principal source was the Nez

Percé Indians, whose large herds came from Spanish stock and could be purchased at Fort Walla Walla (Fort Nez Perces) with trade goods such as ammunition, tobacco, and blankets. In July 1825, Chief Factor John McLoughlin ordered Chief Trader John Warren Dease, bourgeois at Fort Walla Walla, to buy two hundred horses. Of these, one hundred were for New Caledonia, thirty for Fort Thompson, and seventy for Fort Alexandria, including some for breeding. The Snake River and southern expeditions also needed a continuing horse supply. That summer, Dease bought 250 horses.[173] From that time on, McLoughlin's correspondence carried orders requiring the purchase of horses to fill the needs of the brigades and other expeditions.

Of the horses destined for Alexandria and Thompson, significant losses resulted from straying and hardships during the long drive. The route was difficult, with horses falling from high narrow trails or becoming bogged down in muskeg or deep snow. The lack of skill and experience of the boatmen- and laborers-turned-into-horsemen was a handicap on the horse section of the trail. Anyone who has packed horses, even over relatively short distances, knows how critical is the fitting of saddles to individual horses' backs and the persistent care of their feet and legs. Unshod as they were, horses were often footsore and lame. Sore backs, worn hooves, malnutrition, cold or adverse weather, killing by starving Indians, and fatigue were always critical problems. Nevertheless, between 1826 and 1846, the horse brigades, demanding as they were, became routine and, in the long term, profitable.

A rigid timetable developed: when southbound, it was important to leave Alexandria as early in the year as possible so the brigade could reach Fort Vancouver, deliver the returns, load the outfits, and get back to Fort Alexander in the autumn, allowing supplies needed for the Indian winter fur hunts to reach the northern posts before winter.

They generally packed some twenty miles each day. Walla Walla bourgeois John Dease found that stops for resting and feeding of up to three hours made the animals "less liable in warm Weather to get their backs injured by the loads."[174] The brigades were on the trail for three weeks from Alexandria to Fort Okanagan, and three weeks on the return.

The brigades grew larger as experience and trail improved, as these examples illustrate:

Year	Leave Alexandria	Horses	Men	Effective men
1829	May 9	81	30	22
1831	May 14	90	24	21
1834	May 18	99	24	24 (estimated)

The canoe/bateaux transit from Fort Okanagan to Fort Vancouver on the Columbia River was a different task. With the start of the dangerous annual brigade voyages, the commercial use of the Columbia had begun. Fort Colvile, 150 miles upriver from Fort Okanagan and just below Kettle Falls, was the center of boatbuilding on the upper river. In addition to building boats and fur trading, Fort Colvile was also the primary post for crop growing, stock rearing, horse trading, brigade and express transporting, and the outfitting of Flathead and Kootenay posts.[175]

In New Caledonia, the actual time that "gentlemen and servants" of the HBC spent in trading for fur production was relatively small. There was much leisure. Arduous trips taken whenever possible just to visit another bourgeois were not unusual. As everywhere else, it was not surprising that liaisons and marriages with native women provided essential companionship and relief. Despite the often severe conditions of New Caledonia traders' lives, production held a top priority.

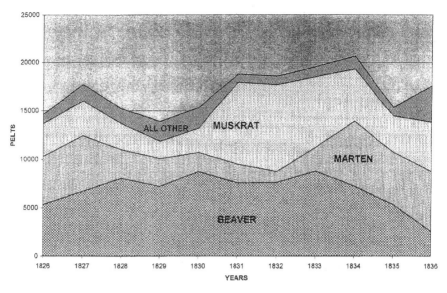

Fig. 7.2 New Caledonia fur production,

Although this chart by the author illustrates New Caledonia production, New Caledonia always was a minor fur producer compared to most other trading districts in Canada.

As an example of competition, and of the humor that must have been a psychological restorative from the arduous and boring aspects of fort life, Morice cited Samuel Black at Kamloops. He deduced that Black "must have been a good-natured man who saw life through rose colored glasses, and had not a little sense of the ludicrous." Alexander Fisher wrote to Black at Fort Alexander:

Lolo [Black's interpreter] tells me of the many tricks wherewith you deceive the Indians, such as making holy water in wash hand-basins, dressing up your cook to make him hold it, walking about the house with a whitewash brush in your hand with many mumblings and magical words, sprinkling the natives in said holy water, telling them that if they do not come to your place to dance and bring their furs with them this fall they will be swallowed up like another Sodom into a fiery furnace or a boiling cauldron...as some of these poor devils may have resisted such an imposition on their understanding which you practice in order to get their furs...I shall...make truth triumph against jugglery, tricks, and profanations of God's holy rites and sacraments.[176]

In February 1841, an Indian murdered Samuel Black. Chief Factor Archibald McDonald wrote to Pierre Pambrun at Walla Walla, "To this melancholy no direct cause can be assigned, unless it could be traced to their superstition & the villainous practices of their man of medicine."[177]

CHAPTER 8:

RUSSIANS IN ALASKAN WATERS

"You are to proceed…along the land that lies to the north, and according to the expectations (since the end is not known), it appears that land [is] part of America. You are to search for the place where it is joined to America, and proceed to some settlement that belongs to a European power, or if you sight some European ship, find out from it what the coast is called, and write it down; go ashore yourself and obtain accurate information; locate it on a map and return here."[178]

So Peter the Great, czar of Russia from 1682 to 1725, instructed an imperial expedition. The czar had formed a navy, made St. Petersburg his capital, and gained access to a warm water port, Kronstad. In 1689, Peter made the Treaty of Nerchinsk with China, in which he lost the Amur maritime region but gained the right to trade for legendary Chinese riches. He died on February 8, 1725. Catherine I, his widow, continued his policies until her death in May 1727.

Vitus Bering, a Danish navigator in the service of the Russian Imperial Navy, commanded this First Kamchatka Expedition of 1725–30.[179] Bering led the expedition overland from St. Petersburg, across Siberia, to Russia's Kamchatka Peninsula and the shore of the Pacific Ocean. That part of the trip took three years—over four thousand miles from the Ural

Mountains to the sea in the east. The expedition requisitioned men, supplies—and furs—along the way, devastating native communities, farms, and military posts.[180]

Bering's expedition constructed the *Gabriel* at Okhotsk and on July 14, 1728, set sail. Rounding Kamchatka, they sailed north by northeast. On August 10, the feast day of Saint Lawrence, they passed an island in the Bering Sea and named it after the saint. Three days later, on August 13, they sailed through the Bering Strait into the Chukchi Sea, but poor visibility hid the Diomede Islands in the strait and the North American continent on the eastern side of the strait. Three days later, on August 16, they reached the northern latitude of 67° 25'—evidence that they must be in the Arctic Ocean and therefore proof that the Asian and North American continents were not joined. They returned to St. Petersburg.

Empress Anna Ivanova, niece of Peter the Great, announced the Second Kamchatka Expedition in 1732. Delays kept that expedition in St. Petersburg until 1737, but finally Vitus Bering and his command crossed Siberia again and built two ships, the *St. Peter* and the *St. Paul.* Bering, commanding the *St. Peter*, saw and named Alaska's Mount St. Elias on July 16, 1741. The *St. Peter* wrecked, and Bering died on the Commander Islands off Kamchatka; the survivors, marooned, reached Kamchatka in September 1742.

Fig. 8.1 Aleuts and their baidarkas. Edward S. Curtis Collection, Photographic prints, 1920-1930. Reproduction # LC-usz 62-123456. Courtesy Library of Congress

Along the Aleutian Islands, the Aleuts, who called themselves Unangan (people of the coast), hunted sea otter, sea lions, seals, whales, and fish. Women used the intestines of these mammals to make weather-resistant clothing. The Aleuts with their baidarkas and harpoons assembled in spring at predetermined locations, and in April or May, they embarked in groups of thirty to a hundred watercraft to hunt sea otter, sometimes paddling more than a thousand miles during the chase, which required the utmost experience, dexterity, and patience.[181]

The Aleuts were expert at navigating the sea, following sea currents despite the almost continuous dense fogs. At home they lived in the traditional Aleut barabara (sometimes called a ulax), a sod-covered hut partially excavated and partially framed with whale ribs or wood planks usually salvaged from driftwood. Aleut barabaras rarely exceeded twenty-one feet long, fourteen feet wide, and the height of a man. They were divided into two parts: the living quarters and the sloping entryway used for cooking, drying clothes, and storage. Light came to the clean, neat rooms through a frame window, which was opened to the elements in good weather and covered with an animal membrane in bad weather.[182]

The *St. Peter* survivors and the men from the *St. Paul* returned to St. Petersburg with the results of the expedition, bringing 1,500 sea-otter pelts. They had established Russia's claim to the lands in North America, and with the sea-otter pelts, had provided financial motivation to hold those lands. By the Nerchinsk Treaty of 1689, Russia had access to China's porcelain, cloth, tea, and foodstuffs through the Mongolian frontier town of Kyakhta on the Selenga River. The Russians had had no readily available market for their furs. This Chinese trade made Irkutsk the rich capital of eastern Siberia.

The *promyshlenniki*, Siberian fur trappers and traders, had also taken note of the sea-otter pelts. Starting in 1743, the brutal, hardy, and ruthless promyshlenniki began hunting sea otter. Soon twenty-five to thirty-nine different Siberian companies had hundreds of men on fleets of ships made of planks assembled with thongs, sailing annually to the Aleutians. A later witness to these hunts described the otter, whose skin was too valuable for the animal's own sake:

It is, when adult, an animal that will measure from three and a half to four and a half feet in length from nose to root of its short, stumpy tail. The general contour of the body is strongly suggestive of the beaver...the skin lies over its body in loose folds, so that when taken hold of in lifting the carcass out of the water, it is slack and draws up like the elastic hide on the nape of a young dog. This pelt, when removed in skinning, is cut only at the posterior, and the body is drawn forth, turning the skin inside out. In that shape it is partially stretched, air-dried, and is so lengthened by this process that it gives the erroneous impression of having been taken from an animal the frame of which was at least six feet in length, with the proportionate girth and shape of a mink or weasel.[183]

So luxuriant, brilliant, and warm were the coats of the sea otter that they were in immediate demand, particularly by the Chinese. Their fur is the finest and thickest of any mammal, a glossy brown or black, interspersed with silver, and nearly a million hairs per square inch. "The coat is very dense, with thick, soft under fur, long guard hairs, beautiful and durable. A full grown prime skin, which has been stretched before drying is about five feet long, and twenty four to thirty inches wide...having a rich, jet black, glossy surface, and exhibiting a silver color when blown open."[184]

Because the sea otter lived entirely in the sea, floating in groups, or rafts, of ten to a hundred, and dived to 250 feet for mussels, urchins, crabs, and fish, they were difficult to find and hunt, except in summer when they languished in bays between headlands. They dwelled in shallow water, but rafts could be far out to sea. They found food on the ocean floor, but ate, groomed, and socialized on the sea surface. Their habitat in North America extended from the tip of the Aleutians, along the coast to the Gulf of California.[185]

A Russian merchant who spent three years in the Aleutians in 1757–62 described how natives hunted sea otter:

They hunt sea otters out at sea using slender arrows about an arshin-and-a-half long. [An arshin is a Russian unit of length measuring twenty-eight inches.] At the end is fastened a sharp bone arrowhead...ridged on both sides. These they hurl from throwing boards. Once a sea otter has been hit, they pursue the animal in small hide baidarkas with one, two or three men in each, following the animal wherever it goes until it is exhausted.[186]

Aleuts, representing an eight-thousand-year-old culture, preferred to locate their villages on bays separated by a neck of land that gave them wind protection and an escape route, and on which there was water and the high ground needed for a lookout for possible enemies. A good salmon stream was essential. Though the Aleutian Islanders represent a separate language and culture, all were coastal people who got their food from the sea, augmented with berries and kelp. Anthropologists have determined that only the Aleutian Islanders are Aleuts, while the natives of Kodiak Island and Prince William Sound are really Eskimos.[187]

There were several patrilineal clans in each Aleutian village, with men and boys privileged to rule. Polygamy was a normal condition of family life. In Aleut society there were heredity nobles, commoners, and slaves. The shape of wooden hats worn at sea also indicated rank, and the visors protected from the glare of the sun and water. Leaders came from the noble class. Living space in the twenty-one-foot-long barabaras was allocated by rank in the clan. Different villages, often from different islands, fought over fishing and hunting areas, and like Plains tribes, they took prisoners from other bands or communities.[188]

The Russians' success in hunting the sea otter depended upon the Aleuts, for only the indigenous people had knowledge of the sea otter and experience in hunting this animal. The Aleuts also had the baidarka (also spelled bidarka), a wooden-frame skin boat covered with sea-lion skin and sealed with seal oil. Most otter hunters traveled in pairs, in a two-man baidarka. A Russian ship would accompany a flotilla of baidarkas to the pelagic hunting grounds. Water would gradually soak the skins, limiting a trip to a day or two. Promyshlenniki took native women and children hostage in order to force the Aleut men to hunt in teams under the command of a promyshlenniki foreman. Resistance by the natives meant violent death at the hands of the promyshlenniki, who were too few in number to hunt safely.

The promyshlenniki took their annual catch to Okhotsk in the early decades, before Russia established communities on their North American claim. The pelts went inland to the Chinese-Siberian-border trade center of Kyakhta, and there were traded for the Chinese goods so popular in Russia.

The Russians used the natives so ruthlessly and extensively that the natives could not engage in normal subsistence hunting, fishing, and gathering. Nor could they rebuild shelters that the Russians had burned to encourage the village's men to hunt. Thus, starvation became common. Lacking firearms, the Aleuts were easily bullied. As the number of sea otter declined, the Russians increased their take of fur seals. Russians also harvested walrus for the tusks (sold in Turkey and Persia) and sea lion, whose thick, tough hides were used for baidarkas.

Between 1733 and 1781, many small companies from eastern Siberia attempted to exploit the riches in Alaska. Russian entrepreneur Grigori Ivanovich Shelikov and later his wife, Natalya Alexyevna, organized the most famous of these. Natalya was, according to one historian, "a clever and astute woman with great capacity for intrigue, and the first white woman to set foot on North America's Northwest Coast."[189] She accompanied Shelikov in the building of Kodiak post in 1773.

Later development in Alaska demonstrated clearly that Shelikov's greatest contribution to the growth of the Russian fur trade in America was to send Aleksandr Andreyevich Baranov, an Irkutsk merchant, to Kodiak Island in 1794, to manage Shelikov's business. He was to establish a settlement, build a shipyard, and introduce agriculture. Also that same year, Russian Orthodox missionaries came to Kodiak.

For twelve years, Baranov contended with few or no supplies shipped from Kronstadt, the St. Petersburg seaport. He overcame the obstacle by constructing what he needed in the wilderness. He was virtually saved by itinerant American ships, such as the trader that arrived with Joseph

O'Cain as mate. Also in 1792, Shelikov sent the *Eagle*, a ship with none of the supplies that Shelikov had promised, but with James Shields, an Englishman whom Baranov persuaded to teach him navigation and to remain to help him build ships in Alaskan waters. Baranov was short of every kind of supply. A Shelikov ship was wrecked at Unalaska and a total loss. He had neither provisions nor trade goods, and the sea otters had been swept from the Aleutians. Competition was increasing from British ships and from other Russian companies, whose men robbed his own. He needed a ship and selected a place to build one near present-day Seward, where there was access to wood and a suitable launching site.

Baranov used natural materials and iron from salvaged wrecks; searched for ore in the mountains, but could not smelt it; made turpentine from the trees; built a sawmill; mixed paints with whale oil, tinting it with rust; sent men for copper from Copper River; and burned bricks to line Russian stoves. A major problem was keeping laborers busy during the winter while living on dried salmon. But in August 1774, he launched the *Phoenix*. "She had three masts and two decks and stood seventy-nine feet long in the upper deck, just as Baranov had planned, and she was strong and sound and her lines looked true and reasonably fast."[190]

With the launching, Baranov's prestige was such that the onetime Kenaitz chief storyteller became Baranov's proud father-in-law. Baranov married his daughter, a beauty by any standard. Baranov renamed her Anna Grigoryevna, taught her the Russian women's style, treated her with respect, and introduced her to Christianity. Anna became the mother of Baranov's two children, Antipar Alexandrovich in 1797 and Irina Alexandrovna in 1802, the primary joys of his life.

After launching the *Phoenix*, he built two smaller vessels, the *Olga* and *Oren*. All three were a product of Baranov's ingenuity and determination. The *Phoenix* not only provided transportation for furs and escort for hunting baidarkas, but established his reputation among the Aleuts and Kenaitz Indians of the Kenai Peninsula.[191]

Shelikov's support turned out to be only talk. He died in 1798, and Natalya managed to unite competing companies into the United American Company. She returned to St. Petersburg and through her intrigues and the efforts of a brilliant court favorite, Chamberlain Nikolai Petrovich Rezanov, the Russian-American Company (RAC) was created. Czar Paul I signed the new charter. Natalya and Baranov were elevated to the nobility, which gave Baranov much-needed rank and later provided for his children's education in Russia.

The charter created a mercantile company with colonizing and governing powers. It also represented Russian political ambitions in the Pacific. The czar was the principal patron. He and various court favorites were shareholders. Employees or agents of the royal court were placed in charge of company affairs and policy decisions. This gave them profit-sharing and pension benefits. In America, all subordinates were Russian or Creole (mixed Russian and Indian parentage). The Russian Orthodox Church was part of the system.

The charter was valid for twenty years; Russia renewed it twice—in 1821 and 1841. The charter gave the Russian-American Company exclusive rights from Attu Island in the Aleutians to latitude 54° 40' on the mainland coast. It could develop trade relations with all countries bordering the North Pacific. It had diverse rights and duties, including punishment of employees, granting awards, purchasing arms and ammunition from government depots, and monopolizing the sale of furs. The company had to keep the czar informed of its operations, spread the Russian Orthodox faith, and establish colonies. In addition, the company was to provide shelter, clothing, food, and medical care to employees; treat natives humanely as lawful Russian subjects; pay natives reasonable wages; offer education; and keep a record of native-Russian marriages.

Natives were to be able to fish and hunt on their own lands.[192] However, a consequence was the extension of strictly observed, rigid Russian
social classification, with Russian employees at the top and the network
of Kolosh (Tlingit) local leaders, the *toions*, at the bottom, though they
performed absolutely vital local community tasks.

Baranov had to deal with competing companies and with vain, arrogant, and virtually useless noble naval officers and priests sent out from
St. Petersburg to Kodiak. Supplies he had ordered did not come from
either Okhotsk or St. Petersburg. He was aware that American and British ships were taking large loads of otter and other furs to Canton and
were providing guns to natives.

Seeing the need to establish a more southern base to offset English and
American shipborne traders and to take advantage of better weather and
more favorable tides, Baranov decided to build a fort at the bay later named
Sitka, to be called Mikhailovstk (St. Michael's, not to be confused with the
St. Michael's established in 1833 by the RAC on the south side of Norton
Sound). He arrived there in the *Olga*, which Shields had taught him to
navigate. With him were four hundred Aleut males, twenty Aleut wives,
and thirty of his best Russians. He no doubt expected to increase trading
for land-based furbearers and to extend the sea otter hunting southward.
There the RAC met its veritable nemesis: the Na-Dene-speaking Tlingit
Indians, whom Russians called Kolosh. As Baranov stepped ashore:

A tense silence fell on the forest. A file of twenty or more Kolosh warriors had stepped out of the woods, and stood, with folded arms, watching them. The Aleut women whimpered......They were, in physique,
culture, and leadership, the aristocrats of the Northwest Coast....
Tall men, well over six feet, their muscles rippled beneath their naked
bronze skins like those of a panther. Several of the twenty warriors wore
short beards two or three inches long; their long, coarse, black hair

was drawn into knots at the backs of their high, conical skulls, powdered with goose down and surmounted by a single black-and-yellow feather. Their attitude seemed neither threatening nor disapproving; it was merely silently questioning.[193]

With an interpreter, Baranov stepped forth, and by this characteristically bold approach to the Tlingit, he announced he had come to live, not trade. After a harangue, he bought land from the Tlingit chief Ska-outlelt for erection of the fort.

The Russians now were meeting the Tlingit, who in their large canoes virtually dominated the Alaskan coast from Yakutat to the Queen Charlotte Islands off the west coast of Vancouver Island between the latitude 56 and 58. The Russians would never defeat them. Their culture was the most complex among North American natives. The Russians learned that the Tlingit were savage, brave, cunning, vengeful, tenacious, and able to endure pain and deprivation. Above all, they were intensely proud and independent.[194] Ever ferocious, they could always protect their middleman role, either on the coast or with the inland Indians who traded along the coastal rivers.

Tlingit women could be quite fair and attractive, though they sat continuously at work, legs tucked under, and consequently their walk was clumsy and ugly in the Russians' eyes. They were expert basket makers and owned and dominated the household and the food. They were loving mothers, whose sacred inalienable right was bringing up children in a matriarchal kinship system. The women were hard bargainers with the Russians, who desperately needed the land's produce, such as wild berries.

The Kolosh and other Alaskan tribes had reason to hate the Russians. They tried to make the Kolosh slaves; they exploited, abused, and tried to prevent their trade with the Americans and British; they restrained their mobility; and they brought smallpox and venereal disease, among other diseases. Eventually, however, the Russians did introduce some European food and drink, tobacco, and tools, and did convert many to Orthodox Christianity, which is still prominent in southern Alaska.

The Tlingit belonged to one of two moieties, the Raven or Eagle, which consisted of kinship-group clans. The clan governed the social, ceremonial, and political life of the Tlingit, and was a cohesive, functioning unit. Clans were made up of "houses," which were both a physical plank structure and its matrilineage. Each house had a formal name and included the leader, his wives, his brothers, their wives, and children. Important artistic crests symbolized both the social organization and spiritual relationship with wildlife and the environment. The Tlingit held slaves, captured in war or purchased from more southern tribes. The Tlingit potlatch was important as a ritualized competition in which clan leaders increased their status through the opulent consumption and distribution of goods and destruction of property. Slaves did the hard work and could be sacrificed.

The Tlingit had traded since ancient times with their inland Athapaskan-speaking neighbors. The Tlingit were middlemen for Asiatic iron and controlled the trade for superior baskets and robes, ermine, and placer copper, all indigenous goods from both inland and shore. Trade was stimulated by the search for furs, and the Tlingit maintained frequent contact. On the coast, traders wanted dressed deer and moose hides, ermine pelts, tailored skin clothing, and coppers from upriver inland tribes. The Tlingit had long used iron salvaged from flotsam for weapons heads.[195]

Baranov completed the construction of Fort St. Michael in the fall and winter of 1799–1800. While building the fort, five American ships came in. He established congenial and profitable trade relations with all of them, while reminding them that Russia claimed the waters in which they sailed.

On June 20, 1802, Vedvednikov, whom Baranov had left in charge when he departed for Kodiak two years earlier, had relaxed Russian discipline at Fort St. Michael for a holiday. The Tlingit, armed with British and American guns, attacked. They reduced the fort and all the buildings to ashes, killing twenty Russians and up to one hundred and thirty Aleuts, and capturing twenty Aleut women and the fort's hunting-master, Vassili Tarkenov. They took as many as four thousand sea-otter pelts.

In war, Tlingit chiefs were ordinarily the commanders, but they could delegate leadership to other war chiefs. All wore cuirasses of rods bound closely together with sinews or vests of double- or triple-folded elk or moose hides for which they had traded. As armor, the cuirasses could stop arrows, lances, and even musket and pistol balls at longer ranges. Slaves and booty were a war acquisition, but extermination of an enemy and acquisition of hunting and fishing areas was usually the objective; these could be preceded by treacherous peacemaking. Secret rituals, training, and personal tactics were important. The men depended largely upon achieving surprise, often using night attacks, organized so that they did not attack each other. There were heavy casualties. After a successful attack, the warriors took trophy heads home for display. In defense, they had positions prepared in advance, using steep-sided hills or islets. They could not withstand a protracted siege. When necessary, they would break up into small groups, melt into the woods, and pursue guerilla warfare. When traders introduced firearms, warfare intensified. While lack of skill with guns and limitations on ammunition may have limited their effectiveness, the roar of gunfire in night attacks enhanced the success of the attackers.

After the battle at St. Michael's, three ships arrived: the *Alert*, with American Captain John Ebbets; the *Unicorn*, with British Captain Henry Barber; and the *Caroline*, with Boston Captain William Sturgis. By threatening to hang Chief Ska-out-lelt, and hanging a sub-chief, both of whom a shore party had captured, Barber and Ebbets forced the return of the Aleut women, Tarkenov, and forty or fifty packs of furs. Sturgis decided that the Tlingit were his customers and that the Russians had gotten about what they deserved, so he took no part.

British Captain Barber sailed to Kodiak and sought a ransom for his rescued passengers, claiming that Russia and England were at war. Baranov did not accept the bluff, and with his guns persuaded Barber to turn over the passengers and furs worth ten thousand rubles. Barber's action was not surprising. It was Barber's ruthless and crooked tactics earlier that had inflamed the Kolosh.[196]

Having learned of the sack of St. Michael's, Baranov in 1804 assembled a force and went to Sitka. There he found three of his ships, a large baidarka fleet, and an even greater surprise, the Russian 450-ton frigate *Neva*, commanded by the competent British Navy-trained Captain-Lieutenant Lurii F. Lisianski. With this force, he recaptured the site and chased the Kolosh from the high ground, where he intended to build his redoubt. The Kolosh objected, but Baranov reminded them that he had come originally in peace, seeking to buy ground, and that they had preferred war and no longer enjoyed his trust.

Baranov buried the bodies of those killed and took possession of Sitka Island, where, on the high ground, he built a fortress and the headquarters of the Russian-American Company, and named it New Archangel. The following winter was a miserable time at New Archangel, with lack of food, scurvy, and constant Tlingit harassment. Baranov wore a suit of chain mail whenever he went outside the fortress. Yet later, on June 10, 1805, the *Neva* set sail for Kronstad, via Canton, with 3,000 sea otter, 150,000 sealskins, and other fur valued at 450,000 rubles.[197]

Baranov's style had started paying off by 1803. Twenty-three different native tribes had accepted the authority of the Russians in central Alaska, on the Aleutians, and along the coast, including the Kenaitz, relatives of the Tlingit, and the Tlingit themselves. Yet throughout the Russian-American Company's rule of Russia's colonies in North America, "the Tlingit...confined the invaders to the coastal lowlands and prevented any extended exploration of the interior of Alaska."[198] The Russians were thus forced to be hunters for furs from the sea with the Aleut, rather than become traders.

Baranov had long been seeking relief from the governorship, citing age and poor physical condition. His authority was still compromised by the arrogance of naval cadets sent to serve and officers sent to "inspect"; by the treasonous disloyalty of the northern clergy, who even participated in an attempt to assassinate him; and always by the hostility of the Tlingit. Into this scene, in 1805, came the noble, handsome, and exceptionally intelligent Chamberlain Nikkolai Petrovich Rezanov with his manservant, his personal physician, and two naval aides. As a director of the Russian-American Company and a close associate of Czar Alexander with the high rank of chamberlain, he came to Sitka prepared to dismiss Baranov.

Meeting Baranov, Rezanov considered him an "amazing man" in many respects, whose capabilities had made a powerful impact on the colonies. He commented:

> I could not but look with respect on a man who devoted his life to the improvement of trade in its various forms. He had already lived in America for twelve years, in the company of wild and primitive people, surrounded by constant danger. He had been struggling with the deep-rooted depravity of the Russians living there, working constantly, in need of many things....His firmness of spirit and constant presence of mind are the reasons why the savages respect him without loving him, and the fame of the name of Baranov resounds among all the savage peoples who live on the northwest coast of America.[199]

Baranov had the disadvantage of lower rank, but, according to his biographer, "there comes a time when suffering and hardships lend a man a dignity that no social or political distinctions can affront."[200] Rezanov did not find a humble Baranov, for he could not have governed effectively had he remained humble in the harsh social and physical environment of Russian America.

Rezanov not only retained Baranov as governor, but also charged him with encouraging local artisans, paying close attention to the health of employees coming from Russia, and enlisting natives in defense forces. He ordered Baranov to establish a port captain, acquire American ships, and build a sawmill. He promised to review the cost of Russian goods, with a fair markup, and to ensure that an effective channel was established for expressing colonials' needs.

The problem of food shortages in Sitka became so acute in February 1806 that Rezanov sailed in the *Juno* to San Francisco for supplies. After considerable difficulty because of the Spanish court's hauteur and the California authorities' fear of the Spanish court, he established good relations with the defense commander, Don Luis de Arguello, and got food for his crew.

When the Spanish governor, Don Arillaga, refused to see him in Monterey, Rezanov and his officers concentrated on Commandante Don Arguello's hospitality at the Presidio San Francisco. Rezanov met and fell in love with de Arguello's daughter, Doña Concepcion, and persuaded her that she should live in the glory of the Russian court; they were engaged despite the Spanish opposition to "mixed" marriages, and the Commandante finally agreed to provide supplies, with his own men loading the ship. Doña's brothers helped. Rezanov left California on May 8, 1806, promising Doña he would return in two years, but that she was not to wait longer than that. He arrived in New Archangel in early June. Though scurvy had raged among both natives and Russians, the herring had arrived in March, and now with Rezanov's food, sold at low prices, the colony was materially helped.

Had Rezanov reached St. Petersburg, his recommendations would have had more effect and could have drastically improved company life and operations much earlier. However, after being injured in a fall from a horse, he tried to travel too fast. Weakened by three years of disappointment, hard work, and care, he died in Krasnoyarsk on March 1, 1807. The beneficial results of Rezanov's and others' inspections occurred slowly. The Russian-American Company eventually made drastic reorganizations, simplifying the Siberian supply system and relying less on the voyages from Kronstad. When Rezanov failed to return, Doña Concepcion entered a nunnery.

In 1806, several American and British vessels arrived in New Archangel, now Sitka, and in plain view of the Russians, bartered more than two thousand sea otters from the natives. They paid the Tlingit with more and better goods than the Russians had to offer. By this method, the English completely disrupted the Russian trade, all the while complaining that the Americans were cutting them out of the fur trade. When the Russians protested the Americans trading guns, powder, and ammunition, the Americans responded that after fifteen thousand miles to get there, they had to market to whomever paid best. One visitor commented, "The Russians are not at all liked by the native Indians—the Americans are greatly preferred."[201] Significantly, as Khlebnikova reported, English and American vessels had already been putting in to the coast for ten years and had earned profits estimated at three million rubles.[202]

Baranov continued sea otter and seal hunting as far south as San Francisco, contracting with, and depending upon, American captains using native hunters. After Rezanov left in 1806, Baranov, worn out, returned to Kodiak, leaving Kuskov in command at Sitka. In Kodiak, he learned that his Russian wife had died; he wrote to the chairman of the company's board, asking him to intercede with the czar to recognize his children Antipar and Irina and his native wife, Anna Grigoryevna. The czar approved and titled Anna "The Princess of Denai." This enabled Baranov's children to enter nobles' schools.

Later, Baranov returned to Sitka to renew some of the plans he and Rezanov had developed. He sent his agent, Kuskov, to establish the post, Fort Ross, at Little Bodega Bay, California, during 1811 and 1812. There they tried agriculture, trapping, trading, ship relief, shipbuilding and other crafts, but it was never really productive or profitable, due to the poor soil in the area.

Between 1797 and 1820, primarily under Baranov's management, exports from Russian America were remarkably profitable. Of the total trade of $32,753,400 (U.S. dollars circa 1830), $7,296,004 was traded by foreign ships at Canton. The primary trade, through Okhotsk to Kyakhta was $25,457,396. In addition, the royal treasury received $2,000,000 in duty payments. The Chinese goods traded were black and aromatic tea, nankeen, some silk, and sugar candy.[203]

According to Baranov's biographer:

Baranov had received shipments worth 2,800,000 rubles but primarily through American captains had sold at Canton 3,648,002 rubles' worth in [fur] trade and through Irkutsk 16,376,696 rubles worth....Net earnings had been seven and a half million, of which four and a quarter were distributed to stockholders as dividends....Russian-American Company shares were quoted at 592.53, with a par value of 100....In the cash accounts, involving millions, wrote Khlebnikov [auditing bookkeeper], "I found not one single discrepancy."[204]

Commander Golvonin, upon inspecting Baranov's establishment, was impressed by what he found, and persuaded Baranov to leave to take a position as advisor to the company's board of directors in St. Petersburg.

Baranov left aboard the *Kutusov* with the always-arrogant Captain Hagemeister, but while passing Sumatra, became terminally ill and was buried at sea on April 12, 1819.[205]

Subsequently, the Russian-American Company's financial problems became apparent. By 1821, the total value of furs and related exports was about $3,275,000 at the various prices existing at the time. This represented a gross gain over capitalization of 265 percent. Though its profits were minimal, the Russian-American Company paid managers in St. Petersburg 9 percent or 10 percent on capital. These apparently excessive payments from 1824 through 1842 contributed significantly to the company's financial problems.

By retaining authority in St. Petersburg, considerations of the empire often delayed trading decisions. After Baranov, a number of Russian naval officers followed as governors of the Russian-American Company and Russian America. "Between 1824 and 1838 colonial expenses rose 91 percent but colonial revenues rose only 13 percent."[206]

Baron Ferdinand Petrovich Wrangell, who was thirty-two when he arrived and served from January 1, 1830, to October 29, 1835, left a commendable record. He was a noted Arctic explorer, and had made two round-the-world trips. He was far better educated than Baranov, and arrived with the advantage of the authority of the nobility. He was most significant to the later coastal fur trade and dealings with the Hudson's Bay Company. Wrangell, his wife, Elizabeth, and their infant daughter, Marie Louise, had traveled across Siberia, four thousand miles to Okhotsk.

Baroness Vasil'evna Wrangell, the first educated woman after Natalya Shelikova and the first Russian-American Company governor's wife to come to Alaska, brought principles of family order from which a moral direction emerged among those serving the company far from home. The roughneck Russians loved her, and "the fierce elders of the Sitka Kolosh tribe…forgot their enmity for the Russians and praised her virtues. With ease and confidence she strolled with her women companions to pick berries" or to visit the site of old Fort Sitka's ruins. "In any weather, the baroness was seen making her way through the muddy streets to visit a sick woman or child."[207]

Governor Wrangell, visiting the colony in 1833, wrote, "The Yankees, who have captured the California trade, have brought in all kinds of things that people need...at such low prices that we simply cannot compete with them."[208] Moreover, after 1833, fur seals and sea lions became so scarce on the Farallon group of islands off the coast of San Francisco that Russians ceased hunting altogether. These factors led to the sale of Fort Ross, and in 1841 the land, cattle, and buildings were sold to John Augustus Sutter at Sutter's Fort, located at the confluence of the American and Sacramento rivers, for $30,000. Selecting a few examples for comparison, the second charter period, 1821–41, resulted in about one-third of the sea otter shipped under the first charter, nearly five times as many beaver, only about one-third the number of fur seals, more than one-and-a-half times as many mink, more than two-and-a-half times the number of walrus tusks, only a fourth as much whale bone, more than one-and-a-half times as many foxes, and less than one-sixth as many pelts of all kinds. There was a marked decline in the most valuable pelt, the sea otter, and in fur seals. The substantial increase in land-based beaver pelts indicated a greater trapping effort inland, and on the coast, more aggressive trading along the rivers leading to interior Indians.[209] The Russians found the Aleuts to be expert whalers, which accounts for the exports of whalebone.

Wrangell succeeded in turning the Russian-American Company's interest to the conservation of furbearers, which had clearly been declining

Table 8.1 Export of peltries, walrus tusks, whalebone, and castoreum during two charters of the Russian-American Company: 1789-1821 and 1821-1841

ITEM	FIRST CHARTER	SECOND CHARTER	DIFFERENCE second minus first
Sea otter	72,894	25,416	-47,478
River Beaver	34,546	162,034	127,488
Beaver Tail	59,530	0	-59,530
Otter	14,969	29,442	14,473
Fur Seal	1,232,374	458,502	-773,872
Black & Silver Fox	13,702	17,913	4,211
Blue Fox	21,890	0	-21,890
Sable	17,298	15,666	-1,632
Wolverine	1,151	1,564	413
Lynx	1,389	4,253	2,864
Mink	4,802	15,481	10,679
Blue Polar Fox	36,362	55,714	19,352
White Polar Fox	4,234	13,638	9,404
Wolf	121	201	80
Bear	1,602	5,355	3,753
Otter Tail	23,506	0	23,506
Cross Foxes	46,262	0	-46,262
Red Fox	30,950	45,947	14,997
Muskrat	4,491	0	-4,491
Sea Lion	27	0	-27
TOTAL PELTS EXPORTED	1,547,568	905,585	-641,983
Walrus Tusks	55374 lb.	234751 lb.	181377 lb.
Whale Bone	42356 lb.	124760 lb.	82408 lb.
Castoreum	21.5 lb.		-21.5 lb.

Source: Data from P. A. Tikhemenev, History of the Russian American Company, 5,7

in numbers. He restricted the killing of cub seals and females with cubs. The results were beneficial; by 1841 on St. Paul's Island, eight thousand fur seals were taken without any risk to the herd, since in any one year, the population was observed to increase. Shortage of furbearers along the

Inside Passage stimulated explorations of the Nushagak, Kuskokwim, and Yukon rivers, and then only in the 1820s through the 1840s.

In 1833, Baron Wrangell reported that in all of Russian America, there was a population of 10,659. Of these, 652 were European, 991 were creoles, and the remaining 8,882 were Aleuts and Tlingit. Some 134 Tlingit and Aleuts were employed at New Archangel. Overall, numbers of men and women were about equal, though at Sitka in Russian-American Company employ, there were 591 men and 256 women.[210] Most of the Russians were lower- to middle-class townsmen; some were even criminals from Siberia. Because of a lack of Russians, the Creoles formed an important part of the Russian company's labor force.[211] The Russian hunters remained in satisfactory health, despite their harsh lives, though newcomers suffered generally from scurvy. Natives suffered from colic, festering sores, cancer, and syphilis. There were few epidemics, though periodically, smallpox took a heavy toll south of Sitka until the natives could be convinced of the importance of vaccination.

Baron Wrangell made substantial administrative changes. He began audits of all accounts, continued the establishment of schools and hospitals, and generally improved employee working conditions. He operated a skilled dockyard, retimbering the *American Lady Wrangell* and providing the fine workshops and other shipbuilding facilities that could repair damage to foreign ships.[212] He moved Father Veniaminov, later Bishop Innokentii, from Kodiak to Sitka. During his governorship, competition with the Hudson's Bay Company came into focus. Along the coast, relations with the English became critically important. Though the indifference at St. Petersburg doomed Russian Alaska, the remarkable Baron Wrangell improved and prolonged the company's situation.[213]

CHAPTER 9:

HORSES IN INDIAN LIFE

The Plains Indians developed a unique lifestyle based on the use of the horse after its spread northward in the eighteenth century. The horse changed their everyday life and created the mobile plains Indian. Native people living on the Great Plains at the beginning of the nineteenth century had been pushed there as more eastern tribes either expanded to the west or were pushed there by advancing white settlement. Most were agricultural tribes, growing and trading corn, beans, and squash, but the arrival of horses allowed them to expand their hunting areas into a more successful year-round food supply.

The Great Plains, which extends westward from the Mississippi River valley to the Rocky Mountains, and from the South Saskatchewan River in the north to Mexico in the south, is a windswept sea of grasses, with trees usually along streams. Bison, game animals, and the growing herds of horses fed on long grass in the eastern regions where there was more rainfall, and the more nutritious short grass westward.

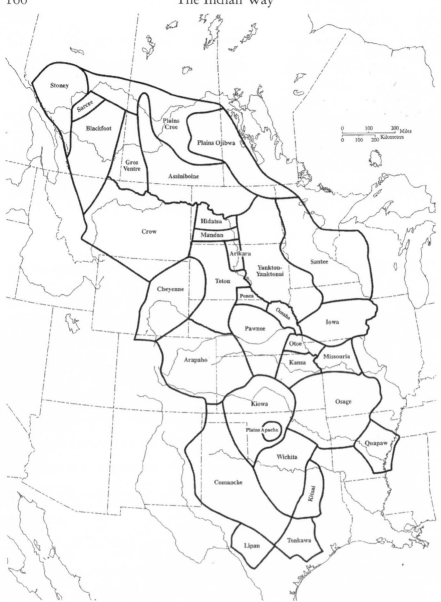

Fig. 9.1 Plains tribal territories. Handbook of North American Indians, vol. 15.
Courtesy Smithsonian Institution

With few exceptions, the Indians of the Great Plains most involved
with fur traders and trappers were those whose trading skills had already
won them wealth and power in their region. On the southern plains, controlled by Spain until 1821, the Comanche, Wichita, Apache, and Ute

dominated the trade of horses. The Pawnee and Cheyenne were powerful in the center, and the Teton Sioux, Crow, and Blackfoot dominated in the north.

Regional trade centers among the tribes were the hub of trade life throughout the plains. The Pecos and Zuni trade centers in the south, the Shoshone rendezvous and great horse fair in the central area near the Rocky Mountains, and the agricultural Arikara villages, a trade center near the mouth of the Grand River on the Missouri, were all important sources of both horses and food for early traders going up the Platte and Missouri rivers. At the Dakota rendezvous, near where the Big Sioux and James rivers come into the Missouri River, the Yanktonai Sioux, the Sisseton, and the Yankton met the Teton to trade. The agricultural Mandan-Hidatsa village was a trade center on the upper Missouri, and it was from there that the Cree and Assiniboin traded for horses.

John C. Ewers of the Smithsonian Bureau of Ethnology noted in Bulletin 159, *The Horse in Blackfoot Indian Culture*, that "horses were first diffused northward and eastward to those tribes on the periphery of the Spanish settlements of the Southwest." He agreed with American Indian historian Clark Wissler that the first tribes to get them would be the Ute, Apache, Kiowa, and Caddo. Spanish records dated in 1659 reported that the Apache carried off as many as three hundred head of livestock in a single raid.[214] From then on, the principal method of diffusion northward was Indian raiding.

Many tribes became known for their raiding success. The Comanche, with some of the largest herds, also were the target of raiding tribes from as far north as the Blackfoot on the northern plains. The Kiowa and Apache raided Spanish and Comanche herds, sending a flow of horses northward east of the Rockies, through the Northern Kiowa, Cheyenne, Arapaho, and Mandan tribes. West of the Rockies, the Ute passed horses north to the Shoshone. The Shoshone traded horses on to the Salish and

the Piegan. The Flathead horses, first obtained about 1720, made possible their forays into bison country. The buffalo horse acquired prime
value, and horses became a major measure of wealth.

Native ponies ate only grass; U.S. Army cavalrymen considered them
superior to Army grain-fed horses. The Army animals also were stabled,
whereas the Indian horses were usually corralled, tethered, or herded on
the prairie. Their finest horses found winter shelter in tribal lodges. In
winter, when grass was not available, Indians and knowledgeable whites
alike fed their horses the inner bark of the round-leafed cottonwood. In
emergencies, horses became reliable food for both Indian and trapper.

Nez Percé country, along the Snake River west of the Rockies, proved
to be great horse land, with well-watered pastures during the summer
months and protected valleys during winter. Natural barriers prevented
the herds from straying and protected them from enemy raiders. By 1800,
Nez Percé horses were famous west of the Continental Divide and east
to the Dakotas. The Nez Percé practiced selective breeding, apparently
without being taught, although it is possible that someone trained on
the Spanish ranches near Santa Fe traveled to the Nez Percé country and
taught them the techniques. Lewis and Clark, coming in 1805, found the
Nez Percé horsemen quite skillful. This combination of favorable environment and intelligent management produced good-sized, well-built
stock quite different from the undersized ponies of the northern plains.

The Nez Percé also raised large numbers of spotted horses (now known
as Appaloosas) from selected animals, mainly for war and parade, and are
credited with a breeding program that expanded the Appaloosa population. Historian Francis Haines noted that the Appaloosa were not new;
they had held a high rank in the legends of Persia.[215]

In the northern plains, according to Ewers, "The adult male Indian
pony averaged a little under 14 hands in height, weighed about 700
pounds, possessed a large head in proportion to its body, good eyes, neck

and head joined like the two parts of a hammer, large round barrel, relatively heavy shoulders and hips; small fine, strong limbs and small feet. Indian ponies exhibited a wide range of solid and mixed colors."[216]

Colonel Phillipe St. Regis de Trobriand, who commanded Fort Stevenson, Dakota Territory, from 1867 to 1869, wrote: "The Indian pony can cover a distance from sixty to eighty miles between sunrise and sunset, while most of our horses are tired out at the end of thirty or forty miles....The movement of Indian horses is lighter, swifter, and longer range than that of our cavalry, which means that they always get away from us."[217]

Various tribes used the horse first as a beast of burden, carrying pack loads, using the "parfleche" in pairs, parfleche being a Canadian French term for a "folded envelope of tough, long wearing, and waterproof rawhide."[218] Indians made them to fold over a horse's back to hold personal items. Women of many tribes had used dogs to carry baggage and were quick to change to the horse. In moving camp, or supporting war, horses pulled a travois: two long poles fastened to the saddle and attached to a platform of sorts that was dragged behind and carried baggage and children. Lodge poles, fastened over the horse's withers using a thick pad, were dragged in a similar manner, except that martingales, a strap loosely around a horses neck, and cruppers, a strap under the horses tail, to prevent packs from sliding, were also used.

The most active riders favored pad saddles: folded pads stuffed with buffalo or deer hair and secured by a girth. Primarily youths used wooden, leather-covered stirrups suspended from the same tabs as the girth. Indian women carved the wooden saddles to fit the horse's back and covered them with rawhide pads, which rode on either side of the backbone. Often saddles were carved to fit a particular horse. Women's saddles had high horns and pommels. Whenever Spanish or American leather saddles were available, Indians preferred them, and they were seen as early as 1787.

Before white contact, bridles, referred to as "war bridles," consisted of braided rawhide fastened to the horse's lower jaw with a couple of half hitches. The reins, part of the single braided rope, were joined by a honda at one end, the other passing to the rider's hand. The Blackfoot used the braided lariat with a fixed loop.[219]

The Apache, living on the borders of the Spanish settlements, may have been the first tribe to ride horses. Unique on the plains, the Apache learned to care for their horses. As Bertha Dutton wrote in *American Indians of the Southwest,* "Their horses were well cared for, never ridden to death."[220] Slaves of the Apaches, particularly boys captured from neighboring tribes, were trained to live among the horses to protect them from raiders.

Acceptance of the horse and the development of peerless Indian equestrian skill appear unparalleled in equine history; it defined life on the prairies. As Ewers wrote, "The speed with which this novelty was taken over is the more surprising in view of the revolutionary effects on many aspects of native life."[221] The remarkable horsemanship of the Plains warriors in the buffalo hunt and in war has long been admired by horsemen everywhere. These riding skills, which involved shooting accurately with bow and arrow, flintlock, percussion lock, and repeating rifles, and at the same time avoiding either the buffalo's charge or the enemy's weapons, began with childhood play and training, as reported by Dr. Gilbert L. Wilson.

In 1908 Wilson began his study the Hidatsa (Minnetaree) of North Dakota. Their position along the Missouri River, in an area where buffalo had been the foundation of their food supply and where corn grown by the women had increased their trading opportunities, enabled the

Hidatsa and Mandan to be the center of a large trading network to obtain both horses and European trade goods.

Wilson asked, "Should we not seek to know how every art, every material complex of his culture is seen by primitive man himself, how it is proportioned in his thinking, and what superstitions and interpretations he gives to it?"[222] To answer that question, Wilson needed and received Indian help. He spent ten summers at the Hidatsa town of Independence in the Berthold Indian Reservation, remote and removed from white society, even by Dakota standards. He boarded with Rev. Edward Goodbird's Hidatsa family, eating with the family and sleeping on the floor of the chapel for the summers of his study, finished in 1918.

Goodbird was Wilson's interpreter. Born about 1869, Goodbird was the son of Maxidiwiac, or Buffalo-Bird-Woman. His maternal grandfather was Small-Ankle, "an able and progressive leader of the Hidatsa in the trying time of the tribe's removal to what is now the Fort Berthold Reservation."[223] One of the first reservation students to attend the reservation mission school, Goodbird had become pastor of the Congregational chapel at Independence. He wrote and spoke English, but retained the natural idiom so important to revealing an aboriginal viewpoint.

Goodbird's mother, Buffalo-Bird-Woman, was born about 1840, and Wilson said of her: "She is conservative, holding native beliefs—but she realizes that the young must adopt civilized ways or perish. She speaks no English, but she has a quick intelligence and a memory that is marvelous. Her patience and loyal interest in these studies has been invaluable."[224]

Buffalo-Bird-Woman's brother, Wolf-Chief, was born the summer of 1849. He was a tribal war leader who saw the value of civilized culture; he attended mission school, and even hired a white man to live with him and teach him English. As the owner of a trading store for many years, he was, in Wilson's words, "a reliable authority in matters pertaining to men's customs and occupations, and, unlike so many of his tribesmen, does not fear to give information of native religious beliefs."[225]

Wolf-Chief did not know when the Hidatsa obtained horses, but Pierre Gaultier de Varennes, Sieur de la Verendrye, found horses with Mandan village tribes in 1741. When Wolf-Chief was about ten, he and his father were watching their herd. Wolf-Chief's father told him, "These horses are gods, or mystery beings. They have supernatural power. If one cares for them properly and seeks good grazing and water for them, they will increase rapidly. I am sure, my son, that if you will remember [this] your horses will increase and all will know that you are a good raiser of horses."

As Goodbird described, the care began with the colt. When a colt was foaled, Wolf-Chief and his father rubbed the colt with dried dung of antelope, elk, or jack-rabbit, which would absorb the gummy moisture and thereby dry the colt. The dung had to be from a speedy animal, so the horse would grow up to be a speedy runner.

After the mare bit off the umbilical cord, the owner broke off the soft yellow pads from the bottoms of the colt's hoofs and used his thumb and forefinger to press the softer inside part of the hoof to make the shape symmetrical. Father and son would guard a colt for the first ten days, protecting it against wolves and injury by other horses. The colt's initial deposits of dung were used as yellow paint on arrow shafts.

The Hidatsa may have learned from the Nez Percé on the Columbia Plateau to castrate colts. According to Wolf-Chief, a colt born in the month of May might be castrated at five months, but in general, colts were castrated at the age of two years. Certain men who had learned the art were brought in to do the deed. The castrator's fee, as Wilson recorded, consisted of a knife, a rawhide rope, and the tanned skin from a buffalo's belly, worked with porcupine quills or painted with white clay. The skin became a saddle blanket; the rope became the lead for the horse, and the knife became the tool for the operation.

Paraphrasing Goodbird: The best stallions were kept for breeding, and a breeding stallion visited mares and herds of other Indian tribes, at no charge. After a mare was bred and seen to be gravid, her owner was careful, when riding her, to sit well forward; and he was especially careful to see that she was never ridden double. A mare ridden double, or with the rider seated too far back, would be likely to cast her colt before her time. If a gravid mare was irritable, they believed she carried a colt; if gentle, a mare. Mares were usually bred in May and foaled in May. Continuing from Goodbird's report:

Training: A colt was broken at two years of age, for a three-year-old is nearly grown, and is then hard to break. Colts are broken by boys fourteen to seventeen years old, but eleven year old boys have helped. Several of us drove a herd down by the Missouri at a place where the current was rather swift, and so likely to prevent a swimming colt from getting back to shore too easily.

I roped a two-year-old and drove him into deep water; swimming out to the colt, I mounted him and made him swim with me on his back. Now a two-year-old still suckles his mare, and frightened at my weight, the colt tried to make shore, where he knew his mare was. I clung to his back, forcing him to swim until, reaching shallow water, his feet touched ground, when he soon struggled to land. By this time I have dismounted. Following the colt, I drove him again into deep water, and repeated the lesson; and so for two or three hours, until the colt was weary. The last time the colt came out, I stayed on his back.

Fig. 9.2 Native boy breaking colt.

Source: John C. Ewers, *The Horse in Blackfoot Indian Culture.* 61. Smithsonian
Institution.

Only one boy mounted a swimming colt, for under the weight of two a
colt would sink. A horse drowns more easily than a man. "If a horse sinks
until water runs into his ears, he grows weak," we Indians say.

As the colt reached shore the last time, another boy mounted behind
me; and together we rode the poor beast back and forth over the low-
lying sandbank covered with soft mud. There are many such sandbanks
along the Missouri; a slight rise in the river covers them with several
inches of soft mud. We rode the colt over such ground until it was utterly
exhausted.

We always rode bareback when breaking a colt. We continued these two
or three hour lessons for three successive days, after which we considered
the colt broken; it was usually safe to mount and ride him on land.

Colts were trained to swim, to stop and turn, to prance from side to side, and to leap over a fallen enemy. Boys learned to drop to a pony's side to avoid attack, holding on with the inside of a thigh. War horses could turn sharply, with a mere shift of the rider's weight, or with the use of a single rein.

In summer, boys managed the grazing herd, always alert for enemies, such as the Sioux. Small Ankle said, "We drove the horses to the Missouri to water them. We patted the colts as they drank so as to accustom them to being handled. They soon grew so tame that we could catch them in the prairie or the hills without trouble. The Missouri is a deep stream, not very shallow even near the shore. A young colt was helpless in water shallow enough for a man to stand upright. If a colt was a bit wild, we drove him into deeper water where a lad waded out to him and caught him; for not being able to touch bottom, the colt could not escape. We then petted and stroked him, until he became gentle.

The best horses were stabled in the family lodge, in a corral to the left of the entrance. While guarding the herd, the boys made lunch by killing cowbirds with blunt arrows, and snaring gophers, which they cooked on the spot. While the horses grazed, Small Ankle would go among them weeping and praying to the horses. "You are my gods. I take good care of you. I want to own many horses in my lifetime." At the day's end, they brought the horses home, placing them in their father's care. Mother provided a supper of hominy of yellow corn, boiled with beans, and seasoned with alkali salt.

In winter horses were driven to a sheltered place where there was unburned grass. In our winter camp we made earth lodges, smaller than in the village, and constructed to be more temporary. There was a small corral inside for our best horses, and another outside in the village. The area selected was protected, with nearby timber for lodge building and cottonwood for horse feed. We fed our best horses cottonwood bark, twigs, and small branches. This was emergency feed. The women cut down the round leafed cottonwood trees when grass was not available. They preferred going where there was grass under the snow which the horses could get by pawing away the snow. When possible women would scrape away snow and make small bales of grass.

This was the Plains horse culture the fur traders and trappers faced. Though they rarely could equal the skill the Indian riders took for granted for war and hunting, or never were able to equal the Indian rider's feats of horsemanship, they did gain from the availability of horses, and learn from observing the Indian's capabilities.

CHAPTER 10:

THE SASKATCHEWAN

The North Saskatchewan River was the original route for transporting goods, furs, personnel, and messages between the Pacific Coast and York Factory, via Fort Edmonton. Two branches of the Saskatchewan River, flowing in deep, wide valleys defined its configuration, scope, and style. The South Saskatchewan rises in the Rockies as the Oldman and Bow rivers and flows over the treeless prairies northeast to its junction with the North Saskatchewan about thirty-five miles east of present-day Prince Albert. The North Saskatchewan also rises in the Rockies west of Fort Edmonton and flows generally east. Throughout its length, it had no falls or rapids then that could not be cordelled up or lined down, making river transport relatively easy.

The Saskatchewan River ended at the Grand Rapids. There it descended into Cedar Lake immediately northwest of Lake Winnipeg. From north to south, the Saskatchewan District of Hudson's Bay Company extended from the shores of Lesser Slave Lake to the Coteaus (hills along the north shores) of the Missouri in present-day North and South Dakota and Montana, forming the east-west Continental Divide.[227] HBC Governor Simpson considered the Saskatchewan District the most productive district. He and the Northern Department Council further divided it, creating the Swan District east of longitude 105.

The river drained what was essentially Cree country. The Cree were the dominant tribe west of Hudson's Bay. There are nine dialects of Cree, which belongs to the Algonquian language family. As David Mandelbaum wrote in *The Plains Cree*, "The immense territory inhabited by the Cree at this time [1820] is greater than that dominated by any other North American tribe, though half of the Cree population had been swept away by the smallpox epidemic of 1780–1782."[228] The Western Woods Cree lived in the northern portions of what became the provinces of Ontario, Manitoba, and Saskatchewan. The Swampy Cree lived in the lowlands west of Hudson's Bay, as far as Cumberland House. By the eighteenth and nineteenth centuries, various groups known as the Plains Cree had moved into western Saskatchewan and eastern Alberta and south to Montana and western North Dakota.

Although the Cree had controlled the middleman trade from Hudson's Bay westward, they had, by the nineteenth century, also become producers and traders of fur-trader provisions. Cumberland House, on Pine Island near the eastern end of the Saskatchewan River, is the oldest permanent settlement and oldest Hudson's Bay Company post in Saskatchewan. It was established by Samuel Hearne as a supply point in 1774. Its permanent traders and the canoe brigades passing through depended frequently upon the ability of the Woodland Cree to provide meat from large animals as a primary provision. As foot hunters, the Cree were the best, attaining a skill with their Northwest guns comparable to the accuracy of rifles. When a drought occurred, as in 1832, Cree assistance was essential. The Cree at that time were sufficiently independent of the traders' goods and produce that they could trade when it suited their convenience, or even in an emergency, as when the local Cree needed food. But they made it clear that they would follow their own priorities.

According to the oral history of Cree, "Old Men," compiled by historian Edward Ahenakew, who had Cree, Cree-Assiniboin, and French ancestors, the Plains Cree had moved westward in search of furs into the lands of the Blackfoot, and though they traded with them, providing guns, they remained enemies, pressuring them to the west and south. Among the Plains Cree and these other tribes, a truce was rare and brief. There was no peace for the Cree from the constant threat of these neighboring tribes.[229] Ahenakew presented a composite view of the people:

> I am a Plains Cree, and on the prairies I can believe that I am the centre of the world—my world....I claim that our life on the prairie has bred into the Plains Cree a freedom that...has made us, on the whole, of a daring and reckless temperament....I will always say that it is not so much in the man himself as in the place where he lives that the true difference lays... the place where a man lives can shape his character.[230]

Plains Cree bands were kinship groups in eight to twelve bands of fluid composition, each with a headman and a loosely defined hunting territory. They lived in buffalo-hide tepees with three-pole foundations. Buffalo was their staple food. To help maintain the buffalo herd, the Cree burned the grasslands to encourage higher yield and earlier growth. Women snared a variety of small game and gathered roots, such as the prairie turnip, and various berries. They dried most of them for winter. Bands took names from their areas, such as Upstream, Calling River, and Touchwood Hills People.[231] Among the famous Cree leaders were Red Fox, a wise man and war chief, and Eyes Open, a more prudent financier than war leader. Eyes on Each Side, also known as Broken Arm, represented his people in a meeting with President Andrew Jackson. On returning home, he disparaged the whites' accomplishments, and thereby avoided the criticism of natives who did not believe what they heard about the whites; such disbelief and ridicule had already greeted Indian people who returned from the lands held by white people.

The Cree men were companionable with their women, regularly consulted them, and shared many camp tasks. David Thompson observed that polygamous marriages among the Cree usually were the result of a man accepting responsibility for another man's widow, though polygamy was common, greatly lessening the labor of an individual wife.

Concerning religion, Mandelbaum wrote that the concept of a single, all-powerful Creator was dominant in Plains Cree religious ideology. Every prayer for supernatural aid had to begin with an invocation to Great Manito, who controlled all. He did not appear in visions and was considered to be too great, too awesome, to be asked directly for his blessing. There were many intermediaries between the Creator and man. As examples, there was a bear spirit power, a horse spirit power, and one for the maple tree. When a spirit appeared to an individual in a vision, it became that person's *pawaka or life guide.* There were unpleasant spirits, such as coyote, who would take a man's wife and child in payment for certain abilities granted to a man. Shamanism could be practiced in varying forms by a good number of people.[232]

Their trading partners and sometimes enemies on the south were the Assiniboin, who were also moving westward. It is often said that although the Cree obtained horses primarily from the Assiniboin, in the mid- to late-eighteenth century, they never equaled the equestrian skills of other seminomadic people, such as the Blackfoot. However, they did adopt much of the Plains culture, including warring, raiding, and using buffalo for food, clothing, shelter, tools, equipment, and fuel.[233]

The Cree's horse-trading alliance with the Assiniboin enabled both tribes to move out onto the plains. They continued to move westward and southward in the face of Sioux and Blackfoot hostility, until they reached the upper South Saskatchewan, home of the Blackfoot Confederation, and the valley of the Missouri, in Sioux territory. David Mandelbaum of the Canadian Plains Research Center concluded, "From

1740 to 1820, the Cree were expanding to their widest limits....The final era found the invaders firmly established in the plains as a true Plains tribe....The quest for furs brought the Cree to the prairies; the congenial mode of Plains life induced some of them to stay there."[234]

George Catlin, Indian historian and painter, reckoned that Cree bands trading at Fort Union in 1832 totaled three thousand souls.[235] They waged an unremitting warfare westward with the Blackfoot, were probably taking on new cultural forms, and were periodically decimated by smallpox. The Cree trading chiefs brought guns to the Blackfoot, who sought them to attack the Kutenai, Flathead, and Shoshone, all of whom lived in the Pacific drainage.

Because the Cree were able to overawe their opponents with their guns, they were able to conquer the western tribes they met. But as the other tribes obtained guns, Cree ascendancy disappeared. Their power waned from disease, guns in the hands of enemies, dependence on fur traders, and fondness for liquor. However, the Plains Cree provided most of the furs harvested in the Saskatchewan District.

Chief Factor John Rowand ran a highly profitable district and gave American fur traders keen competition. Living at Edmonton House, he dominated the Saskatchewan District and the fur trade with Cree and other tribes. His biographer, James G. MacGregor, called him the "Czar of the Prairies." HBC Governor George Simpson wrote to Rowand on December 18, 1830: "We have so frequently gone into the affairs of the Saskatchewan...before you were appointed to the charge of that Department [sic] it yielded a loss instead of a gain, but by your superior management it became the most profitable in the Indian country."[236]

Rowand brought a lot of experience to the job. Born in Montreal in 1789, he grew up around the fur trade, and learned the names of men and places along the canoe trails westward. He had heard the fascinating tales of Sault St. Marie, Fort William, Lake Winnipeg, the Saskatchewan, and the Rockies. Possessing some culture and education, he had great prospects when he joined North West Company as an apprentice in 1803.

Rowand routinely traveled the canoe trails or rode on horseback beside streams throughout the Saskatchewan basin. He met Cree, Assiniboin, and Blackfoot. Adept at languages, he soon could make himself understood. Though languages at a post were a babel of many tongues, both European and native, the principal native trading language in the region was Cree. The voyageurs and laborers about him were generally French-speaking Métis, and some English-speaking "country born."

In the summer of 1810, Rowand was at Edmonton—this time working under Alexander Henry, the younger, who was leading a North West Company challenge to Hudson's Bay Company's monopoly. There Rowand met and married Louise Umphreville, daughter of trader Edward Umphreville, who had left the country, and his mixed-descent wife.[237] Rowand worked up and down the Saskatchewan. He became a full partner in the North West Company. Stationed at Edmonton, he participated in the fairly congenial competition with rival Hudson's Bay Company.

Fort Edmonton, built on the bluffs where the Alberta Parliament buildings now stand, was the last of a number of forts built. It was first Fort Augustus, built by the North West Company in 1794, and followed by various other Hudson's Bay Company and North West Company forts, abandoned or destroyed by the Blackfoot. Chief Trader Rowand built the new Fort Edmonton in 1808, which was abandoned in 1810, and finally, before 1819, built for the North West Company what became the primary Hudson's Bay Company depot. It was the principal resupply point for staging brigade travel between York Factory and Fort Vancouver.[238]

When the two companies merged in 1821, Rowand became a chief trader of the Hudson's Bay Company. With the chief competitor now consumed through the merger, Rowand turned the Hudson's Bay Company operation to profit. He reduced costs and encouraged the Cree and other Plains tribes to hunt furs and robes "on and across the Mountains and toward the Banks of the Missouri."[239]

Fort Edmonton was ideally located to collect meat and pemmican for provisions, and as a vital trade center. Rowand's final fort, famously known as Rowand's huge "Big House," contained a huge, garishly painted ballroom that Rowand used for entertaining visiting chiefs. Visitors looked with awe and wonder at the ceiling decorated with fantastic gilt scrolls. Rowand's fort had a dozen warehouses, residences, workshops, and an icehouse for storing winter provisions. There were pickets, a battlement, gateways, a flagstaff, and a commanding location high above the river.

In the summer of 1822, Rowand went on an expedition to the upper South Saskatchewan and Bow rivers area. Donald McKenzie, who had served both the North West and Hudson's Bay companies in the Columbia basin, was in command. This first Bow River expedition started from Fort Carleton. Simpson had instructed the team to determine the availability of beaver in the prairie that the Blackfoot and Piegan hunted between Rocky Mountain House and the Missouri. They met members of the Blackfoot Confederacy for the first time near the Great Sand Hills (in Saskatchewan). Hearty, heavy-set Rowand demonstrated strong, skillful tactics in dealing with the Blackfoot, and he became rather famous over the years for being able to deal with them, a tribe notable for its disdain for the whites.

A few miles below the junction of the Bow and Oldman rivers, headwaters of the South Saskatchewan, the party stopped and built a post to use as a base for further explorations. They called it Chesterfield House. From here McKenzie sent out parties to the west and southwest, as far as the Teton River. They crossed the Teton about fifty miles north of the Great Falls of the Missouri. All these parties returned and reported that there was not enough beaver to merit further effort in that direction. Among other accomplishments, this expedition welded the various former North West Company men and the long-standing Hudson's Bay Company men into a strong and lasting relationship.

As the story of the 1822 expedition suggests, Hudson's Bay Company traders in the Saskatchewan District dealt with natives other than the Plains Cree. They also traded with Woodland Cree, Assiniboin, tribes of the Blackfoot Confederacy, and the Sarcee, a relatively small tribe on the northern plains that often affiliated with the Blackfoot.

Governor Simpson wisely promoted Rowand to chief factor in 1826.[240] As chief factor, Rowand supervised all trading posts in the Saskatchewan District above Cumberland House, which came under the Winnipeg District. In 1833, these posts were Fort Edmonton, Fort Carlton (sometimes called Carlton House), Fort Pitt, Piegan House, Rocky Mountain House, Fort Assiniboin, and Lesser Slave Lake Post. Fort Carlton was about half way between Cumberland House and Fort Edmonton. It was a provisioning and transport post that provided about three hundred bags of pemmican annually. It received goods from Red River carts and forwarded them onward via water routes. Fort Pitt was on the north side of the Saskatchewan River. It was also a provisioning post, providing dried meat. Lesser Slave Lake Post (later Fort Grouard) was at the west end of the lake, and lots of furs were traded to the company at that post. Rocky Mountain House, built originally by the North West Company in 1802, was located on the north side of the Saskatchewan, about eighty miles west of present-day Red Deer, Alberta.

In 1790, Hudson's Bay Company had built another Carlton House on the east side of the Assiniboine River near the confluence of the Whitesand River. The fort was built to accommodate and protect the diverse furs obtained from trade with the Cree and Saulteaux (Ojibwa): muskrat, mink, fisher, badger, beaver, otter, wolverine, wolf, red fox, silver fox, cross fox, various bears, moose hide, swan skins, and skunk. To the south lay the prairie and the buffalo.

Providing adequate provisions to men who traveled after furs and buffalo robes was an important function of every trading post, and the main provision was pemmican. This concentrated food could last for years in storage. A day's ration of pemmican for one man was one and a half pounds, which was equivalent to eight pounds of fish or fresh meat. While fur traders often hunted en route, the pressure of time and the occasional scarcity of game made reliance on hunting hazardous at best. Elk and deer and, on the Pacific Coast, salmon were also used in making pemmican. Historian Susan Hartmann quotes Pretty Shield, a Crow woman, describing the making of pemmican:

> We cut good, lean meat into strips and dried it a little: then roasted it until it looked brown. After this was done we pounded the dry meat with stone hammers....Next we soaked ripe chokeberries in water, and then used this water to boil crushed bones. When the kettle of boiled bones was cool we skimmed off the grease from the bone marrow, mixed it with the pounded meat, poured this into buffalo heart-skins, and let it get solid.[241]

Hartmann commented that "such labor, if it were well done, could produce 55 pounds of pemmican and 45 pounds of jerky from a single buffalo cow."[242]

The most famous pemmican meal of the voyageurs was "rubbiboo," a thick soup made with potatoes. As a noon meal when stops were not allowed, pemmican was eaten cold. Not everyone found pemmican an attractive meal. Historian H. M. Robison, who wrote for *Harper's Magazine* in 1879, described a pemmican meal:

> Take the scrapings from the driest outside corner of a very stale piece of cold roast-beef, add to it lumps of tallowy, rancid fat, then garnish all with long human hairs, on which string pieces, like beads upon a necklace, and short hairs of dogs or oxen, or both, and you have a fair imitation

of common pemmican. Indeed…[one may wonder] whether the hair on the buffaloes from which the pemmican is made does not grow on the inside of the skin. The abundance of small stones or pebbles in pemmican also indicates the discovery of a new buffalo diet heretofore unknown to naturalists. Carefully made pemmican, flavored with berries and sugar, is nearly good; but of most persons new to the diet, it may be said that, in two senses, a little of it goes a long way.[243]

Blankets, guns, sugar, and flour could be shipped to trading posts. Other provisions could not. HBC's Governor and Committee in London emphasized the need of the men who directed all departments and posts "to use their utmost endeavor to collect large quantities of leather… buffalo robes, pack cords, snow shoe ties [and] leather tents as they are articles absolutely necessary for the trade, and cannot be purchased in Europe or Canada."[244] Many of these items were used on site, and many were shipped across the Rockies to posts in New Caledonia, where they were greatly needed on the Brigade Trail for packing horses.

Governor Simpson considered the Saskatchewan District the most important of all, partly because it produced so many furs and buffalo robes and thereby much profit, and partly because it encompassed the prime travel route between Hudson's Bay and the Rockies. The district also traded with natives for fish and game provisions for the several posts. But provisioning often proved inadequate. Simpson noted in 1827, for example, that provisioning had "again entirely failed in the Saskatchewan," and the various posts were dependent on local agricultural efforts, particularly in "barley, pease [peas], and flour."[245]

The Saskatchewan basin produced so many furs and robes that a decline in production prompted Hudson's Bay Company to begin conservation measures in the 1830s. To protect the rich region in the northern plains, the Northern Council restricted beaver returns. Athabasca could produce annually only 5,000 beaver, Saskatchewan only 5,500, and English River, 650. Seven other districts were also restricted to less than 500, for a total of 12,670.[246]

In 1833 the Northern Council urged that "Gentlemen in charge of Districts and Posts, except such as are exposed to opposition [meaning Americans along the Upper Missouri], exert their utmost efforts in discouraging the hunting of Cub Beaver and beaver out of season, and that no beaver traps be issued from the depot, except for sale to the Piegan, and that in any case where an unusual proportion of Cub or unseasoned Beaver appears, the fact be reported to the Governor and Committee."[247] Regulations became even stricter in the next decade.

Into the 1830s, traders from Hudson's Bay routinely relied on the Woodland Cree to provide meat from large animals as a primary provision—despite the large gardens maintained by post personnel. When a drought occurred, as it did in 1832, Cree assistance was essential. And when fish and game were scarce, the Cree depended on the post for food. Cree and traders lived a mutually exploitive existence, increasing the number of Indian families who lived at or near the post.

The white community, as well as the number of Cree, grew initially to the advantage of both. In a well-researched study, historian Paul Thistle described it in detail. "During the twenty year period between 1821 and 1840, however, reference to Indian 'starvation' became more frequent in Cumberland House journals," he wrote.[248] And traders learned that the word "starvation" was often used as a bargaining chip.

But increasingly the Cree and Métis in the area could live by their own hunting and fishing, and work for the fur company whenever they wanted trade goods. By the 1830s, they had come to trade when it suited their convenience or needs, or when they needed food. Hudson's Bay Company factors could no longer depend on them to work when the company wanted or needed labor. Yet the Cree wanted European goods and said so. The permanent white settlement at Cumberland felt overwhelmed by number, independence, and demands of the natives settled there.

The problem was beyond the authority of Rowand as chief factor of the Saskatchewan District, who kept company officials informed of the situation. As the committee in London wrote on February 27, 1822:

> It has become a matter of serious importance to determine on the most proper measures to be adopted with regard to the men who have large families and who must be discharged, and with the numerous halfbreed children whose parents have died or deserted them. These people form a burden which cannot be got rid of without expense, and, if allowed to remain in their present condition, they will become dangerous to the Peace of the Country and safety of the Trading Posts. It will therefore be both prudent and economical to incur some expense in placing these people where they maintain themselves and be civilized and instructed in Religion. We consider that all these people ought to be removed to Red River.[249]

The committee emphasized "civilization": civilizing the aborigines. "T'is only this way that they can be gradually civilized, and if the children are educated along with those of the settlers, and accustomed to labor, they will in the course of a generation lose much of their Indian habits."[250] The committee failed to note that native children might have been educated with white children at Cumberland House. In London, they could not imagine the prejudices present in native-white communities.

Another major challenge for Hudson's Bay Company in the Saskatchewan District was competition from American fur traders. When in July 1831, for example, Simpson reported that the chances of war against the Rocky Mountain House had increased, since the Mountain Crow had attacked another tribe en route to the house to trade, his concern was clearly business: "Their skins will of course fall into the hands of the American adventurers on the Missouri." He reported that another tribe en route to the establishment (a term used for any HBC activity) traded three hundred to four hundred skins to the "Coutenais"—the Kutenai—and he predicted that those skins would "find their way to Fort Vancouver in the course of the season."[251] That was good for business at Hudson's Bay Company.

Simpson also deplored "the large body of people required to protect Forts Edmonton, Carleton, Pitt and Rocky Mountain House being visited by some of the most formidable and turbulent tribes in the country"—not hostile, but "alert for plunder."[252] Rowand had built Fort Pitt on the south bank of the North Saskatchewan River, about 109.05° west. It was not only the best provisioning post in the department, but it had also drawn several bands from the plains to the thick woods, where they were usefully employed.

Simpson expressed other competitive concerns. There were reports that the Americans in 1829 were building a fort at the mouth of the Yellowstone (apparently Fort Union). He believed the new fort would probably greatly injure the trade of the Saskatchewan District. Of course he knew that the Cree had traded with Hudson's Bay Company for a century and a half before the American Fur Company built Fort Union in 1829, but HBC had lost territory to American traders farther east, so he recognized a real business threat from Fort Union.

The American competition extended beyond Fort Union. Simpson informed London in a letter that "the American traders appear to have altered their system in regard to them [the Blackfoot] and conciliatory treatment…so that they are likely to become formidable rivals to us… their hunting grounds being chiefly within what is understood to be American boundaries." Simpson feared that despite all of the "Honable

Coy's" efforts, the Americans would soon "deprive us of a large proportion of their furs."[253]

In June 1832, Rowand was implementing the Edmonton House's
"Outfit 1833." He also concerned himself with the American competition. He knew the Piegan and the Americans were trading on the Missouri. Rowand used a somewhat renegade trader named Jamie "Jock"
Bird. Bird was the mixed-descent son of a Hudson's Bay Company chief
factor, James Bird, and his Cree wife, Elizabeth. The younger Bird entered
the employment of Hudson's Bay Company in 1809 at Fort Edmonton.
He began as an apprentice clerk, a position that reflected his education,
which was a result of his father's rank. During the years following, he
worked as an assistant trader, clerk, and interpreter. A natural and skillful linguist, he spoke fluently in English, French, Blackfoot, Gros Ventre,
Assiniboine, Cree, and Sarsi.[254]

Bird was an unusually talented representative of the shifting loyalties
among Hudson's Bay Company and American Fur Company employees, and among freemen, whether white, Métis, or native. According to
Rowand's biographer, Bird "wandered with the Piegan [and] flirted with
the Americans." He was "capable and fearless, at times, and sullen and
treacherous at others....Neither fear, shame, flattery, nor money could
overcome his resentment at being treated as a half-breed at Edmonton
House."[255] Yet Bird obtained contraband furs from the Americans, and
Rowand and Simpson gladly accepted them.

In his August 1832 report to the committee in London, Governor
Simpson said the Saskatchewan District "extends over a very large tract of
country—sending forth very large returns and yielding handsome profits."[256] Yet, he added, the profits were not proportionate to the capital
cost, compared with other parts of the country. He attributed this to
the hostile tribes around some of the posts "and in contesting the trade
with our American opponents who are making great efforts to obtain

a footing among the Piegan, Blood, and other Plains tribes, that have been for ages in the habit of frequenting our Establishments on the Saskatchewan."[257]

By 1832, American Fur Company's posts on the Missouri were well established in trading with the Piegan and other Blackfoot tribes, and were drawing off trade from the Saskatchewan District. The American traders persuaded Bird to join them. When Bird left Hudson's Bay Company without notice, he took a few thousand furs to the Americans. He then persuaded the Piegan that the Americans were partners, not opponents, of their old Saskatchewan friend Rowand. Simpson concluded, "Thus I am concerned we have lost a large proportion of the hunts of this valuable tribe."[258] Despite Hudson's Bay Company's general ability to provide trade goods cheaper than the Americans, by 1833, American Fur Company's Upper Missouri Outfit had acquired virtually all of the upper Missouri trade. But the willingness of Hudson's Bay Company to extract furs from American trading or trapping never abated.

After Bird's defection to American Fur Company, Simpson reported that Rowand had volunteered to take a team of about twenty men and go "amidst the numerous warlike and bloodthirsty tribes who occupied the plains between the Saskatchewan and the Missouri."[259] Simpson called this effort a "forlorn hope," but he and the council decided to let Rowand go and to have him build a post for the convenience of the Piegan on the Bow River (west of modern Calgary).

As reported in the *Fort Edmonton Journal* of Monday, June 4, 1832: "An expedition under the immediate charge of Mr. Chief Factor John Rowand, assisted by Messrs. George McDougal and Henry Fisher with the complement of fourteen men and a boy, for the purpose of ascertaining the cause of the Piegan having left off trading with us as usual, and in order to get them back to their old station, from which, it is supposed, they have been drawn away by the persuasions of James Bird who has deserted the service; [the expedition] has been set on foot, and the men all well equipped with arms, and a suitable outfit for trade have taken the lead, they are encamped about two miles south of this place across the Saskatchewan, where Mr. Rowand and the rest of the Gentlemen will overtake them on the morrow."[260]

On Monday, August 4, Chief Factor Rowand returned to Edmonton from his southwestern search for furs. A journalist reported on his courage and hardiness during the expedition:

This evening Mr. Chief Factor Rowand and Mr. George McDougal accompanied by seven men arrived from their tour to the Missouri—[Henry Fisher had been left on the Missouri to persuade the natives to trade with the Hudson's Bay Company]—where they saw the Piegans headed by their chiefs. Endeavors were made to get them back to their own station, and it is supposed they will do so—though the Americans, whom they met near the Sweet Grass Hills [south of the border in north-central Montana] will on the other hand try to stop them from coming in order to make as much as they can while in that quarter.

During this time Mr. Rowand was surrounded by aborigines who were endeavoring to appease his anger and stop him from shooting, which they supposed was his intention. Every precaution had been taken for the safety of the [expedition] party, and we are happy to learn that during the whole route nothing of any serious consequences had been met with....In the course of the summer they met the Kootenai's Chief [sic]who received them with good will. That Chief was at the head of thirty-three men, and from them they exchanged some lean horses for good fat ones, giving ammunition and tobacco to boot.[261]

This small supply of ammunition given to the Kutenai was the means of saving them from real danger. A few days afterward, they were attacked by at least a thousand Blood and Blackfoot, "whose love of horses does not stop them from making mischief toward friends or foe. They immediately began to pillage the Kootenais, who defended themselves with such bravery that after having seven of themselves wounded made their enemies retreat with the loss of eight killed and above twenty wounded—The Kootenais returned to their lands with great joy, having escaped from such a most dangerous situation."[262]

Rowand had begun the construction of the Piegan Post on the north bank of the Bow River. He left ten men to finish the job. American-born Henry Fisher, a former North West Company trader who had had considerable experience with the Blackfoot, supervised nine workers. Only forty tents of Piegan had come to trade, despite Rowand's exertions. It appeared that they preferred the American Fur Company trade at Fort Union. In January 1834, Chief Factor James F. Harriott closed Piegan Post and sent most of its staff to reopen and occupy Rocky Mountain House.

In his 1835 report, Simpson stated that though it was considered necessary to compete with the Americans, the company had gained few American furs, and those at great cost and risk to lives and property. He further explained, "The ordinary trade of the Piegans, previous to the late opposition on the Missouri, was 3000 Beaver, and it has been known as high as 5000, but since the contest they are enabled, by means of the very high prices given for skins, and the large presents they receive, to obtain all the supplies they require for less than one third the quantity they usually brought to market." Simpson' report about Bird concluded that despite his exceedingly high terms, bad character, and unreasonable demands," it was better to have him work for HBC again than against them, and that HBC was indebted to him for bringing in five hundred beaver the previous winter that would have otherwise gone to the Americans."[263]

Buffalo robes were coming to the fore as a money-making item, and the Americans could ship them to market via the Missouri and Mississippi much cheaper than Hudson's Bay Company could ship them down the Saskatchewan, to Hudson's Bay or Montreal, and then to England. The faster and cheaper water route up the Mississippi from New Orleans allowed the Americans to obtain good supplies cheaper than Hudson's Bay Company could, even with the tariff the U.S. government levied on imports from England.

Despite the previously successful conservation measures discussed earlier in this chapter, the availability of furbearers in the Saskatchewan District was deteriorating. Simpson commented that although muskrats were numerous, beaver were getting scarce, and at Lesser Slave Lake Post, once a prime marten source, returns had been reduced by 90 percent. According to Simpson, Indian trappers were violating the company's conservation policy. For example, they trapped cub beaver, which prevented rebuilding the number of mature beaver. HBC did not impose conservation measures on posts "exposed to opposition traps" (that is, American competition). Buffalo remained as available as ever, depending on weather and pasture conditions.

Summarizing, Simpson said he believed the Saskatchewan would continue to be profitable at about the same level as in 1832–33. Beaver returns of the Saskatchewan Department were as follows: 1831, 6,969; 1832, 4,962; 1833, 4,309; 1834, 4,604; and 1835, 2,675. Lesser Slave Lake peaked at 4,257 beaver in 1823, but two years later had declined to 744, and thereafter was no longer reported, though its returns may have been included in the Saskatchewan Department report.[264]

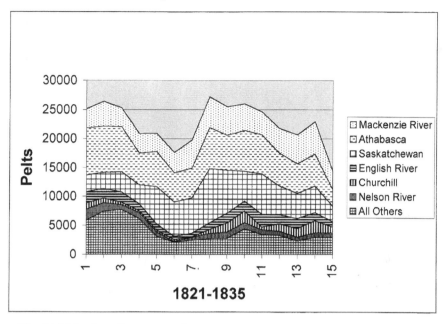

Fig. 10.1 Northern Department beaver returns

By 1835, Rowand's Saskatchewan District had served as a trail to the subarctic, a transcontinental express route, a lucrative fur source, and an area of American competition. There remained the old posts, the fading beaver market, indigenous people, and the buffalo. Rowand and his boss Simpson had forged a lifelong friendship. Simpson wrote of Rowand: "Of a fiery disposition, and as bold as a lion. An excellent Trader who has the peculiar talent of attracting the fiercest to him while he rules them with a Rod of iron and so daring that he beards their Chiefs in the open camp while surrounded by their warriors."[265]

CHAPTER 11:

THE MISSOURI FROM ST. LOUIS TO FORT UNION

John Jacob Astor had spent the twenty years between 1808 and 1828 gaining control of the Great Lakes and upper Mississippi fur trade. Lewis and Clark's exploration in 1803–06 had whetted Astor's appetite for entering the Pacific trade, which had already brought fortunes to Boston merchants. He saw an opportunity in establishing a trading post on the coast, provisioned by ships sailing around Cape Horn. The task required winning over unknown Indian tribes and bands, and gaining the cooperation and support of the Cabanné, Chouteau, Gratiot, and Pratte families, who made up the long-established St. Louis fur business.

The Chouteau family came to St. Louis in the mid-eighteenth century. Auguste and Pierre Chouteau Sr. built Fort Carondelet on the Osage River, worked out agreeable treaties with the Osage, and from that success began a fur-trade empire in the West. They traded with tribes from north to south along the Missouri, Arkansas, Platte, Red, and Canadian rivers. The Osage in particular were an agricultural and powerful warrior tribe whose members acted as middlemen between the Chouteaus and tribes on the Great Plains. The Caddo in the south and the Pawnee farther north were also successful middlemen.

One of the first French traders was Jacques d'Eglise, who travelled up the Missouri River from St. Louis to the Mandan villages. Following the same practices used by the French in Canada, the traders lived in villages, married native women, and adapted their trading techniques to those used by the tribes. In the next fifty years, possibly hundreds of men explored the upper Missouri and into the Rocky Mountains, giving them the knowledge to serve as guides for those who came later.

From the time of Lewis and Clark until 1820, the fur trade west of the Mississippi River slowed to a crawl. Meriwether Lewis was appointed governor of the Louisiana Territory in 1808. He favored the policy of building government trading factories guarded by military posts to protect the aborigine from dishonest traders. For the area beyond the Mandan villages, he proposed giving an exclusive trading license to one company. The license was issued to Manuel Lisa and his partners, including William Clark and Andrew Henry, among others, and they became the St. Louis Missouri Fur Company.

The French-Canadian and British traders from the north who came down the Mississippi River and up the Missouri and adjourning streams continued to provide guns, blankets, and other goods in exchange for beaver from all of the northern tribes. During the War of 1812, General William Clark, now the governor of the territory, gave trade goods to Manuel Lisa to establish a post known as Fort Lisa north of Council Bluffs. The post was to keep the Teton Sioux and Omaha friendly toward the Americans and prevent them from supporting the British.

The British made a substantial effort to acquire the loyalty and trade of upper Missouri aboriginals during the War of 1812. In a letter to General Clark dated July 1, 1817, Manuel Lisa resigned his appointment as Indian agent of the upper Missouri, believing he was the primary force in retaining Indian loyalty to the United States. Lisa wrote:

Your excellency will remember that more than a year before the war broke out, I gave you intelligence that the wampum the British were carrying was extending British influence along the banks of the Missouri, and that all of the nations of this great river were excited to join the universal confederacy then setting on foot, of which the Prophet was the instrument, and British traders the soul. The Indians of the Missouri are to those of the Mississippi as four is to one. Their weight would be great if thrown against us. They did not arm against the Republic; on the contrary, they armed against the British and struck the Iowa, the allies of that power.[266]

Lisa was a prime power on the Missouri until his death on August 11, 1820, when Joshua Pilcher took over management of the often-reorganized Missouri Fur Company. "Thus closed the career of the most active and indefatigable trader that St. Louis ever produced," wrote historian Hiram Chittenden. He explained Lisa's success as follows: "Privation, hardship, incessant toil, were his constant portion. He could put his hand to the oar, if necessary, among his voyageurs, lead them in their songs, and cheer them to exertions which would otherwise been unendurable.... During the last thirteen years of his life, he ascended and descended the Missouri twelve times. In all he could not have traveled less than twenty six thousand miles by river."[267]

After the war, Clark negotiated treaties with the Teton Sioux, the Grand Pawnee and others to assure them that they were now under the protection of the U.S. government. In 1816, Congress excluded foreigners from trading on U.S. soil without an American sponsor.

Freed by the Battle of New Orleans, the Mississippi was open to the sea, and on July 27, 1817, the steamboat *Pike* from New Orleans tied up at the St. Louis docks. Two years later, the *Independence* launched steamboat travel on the Missouri by navigating from St. Louis to Franklin, Missouri. This greatly reduced the cost of transporting goods and furs from the upper Missouri River to New York, and later permitted the transport of heavy buffalo robes, making them an important item of trade.

John Jacob Astor's effort to expand generated competition, for the western tribes and bands were already trading, some with the French firms Cabanné and Company and Berthold and Chouteau; some with the Missouri Fur Company; some with smaller firms, such as the Boston investors in Stone, Bostwick, and Company. Also, entrepreneur General William H. Ashley would soon be sending an expedition into the Rocky Mountains.

All feared, even hated, Astor, but respected his power. In 1822 he ordered Ramsay Crooks to begin their move into St. Louis. In 1823, the American Fur Company bought Stone, Bostwick, and Company and their trading commitments out of St. Louis, and agreed with Bernard Pratte and Company to import their European goods and to sell their furs.

Separately, the newly arrived Columbia Fur Company was proving to be a formidable, efficient, highly profitable, and expert competition. It was organized by former North West Company men, particularly Kenneth McKenzie, manager, and Honoré Picotte, James Kipp, Joseph Renville, Daniel Lamont, and William Llaidlaw. By organizing under the name of the American trader William P. Tilton, the company qualified for a license, which William Clark granted on June 17, 1822, for trading with Dakota tribes on the Minnesota River, and with the Mandan, Hidatsa, and Crow at their villages.[268]

Columbia Fur Company headquarters was on Lake Traverse between the Minnesota and Red rivers. From Lake Traverse they erected posts at strategic places along the "upper Missouri"—that part of the river above the mouth of the Big Sioux River. This included Fort Tecumseh, established in 1822 near present-day Pierre, South Dakota, and posts at the Missouri River confluence of the Big Knife, Teton, James, Niobrara, White, Vermilion, and Big Sioux rivers.

From these posts they obtained enough beavers, muskrats, and buffalo robes, that after their first two years, although they had been $50,000 in debt, they gained in a single season enough to pay their debts, "leaving much money for themselves."[269] Their gross annual income during 1825–27 was from $150,000 to $200,000. About one-half came from buffalo robes. Their outlay for trade goods and supplies did not exceed $25,000 annually. The difference went to debt reduction and profit.

Astor and Ramsay Crooks recognized that Kenneth McKenzie's Columbia Fur Company offered the greatest competition on the upper Missouri river. Crooks and McKenzie finally reached an agreement after difficult negotiations in 1827. The Columbia Fur Company would withdraw from the Great Lakes and upper Mississippi. It would assume control of the Missouri above its confluence with the Big Sioux, and become known as the Upper Missouri Outfit of the Western Department of the American Fur Company. Astor now controlled the Missouri trade.

Bernard Pratte and Pierre Chouteau Jr., of Bernard Pratte and Company of St. Louis, realized they could not continue to oppose the advance of the American Fur Company. The name Chouteau had been dominant in St. Louis society and in St. Louis business, primarily the fur trade.[270] The most prominent Chouteau in the 1820s was third-generation Pierre Chouteau Jr., known as "Cadet." He then was a partner in Bernard Pratte and Company, which he and his brother-in-law Bartholomew Berthold had first organized under their names in 1813. In 1823 J. P. Cabanné joined the firm, and it became known as Bernard Pratte and Company. Astor then made another wise move; after lengthy negotiations on December 20, 1826, in New York, Ramsay Crooks and Cadet Chouteau Jr. agreed to unite the American Fur Company and Bernard Pratte and Company, forming the Western Department of the American Fur Company.[271]

Under this agreement, Bernard Pratte and Company would be general superintendent and American Fur Company's director of Indian affairs in Indian country, with Chouteau receiving an annual salary of $2000 annually. The two companies would share profit and loss equally on the Mississippi below Prairie du Chien, and all of the Missouri. This agreement was good for four years, or until the 1831 fur returns. It was a big business; and although ledger accounts on microfilm today are partly illegible, they numbered about five hundred separate accounts.

With their new Upper Missouri Outfit, Astor, Crooks, Chouteau, and Kenneth McKenzie now faced the mostly nomadic red people whom the mountain men talked about. The task was to trade with the Caddoan, Arikara, and Pawnee, and the Siouan speakers, including the Santee and Yankton Dakota and the Teton tribes. The Assiniboin, Cree, Crow, Hidatsa, and Mandan were also Siouan. Finally, there were the Algonquin-speaking Blackfoot Confederation, made up of the Blackfoot proper, Blood, Piegan, and Gros Ventre.[272]

The number of people in the trading area can only be estimated. Determining native population is extremely conjectural; James Mooney is considered the most authoritative. He estimated the population of the seven Sioux nations at 25,000 in 1870. Of these, 15,000 lived on the plains. AFC trader Edwin Thompson Denig estimated the Sioux in 1833 had 2,360 lodges, with five persons per lodge, for a total of 11,800.[273] The 1833 estimate is for the population that had been reestablished after the sweeping epidemics of 1780 and before the disastrous smallpox epidemic of 1837 on the upper Missouri.

In forming the Upper Missouri Outfit, Astor retained the skilled traders of both ventures—Pratte and McKenzie—and employed them in the new Outfit. When North West Company merged into Hudson's Bay Company in 1821, McKenzie had lost his job. Initially a clerk at NWC, he immigrated to the United States to organize the Columbia Fur Company. He became the head of the new Upper Missouri Outfit.

The mergers creating the Western Department and the Upper Missouri Outfit made the American Fur Company an important presence in St. Louis and were key to developing the western trade. McKenzie was eager to emulate Ashley's famous success in the Rockies.

Chouteau, then head of the Western Department, prevailed over McKenzie's eagerness preventing him from going to the Rockies, and the new Upper Missouri Outfit proceeded to establish trading forts in the traditional manner along the upper Missouri River, from the Big Sioux to the Rockies.

In order to obtain control of Columbia Fur Company supplies McKenzie then rode 250 miles to Fort Tecumseh, across the river from today's Pierre, South Dakota.[274] Gradually, the Upper Missouri Outfit opened Forts Pierre, Clark, Union, and McKenzie on the Missouri to trade with the Assiniboin, Cree, and various other tribes, and Fort Cass on the Yellowstone to trade with the Crow.

McKenzie's plans for spring 1828 required James Kipp to proceed to the mouth of the Yellowstone River with a work crew from the Mandan villages and begin the construction of a forward base. By the fall of 1828, they had built temporary housing, decided on a site on the Missouri River about five miles above the confluence with the Yellowstone, and began the construction of Fort Union, which would become the prime depot and trade center of the Upper Missouri Outfit. From there McKenzie would invade the richest beaver lands of the Missouri River, the lands of the Blackfoot.

The Mandan had long been a trading tribe whose permanent settlements on the Missouri, Heart, Knife, and James rivers served as trade centers for other bands and tribes, and more recently, for white fur-traders.

The most important Mandan village in the early 1830s was Mih-Tutta-Hang-Kush, located on the west bank of the Missouri, north of the site where Bismarck, North Dakota, was later established. Founded in 1822, this Mandan village included farmers, as well as hunters. The Mandan, like the Arikara, farmed the "bottoms" or flats of the Missouri and the streams feeding that river. The farm produce attracted the Sioux, Cheyenne, and Pawnee to trade during mutually beneficial truces. Mandan agricultural products included maize, beans, French beans, gourds, sunflowers, and tobacco, which they traded for dressed skins, meat, and horses.

Upper Missouri Outfit's James Kipp built Fort Clark, a trading post, in 1830–31. An educated man for the time, Kipp was married to Earth Woman, daughter of Four Bears. He became fluent in the Mandan language. He did not become a partner in the Upper Missouri Outfit until 1842.[275]

Kipp traveled so much between forts and to and from St. Louis that he became a master at handling the keelboat. A keelboat was forty to forty-eight feet long, seven to ten feet in beam, and sharp at both ends, where the keel, or centerboard, ran the boat's length. It was flat bottomed, and drew only two feet of water when loaded. In the fur trade, its load was usually about thirty tons, but could go as high as fifty. The cargo or passengers occupied the middle, which sometimes was protected from weather by a shelter or cabin. Along each gunwale ran a narrow, cleated walkway or "passé avant"; crewmen set their poles on the river bottom and walked its length repeatedly while poling. Four to twelve oarsmen sat on seats in the bow and provided propulsion in water too deep to pole, or with banks too difficult to use the cordelle, the principal power. Some boats carried a sail for use when wind permitted. The captain, or "patroon," was also the steersman. He manned a long oar in the stern, working from an elevated platform, or from the cabin roof. Keelboating was slow and averaged twelve to fifteen miles a day. A trip from St. Louis to Fort Clark would literally take months. Keelboats were the dependable boat of the Missouri River trade until the development of a steamboat able to navigate shallow waters.

Kipp had gone upriver to build another fort when, in 1832, American Fur Company's brand-new steamboat, *Yellow Stone,* arrived at Fort Clark. The keelboat remained in use for a while as a lighter craft for relatively short distances, but on the long trips, it was no match for the steamboat. The *Yellow Stone* had been built in Louisville in the winter of 1830–31 largely at Kenneth McKenzie's urging. On March 26, 1832, the *Yellow Stone*, with the Western Department's chief, Pierre Chouteau Jr., and artist George Catlin aboard, left St. Louis for the upper Missouri. *Yellow Stone* arrived at Fort Tecumseh on May 31. Despite a federal law banning alcohol trade with Native Americans, the *Yellow Stone* brought 1,500 gallons of liquor for trade, as well as other goods. The steamer unloaded goods at the fort, located beside the eroding river banks, and went to visit the nearby the construction site of a new fort, Fort Pierre, which replaced Tecumseh later that year. For its return trip, the *Yellow Stone* took on board a hundred packs of beaver pelts and bison robes, and steamed from back down to St. Louis, arriving there on July 7. Scenes from the voyage were recorded by Catlin.

The *Yellow Stone* changed river-borne commerce and marked a fascinating extension of the Mississippi River steamboat commerce. Writing from Belleview, France, in November, Astor said to Chouteau, "Your voyage in the *Yellowstone*[*sic*] attracted much attention in Europe, and has been noted in all the papers here."[276] Of greater importance, the local Indian people were so impressed with the *Yellow Stone* that they announced to the HBC traders on the Saskatchewan River that the company could no longer compete with the Americans, to whom they thenceforth took their skins.

In addition to the insights that artist Catlin provided by his drawings and paintings of the tribes he encountered on this voyage and others, this period's understanding benefited from the journals of naturalist and ethnographer Prince Alexander Philip Maximilian, who traveled upriver on the American Fur Company vessel as its guest the following year. Maximilian, of the German province of Wied; his retainer, David Dreidoppel; and his employee, companion, and painter, Karl Bodmer, left St. Louis for the upper Missouri aboard the *Yellow Stone* on April 10, 1833. Throughout the trip, which advanced as far as Fort McKenzie, seven miles above the Marias River, Maximilian observed in detail and recorded in his journal the natural variety and fecundity of the Missouri River valley. His observations of aborigines and their life are remarkably keen and thorough, considering the relatively short stops en route to Fort McKenzie, where he wintered. Maximilian's journals, offer a firsthand view of sights, the various tribes, and activities upriver as far as Fort McKenzie.

Fort Pierre, the first company stop, was built by Pierre Chouteau and named after him. The fort was on lands of the Sioux, who had pushed the Arikara out of the area in the eighteenth century. William Laidlaw was fort manager. At Fort Pierre, the passengers transferred from the *Yellow Stone*, which turned around at that point, to the *Assiniboin*, the second steamship, which plied the waters of the Missouri above Fort Pierre. Outbound furs went onto the *Yellow Stone*, and supplies bound upriver went with the passengers onto the *Assiniboin*.

As Maximilian left Fort Pierre on the *Assiniboin*, he found himself berthed among the "important travelers...in an airy stern cabin with eight beds."[277] Delayed by sandbars, they reached the vacant Arikara villages near the mouth of the Grand River on June 12. The Arikara had left the Missouri valley the year before to join the Pawnee in their ancestral home, reportedly in fear of trouble with the Mandan or because of drought or, as traders familiar with them believed, because of the continuous threat of the Sioux.

The Arikara, or Ree, lived in the early nineteenth century along the Missouri in present-day North and South Dakota, where they had come in ancient times after splitting from the Pawnee. Pierre-Antoine Tabeau, trading with the Arikara when Louis and Clark arrived in 1804, noted that they had rejected the formerly deified French, and "thus they have passed today from one extreme to the others and we are indeed nothing in their eyes." They were impressed only by York, "a large, fine man, black as a bear." A Hidatsa chief said of Lewis and Clark's men during their wintering with the Mandans, "There are only two sensible men amongst them: The worker in iron and the mender of guns." Jean Baptiste Truteau believed that, at that time, they were interested only in the trade goods the whites could provide.[278]

The Arikara were agriculturalists, famous for growing primarily corn and squash. The vegetables provided winter subsistence when buffalo were absent, and were trade items with the fur traders and even with the Arikara enemies, the nomadic Sioux, who, when not trading, were a constant threat. Women raised and traded the corn and squash, getting household items, personal decorations, and tools, as well as ammunition and tobacco for their husbands. Planting and growing were accompanied by extensive superstitious rites. The corn grew in short stalks, and the kernels were small, hard, and thick shelled. Their squash grew large and were dried for storage or eaten green.

The Arikara stored their harvest by burying it in cellars under their huts, or in the field. They also stored dried fish, which the men caught by planting pens made of willows in Missouri eddies, using meat as bait. In spring, they collected drowned buffalo, eating the putrefied meat raw. During the spring fishing season, women ventured out on ice cakes to collect driftwood, attaching cords so trees could be hauled in to shore.

From buffalo hides, Arikara women made bullboats, in which they were expert, using them in the very roughest Missouri waters. All were expert swimmers.[279]

The homes of the Arikara were huts based on four posts, whose branches supported cross members, interspersed with small twigs and overlaid with thick mud. Inside was a bench along the walls for sitting and sleeping, while the center was excavated, providing standing room. A hole cut in the roof allowed smoke to escape, and a side door was cut large enough to admit a horse.

When the Sioux and Arikara met to trade, it was a joyous occasion with gambling, young love, and dancing, though the Sioux always displayed a menacing attitude toward both play and trade. As farmers and fishermen, the Arikara kept few horses for their own use but were key middlemen in horse trading. When in 1823 the Arikara left the Missouri, after confrontations with fur traders and the U.S. Army, they rejoined the Pawnee on the Platte, adopting a nomadic Plains life. They subsisted on buffalo, other game, and roots.

After passing the Arikara village about June 12, 1833, those aboard the *Assiniboin* encountered a Yankton war party, "considered the most perfidious and dangerous of all the Sioux."[280] They sought Kenneth McKenzie's help in mediating an argument between the Yankton and the Mandan. McKenzie found common ground between the tribes, and emphasized the importance of living in peace, as other tribes on the Missouri did, and not killing white men.

The *Assiniboin* reached the Mandan village Mih-Tutta-Hang-Kush and American Fur Company's Fort Clark on June 18. Maximilian and the others on board saw the Mandan residential village north of the fort and a Crow transient village behind the fort. Unlike most Sioux, the Mandan were not nomadic; they lived off the rivers, land, and trade, rather than following the buffalo, though they did hunt buffalo. And unlike the Arikara, the Mandan had welcomed trade with the whites since contact was established in 1738, when Pierre Verendrye, of earliest historical record, visited there. (Three years later, on March 30, 1741, Verendrye's son, Chevalier de la Verendrye, placed an inscribed lead plate on a knoll across the river from present-day Pierre, South Dakota. It was discovered on November 16, 1913, and is now in the collection of the South Dakota Historical Society.) When the *Assiniboin* arrived, Mandans were sitting in family groups on the ground, watching and apparently commenting on the arrivals. Maximilian wrote, "Here we saw remarkably tall and handsome men, and fine dresses, for they had done their utmost to adorn themselves."[281]

Maximilian wrote much about the Mandan lifestyle, including unique aspects that contributed so much to the Missouri fur trade. Mandan men and women were generally above middle height, but not then considered handsome. They were proud and conscious of their personal honor, but also displayed a good sense of humor. They took daily baths, summer and winter, even breaking the Missouri River ice if necessary. According to Maximilian:

> Their lifestyle, good sense, and clear judgment rejected in large measure the white man's passion and ruthlessness in search of gain. When they observed the difference between the acts of the whites and their Christian evangelism, they were inclined to pause in abandoning the beliefs and rites of their ancestors. Their superstitions were as profound as those of any American aboriginal.[282]

Superstition found expression in dance, and the Mandan also had ceremonial dances to express hope, commendation, joy, accomplishment, and disappointment. Warfare was an important part of life on the plains, for the Mandan as well as other tribes. Attaining an honorable manhood among the Mandan required self-torture (made famous in the film *A Man*

Called Horse), but also required prowess in war and hunting. Through childhood games and youthful competitions, Mandan males became fine horsemen and expert warriors. As was common throughout the plains, a Mandan war party might try to capture horses, simply "count coup" (touch), or bloodily attack the enemy.

Mandan women had roles in war. They accompanied war expeditions, managed the transportation of supplies, and made and maintained camp. In warfare, women as well as men dismembered and mutilated fallen enemies and took scalps. Male warriors, including the great Four Bears, saw nothing dishonorable in killing women, either for revenge or in battle.

As fur-trader Denig wrote, "If possible, in battle [the Crows] take the women and children prisoners, instead of dashing their brains out as the rest of the tribes do....In thus raising the children of their enemies, they in a manner supply the loss of a portion killed in war....The women, after a year's residence and understanding of the language, will not return to their people when given their liberty."[283] Though death was always a possibility in battle, in general, capture was in fact more likely for women on the Great Plains. Captured women became valuable pawns in intertribal trade, and some became slaves.

Like military societies in general, the Mandan treated women as less important than men. Mandan men occasionally treated their women so brutally that some women chose suicide. The men similarly approached sexual relationships very causally, giving whites the impression that Mandan women were promiscuous. Even in marriage, a woman was treated as property rather than as a person, for the aspiring groom gave gifts, often horses, to the prospective father-in-law. After marriage, neither the husband nor the wife, but the wife's father became the principal figure in the family. To him, for example, went the first choice of any game brought in.

In addition to their agricultural produce, the Mandan also ate the meat of the young, fat bear (a favorite), wolf, fox, turtle, and beaver, whose tail was considered a delicacy (as it was elsewhere in North America). The buffalo, a staple food, also provided many other necessities, such as robes. The Mandan suffered hunger when the buffalo did not come near. They avoided eating horses, carrion eaters, and serpents, and disliked the fur-trader's pemmican. Heavily sweetened coffee and tea had become favorite drinks. They avoided liquor, despite its constant availability from traders.[284] The liquor at Fort Clark thus went to other tribes in trade.

Among the Mandan at Mih-Tutta-Hang-Kush in 1833 was the great chief, Mato-Tope or "Four Bears," who with the strength of four bears had once charged the Assiniboin in battle. Karl Bodmer, and a few years later, George Catlin, painted this friend and protector of the whites. But Four Bears died holding them responsible for the smallpox epidemic that killed him and many of his people in 1837. As the resident trader at nearby Fort Clark at the time, Francis A. Chardon kept a diary of the trade, visitors, and the smallpox epidemic. The smallpox arrived on the steamboat *St. Peters*. The few Mandan survivors fled the village, and the next year, some of the Arikara moved up the Missouri to the site and remained there for a couple of decades.

Fig. 11.1 Chief Four Bears

George Catlin. *Letters and notes on the manners,customs, and conditions of North American Indians*, Plate 64. Reproduced by permission of Dover Publications.

When Maximilian arrived at Fort Clark in 1833, haughty Crow horsemen were seated on beautiful panther skins used as horse blankets. Behind the relatively small Fort Clark were seventy Crow tepees set up in no regular order. These Crow were the Belantse-etea band, here to trade. They also farmed, but they were buffalo hunters, too, and thus more nomadic than the Minnetaree and downstream Arikara. "A great number of horses were grazing all around," noted Maximilian. "Indians of both sexes stopped us to shake hands....Among the young women we observed some who were very pretty, the white of whose sparkling hazel eyes formed a striking contrast with the vermilion faces." When Indian Agent John F. A. Sanford complimented Minnetaree Chief Rotten Belly by presenting a medal and gifts, Rotten Belly received them solemnly, but apparently not in the attitude intended. Historians Davis Thomas and Daren Ronnefeldt noted in their book about Maxmillian's journey, *People of the First Man* that "these people consider such presents as a tribute due to them, and proof of weakness. The Crows...are said to despise the whites, whom they would supposedly rob but not kill."[285]

The Minnetaree had ridden down the Missouri banks to Fort Clark. The Mandan and Dakota Sioux called them Minnetaree, but they were also known as Hidatsa and as Gros Ventre, or "Big Bellies," specifically Gros Ventre of the Prairies, to distinguish them from the Gros Ventre or Atsina of the Blackfoot Confederation.

Maximilian and Bodmer lived with the Hidatsa at Fort Clark during the winter of 1833–34. Maximilian's ethnological description of their life and Bodmer's paintings give by far the most accurate, uninhibited picture of Missouri aboriginal life at that time. Maximilian found the Hidatsa, or Minnetaree, to be "in fact, the tallest and best formed Indians on the Missouri, and in this respect, as well as in the elegance of their costume, the Crow alone approach them....The expression of their remarkable countenances...was very various; in some, it was cold and disdainful; in others, intense curiosity; in others, again, good nature and simplicity."[286] The native people involved in the upper Missouri trade, including those nomads who were found as far south as the Platte River, appear as the classical warrior-nomad of the plains. Either in raids for "capturing" horses or counting coup, or in wise council, the typical chief is portrayed in the long trailing-feather headdress.

Traveling up river, the *Assiniboin*, like the *Yellow Stone* before it, struggled against the sandbars, snags, mosquitoes, winds, and currents. The *Assiniboin* was newer and better than the *Yellow Stone* and had cost nearly twice as much, $13,500. En route between forts, the *Assiniboin* stopped at nights, and the travelers made camp. Maximilian wrote of the ambience at one camp:

> [We] saw wolves, wild sheep, and a multitude of bats...which flew rapidly over the bright mirror of the river, and halted for the night at a sandy flat below a high bank, where I had the first watch....I amused myself with contemplating the grotesque ghost-like formation of the white sand-stone of the Stone Walls....We often heard the noise made by the buffalo crossing the river. The forests on the bank to the right and left resounded with the whistling of the elks, alternating with the howling of the wolves; and the shrill cry of the owl completed the nocturnal chorus of the wilderness.[287]

The *Assiniboin* arrived at Fort Union on June 24, 1833, seventy-five days out of St. Louis. Maximilian observed "Fort Union, on a verdant plain, with the handsome American flag, gilded by the last rays of evening, floating in an azure sky, while a herd of horses grazing animated the peaceful scene."[288]

Part of the peaceful response by the Indians to the arrival of whites resulted from the steamboat itself. Only in its second year on the upper Missouri, this technology was beyond anything the aboriginals understood. The steamboat increased their respect for Americans. Some tribes declared that they could no longer trade with Hudson's Bay Company as long as the "fireboat walked on the waters."

On the arrival of the *Assiniboin*, cannon and musketry salutes were given and returned. James Archdale Hamilton, McKenzie's deputy, greeted the passengers and crew. Hamilton was an educated, sophisticated Englishman who had been in charge of the fort during McKenzie's absence. Hamilton dressed formally at all times, even bathed and wore a clean shirt daily. Since he also kept his background a secret, other traders speculated that he might be a nobleman under an assumed name. His boss, McKenzie, arrived with Maximilian and the other passengers of the *Assiniboin*. Most of the fort turned out to welcome the steamboat. At the time, according to one historical account, Fort Union's population included "Americans, Englishmen, Germans, Frenchmen, Russians, Spaniards and Italians, about a hundred in number, with many Indians and half-breed women and children."[289]

The artist George Catlin, who had arrived at Fort Union on the steamboat *Yellow Stone* a year earlier, had enthusiastically described the fort, which was shielded by a palisade of vertical squared poplar logs about sixteen feet high, planted three feet in the ground. According to Catlin, the palisade enclosed an area 220 feet by 240 feet. Cannons were mounted on stone bastions at the northeast and southwest corners. The fort provided protection both from possible attack and from the persistent, strong, shifting winds.

Maximilian observed that one cannon covered the large folding gate of the main entrance on the river, or south, side. Opposite the entrance, inside the palisade, was the bourgeois' residence on the north wall. It was a one-story house with two glass windows on either side of the entrance. Constructed of poplar with a clapboard front and kitchen out behind, it was a commodious residence for the time and place, with a spacious roof and a large loft. Lining the west palisade were employee quarters. On the east side of the fort were workshops, storage, stables, a powder magazine, and a trade room. In the center of the fort, in the courtyard, was a tall flagpole, around which were several tepees. Maximilian noted "fifty or sixty horses, some mules…, cattle, swine, goats, fowls and domestic animals. The cattle are very fine, and the cows yield abundance of milk."[290] The animals had been brought inside the fort for the night; they were herded outside the fort each day.

Known as the "King of the Missouri," the bourgeois, Kenneth McKenzie, lived in style; after all, he earned $2,000 a year! McKenzie's table was loaded with dairy products, buffalo, other game, fowl, mutton, and beef, and an abundance of brandies and imported wines. There was plenty of meat for the fort. Hunters provided buffalo; 600–800 were consumed at Fort Union each year. Vegetables came through trade with the Mandan or the Minnetaree. McKenzie presided over meals for top staff and guests at the fort. The American Fur Company men dressed formally for dinner. Those with native wives decked their women in St. Louis fashions. Catlin observed that at breakfast no one ate until McKenzie arrived about nine and seated himself at the head of the table, possibly following the style of his former North West Company society. At all meals, diners sat in strict order of rank.[291]

Farther up the Missouri river, seven miles above the mouth of the Marias River, stood Fort McKenzie, the westernmost post of the outfit and the destination of Prince Maximilian's scientific expedition. Maximilian documented the fur trade, incidental to his ethnological and geological observations.

CHAPTER 12:

FORT UNION AND BEYOND

Chat-Kay was an Assiniboin chief in 1833. French traders called him "Du Gauche," French for left-handed and his people the "Gens de Gauche," or People of the Left-Handed.

While still young, Du Gauche had gained fame by cleverly using poisons to eliminate opposition. He transformed this skill, into a reputation for prophecy. Ambitious to be chief, he needed success in war. Du Gauche succeeded by prophesying the attacks of neighboring tribes and predicting the victor. Rather than lead in battle, De Gauche took a prominent position remote from the battle, and with fife and drum conducted his medicine ceremonies. If retreat became evident, he found others to blame and retained his mystic authority, enhanced through time and legend. Thus he became a chief.[292]

The Piegan, a tribe of the Blackfoot Confederacy, were longtime enemies of the Assiniboin and Cree, and lived generally to the northwest of the upper Missouri. At dawn on August 28, 1833, Du Gauche led a Cree and Assiniboin force against a Piegan camp outside Fort McKenzie. They achieved complete surprise.

The naturalist Prince Maximilian described the battle as a typical battle of Indian warfare. The shaman "Left Hand" led a combined force of six hundred Assiniboin and Cree against a Blackfoot group of the Piegan. The Assiniboin surrounded the fort and the Blackfoot camp of eighteen or twenty tents outside the fort. The Blackfoot spent the night in singing and drinking, and the Assiniboin attacked at dawn. According to Maximilian, the Assiniboin "cut up the tents of the Blackfeet with knives, discharged their guns and arrows at them, and killed or wounded many of the inmates, roused from their sleep by this unexpected attack."[293]

Confusion reigned inside the fort, with Blackfoot coming in for ammunition and going out to return to the fight. Maximilian described the scene: "Mr. Mitchell and Berger, the interpreter, were employed in admitting the Blackfoot [Piegan] women and children, who were assembled at the door of the fort, when a hostile Indian, with his bow bent, appeared before the gate, and exclaimed, 'White man, make room I will shoot those enemies!'" [294] This exclamation showed that the attack was not directed against the whites, but only against the Blackfoot. The message was clear: whites must not take sides in native warfare. Maximilian continued:

When the Assiniboin saw that their fire was returned, they retreated about 300 paces, and an irregular firing continued, during which several people from the neighborhood joined the ranks of the Blackfeet....At the very beginning of the engagement, the Blackfeet had dispatched messengers on horseback to the great camp of their nation, which was eight or ten miles off, to summon warriors to their aid....They came galloping in groups, from three to twenty together, their horses covered with foam, and they themselves in their finest apparel, with all kinds of ornaments and arms, bows and quivers on their backs, guns in their hands, furnished with their medicines, with feathers on their heads; some had splendid crowns of black and white eagle, and a large hood of feathers hanging down behind, on fine panther skins lined with red; the upper part of their bodies partly naked, with a long strip of wolf's skin thrown across the shoulder, and carrying shields adorned with feathers and pieces of colored cloth...shouting, singing, and uttering their war-whoop; but a great part of them stopped at the fort, received powder and balls, and, with their guns and bows, shot at the disfigured remains of the Assiniboin who were slain, and which were now so pierced and burnt as scarcely to retain any semblance of the human form. The Indians had fired quite at random; otherwise the loss must have been much greater on both sides. A number of wounded men, women, and children, were laid or placed against the walls; others, in a deplorable condition, were pulled about by their relations, amid tears and lamentations....We endeavored to assist the wounded...but very little could be done, for instead of suffering the wounded, who were exhausted by the loss of blood, their relations continually pulled them about, sounded large bells, rattled their medicine or amulets, among which were bears' paws, which the White Buffalo wore on his breast.

The Indian who was killed near the fort especially interested me, because I wished to obtain his skull. The scalp had already been taken off, and several Blackfeet were engaged in venting their rage on the dead body. The men fired their guns at it, the women and children beat it with clubs, and pelted it with stones; the fury of the latter was particularly directed against the privy parts. Before I could obtain my wish, not a trace of the head was to be seen.[295]

Maximilian further reported that during the battle, the Piegan came to David Mitchell, veteran AFC trader in charge of Fort McKenzie, seeking assistance. Mitchell took a group of expert riflemen and hunters to another Blackfoot camp on a hill nearby, asking for help. The Blackfoot responded to the call and the enemy was driven back to the Marias River, where they maintained their ground. It was generally observed that the Assiniboin fought better than the Blackfeet, many of whom did not leave the fort the whole day. Mitchell, always in advance of the Blackfeet, "shamed the Blackfeet whose numbers had increased to 500 or 600 calling out, 'Why did they lag behind?'...Now was the time to show their courage."[296]

Du Gauche, perhaps offended by Mitchell's getting support for the Piegan, decided to trade elsewhere. Later that fall, according to Maximilian, he went "northwards with a hundred tents to the English, in order to trade with the HBC."[297] This competition across the forty-ninth parallel was as long-standing on the upper Missouri as it had been on the upper Mississippi, and one which all too often was waged with liquor as the principal inducement. As we have noted, both governments prohibited liquor, but they and the companies alike recognized its use as a necessary, if evil, road to profit.

Whether or not the Piegan were motivated by Du Gauche's movement north, their beaver deliveries to the HBC's Rocky Mountain House on the North Saskatchewan about eighty miles west of present-day Red Deer, Alberta, peaked that year at "almost 9,400 fine beaver pelts and a profit of 20,000 pounds sterling....As Governor Simpson reported...it is not only the riches of the Hon'ble Company's Territory we are collecting, but those likewise of the United States. While the fur resources of the North Saskatchewan were recuperating from years of over-trapping, the Hudson's Bay Company was draining off the wealth of the upper Missouri region....A new competitor in the field, however, would rudely shake the Hudson's Bay Company out of its luxuriant lethargy."[298]

Fort Union was in Assiniboin country. The Assiniboin were nomadic hunters without permanent villages who separated from the Sioux in the eighteenth century. In the nineteenth century they were closely affiliated with the Plains Cree. In 1833, they occupied roughly 20,000 square miles that may be said to be one great plain with hills and timber occurring only along rivers. They camped in Canada along the Assiniboin and Saskatchewan rivers and south to the Milk and Missouri rivers in Montana. The clear, dry climate may be the healthiest in the world.

In 1833, when bands had reached the Missouri River, they numbered in all about a thousand lodges. Edwin Thompson Denig, trader for the

American Fur Company at Fort Union, lived among the Assiniboin for twenty-one years. In response to a request from Superintendent of Indian Affairs Henry Schoolcraft, he compiled a thorough description of life at Fort Union in general and of the Assiniboin in particular.

The traders witnessed the effect of the smallpox epidemic on that tribe. After the epidemic of 1837, the tribe was reduced to about four hundred lodges. Denig wrote that of these, "200 were saved by having been inoculated by the Hudson's Bay Company." [299] In addition to Du Gauche, described earlier in this chapter, there were good leaders of the Assiniboin. Among them were The Knife, Grey Eyes, and Wind Blanket. Their principal war experience was in Blackfoot country, and in general, they were winners. Denig believed that although they were originally seen as lazy, thieving, malicious, and governed by little home regulation, trade improved them, and "they are among the best Indians of the Upper Missouri....They are affectionate to children, urbane to strangers, distant in their manners to each other, unless to kindred, and very revengeful when roused." Denig found but few handsome women among them, rare in virtue, though very shy and modest. [300]

As hunters, most of the men owned guns, acquired from fur traders out of Mackinac. They were expert in construction and use of the pound, or surround, for killing buffalo. As anthropologist Shepard Krech III described, buffalo hunts using the cliff or surround could kill not merely dozens, but hundreds of animals. All had to be killed: shot with bows and arrows, killed with guns, stabbed with lances, or smacked on the head with stone mauls. [301]

On the prairie, the Assiniboin were, like the Crow, horse stealers and robbers. In general, Maximilian found that the Assiniboin observed the customs and superstitions of the Sioux, including a love of games and gambling. Some of the Assiniboin men were traders, trading horses to the Cree. Maximilian observed, "They keep on good terms with the fur company, for their own interest."[302]

The Piegan camp at Fort McKenzie was the result of McKenzie's important breakthrough with the Blackfoot tribes, a hazardous operation at best. The Blackfoot and allied Gros Ventre—Atsina—attacked fur trappers repeatedly. They were the first to obtain both guns and horses.

The Blackfoot dominated the upper Missouri. To use the term "Blackfoot" for all of these tribes can be misleading. In the Blackfoot Confederacy, there were four distinct bands: the Blackfoot proper, called North Blackfoot, or Siksika; the Piegan, or Pikuni; the Bloods, or Kaina; and the Gros Ventres, also called the Falls, or Atsina. An Athabaskan tribe known as the Sarsi, also at home on the upper reaches of the South Saskatchewan, attached themselves to the Blackfoot Confederacy for protection, spoke the Blackfoot dialect, and finally settled west of Calgary.

These tribes ranged throughout southwestern Alberta and northern Montana, living east of the Rockies. But they made long-distance forays. They rode into the mountains and valleys west of the Continental Divide, where they attacked their traditional enemies, the Kutenai, the Shoshone, the Flathead (or, as they prefer to be called, the Salish), and any small groups of trappers they might find. Though these Blackfoot tribes spoke a common language, had a tradition of common origin, common customs, and intermarriage, they found reason to feud. When camped together, they pitched their tepees in different circles, and governed themselves by civil chiefs and war chiefs, who had "no power beyond their influence, which would immediately cease by any act of authority and they are all very careful not to arrogate any superiority over others."[303]

Oscar Lewis, in his vivid summary of tribal relationships, wrote that the various tribes that comprised the Blackfoot cooperated in war and defense: "The tribes were united before their common enemies, the Assiniboin and Cree on the east, and the Shoshoni on the west, but each had particular enemies against whom they concentrated their efforts. The Piegan defended the western and southern frontiers from the Kutenai, Flathead, and Nez Percé; the Blood fought the Crow, and, together with the Siksika, the Cree."[304]

The Blackfoot jealously guarded the Missouri from the Marias River westward, including the tributaries above the Great Falls, and as far south as the Three Forks. Trouble began when Lewis and Clark returned from the Pacific. When some Piegan tried to steal horses and guns from Captain Meriwether Lewis's party, which was exploring the Marias River, Lewis shot one and Reuben Field stabbed another.[305] This act generated long-lasting Blackfoot anger at the Americans. The historian Bernard DeVoto offers this description:

> The Blackfoot proper were capricious: no one could predict their attitude an hour in advance. The Piegan were a little more genial; they were the ones who had listened to McKenzie's emissaries, begun the trade, and kept it going. The Bloods were the most Teutonic of all. Nobody liked them, including their friends. They were the first to take offense, the first to break a truce, the first to murder. They did all three while Maximilian was at Fort McKenzie.[306]

The allegations of British incitement against the American traders are often cited as another source of Blackfoot hatred. The Piegan were the only Blackfoot tribe inclined to trap. The other tribes fought all trappers in order to protect the profits from their middleman role. However, while Hudson's Bay Company traders made persistent efforts to compete for Piegan trade, persuasion appears to have been their principal method. But everyone used liquor a matter of contentious concern to both British and American authorities.

Though the Blackfoot area is generally described as being east of the Rockies and from the Athabasca to the Missouri, they ranged and raided much farther. The Gros Ventres attacked at Pierre's Hole after the trapper rendezvous there in 1832. Warren A. Ferris, mountain man and author of *Life in the Rocky Mountains*, witnessed the Blackfoot attack on mountain men in Cache Valley near Bear Lake in the winter of 1832–33.[307]

Kenneth McKenzie overcame Blackfoot hostility and made their trade profitable. His opportunity came when a Métis, Jacques Berger, a veteran Hudson's Bay Company trader, wandered into Fort Union in late summer 1830. Berger had lived in Piegan camps. They thought of him as their brother. He was fluent in their dialects and had absorbed a profound grasp of their thoughts and ways. When he arrived at Fort Union, he had no loyalty to the Hudson's Bay Company or to anyone else. He came to Fort Union because he had heard of it and wanted to see for himself.[308]

McKenzie, though at first suspicious and probably fearing some sort of Hudson's Bay Company trap, nevertheless saw in him a possible opportunity to trade with the Blackfoot tribes. McKenzie asked him to assemble a party and seek out the Blackfoot, determine their attitudes, and try to bring them to visit Fort Union. Berger was interested only in trading; he undertook the task merely because it sounded interesting. He and his party of four left in the autumn or early winter of 1830; at Fort Union, his trip was considered a forlorn hope. For four months they traveled upriver in the early winter, always displaying the stars and stripes.

While they were camped on the headwaters of Badger Creek, a tributary of the Marias River, a passing Piegan party discovered them. Berger advanced to the party alone, displaying the American flag. They recognized him with enthusiastic greetings and agreed to take him to their winter village on the Sun River. After long discussion, he finally persuaded them to send a group of about one hundred to Fort Union.

The way was long, more than 450 miles, representing a trip of eighteen to twenty days. After several days, and threats by the warriors to turn back, Berger bet his scalp and horses that they would reach the fort the next day. They reached Fort Union the next afternoon to McKenzie's hospitable reception, well-marked by presents and ceremony.

During the Piegan party's stay, McKenzie persuaded them of the advantages of having trading posts along the Missouri River in their own domain rather than the more distant Saskatchewan. They agreed because McKenzie offered them a real trade in which they hunted for the furs and robes and bartered them at a fort, as they had done with Hudson's Bay Company. McKenzie promised to have a post built by the next autumn, 1831. To show good faith, he sent a clerk and four or five men with them to trade during the winter.

McKenzie evidently was aided in his argument by a famous chameleon of the HBC. As described in an earlier chapter, Jamie "Jock" Bird was a person of mixed descent, the son of retired Chief Factor James Bird. He was fiercely independent and had lived with and greatly influenced the Blackfeet on behalf of the HBC. He found it convenient at this time to switch from the HBC to the AFC. McKenzie used Bird to influence the Piegan further in trading with the Americans, persuading them that all whites were brothers, and that the company made little difference.

McKenzie took credit for "negotiating" a treaty between the Assiniboin and the Blackfoot, who had been at war as long as any could remember. The treaty promised protection for trading throughout the region. The flowery treaty was obviously drawn with the expert understanding Berger possessed of aboriginal psychology. It was a masterpiece, and proclaimed peace in flowery and flattering language. McKenzie promised they would smoke the calumet in friendship and safety. They would hail each other as brothers, seeking approval of the Great Spirit.[309]

McKenzie then sent James Kipp and twenty-five men upriver to build a post at the mouth of the Marias River. In 1831, Kipp asked the Blackfoot to return after seventy-five days, when the post would be built. At the exact expiration of that time, they returned to find the fort named

Fort Piegan. Kipp was ready to trade, but he was aware that liberality would be necessary to turn these bands away from trading with the Hudson's Bay Company. He treated them to a binge with a barrel of whiskey made into two hundred gallons of Blackfoot rum. Thereafter, when trading began, the Piegans found the prices better than with HBC to the north, and in a few days, Kipp had obtained 6,450 pounds of beaver, worth $46,000 at St. Louis.[310]

During the winter of 1831–32, as Ewers described:

A large force of Blood Indians besieged the fort, intent on destroying it and taking the furs that had been traded by the Piegan. For eleven days Kipp held his fire, hoping to conciliate the attackers and secure their trade. [Finally] Kipp charged a four-pound cannon heavily loaded with grape-shot and fired it at a huge cottonwood tree growing near the fort. The thunder of this discharge and the shower of broken limbs and splintered wood that rained down from the tree frightened the Indians so that they fled in every direction. Shortly thereafter two Blood chiefs came to the fort. They blamed Hudson's Bay Company agents for talking them into attacking Kipp's Post. Clever Kipp reminded them that he had withheld his fire and convinced them of his good intentions. Then the Blood brought him some three thousand buffalo robes which the Canadian traders would not take because they were too heavy for them to transport profitably down the Saskatchewan to York Factory or Montreal. When spring 1832 arrived, Kipp departed down river with his furs and robes, leaving only two or three of his men who had taken native wives. Kipp dismantled much of the post, and shortly after his departure, the Blackfoot burned Fort Piegan.[311]

In the summer of 1832, McKenzie sent David D. Mitchell, an Upper Missouri Outfit partner, to take over the post. He was a cultured man, compared to most traders. In 1828 he had traded at Rock Island for the

Iowa Outfit of the Northern Department, and joined the Upper Missouri Outfit at the high annual salary of $700. Phillips referred to him as "one of the most successful on the upper Missouri."[312] Though he had a native wife at Fort McKenzie, he later married Martha Eliza Berry of Kentucky. In later years he was a famous cavalry officer in the Mexican War and superintendent of Indian Affairs. DeVoto wrote of him, "A man who directed the Blackfoot trade possessed an extremity of courage; one who survived the job an extremity of skill."[313]

En route up the Missouri from Fort Union, and before he reached the mouth of the Musselshell, Mitchell's keelboat, the *Flora*, broke from its mooring in a storm, sank, and lost $30,000 worth of goods, plus all the presents McKenzie had sent for the Blackfoot. On reaching the Marias River and finding Fort Piegan burned, Mitchell went upriver for six more miles, and started the post on the north bank that became Fort McKenzie.

He and his men built the fort in the face of several thousand Blackfoot, some hostile. Mitchell's forceful but patient diplomatic efforts staved off an attack, and the crew, living on a keelboat, managed to get the stockade erected and could then feel safe. Fort McKenzie became the American Fur Company's firm foothold among the Blackfoot.

From 1832 until 1843, Fort McKenzie was one of the American Fur Company's most valuable sources, warehousing "almost 1,000 packs of robes and a wealth of furs, skins, and by-products each year from 1834 to 1840. By 1841, the post was returning 21,000 buffalo robes annually, making it by far the most productive fort in the interior West."[314]

McKenzie's capture of the Piegan trade had an immediate impact on Hudson's Bay Company's operation on the Saskatchewan. Though the Piegan brought 2,500 beaver pelts to Fort Piegan on the Bow River in the first ten days of operation, HBC's Piegan Post and the Rocky Mountain House both had to be shut down. Later revived, Rocky Mountain House lasted until 1875.

Hudson's Bay Company viewed the loss of Piegan trade with alarm. Governor Simpson directed Chief Factor John Rowand at Edmonton House to go south to try to persuade the Piegan to return to the HBC. Rowand, accompanied by George McDowell, Henry Fisher, and fourteen others, left Edmonton House on June 4, 1832. During the next two and a half months, they met American traders in Montana's Sweet Grass Hills and continued to the Missouri River valley. There they met the Piegan and apparently persuaded them to return for some trade with the HBC.[315]

In the summer of 1832, McKenzie sought to establish trading contact with the Crows. He sent Samuel Tulloch to build a fort on the Yellowstone at the mouth of the Big Horn River. Tulloch's post was called Fort Cass, in honor of Secretary of War Lewis Cass, who had become a consistent friend of the AFC.

Tulloch was a former mountain man. He had been a member of John H. Weber's party, which set out from the Big Horn in July 1824, crossed South Pass, made a fall hunt on Bear River, and wintered in Cache Valley. In 1827, McKenzie had sent Tulloch from the upper Missouri to the Rockies to investigate what efforts the Upper Missouri Outfit could make in the mountains.

He was present at the 1827 rendezvous at Bear Lake and left there accompanied by the young Pinkney Sublette. In late March 1828, Pinkney was killed in a Blackfoot skirmish at the mouth of the Portneuf River. Tulloch found plenty of keen competition from Hudson Bay Company's Peter Skene Ogden, whose camp on the Portneuf River he visited on Christmas Eve 1828 and remained until late March 1829. Thus he had a broad grasp of the competing fur-trade organizations and of Indian ways.

From Fort Union, Chief Trader Kenneth McKenzie also outfitted independent trappers who were not employees of the AFC, such as Johnson Gardner, an early mountain man. Gardner's account in Fort Union records for 1831–32 outfits totals $1,942.65 in credit for supplies and trade goods, as shown in Table 12.1. Trade priorities are clearly indicated. It is significant that the greatest expense was for liquor.

Table 12.1 Johnson Gardner Account with
Fort Union, 1831-1832

ITEM	COST IN US $	% of TOTAL COST
Liquor	421.95	21.7
Livestock	360	18.5
Supplies and Equipment	356.5	18.4
Other Trade Goods	208.63	10.7
Food	207.57	10.7
Clothing	139.5	7.2
Blankets	96	5
Tobacco	69.75	3.6
Arms and ammunition	66.25	3.4
Miscellaneous	15.5	0.8
TOTAL	1941.65	100

Source: Johnson Gardner. UMO Fort Union to
American Fur Company, Chouteau Papers,
Missouri Historical Society, St. Louis.

Such credit required specific contractual obligations: Gardner would sell all beaver furs then en cache (in hidden storage) up the Yellowstone River at $4.125 per pound, the weight to be determined on delivery; and all castoreum at $3.00 a pound, dried perineal glands and their secretions used both as bait and for sale to the French as a "fix" for making perfume. Furthermore, McKenzie agreed to furnish three men to accompany Gardner, each with half the usual equipment. McKenzie would in return receive half of the fur take of Gardner and the three men; the other half would go to Gardner. Then McKenzie would buy fall beaver at $3.50 per pound, spring beaver at $4.00 per pound, and castoreum at $3.00 per pound.

By charging for supplies, shipment, and insurance, and by using high beaver prices in Indian trade, Astor made $40.00 per gross for every $2.00 invested. His remote but clear grasp of Indian trading was the real source of his profit.

American production reached a pinnacle of more than 131,000 pelts in 1833, and easily most of it was from the AFC. In that year alone, American exports of furs exceeded $800,000. Though it was of minor significance as part of overall American exports, "it was the most significant activity affecting the domestic and international economies of dozens of Indian societies, from the Missouri to the Pacific, for at least a half century."[316]

In the United States, American Fur Company records were probably accurate, despite being partially lost in a fire in its headquarters in New York. However the records of other companies were not as complete, or were spasmodic. All were significant for annual results.

Each year, Western Department records contained about five hundred separate ledger accounts—not all for the Upper Missouri Outfit. Fort Union and Fort Clark were the only post entries for the Upper Missouri Outfit. Evidently the accounts of the Outfit's other posts were consolidated with those of Forts Union and Clark.

Astor's trade policies related to the availability of goods for trade at the most desirable time. The reliable availability of trade goods when promised was a very important part of retaining the loyalty of the various trading chiefs and tribes. Eventually, Astor's polices had a bearing on profit.[317]

In 1833 the Upper Missouri Outfit employed about five hundred men. UMO partners McKenzie, Laidlaw of Fort Pierre, and Daniel Lamont in St. Louis were Scots. Among clerk-traders, 62.5 percent had French or French North American ancestors. Clerks and interpreters were also French. Among voyageurs, nearly 89 percent had French surnames. There were occasional native employees, and there were black personal servants. Employment in the Upper Missouri Outfit was relatively short, the mean for all ranks being 3.1 years.[318]

Depots stored about $100,000 in goods, and posts stored $15,000 to $20,000. The Upper Missouri Outfit was an increasingly important part of Astor's empire, a key to his selling his shares of the American Fur Company to Chouteau in 1834. Chouteau continued making a fortune in the fur trade, especially in the upper Missouri region.

While there were many aspects to competition, the use of alcoholic beverages, "spirituous liquors," or simply "liquor," was fundamental from the beginning of Indian trade, and was an item of trade used by independents and companies alike. Among the mountain men and particularly among independent trappers and traders, the use of liquor was commonplace. Diluted alcohol flavored with tobacco juice was a strong inducement to trade, and concentrated alcohol was easier to pack than the better distillates.

It was liquor that nearly cost the American Fur Company its licenses for the Upper Missouri Outfit and that resulted in the expulsion of Kenneth McKenzie. The first event was the then-famous "Cabanné Affair," in which John Pierre Cabanné, a resident partner at Council Bluff of Pratt and Chouteau, illegally seized legal boatman's liquor and supplies from independent trader Narcisse LeClerc by overpowering him. LeClerc went to St. Louis and filed charges against the company.[319]

As Ramsay Crooks reported to "Dear Cousin" Pierre Chouteau on February 17, 1833, the Cabanné affair raised a considerable storm in Washington in the War Department. In the same letter he expressed deeper concerns: "We are looked upon by many as an association determined to engross the trade of the Upper Missouri, by fair means if we can, but by foul proceedings if nothing short will ensure our object....With such a reputation, it becomes us to be more than usually circumspect in all we do—every eye is upon us, and whosoever can, will annoy us with all his heart."[320] Crooks saw as the American Fur Company's only hope the possibility that the government would persuade the British to enact and enforce an absolute restriction on use of liquor by the Hudson's Bay Company. The United States had already banned alcohol which reiterated the prohibition of liquor into Indian country, but across its vast distances, it was unable to enforce the law.

Kenneth McKenzie at Fort Union would not give up. He built a still and used Mandan corn to make whiskey, on the excuse that the law prohibited importation only. He did not conceal his distillery. In fact, he wrote to Pierre Chouteau: "I can produce as fine liquor as need to be drank: I believe no law of the U.S. is thereby broken though perhaps we may be made to break up my distillery but liquor I must have or quit."[321] Nathaniel Wyeth, a Fort Union guest en route home from the Rockies, reported the still, which came to General Clark's attention. He simply reported to the War Department.

John Jacob Astor had decided to retire. Chouteau requested that McKenzie come down to St. Louis, presumably to renew his contract, at a time when Chouteau was considering the purchase of the Western Department from the American Fur Company. McKenzie was retired from the Upper Missouri Outfit in 1834. Thus ended his career with the UMO. After a profitable career that literally dried up, he departed for a European sojourn. McKenzie later returned to St. Louis, where he was involved in wholesale liquor trade. On June 1, 1834, Crooks and partners bought the Northern Department from the American Fur Company and retained the American Fur Company name. Chouteau, as Pratte, Chouteau, and Company of St. Louis, bought the Western Department. The American Fur Company retired from western trade.

CHAPTER 13:

INDIANS AND ASHLEY'S RENDEZVOUS SYSTEM

Waterways tied the Indian villages and relatively permanent posts of the fur trade together throughout British North America, the Great Lakes, the Old Northwest, the Missouri, and the Columbia Plateau. Indian horses permitted travel on the plains, separate from river routes. In the second decade of the nineteenth century, William H. Ashley of St. Louis conceived and brought about a new method of providing supplies and trade goods and collecting furs in the wilderness remote from the trading post.

On April 11, 1822, territorial Governor William Clark granted a license to Ashley and Andrew Henry to trade with Indians up the Missouri for one year. In anticipation of his license, Ashley placed the following advertisement in the *Missouri Gazette & Public Advertiser* of St. Louis on February 13, 1822:

> To enterprising young men: The subscriber wishes to engage one hundred young men to ascend the Missouri river to its source, there to be employed for one, two, or three years. For particulars enquire of Major Henry, near the lead mines in the county of Washington, who will ascend with, and command, the party; or of the subscriber near St. Louis.[322]

This first advertisement gave no hint of the eventual outcome. Despite Henry's experience in the Indian trade, the prospective traders and trappers who responded became known as "Ashley's Hundred." The notice attracted the men Ashley and Henry needed, including such later fur-trade greats as Jedediah Smith, David Jackson, Milton and William Sublette, Eddie Rose, Jim Bridger, and Thomas Fitzpatrick. The campaigns that followed in 1822, 1823, and early 1824 are complex because of Indian influence.[323]

William H. Ashley was new to the fur trade. Born a Virginian in 1778, he was, by his twenty-fourth year, a typical American frontier businessman living in Missouri. He speculated in land, mined saltpeter for gunpowder, and became a member of the Missouri militia. During the War of 1812, he advanced in rank to lieutenant colonel, and in 1821, he was appointed a brigadier general of the Missouri Militia. He was also elected lieutenant governor for the state of Missouri. He embarked on the fur trade in 1822, and his spectacular success made him wealthy by 1827.

Ashley and Andrew Henry, commander of the expedition, had been friends since at least 1805. In 1809, Henry had joined Manuel Lisa's St. Louis Missouri Fur Company, and as a field captain, led a large force to the Three Forks of the Missouri. Blackfoot attacks had virtually destroyed the force, killing some. Escaping from the Blackfoot, Henry took a party up the Madison River valley, probably across today's Reynold's Pass, to present-day Henry's Lake, which was named for him, and to the forks of the Snake River near Elgin, Idaho. There he built Henry's Fort, the first American fort west of the Continental Divide. In the spring of 1811, he is believed to have moved northeast to the Yellowstone River and floated down it and the Missouri to deliver his forty packs of furs to Manuel Lisa.[324]

Henry, as a result, could provide the 1822 Ashley/Henry partnership with the knowledge of Indian ways, distances, and the geography of the upper Missouri, Yellowstone River, and tributaries. Ashley and Henry secured credit, bought keelboats, and obtained provisions. With the license to trade, they were ready to proceed up the Missouri River.

"Ashley's Hundred"—actually about 150 men on that first expedition in 1822—traveled in two keelboats. Major Henry commanded the first, which was launched in St. Louis on April 3. Some of the men were hunters who would supply the boat crew and the trappers with fresh meat; they were equipped with horses and guns and usually traveled by land on either side of the river. By mid-August Henry was a hundred miles above the Mandan villages. Somewhere between the villages and the Yellowstone River, a roving band of Assiniboin stole their horse herd. Undeterred, Henry reached the mouth of the Yellowstone by September and began the construction of Fort Henry, the base from which they expected to send out small groups of trappers up the Yellowstone and Missouri rivers. They planned to trap, not trade.

Ashley sent a second keelboat upriver from St. Louis on May 8, filled with provisions, ammunition, guns, and traps. Daniel Moore commanded this party and hunter Jedediah Strong Smith was among the young recruits. Twenty miles below the U.S. government's factory trading post of Fort Osage, the keelboat hit a snag and capsized. The loss included both the boat and $10,000 in cargo. Smith and the rest of the men stayed at the scene of the accident, while Moore went to St. Louis to advise Ashley.[325]

Moore arrived back in St. Louis on June 4. Ashley obtained more credit, purchased replacement supplies, and acquired another keelboat. Eighteen days later, Ashley had hired forty-six additional men, and leaving Moore behind, they proceeded upriver where they picked up the waiting crew camped beside the lower Missouri. As they moved north from there, Jedediah Smith recalled, Ashley stopped and smoked a pipe with the Omahas, Poncas, and Sioux.

On September 8, they arrived at the Arikara villages on the upper Missouri, important to Ashley as a possible source of Indian horses. Ashley decided to split the group. Some would remain on the boat and proceed to the mouth of the Yellowstone River with supplies, and Ashley would try to buy enough horses from the Arikara that he and the rest of the group could travel overland. His overland trail took him past the Mandan villages, where they stopped for a day and held a council with tribal leaders concerning their plans.

On October 1, Ashley joined Henry at the newly constructed Fort Henry at the confluence the Yellowstone and Missouri rivers. Ashley and Henry immediately allocated the supplies needed for two parties to go separate ways for a winter of trapping. Henry would lead a party up the Missouri River, the second party would go up the Yellowstone. Ashley took the available packs of furs already trapped by Henry's men, a pirogue, and voyageurs, and started back downriver to St. Louis. He and his pirogue crew exchanged greetings with his northbound keelboat. He reached St. Louis in the autumn to plan for the following year.

By mid-October the keelboat of supplies arrived at Henry's fort. Among the personnel on board was a literate trapper named Daniel T. Potts, who kept a personal journal in which he recorded much of the detail that is known about the expedition that winter. He wrote, "This is one of the most beautiful situations I ever saw."[326]

Henry immediately organized the men into hunting parties. Smith and fourteen men were sent out to hunt for meat, skins, and whatever beaver they could find, using the horses left by Ashley. Henry sent John H. Weber and a small party in canoes up the Yellowstone to the Powder River to trap. Henry left a few men at the fort, and using the keelboat and canoes, he took another group up the Missouri River. Smith and his hunters returned to the fort with the game needed and then followed Henry's group. They met at the mouth of the Musselshell River and established a winter camp. Smith reports meeting Henry as he was going back downriver; Henry apparently wintered at Fort Henry. The arrival of an immense herd of buffalo that crossed the frozen Missouri and moved past their post on the Musselshell amazed and impressed the men, who could step from their cabin and shoot all the meat needed.[327]

The ice on the Missouri River did not move until April 4, 1823. Two days later, the men were ready to proceed upstream in the hope of trapping to the Three Forks of the Missouri. On their sixth day out, Daniel Potts was injured in a gun accident and Smith left the group to take him back to Fort Henry to recuperate. Meanwhile, Henry took a small group of men and left Fort Henry to ride across country to reinforce the group on the Musselshell. En route, Indians stole four more horses. Henry reunited with the hunting party and led them as far as the mouth of the Smith River. There the Blackfoot attacked. Four of the men were killed, and pelts and horses were taken. The remaining seven escaped downstream by canoe.

This was only one of several Indian attacks on hunting and trapping parties that year. Immel and Jones of the Missouri Fur Company passed Fort Henry in October 1822, and their forty-three men built a fort named Fort Benton at the mouth of the Big Horn River. After wintering on the Big Horn, they moved up the Yellowstone and crossed over, probably at Bridger Pass, up the Gallatin Valley to the Three Forks of the Missouri as soon as the ice was gone in the spring. By May 16, they had completed a very successful twenty-pack hunt and were ready to return to the Yellowstone. A week later a group of Bloods attacked them in a defile. Jones, Immel, and five trappers were killed, four others were wounded, and horses, beaver, and equipment was lost. This was a major disaster for the Missouri Fur Company.[328]

In the meantime, Ashley had organized a second expedition, which left St. Louis on March 15, 1823. He reached the Arikara villages by

May 30, knowing that the tribe had a fickle reputation among whites. Henry had sent Jedediah Smith downriver with a message asking Ashley to trade for more horses with the Arikara. By June 1, Ashley had traded for the needed horses and was ready for a land party to lead the horse herd to Fort Henry. His land party was camped on the beach on the Arikara village side of the river. The Arikara attacked at three o'clock in the morning. All horses were lost, and half the men on the beach were killed or wounded. Immediately after the Arikara attack, Ashley sent Jedediah Smith back upriver to Henry, asking them to provide assistance. Henry and Smith descended the river with all but twenty men, who were left at Fort Henry, meeting Ashley at the mouth of the Cheyenne River about July 2.

Smith was then sent with Henry's furs to St. Louis and reported the attack to General Atkinson, who provided a force of 220 troops under Colonel Leavenworth to punish the Arikara. Smith then returned to Ashley. In the ensuing skirmish, involving not only the troops, but many trappers, Leavenworth failed to pursue, earning the Indians' contempt. Ashley, in November, 1823, referring to the effect of Leavenworth's campaign, wrote, "The Blackfoot Indians will in all probability continue to do us all the injury in their power; the Aricara, the Chians [Cheyennes] and a part of the Sioux, may unite in hostilities against us, or they may pause for a while to ascertain what further steps will be taken by our government for the protection of our citizens. The Mandans, Minnetarie or Hidatsa, Crows and a part of the Sioux, will probably continue to meet us as friends and treat us accordingly."[329]

Ten years later, in 1833, the anthropologist Prince Maximilian said of the incident, "The Arikaras...became extremely arrogant, and henceforth murdered all white men who were so unfortunate as to fall in their way."[330]

Missouri traders believed that the Indians' enmity was traceable to the British. Chittenden wrote, "Whether these suspicions were well founded or not, it was a fact that the firearms with which the Indians attacked the traders came from across the line, and the furs which they took from our people quickly found their way back there in payment."[331]

Ashley and Henry decided to abandon the Missouri and go west overland to the streams of the Rocky Mountains. They stored their remaining goods at Fort Kiowa, about twenty miles above the White River junction. Finding only enough horses to carry their supplies, Henry took a large force that included Johnson Gardner, Daniel S. D. Moore, Moses "Black" Harris, Milton Sublette, Hugh Glass, James Bridger, and about six others back to the Yellowstone. En route the Mandan attacked, but were easily driven off, though two men were killed and two wounded. When Henry reached Henry's Fort, he found that the Blackfeet and Assiniboin had stolen twenty-two of his horses, and later they took seven more. He abandoned the post and moved up the Yellowstone, where he built another Fort Henry. There he was able to purchase forty-seven horses from the Crow. Dividing his party, he sent John H. Weber with thirteen men to trap on the Wind River, on the eastern slope of the Rockies. Weber, later joined by Jedediah Smith, wintered with the Crow on the Wind River.

A month later at Fort Kiowa, Ashley obtained horses from John Pierre Cabanné of the French Fur Company. He sent Jedediah Smith and a party of eleven, including James Clyman, by land to the Powder River. The party, according to Clyman's journal, included William Sublette, Thomas Fitzpatrick, Thomas Eddie, mixed-descent Crow Edward Rose, and two others named Branch and Stone. Three remain anonymous. They started up the White River in present-day South Dakota, and in a desperate struggle against thirst, crossed over to the Cheyenne River. Traveling upstream, they encountered a camp of the Bois Brule Sioux, remained a few days and traded for horses. They got enough for two animals apiece and several spares. They entered the Black Hills apparently through Buffalo Gap.

Cheyenne were camped nearby. Although the Cheyenne ranged widely, this area was their usual hunting grounds. Their legendary or mythological religion originated on nearby Bear Butte, east of the Black Hills. They were in continuous warfare with the Shoshone, Crow, and Pawnee.

Hoping to find beaver that would permit a stop to rest the horses, Smith sent Rose ahead to find the Crow from whom they could get more horses. Smith encountered a grizzly bear, which attacked and left him badly wounded. As Clyman described it:

> Grissly did not hesitate a moment but sprung on the capt taking him by the head first pitc[h]ing sprawling on the earth he gave him a grab by the middle fortunately cat[c]hing him by the ball pouch and Butcher K[n]ife which he broke but breaking several of his ribs and cutting his head badly none of us having any surgical Knowledge what was to be done. [332]

At Smith's order, Clyman sewed up his wounds, including the attachment of the right ear. This gave them a lesson on the "grissly" they would not forget.[333]

Smith traded with the Cheyenne for more horses and continued to the Powder River. Rose arrived with the Crow and horses, which gave them a chance to ride. Still recovering from his grizzly attack and unable to travel at the speed of the Crow, Smith sent Rose and some packs ahead with them. They headed northwest across the Tongue River and into the Big Horn Mountains. Then turning southwest, they crossed the Owl Mountains to the Big Horn River, which, as it turns northwest, becomes the Wind River. They reached the Crow camp on the Wind River. Smith caught up, and they spent the winter of 1823–24 with the western detachment of Henry's party, led by "the moody Captain Weber," as well as with Daniel Potts, who wintered there after trapping up the Big Horn in the fall of 1823. This area became a common wintering ground for Henry's parties and others who trapped the Big Horn.[334]

The Crow, who called themselves Apsáalooke in their language, lived along the Yellowstone tributaries and into the Absaroka Mountains (a variation of Apsáalooke) in the eastern Rockies. The Crow ranged as far north as the Milk River, east to the slopes of the Black Hills, southwest from the Little Missouri River, west along the Sweetwater River to its headwaters east of South Pass, and northwest along the eastern fronts of the Wind River and Absaroka ranges and as far as the Three Forks of the Missouri River. Various estimates place the Crow population at between 300 and 450 lodges in 1833.

A River Crow named Eelápuash (Arapooash)—Rotten or Sore Belly—refused to sign a treaty in 1825 when Colonel Leavenworth and Indian Agent Benjamin O'Fallon toured the upper Missouri after the conflict with the Arapaho. Arapooash defended Crow lands from whites as well as Indians. In 1833, the year before he died in battle against the Blackfoot, Arapooash reportedly gave this description of Crow territory: "The Crow country is good country. The Great Spirit has put it exactly in the right place; while you are in it you fare well; whenever you go out of it, which-ever way you travel you fare worse."[335]

The Crow made the winter and spring interesting for the fur trappers. James Clyman described the huge buffalo hunts in which most of the tribe participated. Men on horseback surrounded herds of buffalo and drove them into a narrow canyon, where they were killed by men lining the walls of the canyon. Old men, women, and children participated in butchering, drying the huge quantities of meat, and protecting the meat from hungry wolves.

The Crow were continually at war with their neighbors, the Black-foot, Sioux, Cheyenne, and Arikara. The Crow also stole horses from the whites, even horses previously traded to them. The Crow, however, would rarely kill a white; according to one report, "they frankly explain by telling us that if they killed, we would not come back, and they would lose the chance of stealing from us. They have no shame about stealing and will talk over their past thefts to you with all possible frankness and indifference."[336]

The Crow traded widely using their own products—furs, skins, skin lodges, and horses—and manufactured items, such as European- and American-made trade articles they had purchased—knives, awls, kettles, guns, and ornaments. They wanted garden produce. For the squash and corn from the Hidatsa, they exchanged horses, articles from western tribes, and clothing made by Crow women. The horse had early given the Crow an edge in trade, as they traded easily with the Shoshone, who brought horses north and passed them on. With the advent of white traders and hunters entering the Rocky Mountains, horses became an even more important trade item. In order to get them, the Crow trapped beaver; according to one historian, "They committed themselves more than any other Plains tribes to the trapping of beaver."[337] The resulting "Crow beaver" were pelts of high quality, having originated as thick-furred mountain beaver, then skillfully prepared by Crow women.

Polygamy was common, and it spread the women's work among more women in the family unit. The work involved in making and decorating skin lodges required the efforts of several women. They were well-known for the beadwork decoration of clothing and household items. The shirts, leggings, and robes they produced found a ready market in all the surrounding tribes.

Although the Crow were typical of warlike Plains Indians, they were known for good treatment of captive females, usually taking them for wives. No one outdid them in the domestic arts. Their lodges were the largest, the best constructed, and the most handsomely ornamented the mountain men saw anywhere. The Crow women were extremely fond of white men. The year they wintered with the Crow must have been a big winter for Jedediah's men. Tough, courageous, sensual, and ribald, the Crows were the best of mentors for men adapting themselves to mountain life.[338]

The Americans did not waste that time among the Crow. Using packs and lines drawn on the floor of the tepee, they learned from the Crow the topography of the mountains to the west. The Crow had traveled back and forth across the mountains for trading and warfare. They also had paid attention to the beaver. The Crow told Smith and Weber that "just across the Wind River Mountains was a country with streams so rich in beaver a man did not require traps to take them. He had only to walk along the banks with a club." Clyman copied those maps into his journal.[339]

To reach those streams, in February 1824, Smith tried to cross the Continental Divide through Union Pass west of the Crow camp, but deep snow defeated them. Smith and party retreated to the southern end of the Wind River Range, crossing a ridge to the Popo Agie River and wilderness region of the Wind River Range of the Rocky Mountains.

Clyman vividly described in his journal the difficulties encountered, including extreme wind, cold, and blowing snow. He and Sublette left the main party to hunt. They selected one buffalo as a target. Their horses were in too poor a condition to run in the wind-swept drifts, so the men crawled toward a buffalo and managed to shoot it. In the cold and wind, they had great difficulty lighting a fire, much less keeping it burning. At one point, Sublette nearly succumbed to the cold, but Clyman finally managed a small blaze, which restored him. Clyman wrote, "I have been thus particular in describing one night near the sumit of the Rockey mounta[n]s although a number similar may and often do occur."[340] The hunters rejoined Smith, and to avoid the wind, the entire party descended the Sweetwater River to a "Kenyon" that provided shelter from wind, wood for fuel, and mountain sheep for food. There they stayed for two or three weeks, until the scarcity of game and the need to get across the Continental Divide for spring trapping dictated they move on.

Smith established a cache for items they might not need during the spring hunt, and designated the spot on the Sweetwater as a June rendezvous. Following the Popo Agie River to the Sweetwater headwaters, they reached South Pass, which though a broad, open prairie, crested at eight thousand feet. Smith gets the credit for first opening the pass to westbound travel, making it part of the route of the Oregon Trail. By March 19, they had reached the Big Sandy River and descended it to the Green River, known as the Seeds-kee-dee, the Crow name for the Prairie Chicken River. Earlier the Spanish from the south had named it the Verde, for the green color of its water. The name Green floated northward and stuck.

Smith divided his eleven-man party for the 1824 spring hunt. He sent Fitzpatrick with three men, including Clyman, northward to the head of the Green River valley. Smith, with six men, headed south, and apparently trapped at Black's Fork; a nearby fork is called Smith's Fork.[341] Fitzpatrick had had a very successful hunt after leaving Jedediah Smith. He had encountered the Shoshone; lost his horses in a raid; regained them; and now, with fur-laden horses, headed east across South Pass.

The Shoshone were not a large tribe. By the early nineteenth century, they were divided into groups by location. The Lemhi band was usually the first one met by the fur trader coming from the Missouri River; they had met Lewis and Clark in 1805. The Blackfoot had driven them out of the plains of southeastern Montana into the mountains of Wyoming and Colorado. The eastern and northern bands hunted buffalo and lived in tepees of buffalo hide. It was they who became the central horse traders of the northern plains. Their large trade network provided them very early with horses from the Utes to the south. The Shoshone rendezvous near the Green or Bear River had been one of the major trading locations. They did not have guns in the early years; their main weapon was a stone club; but with horses they could raid and trade throughout the plains, from the Comanche in the south to the Assiniboin in the north.[342]

The Eastern Shoshone, also called the Green River Snakes, went across South Pass for their buffalo hunting and returned to the Green River to winter. There they were familiar faces to the American fur traders, and were present at rendezvous, trading horses for trade goods. However, they were great wanderers, seldom spending more than eight or ten days in one place, routinely traveling the distances and trails from the east and south branches of the Green and Snake rivers to Bear Lake.[343]

The great chief Wakashie reinvigorated the Eastern Shoshone in the 1820s and 1830s. He was an orphaned Flathead, raised by a Shoshone family. Early in adulthood, he joined the Bannocks, known as enemies of the whites, but later returned to the Shoshone. By 1850 he was head chief, having earned this respect by prowess in war and wisdom in council. Apparently he united the Shoshone in defense against the Plains tribes. In later years, to fight the Sioux and Cheyenne, he served as a U.S. Army scout, and eventually sought to have schools, churches, and hospitals built on Shoshone land. In 1896, he ceded lands near Thermopolis, Wyoming, for public use. He died February 20, 1900, and was buried with full military honors.[344]

Fig. 13.1 Chief Wakashie

Source: Photographed by Rose & Hopkins c1900 LC-usz62-102134. Courtesy of Library of Congress

The Northern Shoshone, often referred to as the Snakes, lived in eastern Idaho, western Wyoming, and northeast Utah, roughly south of the

Salmon River. They often lived and hunted with the Paiute or Bannock near the Portneuf and Snake rivers, and they frequently encountered the Hudson's Bay Company brigades that followed the Snake River into the mountains. The most prominent features of their country were the Sawtooth and Bitterroot ranges and the Snake River plain. They often wintered in the Weber and Cache valleys. The Western Shoshone, who lived from the Great Basin to California, lived on berries, roots, pine nuts, and small game, such as rabbits, fish, and birds. The climate was mild; they did not have animal hides to use, so they built their dwellings of grass.

In the 1820s, the Shoshone celebrated at the rendezvous and stole horses when available. The fur traders became accustomed to the type of encounter that Fitzpatrick had had with the Shoshone.

Thomas Fitzpatrick met Smith and Clyman in June on the Sweetwater as previously planned, and agreed to deliver the furs to Ashley in St. Louis and return with supplies. His party built a bullboat and started their load down the Sweetwater. Damage to the boat forced them to cache furs near Independence Rock. Clyman became separated from the others, and alone found his way across the prairie to Fort Atkinson. Fitzpatrick's bullboat met disaster in Platte River rapids, and he and his two men, believing Clyman to be dead, headed east on foot. They arrived at Fort Atkinson in a pitiable state, ten days after Clyman.

Fitzpatrick immediately wrote to Ashley about South Pass and of trapping prospects on the Green River. He then got horses from Lucien Fontenelle of the AFC, then at Fort Atkinson, and headed back to Independence Rock for the cached furs. He returned to Fort Atkinson with the furs by late October 1824. Lucien Fontenelle, who, according to Chittenden, was one of the best examples of Rocky Mountain partisan, or leader of a group of itinerant hunters and trappers, bought his furs.[345] Smith, in the meantime, had remained west of the Rockies. Though his itinerary has been the subject of conjecture, he did meet HBC's

Alexander Ross and spent Christmas 1824 at Flathead Post, having had a very successful trapping tour.

After a profitable spring hunt in 1824, Weber met Henry on the Big Horn River in a prototype rendezvous involving thirty to forty-five men, delivered his furs, obtained supplies, and departed across South Pass. He had advised Henry that wagons could cross the Continental Divide at South Pass. This news, which Henry passed on, stimulated interest in trapping and trading west of the Continental Divide and traveling overland instead of on the Missouri and Yellowstone. Henry's local trappers had combed a wide area and brought in a good catch of beaver, the largest Henry had ever made. With the returns of both parties, Henry went downriver to St. Louis, delivered his beaver, and retired from the fur trade.

Meanwhile, as documented by Daniel Potts' letters, Weber's large party crossed the Green, traveled to the Bear River, and spent the winter of 1824–25 on Cub Creek, a branch of the Bear River. This became famous as Cache Valley. During that winter, Jim Bridger hiked down the Bear River to the huge lake, which he thought was the Pacific. Potts was with him and referred to it as the "Great Salt Lake."

The trapping crew Henry had sent down the Big Horn River in the fall of 1823 had apparently returned to Fort Henry with their furs and agreed that they could be paid when they next returned to Missouri. Ashley, facing mounting debts from the previous year, laid plans to make another attempt to make a profit in the fur trade by sending supplies to the trappers left in the mountains. Having received Fitzpatrick's news of South Pass, of the successful trapping on the Green River, and of the furs cached at Independence Rock, Ashley determined to resupply both Captain John Weber of Henry's brigade and Jedediah Smith's party, by an expedition he would lead himself.

The principal contributions of William Ashley to the fur trade were two. First was the concept of the Rocky Mountain rendezvous, which became the annual opportunity for receiving supplies, delivering furs, exchanging information, and renewing friendships, without constructing and maintaining a fort. Second, he dealt with the trappers as independent operators, paying for beaver delivered in the mountains at half their value in St. Louis; prices quickly became standardized at $3.00 a pound, from $5.00 to $6.00 per plew. Under this arrangement, trappers had greater incentive. Ashley's overhead was reduced, for he had no staff or fort to support. This was the "Rocky Mountain System." Thomas Fitzpatrick and others, with Ashley, considered that their furs were their own, to do with as they pleased.[346]

On September 24, 1824, with a capitalization of $8,000, Ashley obtained a license to trade with the Snakes at the junction of two rivers within the territory of the United States. From Fort Atkinson, Ashley wrote to William Carr Lane on October 29, 1824:

> I arrived at this place on the 20th....& have remained here since that time, with hopes of Majr Henry's Joining me, and that a difference between the Agents of the US at this post, and the pawney Indians (out of which serious consequences may result) would be amicably settled....I shall therefore have to accompany my party of Mountaineers to their place of destination, and be the first to encounter the hostile disposition of those savages—their dissatisfaction has arisen from Majr O'Fallons demanding of them, the surrender of one of their warriors, who has committed a violent outrage upon a whit[e] man who was at their village. Twenty-nine of their Chief & warriors are here...at present there is no appearance of their being satisfied.[347]

Ashley was the entrepreneur, the businessman, and a strong leader. Without Henry, Ashley would have to rely on his "Mountaineers," who had already spent a year or two in the mountains, particularly Clyman and Fitzpatrick. Ashley left St. Louis with twenty-five men, including Zacharias Ham and James Beckwourth. They rode first to Council Bluffs, where they met Clyman and Fitzpatrick, and continued on to Fort Atkinson.

With Fitzpatrick and Clyman leading the way, the men started up the Platte River with fifty pack horses and a wagon. Ashley had heard of the Pawnees' strong spirit of hostility. Concerned about them, he caught up with his men on November 5, 1824. Before reaching the villages of the Grand Pawnee, they were caught in an early winter snowstorm without food or firewood, since they had expected to either hunt or trade for food with the Indians. By December 3, Ashley reached Plum Point on the Platte and found the encampment of the Grand Pawnee. Some young warriors had harassed them en route, but the council, fresh from their conference with Colonel Leavenworth, welcomed them.

The Pawnee in some way influenced nearly all the traffic along the Platte River valley, from the first trapper explorers to the travelers on the Oregon Trail. The Pawnee were divided into four bands, or tribes: the Skidi or Wolf, the Chaudi or Grand Pawnee, the Kilkehahkis or Republican Pawnee, and the Pitahuerat or Tapage Pawnee. Each band or tribe organized as a large village, although smaller bands traveled on their own and formed smaller villages. The Pawnee numbered between ten thousand and thirty thousand in the early 1820s, when they were the dominant power on the central plains. They were originally an agricultural tribe that had been forced out onto the plains. After the horse arrived, they dominated the middle plains.

Francisco Vasquez de Coronado encountered Pawnee in the Southwest in 1540. Like other Plains tribes, they were governed by councils. Women could attend councils, and could speak if they had performed war deeds similar to those of men. The Grand Pawnee settled along the Platte River in about 1820, but when wood became scarce, they joined other Pawnee people northward.[348] David Thompson wrote that they "raise more than double the quantity of corn and vegetables that is necessary for their own consumption, and furnish their neighbors with the surplus in exchange for peltries."[349] If the supply of horses was not dependable, it was at least a trade commodity. Horses with Spanish brands flowed northward. The Pawnee got their horses from the Cheyenne, who raided southward to the Comanche and the Kiowa.

The Pawnee lived in beehive-shaped thatched huts housing twenty to thirty people. They wore deerskin or buffalo-hide clothing in winter. In summer, women wore only a skirt coming up to the waist. Bare breasts were decorated with tattoos. Pawnee were the most northerly Caddo speakers and famous for their practical astronomy, which they used to determine the time for corn planting, religious observances, and periods of the calendar. Wissler described their philosophy as "in dignity and beauty…compares favorably with that of Greek, Egyptian, and other ancient civilizations." They boasted that they never fought the whites, and they were famous Army scouts later in the nineteenth century.[350]

Petalasharo, born about 1797, was their noted hero who saved the life of a maiden about to be sacrificed in a religious ceremony and forced the abandonment of that practice. His successor, Petalasharo II, required peace with whites and the keeping of treaties.

Ashley met with the Pawnee Council; seeking twenty-five horses, he traded for twenty-three. His party departed along the South Fork, anticipating that there would be more wood by that route, and always seeking beaver sources. They again encountered severe cold and deep snow, but were able to find round-leafed "sweet" cottonwood where they stopped to rehabilitate the horses. By February 4, two months after leaving Fort Atkinson, they followed the Cache la Poudre River into the mountains.

By March 10 they had descended into the valley of the North Platte. Heading northeast, they passed the east side of the Medicine Bow Range, then west, going south of Elk Mountain. They journeyed across the rough southwestern section of Wyoming to a point about 125 miles east of the present-day town of Green River, then west by northwest across the southern end of South Pass. On April 15, they camped on the Big Sandy River in about nine inches of snow. Four days later, they reached the Green River. Ashley noted that from the number of trees cut down, there must have been many beaver. (We later learn that Donald McKenzie and his North West Company crew had trapped it in 1821–22).

Here Ashley divided his force. Clyman, with six men, would trap upstream to the sources of the Siskadee. Zacharias Ham, one of Ashley's most respected trappers, would go westward toward the mountains with seven men, and Fitzpatrick would take six to the south. Before parting, each leader designated a deputy to act if necessary. Ashley directed that all would meet at a river entering the Green River from the west, marked either by peeling trees or a rock-topped five-foot mound, the top colored by vermillion. To the northwest, he would bury further instructions a foot deep. This designated the site of the 1825 rendezvous.[351]

On Wednesday, April 22, they finished a buffalo-hide boat measuring sixteen feet by seven feet. Ashley, with seven men, all the trade goods, and the men's supplies, headed down the largely unknown Green River. He had not drifted far before he decided another boat was needed to permit hunting and to carry the load. This they finished on April 24.

Here he entered on one of the great wild-river descents in Western history. As he described it, "We proceeded down the river which is closely confined between two very high mountains." Ashley was viewing Flaming Gorge, into the maw of which the Green disappears just below Henry's Fork.[352] This remarkable trip continued until May 16, when they camped at present-day Ashley's Fork, just above Stewart Lake, where Ashley deposited a cache.

Commenting on the canyon trip, Ashley wrote, "In the course of our passage through several ranges of mountains we performed sixteen portages, the most of which were attended with the utmost difficulty and labor." Remarkably, with their two bullboats, they had survived several severe rapids, rocks, falls, swamping, and drenching of supplies. Halfway down, on the eighth, he commented, "As we passed along between these massy walls, which in a great degree excluded from us the rays of heaven, and presented a surface as impassable as their body was impregnable; I was forcibly struck with the gloom which spread over the countenances of my men; they seemed to anticipate...a dreadful termination of our voyage."[353]

On May 16, Ashley cached the remainder of his goods. By May 21, Ashley had reached the junction of the Green and White river in a flat valley marked by huge, ancient round-leafed cottonwoods, which was the wintering place of Canadian Etienne Provost, a wanderer of the fur trade, then from Taos. This river junction was used in later years by many others.

There on May 21, they met two men from Taos, part of Etienne Provost's and Francois LeClerc's brigade of twenty to thirty men. Provost,[354] a famous independent who later worked for the Western Department of the American Fur Company, had arrived in the area a year earlier.[355] In a surprise attack by Snake Indians near Utah Lake, he had lost seven or eight men. He returned to the area in 1825, and on the Weber River, met Hudson's Bay Company's Peter Skene Ogden and his brigade, and Ashley's men under John Weber, including Johnson Gardner and his party, all of whom had wintered in the Cache Valley.

Ashley now began a clockwise circuit of the Uinta Mountains by land. Ascending the Duchesne River, he met a friendly band of Utah Indians from whom he bought seven horses. He got five more "from the camp of the Frenchmen." On June 7, he arranged for Provost to return to the Green, recover his cached goods, and bring them to Ashley. Provost returned with Ashley's goods on June 15. This was a great break for Ashley, because Provost not only forwarded his cached goods, but then guided him around the Uinta Mountains to the Green River. Ashley, eager to reach the site of his rendezvous at the appointed time, followed the Strawberry River, a branch of the Duchesne, westward; then turning north; he crossed the Wasatch Divide, and on the twenty-third, camped below the forks of Chalk Creek, east of the Weber River. He then crossed to the Bear River and to Muddy Creek. He reached the Green River and moved to the previously designated rendezvous site. He then went up Henry's Fork, about twenty miles, to Burnt Creek, to take advantage of the superior forage, arriving there on July 1.

As word of the rendezvous had spread, by the time Ashley arrived at Burnt Creek, he and his twenty-five men had been joined by twenty-nine deserters from Hudson's Bay Company and some of their women and children, thirteen of Etienne Provost's men, seven of Jedediah Smith's, and twenty-five to thirty of the men with John Weber. Also joining them were the parties led by Fitzpatrick, Clyman, and Zacharias Ham, and a number of independents—in all about 120 mountain men.[356] Ashley immediately opened his goods to what Jim Beckwourth described as a:

> little town numbering at least eight hundred souls, of whom one half were [Indian] women and children. There were some among us who had not seen any groceries such as coffee, sugar, etc., for several months. The whiskey went off as freely as water, even at the exorbitant price he sold it for. All kinds of sports were indulged in with a heartiness that would have astonished more civilized societies.[357]

For Ashley, the rendezvous lasted but one day. He had brought loads of supplies and about fifty different types of trade goods, summarized as ammunition, axes, cloth of various types, coffee, whiskey, fish hooks, gun parts, guns, horse tack, kettles, pipes, and tools. He bought furs from the trappers, mostly at the standard mountain price of $3.00 per pound, and left with 8,829 pelts, which in St. Louis weighed 9,700 pounds, valued at $48,000.[358] He divided the party, with instructions to those who remained to meet in Cache Valley the following summer. He left for St. Louis on July 2 with Jedediah Smith, who, Morgan believes, had agreed at the rendezvous to join Ashley in a partnership, since he was to return to the Rockies with supplies for the coming year.[359]

Ashley wrote of the journey:

On the 2nd day [of] July, I set out on my way homewards with 50 men, 25 of whom were to accompany me to a navigable point of the Big Horn River thence to return with the horses employed in the transportation of furs. I had forty packs of beaver cached a few miles east of our direct route [probably on the Sweetwater, left by Smith in 1824]. I took with me 20 men...raised the cache, and proceeded in a direction to join the other party, but previous to joining them, I was twice attacked by Indians.[360]

The first attack, by Blackfeet, ran off all the horses, but failed to take the camp. An express to Ashley's main group brought horses. The next night Crows attacked, resulting in one killed and one wounded. Ashley continued on to the point of embarkation on the Big Horn above the Wind River Canyon, arriving there on July 7, and sent the twenty men back to the mountains. His crew then made bullboats, loaded their furs, and embarked down the Yellowstone to its mouth.

There, twelve days later, on August 19, he met the treaty-making "Yellowstone Expedition" of General Atkinson and Indian Agent O'Fallon. Leaving them, he floated down the Missouri without incident and reached St. Louis on October 4. The *Missouri Advocate and St. Louis Enquirer* for October 8, 1825, wrote:

By the effort of heroic enterprise Gen'l Ashley has indemnified himself for all the losses occasioned by the murderous attack of the Arikaras in the summer of 1823....Gen'l Ashley fell in with a party in the service of the Hudson's Bay Company, who are believed to have 1000 men in their employment west of the Rocky Mountains. The riches which this company are carrying out of the territory of the United States are immense...the single party met with, had taken beaver to the amount of $200,000.[361]

That year, HBC Peter Skene Ogden's party alone took out 3,188 pelts, which valued in St. Louis at $5.00 a pound would have been $38,880.[362]

Among Ashley's "hundred young men" were fortune seekers, romantics inspired by tales of the West filtering eastward from Lewis and Clark, or those escaping the law of the more settled States. During the rendezvous heyday, there may have been from six hundred to a thousand trappers scouring the ponds and streams, canyons, and valleys of the Rockies, each bringing in his own furs to sell at the annually designated meeting.

These "mountain men" had the courage, powers of observation, and knowledge of the wilderness that enabled them to survive and find and take the beaver. Men such as Jedediah Smith, William Sublette, Thomas Fitzpatrick, James Clyman, Andrew Drips, Etienne Provost, Jim Bridger, Lucien Fontenelle, and Robert Walker were blessed with a marked capacity for leadership. Not just furs and supplies were traded over the campfires. Tales of the battles, enticements, and persuasion of Indians were freely and imaginatively exchanged.

Their favorite productive haunts, however, were probably guarded as carefully as a fisherman protects his favorite hole. This undoubtedly delayed a comprehensive American grasp of the geography of the country west of the Mississippi, since the mountain men who had the greatest appreciation of its realities for the most part kept their secrets. While these men could find a rendezvous site as easily as a man going to the barn, their knowledge—seldom mapped—trickled down slowly to later explorers. For example, Jedediah Smith's report on the importance of

South Pass came two decades after its first crossing, in 1812 by Robert Stuart from Astoria. It is remarkable how little each knew of what others were doing, and how restricted the flow of information was.

In St. Louis, Ashley and Jedediah Smith wasted no time after returning from the first rendezvous. On November 1, 1825, Smith led an expedition back to the mountains for a two-year stay. It included 60 men, 160 horses and mules, and goods worth $20,000. The party is believed to have included Robert Campbell, Hiram Scott, Jim Beckwourth, Moses "Black" Harris, Louis Vasquez, and A. G. Boone—Daniel Boone's grandson—who had accompanied Ashley as a clerk and bookkeeper, but became a famous mountain man and trader in his own right.

Smith took the expedition from St. Louis west to the Republican River and along it to a point about fifty miles south of Grand Island, Nebraska, where they wintered. They suffered very much for want of provisions. Men deserted and a third of the mules died. At a Pawnee village, they found and unearthed a cache of Indian corn, and when the Pawnee returned, they paid for what they had consumed. Smith and Campbell stayed in the lodge of the Pawnee chief, Ish-ka-ta-pa, and benefited from his hospitality.

Ashley, having heard of the expedition's difficulties along the Republican River, started to follow them on March 8, bringing twenty-five new men, replacements for the mules, and provisions. He caught up with Smith in early April at Grand Island. Ashley sent Smith and Harris on ahead to the trappers who had remained in the mountains, to make arrangements for the coming summer rendezvous at Cache Valley. The rest of the party, with everyone but Ashley walking, continued west along the Platte and finally, at the forks of the Platte, found buffalo.

Following the North Platte and Sweetwater rivers, they crossed South Pass, no doubt following the Sandy River to the Green, and thence along Ham's Fork to the Bear River, which took them to Cache Valley.[363] Sixty to seventy-five of Ashley's trappers came out to meet them. In Cache Valley, Ashley was also met by fifteen lodges of Iroquois, who had left the HBC and brought plenty of beaver. Ashley's trip had taken seventy-eight days. This valley became a favorite mountain-man wintering place. As Daniel Potts wrote:

> This valley had been our chief place of rendezvous and wintering ground. Numerous streams fall through this valley, which, like the others, is surrounded by stupendous mountains, which are unrivalled for beauty and serenity of scenery. You have here a view of all the varieties, plenty of ripe fruit, an abundance of grass just springing up, and buds beginning to shoot, while the higher parts of the mountains are covered with snow, all within 12 miles of this valley. The river passes through a small range of mountains and enters the valley that borders on the Great Salt Lake.[364]

The detailed trapping routes taken by Ashley's men in the mountains during his absence after the first rendezvous are only a matter of conjecture. The assembled trappers arrived in Cache (or Willow) Valley in late May or early June 1826. Ashley remained in Cache Valley only a couple of weeks, trading for 125 packs of beaver, which on his arrival in St. Louis about September 28, the *St. Louis Intelligencer* valued at $60,000.[365]

Ashley had made a fortune and wished to return to his pursuit of commerce and politics. While still at the rendezvous, he sold his interest in the trapping/trading company to a new firm formed by Jedediah Smith, David E. Jackson, and William Sublette. The company became known as Smith, Jackson, and Sublette, with Robert Campbell as clerk. This relationship made Campbell and Sublette fast friends and later business partners.

The articles of agreement, dated July 18, 1826, provided that the new firm would buy all of Ashley and Smith goods then at the rendezvous. Evidently Ashley credited Smith, his partner, with $5,000, leaving a

$7,821 balance due. Ashley gave to Smith, Jackson, and Sublette the services of forty-two hunters whose service would end in July 1827.[366]

Ashley agreed to sell them an inventory of fifty specific goods at specified prices, from coffee and tobacco to beads and gunpowder, to be delivered at Bear Lake no later than July 1, 1827. The total price was to be not less than $7,000 nor more than $15,000. The sale and delivery would be contingent upon Smith, Jackson, and Sublette notifying Ashley of their specific requirements not later than March 1, 1827. Failure to notify him would make the purchase null and void. The new company would sell beaver only to Ashley, paying for the delivered merchandise with beaver at $3.00 per pound, or Ashley would sell the beaver in St. Louis at the best available price, charging $1.125 per pound for transportation. Ashley also agreed that so long as he was furnishing them merchandise, he would supply no other company except those whom he might himself in future employ.[367]

Even more important than the specific terms, this agreement set a pattern followed by others. One group would remain in the mountains and hunt, and another would make the trek to and from St. Louis with furs, bringing back the trade goods procured and delivered in St. Louis. It was critical that the trade goods arrive at the proposed rendezvous at a convenient time. If they were late, the men in the mountains could take no chances, and another provider might make the sale.

By the end of the 1826 rendezvous, the character and nature of the mountain man were well established, though not widely known. As Bernard de Voto colorfully detailed, "The mountain men were a tough race...their courage, skill, and mastery of the conditions of their chosen life was absolute." They would not have been in the wilderness "if they had not responded to the loveliness of the country, and found in their life something precious beyond safety, gain, comfort, and family life."[368]

Though they demonstrated an extreme amount of individualism and gusto, solitude had given them a surpassing gift of friendship, and simple survival sharpened their wits. Mostly illiterate, they were great storytellers, both for information and for entertainment. Shop talk included trapping, hunting, packing, trailing, fighting, geography, fighting or escaping Indians, the availability of water , starvation, trickery and feasts, and always, Indian women. Buffalo was the complete diet. Parts were eaten raw and the fat eaten with the lean. Injuries were not infrequent, usually cured by mountain air; and gunpowder was a frequent internal medicine.[369] Toughness and wilderness savvy were sought and admired.

CHAPTER 14:

THE "FUR DESERT"

T he inland Oregon country was unknown to Europeans when John Jacob Astor's men—the "Astorians"—went to the mouth of the Columbia River in 1811. But the Astorians who traveled overland experienced the mountains, canyons, and turbulent rivers of the Rocky Mountains. The continued presence of the British traders along the Columbia River and increasing numbers of Americans led to an unresolved predicament in the Pacific Northwest. The Convention of 1818, which settled border issues from the War of 1812, gave both Americans and the British free access to the contested area lying west of the Continental Divide.

However, Hudson's Bay Company served as a British agent actively working to keep the Americans from extending the northern boundary of the United States along the forty-ninth parallel from the Continental Divide to the Pacific. To implement this policy, the instruction from London was to strip the country bare of furs in advance of the Americans, thus creating a "fur desert."

The tactics and techniques for conducting a yearlong trapping expedition from the Columbia River into the Rockies were developed by a veritable giant of the Columbia, Donald McKenzie of the North West Company, in 1818. He was born in Scotland and had joined the North West Company in 1800. In Montreal in 1809, he joined Astor's Pacific

Fur Company, and with Wilson Price Hunt traveled overland to Fort Astoria, gaining considerable information about the Snake River country en route. When Astoria was sold, McKenzie rejoined the North West Company and was sent back to Astoria, renamed Fort George.

The council at Fort William appointed him to take charge of the interior of the Columbia Plain. But because of his history with the Astorians, to the men at Fort George, McKenzie was an outsider. James Keith, the traditional manager at the post, described him as "only fit to eat horseflesh, and shoot at a mark."[370] By deliberate obstruction, Keith and his colleagues persistently interfered with McKenzie's desire to trade and trap in the interior. According to Alexander Ross, Keith's view was, "Your plans are wild, you will never succeed, nor do I think any gentleman here will second your views, or be so foolish as to attempt an establishment in the Nez Percé country as a key to your future operations, and without which you cannot move a step." McKenzie responded: "These remarks are uncalled for. I have been there already. Give me the men and goods I require, according to the conditions of the Council. I alone am answerable for the rest."[371]

Keith had misjudged. McKenzie was a huge man, very energetic, liberally educated, extremely hardy, bold, and masterful in his rapport with Indians. The council supported him, and in July 1818, McKenzie departed with Ross as his deputy and ninety-five men, including some treacherous Iroquois, some voyageurs, and the dregs of NWC at Fort George, to build Fort Nez Perces—later Walla Walla. "Never during my day," said Ross, "had a person for the interior left Fort George with such a motley crew, nor under such discouraging circumstances and inadequate means."[372]

On reaching the area of the mouth of the Snake River, McKenzie found the Cayuse, Nez Percé, and Palouse Indians to be antagonistic. During the short time that the Astorians, had spent on the Pacific, they had succeeded in alienating a number of tribes. For example, in 1813,

John Clarke, traveling between Spokane House and the Columbia River, stopped at a Palouse village. While there he showed them two silver goblets he prized. The next day when one was missing, he swore to hang the thief. The band found the thief, and much to their horror, Clarke did hang him.

The Indians never forgot, and for many years reminded whites of the deed. The outrage of the Palouse and other tribes continued. It wasn't until McKenzie took advantage of the euphoria that developed when five hundred warriors were celebrating a victory over their longtime enemies, the Shoshones (Snakes), that he could negotiate a peace agreement. As Ross explained:

His [McKenzie's] open, free, and easy manner often disarmed the most daring savage, and when one expedient failed another was always at hand. When the men stood aloof he caressed their children, which seldom failed to draw a smile of approbation from the rudest. His knowledge of their character armed him with confidence. In the most suspicious places, he would stroll among them, unarmed and alone....He saw at a glance what was working within, and never failed to upset all their designs.[373]

In present-day central Idaho and Washington and Oregon east of the Cascades, the Shahaptin-speaking tribes held sway in the nineteenth century. The most prominent of these were the Nez Percé, Yakima, and the smaller tribes of Cayuse, Klikitat, Palouse, Umatilla, and Walla Walla. The Nez Percé are famous in fur-trade history for their horses, and in American history for their great chief and American citizen, Chief Joseph (1840–1904). His Indian name was In-mut-too-yah-lat (thunder coming up over the land from the water). Among his many expressions of profound wisdom: "It does not require many words to speak the truth."[374] This described his relations with Indians and whites alike.

The Cayuse were excellent horsemen and yearly traveled with the Nez Percé to the prairie east of the Rockies to hunt buffalo. "This Tribe are the

fewest about 50–54 Men but have great influence over the others excel-
ling in bravery hunting & athletic exercise & the first who procured Arms
(Guns) & Ammunition for their Bever [sic] and Horses. They are fond
of domineering & [there are] troublesome characters amongst them."[375]

The Nez Percé in particular were expert in both breeding and raising
horses. However, both Clark and Lewis were critical of them. Clark, near
the Umatilla area, commented: "Both the men and women ride extremely
well. Their bridle is usually a hair rope tied with both ends under the jaw,
and their Saddles Consist of a pad of dressed skin stuffed with goats hair
with wooden sturreps. Almost all horses I have seen…have sore backs."[376]
Lewis later commented, "These indians are cruell horse-masters; they ride
hard, and their saddles are so illy constructed that they cannot avoid
wounding the backs of their horses; but regardless of this they ride them
when the backs of those poor animals are in a horrid condition."[377]

Leaving Ross to finish the job at Walla Walla, McKenzie departed up
the Snake River. With him were 55 men of many different backgrounds,
195 horses, and 300 beaver traps. There was a considerable stock of merchandise for trading, but no provisions or stores of any kind. They lived
off the land. The Iroquois who had moved west with the fur trade were
often at odds with McKenzie; they deserted with goods, traded with
Indian tribes, and even joined them. Nevertheless, in this and two following expeditions, McKenzie was remarkably successful in exploring
the Snake River country, roving "as far south as the Bear River and as far
east as the Green River valley, trapping its productive streams a full three
years before Jedediah Smith penetrated there across South Pass."[378]

McKenzie established friendly relations with the two great Shoshone
chiefs, Pee-eye-em and Ama-Qui-em, during the long winter months of
trapping. The two chiefs were as huge in height and girth as was McKenzie, and proved to be valuable friends. Because of the constant hazard of
Indian attack, often by Blackfeet, McKenzie's method was to establish a

base camp in a desirable area. He then sent out numerous small trapping parties, which could not have defended themselves, but were not too far out to seek the protection of the base camp. The system worked.

To historian Dale Morgan must go the credit for the best appraisal of McKenzie's contribution:

> With a motley group of Iroquois and Abenakis from the St. Lawrence, "Owyhees" from the Sandwich Islands, superannuated freemen (servants whose term of service had expired), and a few Canadian engagés, Mackenzie made history. His bold and imaginative use of his men for trapping rather than for manning trading posts; his system of supply and the transport of his furs, which involved the use of horses in place of the boats to which the fur trade had been wedded; his maintenance of his trapping force in the field almost uninterruptedly for three years—all this displayed genius and laid the groundwork for the revolution which Jedediah Smith and his associates were about to implement in the conduct of the American fur trade. It was left to Donald McKenzie to demonstrate the real potential of the trapping brigade.[379]

McKenzie's third trip ended in 1821 at Flathead Post, where he brought in 4,339 beaver.[380] McKenzie later became a chief factor for the HBC and served as governor of Red River from 1825 until 1833, when he retired to Mayville, New York, where he died in 1851.

Under the reorganized HBC, Finan McDonald took out the next Snake River Brigade, returning in 1823. Alexander Ross, who had been in charge of Spokane House and was looking forward to retirement, was persuaded to take charge of Snake River operations, with a substantial increase in salary. On November 12, 1823, Ross left with the brigade from Spokane House for Flathead House, near present-day Thompson Falls, Montana, where he completed assembling his party to travel to the Snake River beaver-trapping area.

On departing from Flathead House "in the depths of winter," Ross's brigade totaled fifty-five men, consisting of two Americans, seventeen Canadians, five half-breeds from east of the Rockies, twelve Iroquois, two Abnaki Indians, two natives from Nipissing, two Saultman from Lake Huron, two Athabaskan Crees, one Chinook, two Spokanes, two Kutenai, three Flatheads, two Kalispels, one Palouse, and one Snake slave. This variety of engagés from across the breadth of Canada indicates the scope and influence of the HBC. The Spokanes, Flatheads, and others served as interpreters, hunters, and guides, and were probably not of mixed descent. Indians were primarily useful as horse traders; with that, plus their other expedition activities, Ross could count on only twenty trappers at any one time. He commented, "One half, perhaps two thirds of the people I had under my command were more expert at the bow and arrow than at the use of the beaver trap, more accustomed to indolence and free will than to subordination."[381] Accompanying the brigade were 25 women and 65 children, for a total of 146 souls.[382] His brigade equipment included 75 guns, a brass three-pounder, 212 beaver traps, 392 horses, plus powder, ball, and trade goods.

The expedition would not reach the Snake River valley until after an extremely arduous late-winter trip. The Iroquois, who Simpson had earlier insisted be employed and who had been invaluable in canoes and boats as well as on the trail, were often a treacherous and unruly lot who sought to turn back when difficulties were encountered. The expedition reached the confluence of the Blackfoot, Bitterroot, and Clark Fork rivers at "Hell's Gate," in the present-day Missoula area. Here Ross decided to follow the Bitterroot River southward to avoid a possible encounter with the Piegan in the Blackfoot River valley, which was the Piegan "war road" to the Flathead. The Indians who accompanied him were probably also apprehensive of the Piegan and may have known something about the Bitterroot.

By March 12, they reached the present-day village of Sula at the head of the East Fork of the Bitterroot River, 183 miles by modern road from Flathead Post. This place they named "The Valley of Troubles." Ross reconnoitered the present-day Gibbon Pass, first used by Captain William Clark in 1806, but found seven feet of snow. Failing to break a trail using horses, he managed to make a trail across the pass by using mallets to break the snow crust and shovels to move the snow. This extremely arduous task took twenty-one days. On April 14, after thirty-three days at the Valley of Troubles, the brigade, including the women and children, made the strenuous trip to the Beaverhead River valley and camped by one of the hot springs.

They traveled southeast along the Beaverhead, again in dangerous Piegan country, and finally crossed Lemhi Pass into the Salmon River drainage. They found their way down the Little Lost River and into the Snake River plain. They continued trapping in creek valleys of the Salmon River and the Big Lost River, with both the assistance and the harassment of the Snakes, who cheerfully stole their horses whenever possible. These thefts always involved time-consuming recovery operations.

The peace brokered by McKenzie between traditional enemies—the Cayuse and Snakes—allowed the expedition to move safely when they encountered influential Snake chiefs, Pee-eye-em and Ama-ket-sa, and a group of Cayuse Indians. The brigade trapped as far west as the Payette and Weiser rivers. Eventually after trapping the Salmon to its junction with the Lemhi, at Canoe Point, Ross returned to the Three Buttes in the Snake River plain, a well-known landmark. Small bands of Shoshone continued to steal horses, furs, and traps.

"Old Pierre," an Iroquois member of the brigade, and a number of others had been sent off by themselves to trap, and had been attacked by a Snake war party. They lost nine hundred beaver, fifty-four steel traps, twenty-seven horses, five guns, and all their clothing. They were rescued by Jedediah Smith and his small party, and seduced by better prices for

supplies and higher prices for their furs into joining the Americans. The
HBC brigade, American trappers, Iroquois, and Shoshone all met at the
Three Buttes in the Snake River Plain.

Smith and his men joined Ross for the protection of their camp. Ross
found Smith to be a shrewd, intelligent man. He began his return to the
Flathead accompanied by the seven Americans. Going north they encountered Indian opposition and horse stealing, met with Crows, and re-crossed
Lemhi Pass. They then re-crossed Gibbon's Pass, overcoming heat rather
than cold and snow, passed Hell's Gate, and arrived at Flathead House by
the end of November 1824. Governor Simpson promptly appointed Peter
Skene Ogden to relieve Alexander Ross and lead the next brigade.

Peter Skene Ogden, one of nine children, was born in Quebec in 1794.
Before his birth, his parents, who were American Loyalists, fled to England, and then returned to Canada. His father became a prominent judge
in Montreal. Peter was well educated, and his father wanted him to study
law, but he wanted the fur trade. Ogden joined the North West Company
in 1809 as a clerk. He and his friend Samuel Black became two of the
toughest competitors for Hudson's Bay Company traders in remote areas,
even being charged with murder while in the area of Isle a la Crosse.
To avoid a trial, the North West Company sent Ogden to its Columbia
Department in 1818. There he served at Fort George, Spokane House,
and Thompson River Post. In 1821, rejected for appointment in the
merged HBC, he traveled from Thompson River Post to London to make
his case. As a result he was appointed an HBC chief trader to be stationed
at Spokane House, where he arrived in 1823.[383]

The following fall, Governor Simpson came to Spokane House to
review HBC operations. Dr. John McLoughlin had accompanied Simpson
on the cross-continent trip and was to be put in charge of Fort Vancouver.
Simpson made clear to the chief traders what the British purpose was, as
relayed by the Governor and Committee in London:

It is intended that a strong Trapping Expedition be kept up to hunt in the country to the southward of the Columbia, as while we have access thereto it is our interest to reap all the advantage we can for ourselves, and leave it in as bad a state as possible for our successors....Our wish is that it should scour the country wherever Beaver can be found (but on no consideration across the mountains) take its returns to Fort Vancouver annually...and return to its hunting grounds immediately."[384]

But expeditions under Governor Simpson would repeatedly violate London's orders not to trap east of the Rockies.

At Spokane House, Governor Simpson, believing Ross not sufficiently strong as a leader—despite the fact that Ross had overcome many difficulties involving weather, terrain, and treacherous Iroquois trappers, and was returning with more than four thousand pelts—immediately selected Chief Trader Peter Skene Ogden to succeed Ross as commander of the Snake River expeditions and ordered him to go immediately to Flathead House.

Ogden had a gift for leadership; a contemporary described him as "humorous, honest, eccentric, law-defying, the terror of all Indians and the delight of all gay [joyous and lively] fellows."[385] He was to prove an invaluable asset.

Having received Simpson's instructions, Ogden rode hard for Flathead House, arriving there November 1, 1824. Three weeks later, Ross brought in his brigade, accompanied by Smith, Sublette, and five of Ashley's mountain men. Ross reported that Americans were rapidly coming into the valleys and rivers sought by the British west of the Rockies. They were freemen and could trap and trade wherever they wished.

On his first expedition, Ogden left Flathead Post on December 20, 1824, accompanied by the Americans. His party was very diverse, consisting of William Kittson; clerk Charles McKay, an interpreter of the

Piegan language; Francois Rivet, an interpreter of the Flathead language and Ogden's father-in-law; forty-five freemen and boys; ten engagés, and families of thirty women with thirty-five children. Ogden's wife, Julia, with a nursing baby, insisted on coming, pointing out that if the nursing son could travel, so could the other children. The expedition had 22 leather lodges, 268 horses, and 352 traps.[386]

Though he was aware of the dangers and difficulties that lay ahead, Ogden immediately began trapping, and assigned areas to trapping detachments along the entire route. These he maintained even under the most difficult circumstances of terrain, weather, condition of horses, and Indian dangers. Indian raids were always a threat—often the Blackfoot, either for horse stealing or attack. After leaving the Flathead camp near Hell's Gate, he crossed Gibbons Pass into the Big Hole on January 13, despite the snow. In the Big Hole valley, they were constantly in fear of Blackfoot attack. There were plenty of buffalo. Restrained by snow over the Continental Divide, Ogden stayed for sixty days in the camp at the Boiling Fountain, near present-day Jackson, Montana.

Finally, on March 19, Jedediah Smith and his American party left Ogden and crossed Lemhi Pass, then went down the Little Lost River to the Snake River plain, the area marked by the Three Buttes. After sending scouts to track the Americans, Ogden on the twenty-third followed them onto the Snake River plain. Here in early April, while camped on the Snake near the mouth of the Blackfoot River, Julia Ogden provided a famous example of courage and hardihood. Little Charles had a cold and needed goose grease on his chest. Julia had a freeman shoot a goose that fell across the river. She stripped, swam to the goose, and returned with it, though the current carried her somewhat downstream. Reaching a sandbar, she scrambled out. Little Charles got goose grease on his chest and goose broth in his tummy, and he recovered.

By late April, Ogden was on the Bear River, where he completed his first thousand pelts, and may have continued to the present site of Ogden, Utah. He never lost an opportunity to "annoy" American trappers when he knew or suspected their whereabouts. He sought Shoshone Chief Pe-i-em on the Bear River, who was away trading shells. From a large party of Snakes, he learned that an American group had wintered west of Bear Lake on the Cub River and had left early in the spring. This journal entry has fur-trade historical significance, because it identifies the location of John Weber's party that winter.

In late May in Ogden's Hole, now near Ogden, Utah, Ogden encountered a group from Taos: Etienne Provost's party. On May 23 there began an unlikely encounter. Etienne Provost, a free trapper, appeared in the area. He had come from Taos, and camped nearby with fifteen men, including the Iroquois Francois who had deserted Alexander Ross's expedition, some Canadians, and an old Spaniard. Jedediah Smith and his party were believed to be in this area also. In late afternoon, another group, probably a segment of Weber's party, arrived. They were led by Johnson Gardner, who rode into Ogden's camp carrying an American flag. Ogden identified fourteen deserters accompanying Gardner.

> This morning Gardner came to my Tent & after a few words of no import, he questioned me as follows: Do you know in whose Country you are? To which I made answer that I did not as it was not determined between Britain and America to whom it belonged, to which he made answer that it had been ceded to the latter & as I had no license to trap or trade to return from whence I came to this I made answer when we receive orders from the British Government we Shall obey then he replied remain at your peril. [387]

Gardner can be criticized for his rancorous display of antagonism in his altercation with Ogden, but this in itself carried fundamental lessons about the HBC's compensation of their engagés and free trappers. "The true antagonists were neither the North West Company nor the Hudson's Bay Company in opposition to a handful of American free traders, but one aspect of British tradition arrayed against the new social concepts beginning to emanate from the small nation east of the Mississippi."[388]

L. B. Shippee wrote, "While the HBC was a monopoly whose word was law, no chartered organization with monopoly privileges represented the dignity of the United States in the region. Private enterprise, unsupported by legislative grant, undertook to penetrate the country which was affording British stockholders handsome returns."[389]

Ross was particularly contemptuous of "freemen" such as the half-Iroquois John Grey. He described them as "a kind of enlightened Indian, with all of the imperfections but none of the good qualities of their countrymen." He observed that though they lived in a mode comparable to Indians, whites despised them because they became savages.[390] Many of them operated on their own and traded their beaver with the Americans, particularly at rendezvous. The result was that Grey led a number of trappers to desert Ogden, seeking the higher price for beaver and lower price for trade goods and equipment the Americans offered. Three men deserted, leaving their women and children with Ogden's brigade.

By the end of May, Ogden returned to the vicinity of the Three Buttes and the Portneuf River. Camping near Henry's Fork, he received letters that had been carried to him by Flatheads, who often acted as messengers. One letter was from Governor Simpson, telling him to return to Fort George via the Umpqua River. However, Ogden felt that now he was too weak in numbers to travel the longer route. Simpson's order revealed the degree to which the Oregon country was still unknown; there was no direct connection between his location and the Umpqua River.

Late in June he was on the North Fork of the Snake, where he met a group of friendly Piegan. They wanted to trade for ammunition, which

Ogden would not do. He commented that they could get it from the Americans. He was able to dispatch a letter via Iroquois messengers to York Factory, describing his altercation with the Americans and that men had deserted for better American treatment.

By mid-July, Ogden had crossed Monida Pass and was near Jackson, Montana. Until September 12, he remained east of the Continental Divide, in country that the Governor and Committee in London had specifically forbidden to HBC trappers. He made extensive trapping efforts from various camps on the Beaverhead. In late July and early August, he was in the Deer Lodge area, bothered by grizzlies and horse flies so thick that they made the horses "poor." Crossing from the Clark Fork to the Missouri drainage, he learned the Piegan possessed the horses stolen from him on Bear River.

In early September, Ogden heard that the men he had sent under Kittson with a load of furs to Flathead House had safely reached Spokane House. Despite the continuing difficulty in finding adequate forage for horses in the timber, he crossed Gibbon's Pass by September 12, thus returning to jointly shared British-U.S. country. He was still not free of Blackfoot influence, and four days later, the Piegans stole thirty horses. He remained in place near the omnipresent buffalo herds until he could accumulate enough dried buffalo meat to permit returning to Walla Walla. Near the end of September, he sent Charles McKay and J. Hubert to the Flathead Post with 774 large and 298 small beaver and 15 otter. He noted that Snake River beaver pelts were inferior to those he was accustomed to east of the Rockies.

In October, Ogden's party headed west, probably crossed Lemhi Pass and into the Little Lost River valley, which he knew as Day's Defile. During the subsequent trip along the Snake, he observed the Snake River tributaries; this area, the location of Ross's trips, "has been examined and now ascertained to be destitute of Beaver."[392] Continuing along the

Snake, he was three days' march from Fort Nez Perces by October 30, and on his arrival met Chief Factor McLoughlin, who had come from Fort Vancouver to hear the report of Ogden's first Snake River expedition. Discussing the campaign, Ogden was disgusted with his dealings with the Snakes, believing that the Iroquois had trained them too well in the art of trade. He commented, "I would willingly sacrifice a year to two to exterminate the whole Snake tribe, women and children excepted."[393]

Despite Ogden's negative report, the Shoshone had had a long history of successful trading. Their horse fairs had been an important avenue for the movement of horses from the southern plains to the north long before white people were found in the mountains. The Eastern Shoshone, or Green River Snakes, went across South Pass for their buffalo hunting and returned to the Green River to winter. There they became familiar faces to the American fur traders, present at rendezvous and trading horses for trade goods. However, they were great wanderers, seldom spending more than eight or ten days in one place, routinely traveling the distances and trails from the east and southern branches of the Green and Snake rivers to Bear Lake.[394]

Ogden made five more Snake River expeditions, the last taking him to the mouth of the Colorado River. His family remained at Fort Nez Perces with Julia's mother. Returning through California, he obtained a thousand beaver in the San Joaquin Valley, and had a congenial encounter with Ewing Young and Kit Carson, who had come from Taos. During his expeditions, he demonstrated incomparable devotion to duty and accomplished the objective of turning the Snake River valley into a fur desert.

Each campaign followed a pattern that appeared in all of the Snake River expeditions. Ogden's journals reflect the difficulties in detail. There was a wide variation in beaver availability on various streams, with the men often trapping through ice, demonstrating the often admirable, even heroic, willingness to undergo severe hardship. There were periods of starvation when they depended on beaver for sustenance and suffered desperate illness from eating beaver fed on hemlock. Horses were starving and their feet wearing away from ice and snow. The Snake Indians stole horses. They had to be on constant guard against other theft, the "desertion" of freemen to the Americans to take advantage of their better prices, and the danger of attack by Blackfeet.

On a later expedition, Ogden encountered, or nearly missed, parties of American trappers and was proud of his ability to prevent freemen and engagés from deserting to the Americans. His principal encounter was on his second expedition, on March 24, 1826, on the Raft River. He observed that there were about two hundred tents of Snakes, who he thought had spent the winter at peace with the Americans. They had an American flag and were content with American knives and trinkets. All their guns and ammunition were from "our quarter" (British). The Snakes told Ogden that twenty-five tents of Americans were on the Bear River. On April 9, a party of ten Americans met them and camped separately. Ogden drew satisfaction from the fact that the argument of the previous year with Johnson Gardner did not recur.

Ogden felt strongly about the willingness of his men to desert to better American treatment, writing that "it was almost impossible however industrious a man might be to clear his individual expenses, in fact his four horses and traps alone cost him one hundred fifty large Bever... and seldom could a Trapper return to the depot without being obliged to renew both and the former at an advanced price....Although some articles are sold by the Americans higher than we now sell...they pay for Beaver say three dollars per pound delivered in the Snake country."[395] The difference he attributed to the easier American transportation by wagons and water to and beyond St. Louis.

Eventually twenty-three trappers, carrying with them about seven hundred furs, had defected to the American side. Chief Factor McLoughlin acted on Ogden's complaints, and in 1826 instructed Ogden to allow the

freemen to buy reasonable necessities at the same prices as European servants, to sell them their hunting implements at inventory prices, and to
pay them ten shillings for a full-grown beaver. In 1827 the Governor and
Committee in London confirmed McLoughlin's action with a gentle rebuke
to Simpson: "By attempting to make such expeditions too profitable the
whole may be lost and it is extremely desirable to hunt as bare as possible
all the Country South of the Columbia and West of the Mountains."[396]

Another problem along the Snake was the increased sophistication of
Indian traders. On March 21, 1826, Ogden wrote, "100 Indians came
to see us they brought little or nothing to trade Elk or Deer skins they
demanded Horses or Kettles one horse was traded from them miserably
poor which cost 20 skins, not many Years since a horse could have been
obtained for a Knife or Axe, this is the effects of Iroquois remaining
with them to be independent of them for years, they might not again be
taught to bargain on equal terms, but at present we cannot."[397]

The details of Ogden's journals show a complete dedication to reaching his objectives. He had rediscovered the value of having women on the
trail, noting their competition to see who could provide the best-dressed
beaver skins. He deplored having the trips start so late that they could
trap only three of the eight months en route, with no fall hunt due to
the severity of the weather. He also believed that an expedition would be
more successful if it were designed to remain for two years, as the Americans did, and had members to deter Indian attacks.

With his experience, Ogden had occasion to both admire and privately
ridicule the American effort. On the Snake River plain, he had encountered various groups of Americans, including Samuel Tulloch and Robert
Campbell. He commented gloomily on the inequalities still remaining
from Simpson's somewhat moderated policy of supplying the trappers at
a huge company profit:

The price of their beaver is certainly low compared to Americans. With them, beaver large and small average $5 each; with us $2 for large and $1 fore small....An American trapper—from the short distance he has to travel is not obliged to transport provisions—requires only ½ the number of horses and very moderate in his advances. From 3 years prior to the last one, General Ashley transported supplies to this country and in that period has cleared $80,000 and retired, selling the remainder of his goods in hand at an advance of 150 P cent....Three young men, [Jedediah] Smith, [David] Jackson and [William] Sublette purchased them, who have in this first year made $20,000....What a contrast between these young men and myself. They have been only 6 yrs. In the country, and without a doubt, in as many more will be independent men.[398]

Unfortunately in June 1830, Ogden's last expedition ended at The Dalles, where his boat, crew, journals, and five hundred beaver were swallowed by a whirlpool. Simpson, writing to London, complimented him highly and relieved him because of his deteriorated physical condition.

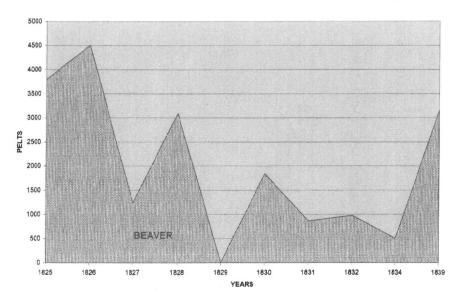

Fig. 14.1 Snake River brigade production 1825–1839

CHAPTER 15:

ROCKY MOUNTAIN FUR COMPANY

The most extensive cooperative intermingling of Indians and mountain men began with Ashley's sale of his fur business to Jedediah Smith, David E. Jackson, and William Sublette in 1826. This sale generated a keen appreciation of the Indian role in the fur trade and opened the way for the emigration of settlers to the Oregon country, thus determining America's present northern boundary from the Rockies to the Pacific.

Smith, Jackson, and Sublette displayed such broad talents as to be considered representative of the mountain men, true pioneering figures in American history. Their firm became well known and respected by Indians, other American companies, independents, and Hudson's Bay Company officials. By October 1, 1827, they had received a quit-claim deed from Ashley for $7,821, indicating that their debt to Ashley was paid.[399]

Indian tribal activities, movements, and viewpoints that largely determined fur-trade patterns during the 1820s and 1830s have been described in earlier chapters. The ubiquitous attacks of the Blackfoot, the friendly support of the Flathead, Nez Percé horses, the unpredictability of the Snakes and the Bannocks, the assistance provided to caravans many times by the Pawnee, and the gradual discovery of ancient native trails are but a few examples. The capability of Indian women in camp, on the trail, and in the preparation of pelts and robes for sale was always a critical asset.

Patterns of friendly support and mutual loyalty did exist between various Indians and traders or trappers west of the Continental Divide and on the plains, but the relationship was stronger between Indians and the more experienced and disciplined American traders and trappers. Above all, the HBC had an advantage in that many HBC people were of mixed descent or the widely employed Iroquois. Courage, patience, and prudence were required, and the experience of HBC traders through two centuries was a priceless asset for HBC operations.

At the 1826 rendezvous, the new Rocky Mountain Fur Company designated the southern end of Bear Lake as the rendezvous site for the next years. They also organized about fifteen fur brigades around their trusted lieutenants, such as Robert Campbell, Thomas Fitzpatrick, Moses "Black" Harris, Jim Bridger, and Jim Beckworth, all of whom had joined the new company. The brigades scattered. Sublette and Jackson headed northwest into the Snake River valley and Jackson's Hole, trading with Snakes, Crows, Sioux, and Flatheads, using about a hundred men. They visited present-day Yellowstone Park after visiting first the lower Snake River to trade for skins and horses. They then followed a "circuitous route" west and southwest into the Snake River valley and back to Bear Lake for the winter of 1826–27.

William Lewis Sublette was born on September 21, 1799, in his maternal grandparents' home near Stanford, Kentucky. His father, Phillip Allen Sublette, had brought his family from Virginia, and in Kentucky, was an entrepreneur and always active in local affairs and politics. Phillip and Isabella moved their family to St. Charles, Missouri, where he established a tavern, dabbled in land, and was a justice of the peace. They had five sons and three daughters. The boys were William, Milton, Andrew, Pinkney, and Solomon, several of whom were involved in the fur trade. William, the oldest, was six feet two inches tall, with sandy hair, fair skin, and blue eyes. He followed his father's business interests, became township constable, and was reelected in August 1822.

Upon the death of his parents, and with his brothers and sisters living with relatives, William responded to Ashley's advertisement and joined the Ashley adventures. After the skirmish with the Arikara on the Missouri River, Sublette traveled with Jedediah Smith through the Black Hills, to Powder River, and to the winter with the Crow in the Wind River Range. Jim Clyman saved his life in a blizzard on the Popo Agie, and for two years, until 1825, he trapped the mountain country. In November 1824, he and Jedediah Smith joined a detachment of Alexander Ross's Snake River expedition and reached Flathead Post on November 26, 1824. There they enjoyed British hospitality. After Christmas, they joined Chief Trader Ogden in his first Snake River expedition. By July 1, 1825, Clyman, Smith, and William Sublette had rejoined Ashley at his first rendezvous.[400]

Among the various provisions of the 1826 sale contract was the requirement to notify Ashley of their 1827 rendezvous needs before March 1, 1827. This provision led to Sublette's almost unbelievable winter walk across the plains to St. Louis. Leaving Jackson to conduct the winter hunt, Sublette and Moses "Black" Harris left Cache Valley on New Year's Day 1827. They traveled on snowshoes with one pack dog. Dried-meat supply was short by the time they reached Ham's Fork. Water was limited to melted snow or ice. They found buffalo on the Sweetwater, and continued through drifted snow, often into the night before they could find a protected hollow in which to build a small fire, on whose embers they could spread their blankets. On arriving at the Platte River, without firewood or food, they feared the opposition of the Pawnee, but in the more wooded, rolling country of Ash Hollow, they altered course and ran into the band of Omaha led by Chief Big Elk. The chief provided food and horses and sent them on their way. Sublette traded a hunting knife with another Indian band for dog which they reluctantly killed for meat.

Sublette left Harris, who had a sprained ankle, with Big Elk, and rode on to St. Louis, arriving there three days late, March 4, 1827. He had traveled more than 1,600 miles, mostly on foot, in midwinter. On arrival, he found Ashley and the French Fur Company, a subsidiary of the American Fur Company, already preparing supplies for the return. Two weeks later, Sublette began his third trip across the plains—his second trip westward—with his supply train. Ashley had started the train, but Sublette caught up, having stopped at St. Charles to get his younger brother, Pinckney. They reached Bear Lake in late June 1827, and had a successful year. They traded 7,000 pounds of beaver for $22,000 in merchandise, having sold beaver pelts to Ashley's agent at the rendezvous for $3.00 per pound. Chouteau, then Astor's representative in St. Louis, later bought them for $4.375 per pound.

The Blackfoot were a constant hazard. At the opening of the 1827 rendezvous, the supply train led by William Sublette had just arrived from St. Louis. As Campbell reported:

> The Blackfoot attacked the Snakes, and the Snake warriors with William Sublette went out to assist them. Tullock was wounded on the wrist, and his hand later withered from the effects of the wound....Sublette behaved bravely. I staid in camp in charge of everything. The families of those killed disposed of all the bodies. One of them placed a buffalo robe on Sublette's tent and said to him, "You are a great warrior. I seen it. My "bonich" behaved coolly.[401]

Sublette continued leading trapping brigades. He demonstrated a remarkable ability to travel. Between 1823 and August 7, 1832, he made fourteen trips between the Rockies and St. Louis. Two were on foot, 1,600 and 1,400 miles respectively, and in midwinter. Two were between St. Louis and Santa Fe. He introduced the use of freight wagons, and drove cattle to provide food until buffalo were encountered. He traveled to New York to procure supplies and confer with the American Fur Company. He formed a partnership with Robert Campbell, and after 1840, when they made their last fur sale in St. Louis, he and Campbell invested in a mercantile business. William became a progressive farmer and maintained an interest in Missouri politics. He died in Pittsburgh, of pneumonia, on July 24, 1845.

As the other partners led brigades throughout the mountains, it fell to Jedediah Smith to explore for beaver to the southwest of Bear Lake. He left on August 15, 1826, beginning an odyssey that would take him to the Mojave Indians near the mouth of the Colorado River, across the Mojave Desert to California, and eventually through Northern California. Ostensibly he was looking for beaver, but probably he intended to determine if the Buenaventura River really existed as a river from Salt Lake to the sea. He passed friendly Utes on August 22, easing the way with gifts.

In early October, he reached the Mojave villages, a veritable oasis. He found the Mojave to be tall, well-built men, wearing only a loincloth. The women were short and stout, the girls pretty, and all wearing only a skirt. The Mojave cultivated the soil, raising corn, beans, pumpkins, watermelons, muskmelons, and a little cotton and wheat. Smith remained there for fifteen days, resting his horses and men. He left the Mojave, taking an age-old road to the sea, guided by two runaways from the California missions. By November 26, 1826, he had reached the San Bernardino Mountains.

In California, Smith met both the kindness of the San Gabriel missionaries and the tyrannical bureaucratic restraints of Governor-General Jose Maria Echeandia, whose actions were fortunately countered by the assistance of an American ship captain, William H. Cunningham. Echeandia finally permitted Smith to leave "the same way he had come." However, Smith and party continued up the central valley, trapping as they went, collecting 1,500 pounds of beaver. Smith anticipated that Spanish soldiers were en route to arrest him. On May 20, he left his men, furs, and horses with his deputy, Harrison G. Rogers, promising to return in four months. Smith, with Silas Gobel and Robert Evans, crossed the Sierras to the rendezvous. They made a strenuous trek across central Nevada, south of the Deep Creek Range, and then northeast to Skull Valley. An enfeebling thirst forced Smith to leave Evans, but he soon found water in Skull Valley, and returned to revive him. Following the south shore of Salt Lake, Smith killed a fat buck on June 30. On July 2, they left the lake, fell in with two hundred lodges of Snakes, and traveled with them to Bear Lake. Smith reached his colleagues at the rendezvous on July 3, 1827, and was welcomed by a salute from the first cannon to cross the plains.[402]

Jedediah Strong Smith was born at Bainbridge, New York, on January 6, 1799. According to Harvey L. Carter,[403] Smith was far from being a typical fur trader. He was strongly religious, with an education comparable to that of other literate mountain men. He realized the importance of exploration. He had strong qualities of leadership, was accustomed to command, and others referred to him as Mr. Smith or Captain Smith. He abstained from smoking and liquor, though he would occasionally take a glass of wine. Biographer Dale Morgan wrote:

> There was an honesty, a directness, an openness that won him friends on brief acquaintance—and there were times during Jedediah Smith's years in the West when much depended upon his ability to make friends. In the world in which he made his mark, courage was a commonplace, and the intricate skills of survival were essential. But intelligence has never been commonplace, in the West or anywhere, and everyone was struck with the quality of Smith's intelligence…and had life been kind to him, the world might have heard much of Jedediah Smith.[404]

Ten days after arriving at the 1827 rendezvous from California, Smith left again. He took eighteen men, including Silas Gobel, and supplies for two years, intending to rejoin the men he had left the previous year, then trap northward along the California-Oregon coast to the Columbia Plateau.[405] Taking a somewhat different route, he followed the Virgin River to the Colorado, then crossed the Colorado to the east side and descended to the Mojave villages.

Unknown to Smith, about a year earlier, Ewing Young and others from Santa Fe had visited the Mojave, and there had been a scrimmage in which a number of Mojave were killed. They remembered it, and when Smith and his party attempted to cross the Colorado, the Mojave attacked those remaining on the east bank, killing ten men and capturing the accompanying Indian women. Smith gave the remaining eight the option of continuing or staying. All eight elected to continue to California.

They crossed the desert, relying on Smith's memory of water holes found on his previous trip, and arrived in the San Bernardino Valley about August 28. From then on, he encountered the abominable bureaucratic arrogance of the Mexican authorities. Only through the willingness of American ship captain John Rodgers Cooper to assume responsibility for his conduct could he reach San Francisco, where his deputy, Harrison Rogers, and the remainder of his men had been alternately jailed or camped since Smith had left them.

"Jedediah by now was prepared to believe anything of this strange people who dwelt along the California coast...everywhere he turned, he saw the iron hand of oppression, and all in the name of republican government and the true faith."[406] Smith sold his beaver to a ship captain, and with only forty-seven traps left, proposed to resume trapping and to drive the 250 horses and mules he had purchased back to the Bear Lake rendezvous along a route that took them north along the Pacific Coast.

Here began one of the remarkable trips in fur trade history, detailed in Dale L. Morgan's *Jedediah Smith, and the Opening of the West*. Including the men waiting for him in California, he had a party of twenty. Smith departed San Francisco Bay in late December, and in almost continuous rain, trapped and herded horses and mules northward amid generally friendly Indians. They were delayed on March 8 when Rogers was mauled by a bear. On April 11, Smith crossed the Sacramento just above the site of Red Bluff, and by April 17 crossed the Hay Fork of the Trinity River. Soon they encountered Indian raids. As they moved north the Indians appeared to be increasingly frightened of strangers. Driving horses and mules was extremely difficult. As Morgan described it, the half-wild horses and mules would go through narrow passes in a squirming mass, frantically trying to keep from being pushed down vertical cliffs. They would get tangled in brush or timber or tied up in cul-de-sacs, their feet, legs, and bodies cruelly mangled by sharp rocks or broken branches.

In early May, the party was moving into the lands of the Hupa Indians, who had been trading with the HBC. On May 19 they camped in view of the ocean. The Indians continued their harassment and persistently shot arrows into the mules and horses, wounding many. Skirmishes with the Indians as they moved prompted members of Smith's party to shoot in retaliation.

Smith found his way through thick brush and ridges and finally reached the vicinity of present-day Crescent City on June 14. A month later, they reached the Umpqua River. Smith, Turner, and Leland went ahead to find a trail, advising Rogers not to let Indians into camp. Unfortunately, Rogers relaxed this rule. The Indians attacked after an argument over an ax, and only Arthur Black, though wounded, escaped. Smith, on returning, saw the result, and turned back, reaching the coast near Tillamook Indian village. From there the Tillamook guided Smith, Turner, and Leland to Fort Vancouver. Black had arrived there two days before, on August 8, 1828.

Chief Factor John McLoughlin, who recognized Smith's personal qualities, graciously received him and was happy to obtain geographic information on the Oregon and California coasts. Through Ogden, they also had come to regard Smith, Jackson, and Sublette as a firm worth reckoning with, even coming to an agreement concerning deserters. McLoughlin sent a force under Alexander Roderick McLeod, who was scheduled to trap along the Oregon coast, to Umpqua to regain Smith's losses and discipline the Indians. He recovered most of Smith's furs and other losses. McLoughlin bought Smith's furs for $20,000, but was sharply critical of their condition.

Smith remained at Fort Vancouver until March 12, 1829, when he traveled to Flathead Lake. There he met Black Harris. They went south, and en route met Jackson, who was looking for him, and at last met Sublette on Henry's Fork on August 5, 1829. There he no doubt learned that during the previous spring, Pinkney Sublette had been killed at the mouth of the Blackfoot River while on a trip to the Salmon River with Samuel Tulloch.

Competition against Smith, Jackson, and Sublette was beginning. Joshua Pilcher sent a party consisting of Lucien Fontenelle, William Henry Vanderburgh, and Charles Bent to the Green River in the summer of 1827. They had forty-five men and a hundred horses. However, they met with defeat. The Crow stole most of their horses, and they cached their goods. When retrieving them later, they found the goods to be spoiled by moisture. They attended the 1828 rendezvous south of Bear Lake and returned home, taking only seventeen packs of beaver. Pilcher's partners and most of his men then returned to Council Bluff.[407]

Pilcher was not willing to give up; he took a small crew to Flathead Lake to winter. In February 1839, his horses stolen, he discharged his men and headed for the HBC post at Fort Colville. From there his association with the HBC involved travel along the HBC express route across

Athabasca Pass and eastward, ending at Brandon House, and thence to the Mandan villages, and by June to St. Louis. His trip was not a complete loss, for he wrote a detailed letter to the U.S. secretary of war, commenting on the geography he had seen and the adverse effects of the Convention of 1818. It was of value in Congress.

After the 1828 rendezvous at Bear Lake, Sublette headed for St. Louis with seventy-five mounted men plus equipment and furs from a year's hunt. With him were Fontenelle, Vanderburgh, and Charles Bent from Pilcher's party. The presence of these men signified evidence of the coming competition from the American Fur Company. Indians attacked near Independence Rock. Several men were killed, furs were lost, and Ashley's agent Hiram Scott was wounded. Sublette, realizing that he had to get their furs to market, left two men with Scott, promising that someone would return for him, and continued on, arriving at Lexington just before September 26, 1828. The two men remaining with Scott started downriver in a bullboat, which capsized at what became Scott's Bluff. The two men, believing Scott was dying, left him and rejoined the caravan, reporting that he was dead.

On March 17, 1829, as Jedediah Smith was leaving Fort Vancouver, Sublette began his fifth trip—his third trip west across the plains—with $9,500 worth of supplies and leading fifty-four men. There were peaceful encounters on the Platte River with the Sioux, Arapahoe, Kiowa, and Cheyenne. Sublette followed the Sweetwater to the Popo Agie River, where there was a small rendezvous. There, on about July 1, he met Robert Campbell, who had all the furs from the company's winter efforts and was returning from trapping in Crow country.

From this partial rendezvous on the Popo Agie, Joseph Meek provided some information about the free, or independent, trappers vs. the hired ones:

The hired trapper was regularly indentured and bound not only to hunt and trap for his employers, but also to perform any duty required of him in camp. The booshway, or the trader, or the partisan, had him under his command, to make him take charge of, load and unload the horses, stand guard, cook, hunt fuel, or, in short, do any and every duty. In return for this toilsome service he received an outfit of traps, arms and ammunition, horses, and whatever his service required. Besides his outfit, he received no more than three or four hundred dollars a year as wages. There was also a class of free trappers who were obliged to agree to a certain stipulated price for their furs before the hunt commenced. But the genuine free trapper regarded himself as greatly the superior of the foregoing classes. He had his own horses and accoutrements, arms, and ammunition. He took what route he thought fit, hunted and trapped when and where he chose; traded with the Indians; sold his furs to whoever offered highest for them; dressed flauntingly, and generally had an Indian wife and half-breed children. He prided himself on the hardihood and courage…the best horse…the wildest adventures…the most narrow escapes.[408]

Meek was well qualified to comment. He trapped and traded in the Rockies from 1829 until 1840, when he led settlers from Fort Hall to the Willamette Valley. When government in the Willamette Valley was organized in 1843, Meek was elected sheriff. He was politically active and became the first Oregon federal marshal.

There was also a deplorable aspect of the independents. While many of them commanded Indian respect, many others, by virtue of their conduct, commanded only enmity. This was true of others in the business, as well. For example, Ashley, though an honorable man, had, by introducing the corps of trappers rather than the trader, generated the resentment of the Indian—not only the Blackfoot, but also other tribes that were normally friendly. Losses among American trappers were considered heavy. Considering all the wilderness hazards in addition to Indian attacks, historical writer Frances Fuller Victor gave the trapper a chance of life of about one in three.[409]

Commenting on trapper-Indian hostility, Victor acknowledged that initially, the relationship could be friendly. However, when the Indian stole what he could not purchase, and the trapper sought punishment, the result was an Indian need for revenge. But the trapper's attitude toward Indian property rights, his exploitation of Indian women, and his instinctive sense of superiority, to say nothing of his propensity for lying, all contributed to the atmosphere of deadly enmity that existed in some areas between the two races. There is no doubt that the white–Indian relationship existing in the Hudson's Bay Company was more mutually beneficial over two centuries, due both to the extensive presence of Métis and the generally enforced company discipline at their posts and in the brigades. It must be remembered that the HBC, under Ogden on the Snake and under the various leaders of the California brigades, followed the same policy—and by trapping as well as trading, generated Indian enmity. The Indians never forgot that their profits would have increased , had they done the trapping, and then traded with the whites. Occasionally, a trapper may have been someone who could not get along in civil society and so escaped to the wilderness. Nevertheless, as we have seen, many upright, thoughtful, and honorable men made up the population of American fur trappers and traders and enhanced Indian participation.

Returning to the Popo Agie mini-rendezvous: Robert Campbell left on July 18, 1829 and headed for St. Louis with forty-five packs of furs. Sublette sent his brother Milton to the Big Horn basin to trap, while he and Smith followed Togwotee Pass across the Wind River Range to Jackson's Hole, and then over Teton Pass to Pierre's Hole, arriving there on August 20 for the 1829 rendezvous. Gowans commented that this must have been a special time for Jedediah Smith, "since most everyone there thought him dead."[410] There was time for reminiscences, and Smith did have $2,400, the result of his two years of western travel.

The fall hunt was truly remarkable by any measure. Sublette led his party to Henry's Fork, and there drove off a Blackfoot attack. Continually harassed, they went to the upper Madison, across the mountains to the Gallatin River, and thence across the Yellowstone River and the Absaroka Range to the Shoshone River and down it to its confluence with the Big Horn, where they met Milton and his forty men. All went to the Wind River to winter.

During the winter of 1829–30, the partners reviewed their situation. As historian John E. Sunder summarized, after four years, they were barely solvent. "They had lost about forty-four men, and by the coming July, 1830, their losses in horses, mules, furs, traps, and equipment would amount to at least $43,500."[411] Profits had suffered from the increased cost of trapping, trading, transportation, and purchase of merchandise, and from salary outlays, business competition, and reduced fur fields. They decided to conduct the 1830 hunt. Sublette, with Black Harris, made another epic trip on snowshoes from their Wind River camp to St. Louis for supplies. They left winter quarters shortly after Christmas and arrived in St. Louis on February 11, 1830. They had hiked more than 1,400 miles, but the trip had been easier, due to milder weather and a more adequate dog-pack train.

On April 10, 1830, Sublette left St. Louis with a different type of brigade. He used ten mule-drawn wagons, each carrying 1,800 pounds, two one-mule dearborns (carriages), twelve head of cattle, and one milk cow. They could have meat until they found the first buffalo. They reached the site of a small rendezvous, just below the junction of the Popo Agie and Wind rivers, on July 16. It had been a good year. Smith, Jackson, and Sublette had made their largest catch, with 170 packs of beaver valued at

$84,499.14. After paying for their supplies, the partners had $17,177.15 each, and $28,000 credit with Ashley.

Early in 1830, Pierre Chouteau Jr. of the Western Department of the American Fur Company launched an expedition to compete with Smith, Jackson, and Sublette. It was led by Andrew Drips and included Lucien Fontenelle and Joseph Robidoux IV. With forty-five men, they left Belleview on the Missouri River on April 30, 1830. Their route was up the Platte and the Sweetwater, and across the Continental Divide at or near South Pass. By June 21 they were camped on the Sandy River, and by June 27 they were on Ham's Fork, near present-day Nutria, Wyoming. Evidently they did not know that Smith, Jackson, and Sublette had designated the junction of the Popo Agie and Wind rivers as the 1830 rendezvous point, about 140 miles away.

From 1771 to about 1870, the large Robidoux family, most of whom were illiterate and kept no journals, was a force to be reckoned with on the fur-trade frontier. Joseph Robidoux III, oldest of the ten children of Joseph II and Catharine Robidoux, was the dominant member of the large fur-trading family, expert in Indian relations, and a genuine mountain man. On this occasion he was a co-leader with Fontenelle and Drips on an AFC expedition to the Rockies to compete with the Rocky Mountain Fur Company.

William H. Vanderburgh, a West Pointer now trading on the Missouri for the Upper Missouri Outfit, was appointed captain by Colonel Leavenworth during the Arikara affair in 1823. At Fort Union, Kenneth McKenzie chose Vanderburgh to lead fifty men from there to Green River in July 1830. Vanderburgh spent the winter on the Powder River, supplied by Etienne Provost from Fort Union. His other activities are apparently unknown until he appeared at the 1832 rendezvous at Pierre's Hole, and participated in the battle of Pierre's Hole. When on July 16, 1830, the Sublette wagons arrived at the rendezvous with their $30,000 worth of trade goods, they created a sensation in the large assembly of trappers.[412] Celebrations, riotous greetings, and general enthusiasm dominated. Fur-trade historians find it difficult to avoid dwelling on the action and color that marked the Rocky Mountain rendezvous. Hafen provided a precise, if restrained, description:

> To [the rendezvous] came fur company caravans from the East, laden with equipment and supplies for hired trappers, and with attractive goods for trade with Indians and independent fur men. The rendezvous was the great occasion of the year for the trapper. Here was opportunity for both barter and recreation. Races and contests of all kinds were arranged; gambling and drinking were indulged in. Beaver skins were money, and with these hairy banknotes all primitive wants could be satisfied. White trappers with Indian wives bedecked their spouses with bright cloth and gewgaws. Most of these Mountain Men were of the openhanded sort who in a few days of prodigal living squandered the earnings of a year. Indian bands came in, set up their lodges, and participated in the wilderness fair. Indeed, the rendezvous was a market day, a fiesta, a carousal, all in one.[413]

The partners—Smith, Jackson, and Sublette—after considering their fur returns and the cost of the 1830 expedition, realized they had enough to pay their notes to Ashley and to provide each of them with a small profit. "Perhaps they could...prepare and send annual supply trains to the rendezvous; then trade, carry, and sell beaver caught by others.... They were weary of cutthroat competition with British fur parties, and of confusion in the Indian administration as reflected in the West....They knew the American Fur Company was broadening its mountain operations....Astor meant business...he meant monopoly."[414] In addition, the three partners had long been away from civilization's comforts and from family. Farming was attractive. They decided to sell out and dissolve their partnership.

On August 4, 1830, Smith, Jackson, and Sublette sold their company to Thomas Fitzpatrick, James Bridger, Milton Sublette, Henry Fraeb, and Jean Baptiste Gervais, who called their new partnership the Rocky Mountain Fur Company (RMFC). Fitzpatrick, who was then thirty-one, and had excelled as a trapping brigade leader, was also clearly the best financial manager and leader. The new partners making up the Rocky Mountain Fur Company agreed to pay upwards of $16,000 to Smith, Jackson, and Sublette on or before June 15, 1831.

Thomas Fitzpatrick, who headed the new Rocky Mountain Fur Company, was born in Ireland in 1799 and got a good fundamental education. He was in America by age seventeen, and at twenty-four joined Ashley's party on the Missouri and fought the Arikaras. In 1835, he and his partners bought Fort William (Fort Laramie). When the Rockies' fur trade faded, he became a guide for missionaries and for General Kearney. In 1846, he was appointed Indian agent for the upper Platte and Arkansas region. Little Raven, an Arapahoe chief, said in 1865 that he had but one fair agent. That was Major Fitzpatrick. Fitzpatrick died of pneumonia in Washington, D.C., on February 7, 1864.[415]

The old partners Smith, Jackson, and Sublette then left the Popo Agie, and following their outbound trail, arrived in St. Louis on October 10. Returning with them were fifty to seventy men, many pack horses and mules, ten wagonloads of peltries, the remaining cattle, and the milk cow. Their arrival was a celebrated public event of note. They settled their accounts with Ashley and the estates of three killed trappers. They had accomplished a monumental first: taking wagons across the overland trail and the Continental Divide. The road to Oregon was largely open.

Apparently aware of some of the significance of their accomplishment, on October 29, they wrote to Secretary of War John H. Eaton. The letter described the feasibility of a wagon route across the Rockies via the South Pass. "Our men were all healthy during the whole time: we suffered nothing by the Indians, and had no accident but the death of one man....Of the mules, we lost but one by fatigue, and two horses stole by the Kanzas Indians; the grass being, along the whole route going and coming, sufficient for the support of the horses and mules." The wagons carried about eighteen hundred pounds each. "The usual progress of the wagons was from fifteen to twenty five miles per day....This is the first time that wagons ever went to the Rocky mountains; and the ease and safety with which it was done prove the facility of communicating over-land with the Pacific ocean."

The letter further described HBC's Fort Vancouver, its population, services available, and marine activity; it was apparently a permanent facility. Further they described the relatively efficient and aggressive HBC trapping and trading system, which they believed produced about thirty thousand beaver skins annually. They explained that "the object of this communication being to state facts to the Government, and to show the facility of crossing the continent to the Great Falls of the Columbia with wagons, the ease of supporting any number of men by driving cattle to supply them where there was no buffalo, and also to show the true nature of the British establishments on the Columbia, and the unequal operation of the convention of 1818."[416]

The new Rocky Mountain Fur Company, as Chittenden commented,[417] is difficult to trace because its numerous bands of trappers penetrated the entire mountain region. A few of the more prominent efforts after the 1830 rendezvous will describe their general pattern. The RMFC dispersed from the Wind River-Popo Agie rendezvous site. Fraeb and Gervais took about thirty men, plus ten free Iroquois and their women and children, back to the Snake River valley. There they encountered friendly opposition in the person of Joseph Robidoux of the AFC, and soon ran into HBC's John Work. They trapped together, though some of the Iroquois left Fraeb and Gervais and joined Robidoux. Fraeb and Gervais made their way back to Cache Valley to winter, where they found four feet of snow.

At the same time, RMFC partners Fitzpatrick, Milton Sublette, and Jim Bridger, with eighty men, ventured again into the Big Hole country and trapped the Three Forks region. They had a successful hunt and safely reached the Yellowstone. Early in March, Fitzpatrick and one other left for St. Louis to purchase the supplies to be delivered at the 1831 rendezvous, planned for Cache [also referred to as Willow] Valley. They arrived in Lexington in early May. During the trip, the eighty-man RMFC party moved to the Tongue River, where the Crow stole fifty-seven horses. In a counterattack, the trappers got them back. After moving to the Powder River, Milton Sublette went to North Park, headwaters of the Platte, and Bridger went to the headwaters of the Laramie Fork. After rejoining, they went to the Snake River and then to Cache Valley to wait for Fitzpatrick and the supplies.

In St. Louis, Fitzpatrick found that Smith and William Sublette had left for Santa Fe with twenty-three wagons loaded with supplies. He joined them, hoping to get supplies in Santa Fe and move them to the RMFC. This was the trip to Santa Fe on which Jedediah Smith was killed by Comanches.[418]

South of the Arkansas River, Fitzpatrick, riding away from the caravan, discovered a small, emaciated Indian boy. Fitzpatrick took him to the wagons, and with proper food and care, he recovered. Fitzpatrick named him Friday and sent him to school in St. Louis. He later returned to his family among the Arapahoe.

The wagon train arrived in Santa Fe on July 4. Fitzpatrick bought $6,000 of their supplies and hauled them northward along the front range of the Rockies with a forty-man pack train and the newly enlisted trapper, Kit Carson.

While waiting for Fitzpatrick, his partners had conducted their spring hunt and returned to Cache Valley to await his arrival. There were large numbers of men in the mountains in those years and a strong demand for the goods at each rendezvous. They needed blankets and were desperate for ammunition, knives, and traps. But worst of all, the tobacco had given out. On the advice of a Crow medicine man, Fraeb left to find Fitzpatrick. They met on the North Platte in late summer. Fitzpatrick returned immediately to St. Louis for the next year's supplies, and Fraeb returned to Cache Valley with Fitzpatrick's load.

Meanwhile, Milton Sublette and Jim Bridger had embarked on their fall hunt. They were aware that in their intended hunting area were forty HBC men, thirty AFC men, and numerous independents. They moved north to the Snake River Plain, then farther to or near the present-day Salmon River. After crossing the Bitterroot Mountains, possibly by Lost Trail Pass, they reached the Deer Lodge valley, then traveled west and northwest until they had passed Flathead Lake and arrived at the headwaters of the North Fork of the Flathead River. They returned to Salmon River to winter, and there found the Flathead and Nez Percé, and finally the supplies obtained by Fraeb. They wintered with the Flathead and Nez Percé, and during a winter Blackfoot attack, lost four or five men.

In St. Louis that winter of 1831–32, Fitzpatrick ran into credit difficulties; the Rocky Mountain Fur Company had not been able to bring in beaver packs, they were still in the mountains. Fitzpatrick finally agreed with William Sublette's terms to take supplies westward in the spring counting on RMFC being able to settle at the 1832 rendezvous.

Sublette and Bridger also found the party of Andrew Drips with forty-eight men of the AFC. Vanderburgh, leading fifty men from Fort Union, was wintering in Cache Valley. In the spring of 1832, the various companies kept in mind the rendezvous to be held at Pierre's Hole and maneuvered so as to be there for the trading. Rivalry was keen. The AFC had the money, and the RMFC the knowledge. As Meek reported:

The American Company's resident partners were ignorant of the country, and were greatly at a loss where to look for the good trapping grounds. These gentlemen, Vanderburg and Dripps [*sic*], were therefore inclined to keep an eye on the movements of the Rocky Mountain Fur Company, whose leaders were acquainted with the whole region lying along the mountains, from the head-waters of the Colorado to the northern branches of the Missouri....The rival company had a habit of turning up in the most unexpected places, and taking advantage of the hard-earned experience of the Rocky Mountain Company's leaders. They tampered with the trappers, and ferreted out the secret of their next rendezvous; they followed on their train, making them pilots to the trapping grounds; they sold goods to the Indians, and what was worse, to the hired trappers.[419]

The RMFC was facing increased competition, fewer furs, greater supply costs, and evidence of a depressed market.

In the winter of 1831–32, Andrew Drips' American Fur Company party was very active. Drips, a trapper for forty years, led forces of the AFC's Western Department and provided the RMFC its most significant competition. But he was universally held in high regard by both Indians and whites. Regardless of the AFC's desire to follow and imitate the RMFC parties, a detailed report of travels of various detachments of Drips' organization in Warren E. Ferris's *Life in the Rockies* reveals that the AFC as well as the RMFC frequented the valleys of the Yellowstone and the Snake, Cache Valley, the Green River and Salmon River tributaries, the Clark Fork system including the Flathead River, and occasionally the Missouri headwaters. Both companies' trappers often visited the sources of beaver in the Rockies. After HBC's Ogden had repeatedly "stripped" the Snake River, the RMFC and AFC still found profitable trapping there.

In early March 1832, Bridger led his party across Lemhi Pass into Horse Prairie and to Red Rock Creek, which, because of the Blackfoot, had not been trapped. Then he crossed Monida Pass to Grey's Lake. Ferris, with the AFC, reported that on May 15, 1832, "In a narrow bottom, beneath the walls of Grey's Creek, we found a party of trappers, headed by [James] Bridger. Their encampment was decked with hundreds of beaver skins, now drying in the sun....There were [in addition] several hundred skins folded and tied up in packs."[420] Bridger informed the visitors that Vanderburgh, coming from the Yellowstone and wintering in Cache Valley, had had a Blackfoot attack, with four men slain and four others missing. Vanderburgh was scheduled to meet Drips at Bear Lake, then both would go to the rendezvous scheduled for Pierre's Hole.

The trapping parties were assembling. William Sublette had been en route from Independence, Missouri, since May 13, 1832. With him were fifty men as well as Thomas Fitzpatrick, Robert Campbell, and young Andrew Sublette. Nathaniel Wyeth had also joined at Independence. At Laramie Creek they met the bankrupt firm of John Gantt and Jefferson Blackwell, and from them obtained 150 beaver skins, which they cached. Near South Pass, Sublette's train met some of Drips' and Fontenelle's men who had just lost horses to an Indian raid. Fitzpatrick advanced alone to check the location of Indian tribes.

Sublette reached Pierre's Hole on July 8, the only supplier to arrive. Fitzpatrick was missing. At Pierre's Hole, Sublette found representatives of the HBC, the AFC, the RMFC, some independents, Nathaniel Wyeth—all together about a thousand people, including Nez Percé and Flatheads who were allies of the RMFC—and two thousand to three thousand horses. Another trader, Robert Newell, counted about six hundred Indians and whites. Ninety AMC trappers under Vanderburgh and Drips were waiting for supplies being brought by Fontenelle from the east and Provost from Fort Union. But Provost made it no farther than Green River, where he came into contact with Fontenelle and Bonneville.

Competition between the AFC and RMFC people was keen. They used different camps, though probably for the need to find forage. [421]

After Captain Sublette's goods were opened and distributed among the trappers and Indians As Joe Meek told, "the usual gay carousal began, and the "fast young men" of the mountains out-vied each other in all manner of mad pranks. In the beginning of their spree, they exhibited many feats of horsemanship and personal strength, which were regarded with admiring wonder by the sober and inexperienced New Englanders under Wyeth's command. And as nothing stimulated the vanity of the mountain men like an audience of this sort, the feats they performed were apt to astonish even themselves. In exhibitions of the kind, the free trappers took the lead and usually carried off the palm, [prize] like the privileged class they were."[422]

In the meantime, Fitzpatrick underwent a death-defying ordeal, later described by George Nidever. Sublette had lost his second in command, Thomas Fitzpatrick, "while crossing Green River. Having gone in advance to reconnoiter, he was cut off by Indians and so hard pressed that he was obliged to abandon his horse and take to the rocks." While out hunting, Nidever and another trapper "met Fitzpatrick crossing the Lewis Fork. He had, by great chance found a saddled and bridled horse that had wandered from Pierre's Hole, but he was shoeless, hatless, and almost naked....For ten days or thereabouts he had wandered about, having in that time eaten no food excepting a very small piece of dried meat."[423]

The 1832 Pierre's Hole rendezvous is more famous for the "battle of Pierre's Hole," actually a skirmish with the Gros Ventres Blackfoot tribe, than for the trade. On July 17, as RMFC trappers left for the Lewis River, they noted an apparently hostile Indian band. A chief came forward, unarmed as sign of peace. Going forward to meet him was Antoine Godin, an Iroquois half-breed, orphaned by the Blackfoot earlier, and with him a Flathead. As the visitor offered his hand, Godin told the Flathead to shoot. The chief fell dead.

The battle followed. The Gros Ventres made a brush and cottonwood-log barricade. Under William Sublette's and Robert Campbell's leadership, the trappers crept close and attacked. Wyeth, realizing that his men were not expert at Indian warfare, had them entrench themselves behind their packs. Later they were very helpful in treating the wounded. He then participated in the battle, leading a group of Nez Percé, and as Joe Meek described the battle, conducted himself with credit.[424] William Sublette was wounded in the arm and shoulder, and Campbell dragged him to safety. Sinclair, leading some free trappers, was killed. Milton Sublette sent a messenger back to the camps for reinforcement, but the day was late, and the Gros Ventres, seeing increasing numbers of enemies, withdrew in darkness, leaving ten dead. The trappers returned to the main camps to nurse their wounded and aid their recovery.

William Sublette left Pierre's Hole with a detailed agreement signed by Fitzpatrick. He had 169 packs, which were the RMFC catch for two years, amounting to 13,719 pounds of beaver, 247 pounds of beaver castoreum, and a few muskrat and otter skins. Sublette charged $.50 per pound for transportation, and after arriving in St. Louis, prepared the pelts for market and began sales. Other charges were 6 percent to 10 percent for interest, 1.5 percent for transport and fire insurance, and cleaning, packaging, and dealer's commissions. Sublette was to pay all the men's wages. The total income from sales was $58,305.75. The specific obligations from various notes to Sublette, including the cost of supplies bought at Pierre's Hole and those that Fitzpatrick bought in Santa Fe, and to Smith, Jackson, and Sublette, stated in the agreement, were $46,751.13. When all charges were accounted for, the RMFC was still in debt to Sublette, who charged 8 percent on the outstanding obligation. This illustrates the grip that Sublette then had on the RMFC.[425]

Campbell—who had escorted the wounded William Sublette away from Pierre's Hole on July 30, partly recovered but with one arm in a sling—arrived in St. Louis on October 3, 1832. There, the men formed the partnership of Sublette and Campbell, effective January 1, 1833, a partnership that lasted until 1842.[426] Their intent was to supply the trappers in the mountains, buy their furs, and set up posts on the upper Missouri in competition with the AFC. In December and January, they traveled to conduct business in New York, and to visit Campbell's brother Hugh in Philadelphia and Ashley in Washington, D.C. Ashley's support of Campbell and Sublette in Congress resulted in their acquiring considerable bank credit.

In New York, they contracted for hardware and arranged for sales of furs with Ashley's broker, Frederick A. Tracy. During the winter, they planned their campaign against the Upper Missouri Outfit. Campbell was to take supplies to the 1833 rendezvous, and Sublette, with loaded keelboats, was to ascend the Missouri and establish posts opposing each UMO post, seeking to out-trade with the Indian tribes. Their final post was to be opposite Fort Union. There Campbell was to meet Sublette on his return from the rendezvous.

While there were many trading and trapping activities in the Rockies during 1832–33, the most significant historical theme among Americans was the ruthless efforts of the AFC brigades to destroy the RMFC and capitalize on its knowledge and skills. So serious was Fitzpatrick's and Bridger's concern about AFC competition, and believing that there were enough furs for both, the two proposed to Vanderburgh and Drips at the 1832 rendezvous that the Rocky Mountain Fur Company trap only east of the mountains, and the AFC trap only west. The AFC leaders turned them down, because, as Chittenden guessed, the newcomers preferred to use their experienced rivals to pilot them to the best beaver country.[427] While the AFC trappers had the advantage of greater financial and market backing, the RMFC had the advantage of greater knowledge of Indian attitudes and the probable location of profitable beaver communities.

AFC trappers Drips and Vanderburgh missed getting their supplies at Pierre's Hole. They traveled to join Fontenelle on Green River, assuming he was bringing the supplies and expecting him to receive their furs. They made successful contact, and Fontenelle headed for Fort Union on August 12 with the furs and a thirty-man pack train. Vanderburgh, Drips, and fifty men quickly returned to Pierre's Hole to take up the trail of Fitzpatrick and Bridger, who had left on July 31, headed for Blackfoot country.[428]

Leaving Pierre's Hole, Fitzpatrick and Bridger had crossed the Snake River plain to the northwest, ascended the Lemhi valley, and crossed Lemhi Pass to the Big Hole in southwestern Montana. Believing that Drips' AFC trappers were following them, they moved north through the Deer Lodge valley and onto Clark's Fork. A reasonable route would have been to follow the Blackfoot River to present-day Rogers Pass, then take the Dearborn River and the Sun River to the present-day Craig, Montana. By September 14, they were on the Missouri, halfway between Helena and Great Falls. There, Vanderburgh, Drips, and their trappers caught up. The two groups camped together, 150 to 200 men, all starving in a location where there were too many men for the available game.[429]

As an early fall sleet storm settled in, Bridger urged all to move southeast to the three forks of the Missouri River. The two camps "followed a road, composed of several trails, a few feet asunder, which was evidently much used by the Blackfeet." They reached the present-day Pipestone Creek, a tributary of the Jefferson River—probably near Whitehall, Montana, and following the present route of U.S. Highway 287 and Montana State Highway 69.[430]

Drips and company headed up the Jefferson, and Bridger's RMFC crew went up the Gallatin. Jim Bridger's biographer, J. Cecil Alter, wrote that "Vanderburgh…had a few years' trapping experience to his credit… there were few furs to be found on Bridger's trail. With the instincts of a gentleman and the initiative of a freeman, Vanderburgh broke away entirely, on September 16, with a force of about fifty men, to operate on his own."[431]

Drips, with fifty of his AFC men, continued southwest along the Ruby River, camping on October 3 near Black Butte. On October 7, seeking meat, they went east ten miles in another snowstorm to the Madison River. The RMFC had trapped the Gallatin and crossed to the Madison.

Ferris reported that on October 14, Vanderburgh and his party camped while traveling from the Madison valley west to an area at about present-day Alder, Montana. Vanderburgh, Pilou, Ferris, and four others left camp to investigate signs of a large Indian force. They were met by the Blackfoot, and in the skirmish, Vanderburgh and Pilou were killed and Ferris wounded. Ferris wrote, expressing his esteem: "Thus fell William Henry Vanderburgh, a gentleman born in Indiana, educated at West Point in the Military Academy.…Bold, daring and fearless, yet cautious, deliberate and prudent… a soldier and a scholar, he died universally beloved and regretted by all who knew him."[432]

Vanderburgh's party, greatly alarmed, retreated westward toward Beaverhead Rock, raised their caches in Horse Prairie, the valley west of present-day Clark Canyon Reservoir, and built a barricade in anticipation of an attack. There they discovered a large Indian encampment of Flathead, whom they promptly joined. By moving to the area of what is now Clark Canyon Reservoir, they rejoined Drips' main party, and then they all left for the Snake River plain to winter. There they discovered that the periodic Blackfoot-Snake war had erupted. Moving around to find warmer weather and grass, they finally, by January 1, 1833, were camped at the forks of the Snake.

In late October 1832, the RMFC, led by Bridger, had moved from the Madison to the Jefferson headwaters, where they met a party of Piegan, who, according to them, had instructions from McKenzie at Fort Union to make peace with the trappers. They displayed a white flag to show their intentions and warned of a large party of Bloods on the warpath. The Piegans' intention was to cross the mountains and exterminate the Flathead, but they were going to kill and rob the whites no more. About a hundred Bloods appeared on October 25, approaching under a white flag. Bridger advanced to the Blood chief and, suddenly suspicious, cocked his rifle. The chief grabbed the rifle, and in the ensuing scramble, the gun fired harmlessly, but Bridger was unhorsed and collected two arrowheads. He carried one in his hip for nearly three years until Dr. Whitman at Walla Walla removed it in August 1835. Evidently the chief took off with the saddled horse as the Bloods departed.[433]

The RMFC men continued their trapping, particularly in the Beaver Head part of Big Hole, and took many skins before heading for winter quarters in the Salmon River valley, where they encountered Captain Bonneville building a small fort, and many friendly Flathead and Nez Percé.

Fitzpatrick left Bridger on the upper Lemhi and departed for the mouth of the Blackfoot River, where there was better forage for their large herd of horses. He was accompanied by Bonneville's Joe Walker, who had also been at Horse Prairie. Milton Sublette, having been almost to Walla Walla, joined Bridger on the Lemhi in early November. Here all RMFC partners were together. Leaving Bridger, Sublette moved to the mouth of the Portneuf River for the rest of the 1832–33 winter, partly, according to Joseph Meek, because his wife, a Snake woman, lived there. According to Victor, Meek was interested because, after Milton Sublette died a couple of years later, Meek married Mrs. Sublette.[434]

In January 1833, when all partners of the RMFC were together, they planned the spring activities in anticipation of the 1833 rendezvous to be held on the Green River. They sent Henry Fraeb eastward in the hope that he would meet Campbell and the RMFC supplies. Fitzpatrick would take charge of furs and supplies on hand and accompany Fraeb as far as the Green River. He would then trap on Black's Fork and nearby streams. Bridger was to trap on the tributaries of the Madison River in what is now Yellowstone Park. He returned by way of Shoshone Lake, Snake River, Jackson's Hole, and southward in Hoback Canyon, to the rendezvous site on the Green River. Milton Sublette, after recovering from a stab wound to his foot, traveled the Big Lost River with Gervais to the Malade River trapping areas.

Indian women played an important part of the fur trade everywhere, but not much has been written about their womanly behavior. Around trapper campfires, there were continuous tales of the wiles of Indian women, which Washington Irving, in his *Bonneville,* tells about. On July 7, 1822, a young Nez Percé woman "strode into the trappers' midst, and quietly seated herself, still holding her horse by a long tether. When asked 'Why?' she said, 'I love the whites, I will go with them.' She was assigned a lodge, and from then on she was one of the camp."[435]

According to another rendezvous tale, Robert Newell, known as "Doctor," won a woman on a wager. On hearing that his Flathead wife was coming with McLeod's party, he said he must get rid of the woman. Accordingly he went and sold her to her previous owner for one hundred dollars.[436]

Eventually the rendezvous of 1833, on the Green River near present-day Daniel, Wyoming, became the center of attention, and apparently all who could make it were there. As Washington Irving described it, "The three rival companies, which, for a year past had been endeavoring to out-trade, out-trap, and out-wit each other, were here camped in close proximity....Never did rival lawyers, after a wrangle at the bar, meet with more social good humor at a circuit dinner. The hunting season over, all past tricks and manoeuvers were forgotten, all feuds and bickerings buried in oblivion."[437]

The greatest excitement came from an attack by mad wolves. Some men and horses were bitten; some of these died in agony of hydrophobia. But despite this distraction and spread of wild concern, important business was conducted.

During this rendezvous, there were two agreements of importance. The first was between Robert Campbell and William Sublette, in which they formally formed a company. "The terms were: 1. The name shall be 'Sublette and Campbell'. 2. Expenses to be mutually furnished, starting with $3000 in cash. Partners may charge interest at 6% on any unfunded surplus. 3. Each party would devote personal attention to the promotion of the joint business during its life. 4. losses equally sustained and profits divided equally."[438]

The other agreement was between the RMFC and Edmund T. Christy, who had come out with Campbell. This firm was to last for one year, and was to be called "Rocky Mountain Fur Company and Christy." The Rocky Mountain Fur Company would contribute horses, mules, and merchandise worth $6,607.82, which was half the value of the company. The twelve men hired would be paid jointly. Furs would be sold at $3.25 per pound, and would be delivered within fifty miles of the rendezvous site. Costs and profits were to be equally shared. Christy would devote his personal services to the company.[439]

The addition of Christy's funds and efforts did not rescue the Rocky Mountain Fur Company from financial pressures. The partnership of Sublette and Campbell had such control over supplies, transportation, and fur sales that they absorbed any possibility of profit for Fitzpatrick,

Milton, Sublette, Bridger, and Christy. After a relatively short life, at the 1834 rendezvous, partners Fraeb and Gervais sold out, and the remaining partners formed a company named Fitzpatrick, Sublette, and Bridger. They took on all of the former company's obligations. When in 1836 Milton Sublette died, Fitzpatrick and Bridger went to work for the AFC.

Hiram Chittenden wrote a very commendatory obituary for the Rocky Mountain Fur Company. He believed that the RMFC, by devoting itself to procuring, rather than trading for beaver, had in effect opened up the west. It had shipped to St. Louis more than a thousand packs of beaver worth about $500,000, losing in the process a hundred lives and supplies worth $100,000. But the partners never made much money. As Chittenden said in closing:

> As a school of adventure the Rocky Mountain Fur Company had no parallel among the business concerns of the mountains. The campaign with the Arikaras...the wanderings of Jedediah Smith, the battle of Pierre's Hole, and innumerable other romantic incidents have made famous the career of this notable company....But perhaps the most important service which the company rendered was as a school for the education of those who were later to assist the government in the exploration of the West. It was to the old members and employees of the Rocky Mountain Fur Company that the government looked mainly for its guides."[440]

CHAPTER 16:

AMERICAN ROCKIES COMPETITION

Nathaniel J. Wyeth, a Boston ice broker, organized a stock company in Cambridge, Massachusetts, in 1831 to take a trapping expedition to the Rockies. Candidly reporting its possible failure in letters to potential supporters and contributing $5,000 himself, he obtained sufficient financing for the trip to Oregon.

The idea of making a fortune in the West was not new to the Bostonian. Hal Kelley, a Boston schoolteacher, had talked endlessly to promote Oregon settlement and greatly influenced Wyeth, at heart an imaginative, idealistic entrepreneur. The courage, determination, and adaptability Wyeth later demonstrated earned respect among American mountain men and the British alike. However, his grasp of geography was so vague that he did not learn until 1832 that his route to Oregon would not go through Santa Fe. He had literally no idea of the life he would lead in western fur-trade country, though he had long been concerned about the apparent British hegemony in Oregon.

On March 10, 1832, Wyeth left Boston with twenty-five men, including a bugler to provide marching music, and by canal boat, railroad, walking, and steamboat, arrived at Independence, Missouri, in time to leave "for the prairies" on May 12. With desertions and additions, he then had a party of twenty-one. Of them, "only eight men of the original party completed the trip [to Oregon], the others deserted or died of exposure, starvation or wounds."[441]

Once in Missouri, Wyeth and his men spent the next two weeks preparing and becoming aware of their unfitness for the trip. Fortunately, William L. Sublette, heading west with a supply expedition, came to their aid. Fearing no competition, "he therefore lent them a ready hand... and offered them the protection of his own party.... To the more timid this unexpected assistance seemed providential and they gave it an exaggerated importance which we may be sure the stubborn Wyeth did not."[442]

Also in St. Louis, planning a trapping expedition to start the following April, was Army Captain Eulalie de Bonneville, a native of France, born on April 14, 1796, and a graduate of West Point. In his company, he had Joseph Reddeford Walker and Michael Sylvestre Cerré, both experienced mountain men. Bonneville had secured a leave of absence for two years from the Army, and in addition, many believe he had been instructed to collect any information that might be useful to the U.S. government.[443] Bonneville led 110 men, 20 wagons drawn by oxen and mules, and a very complete inventory of trade goods and supplies. His financial backing is unknown.

Captain Bonneville left Fort Osage on May 1, 1832, traveled up the Platte and Sweetwater, arriving at the mouth of Horse Creek on the Green River on July 27. Here he built a traditional fur trade fort, bastions and all. It was known as Fort Bonneville, which trappers called "Fort Nonsense" because it was little used. The elevation and cold at Fort Bonneville forced him to disperse his livestock to Bear River for grazing, and to spend the summer moving the rest of the herd through Jackson's Hole, about 250 miles northwest, to the mouth of the Lemhi River in Idaho, arriving at the end of September. There he cached a substantial part of his goods and built another post, little more than shelter. He dispatched three parties to hunt in various directions, all mostly unsuccessful. He did not attend the 1832 Pierre's Hole rendezvous.

Wyeth's route to the 1832 rendezvous must have seemed long and tortuous, though it was a well-known trapper and trader trail. It led up the Platte River, the Sweetwater River, across South Pass, the headwaters of the Green River, and the Hoback River to Jackson's Hole, and along the Snake to Pierre's Hole, which they reached on July 8. Wyeth had learned of the vastness of the country, the skills of the mountain men, the attacks, wiles, and culture of the Indians, starvation, buffalo, and the wild and generous nature of the trappers.

The two hundred Indian lodges, ninety American Fur Company trappers, a hundred of the Rocky Mountain Fur Company men, many free trappers, and two thousand to three thousand horses must have provided a shocking and disquieting spectacle. Since the origin of William Ashley's mountain trapper system, where he both organized the trappers and brought in the supplies, these two functions had split apart. In 1832, William Sublette, later joined by Robert Campbell, brought supplies to the mountains and purchased the furs produced by the RMFC. The AFC sent supplies to their trappers. At this rendezvous, all groups met for the exchange of furs and supplies.

The Wyeth party called a "town meeting" to decide the next step. Wyeth realistically refused to argue and simply asked each man if he wished to go on. All but eleven of his men decided to join others, or to return to St. Louis. Wyeth wrote, "While here I obtained 18 horses in exchange for those which were worn out and for a few toys such as Beads and Blue cloth, Powder and Balls, fish hooks vermillion, old Blanketts. We also supplied ourselves with Buffaloe robes we have now a good outfit and here we found plenty of meat which can be had of the Indians for a trifle."[444] Wyeth's journal, reflecting keen observation of everything around him, his aspirations, and his philosophical ruminations, is a principal source of a contemporary 1832 view of the Indian culture and the fur trade it supported in "the Oregon country."

The loss of his men, although disappointing, apparently did not lessen Wyeth's determination. With his eleven men, he headed southwest on July 24 and crossed the Snake River Range, probably on Pine Creek Pass, which is present-day State Highway 31. By August 5, he was at the mouth of the Portneuf River, near present-day Pocatello, Idaho, following Milton Sublette, Fraeb, Gervais, and their trappers. At that point, he left the Snake River trails and camped on the Raft River on August 14. He commented that it was so dry that percussion caps could not be left in guns in daytime—only at night—or they would go off. This is an important observation, because it indicates the degree to which trappers coming into fur-trapping country had shifted from the flintlock to the percussion-cap rifle. Wyeth continued south of Burley, Idaho, along Goose Creek, which, as he discovered, the HBC had trapped out. He was enthusiastic about the wild service berries and raspberries he found.

Returning to the Snake at the mouth of the Bruneau River, Wyeth noted the good, well-used Indian trail. His course took him along the Owyhee River and back to the Malheur River junction. He trapped up the Malheur for fifty miles, and on returning to the Snake, encountered Milton Sublette and Fraeb of RMFC. He reached Walla Walla on the October 14, and enjoyed the hospitality of P. C. Pambrun, the Hudson's Bay Company clerk in charge. Leaving his horses with Pambrun, he took an HBC barge downriver, and after experiencing the portages at The Dalles and the Cascades, reached Fort Vancouver on October 29. There, the merchant from Boston was impressed and delighted with the gracious and generous hospitality of Chief Factor McLoughlin.

With future projects in mind, Wyeth explored the lower Columbia as far as Astoria, and with the continuing assistance of HBC people, canoed up the Willamette River, portaging the falls. He was much impressed by the valley's richness and the farming success of retired Canadian fur traders.

Wyeth and his men spent the wet, cold winter at Fort Vancouver, and in December he noted that the HBC was building a fort at the mouth of the Nass River in Milbank Sound to compete with American ship-masters. Losing their faith in Wyeth's project, all of his men decided to leave him and work for the HBC for maintenance, until they could find a way home. Wyeth joined HBC employee Francis Ermatinger, who at McLoughlin's direction was heading a trapping expedition to the Flathead country. They canoed up the Columbia and reached Walla Walla on February 14, 1833. Leaving the canoes, he retrieved his horses from Pambrun, and with Ermatinger, was at Fort Colvile by March 26.

Ermatinger's first destination was Flathead Post, near present-day Thompson Falls. He traveled by boat, and Wyeth by horseback. Wyeth arrived on April 7 and Ermatinger five days later. Wyeth was enchanted by the Clark Fork—then called the Flathead—valley: "This valley is the most romantic place imaginable a level plain two miles long by 1 mile wide on the N a range of rocky and snow clad mts. On the S. the Flathead River a rapid current and plenty of good fishing."[445]

Despite the specific command of the HBC Governor and Committee to remain west of the Continental Divide, McLoughlin's orders to Ermatinger were to trap the headwaters of the Missouri. On April 22 they left Flathead Post, and a week later, were at the great Flathead camp near present-day Missoula. Wyeth found the Flatheads, whom he greatly admired, in turmoil over Blackfoot horse raids and attacks, and in preparation for counterattacks into Blackfoot and buffalo country. He found a camp "of 110 lodges, upward of 1000 souls with all of which I had to shake hands…with men, women and children a tedious job." He observed others arriving in preparation for the Blackfoot reprisal and

buffalo hunting. Wyeth wrote in detail about the Indian hand game and
their courteous sportsmanship. The Sabbath was carefully observed. His
journal leaves a valuable record of Flathead Indian life:

> Theft is a thing almost unknown among them and is punished by flogging
> as I am told but have never known an instance of theft among them the
> least thing even to a bead or pin is brought you if found and things that
> we throw away this is sometimes troublesome. I have never seen an Indian
> get in anger with each other or strangers. I think you find among 20 whites
> as many scoundrels as among 1000 of these Indians they have a mild play-
> ful laughing disposition and their qualities are strongly portrayed in their
> countenances. They are polite and unobtrusive and however poor never beg
> except as pay for services and in this way they are moderate and faithful but
> not industrious. They are very brave and fight the Blackfeet who continu-
> ally steal their horses and kill their strag[g]lers with great success beating
> hollow equal numbers. They wear as little clothing as the weather will
> permit. The women are close covered and chaste never cohabiting promis-
> cuously with the men. The young women are good looking and with dress
> and cleanliness would be lovely today about one hundred of them with
> their root diggers in their hands in single file went out to get roots they
> staid about two hours and returned in the same order each time passing
> the chief's lodge....In a lodge or other place, when one speaks the rest pay
> strict attention. When he is done another assents by "yes" or dissents by
> "no" and then states his reasons which are heard as attentively....I have
> never heard an angry word among them [the children] or any quarrelling
> although there are here at least 500 of them together and at play the whole
> time at foot ball bandy and the like sports which give occasion to so many
> quarrels among white children.[446]

Ermatinger's party left the Flathead camp on May 9. Their apparent
route was up the Clark Fork to Deer Lodge country, then south to the

Big Hole, where they camped on "one of the heads of the Missouri."[447] They later crossed Lemhi pass into the Salmon River valley. They were on the Little Lost River by June 2, having been constantly harassed by the Blackfoot. From that point on, they followed a well-used route south to Henry's Fork of the Snake and north through the Hoback Canyon, to the Green River headwaters and Pierre's Hole. By July 15, Wyeth was at Fort Bonneville for the 1833 rendezvous. Wyeth had personally observed the close relationships the Hudson's Bay Company had with the Nez Percé, Flathead, and Kutenai.

For the spring hunt of 1833, Captain Bonneville had sent Cerré to trade with Flathead and Nez Percé (Salish), who also wintered on the Salmon, but without much success. They were firm in their loyalty to the HBC. Bonneville then took a detachment south, intending to trap the Malade (Wood) River. Running into Milton Sublette and J. B. Gervais, also headed for the Malade, dampened his ardor. The snow melted in April, but his hunt was unsatisfactory.

Unfortunately, Bonneville's various dispersed hunting parties in 1833 also met with misfortune. One, led by Antonio Montero and sent to Crow country, was robbed in the exquisitely deceptive Crow style. Some of the men joined the Crow, and some sought protection at Fort Cass, then under veteran AFC trader Samuel Tulloch, who, under AFC policy, probably gave them little. Tulloch's job was to defeat all AFC competition, and it is fair to assume that he had a hand in their robbery by the Crow, as he later was to have in robbing Fitzpatrick.[448]

Bonneville's parties reassembled on the Salmon on June 15 and by mid-July were at the proposed 1833 rendezvous site at Horse Creek. Bonneville had little to show for a year's work—perhaps only twenty-three packs of beaver, most of which he got by trading with AFC and RMFC trappers.

Evidently Ermatinger did not go on to the 1833 rendezvous with his party of twenty-five, for Wyeth wrote that although he would have been proud to show him the exemplary discipline of the American Fur Company and the Campbell RMFC parties, the possibility of robbery exists, and he should not come. "There is a great majority of scoundrels," he said.[449] Wyeth wrote to Ermatinger on the rendezvous business:

> Dripps and Fontenelle arrd July 8th 160 men a good supply of animals.
> Obtained 51 packs of 100 lbs ea Beaver.
> Rocky Mtn Fur Co. 55 packs 55 men well supplied one party not in.
> Beaver sent home by Mr. Campbell.
> Mess. Bonneville & Co. 22 1/2 packs. Few goods few horses and poor
> Capt Cerry [Cerré] goes home B. [Bonneville] Remains.
> Harris party now in hand 7 packs Beaver and are on foot.[450]

After the rendezvous, Bonneville launched the most notable of his accomplishments. He sent Joseph Walker, George Nidever, and Zenas Leonard, among others, to find profit around Salt Lake. Walker's real objective was California.[451]

Joseph Reddeford Walker, a Tennessean and veteran of the Santa Fe Trail, left the Green River rendezvous on July 24, 1833, leading forty of Bonneville's men and about twenty free trappers. He skirted the north shore of Salt Lake and camped on the Humboldt River. To restrain the aggressive thievery of the Digger Indians, he attacked them. The action was criticized as unnecessarily forceful, but Leonard and Nidever later wrote in full support of Walker's action.

Living on starved-lean horse flesh, and usually desperate for water, they finally reached the Sierra Mountains near Carson Lake. Crossing the Sierra, Leonard wrote, "Here we began to encounter...deep chasms which [rivers] through the ages cut in the rocks...some of the precipices appeared to us to more than a mile high." Thus Yosemite Park was discovered. They then found redwood trees, "some of which would measure from sixteen to eighteen fathoms around the trunk at the height of a man's head."[452]

On reaching California, Walker began trapping to make up for their lack of beaver pelts, with yet no possible income. He had also lost both time and horses. He noted California's abundance, friendly Indians, and evidence of white men's earlier presence. On November 20, they reached the Pacific and were delighted to see the American flag at the masthead of the *Lagoda* of Boston. Captain Bradshaw briefed them on California and its people. They were shocked by the Spaniards' cruelty to animals. Zenas Leonard wrote of mules being driven by Santa Fe trappers clear to Missouri, and of the extensive trade in hides and tallow.

On January 13, 1834, now a party of 52 men, 315 horses, 47 beef, and 30 dogs, they started their return to Captain Bonneville. Indians showed them what would later become known as Walker Pass. They traveled up Owen valley to the Humboldt River, and thence to Bonneville's camp at Bear Lake. Bonneville criticized Walker's lack of furs and did not credit him for the geographic information, which was one of Bonneville's stated objectives. Though Bonneville had overstayed his official Army leave, he was reinstated. In spring of 1835, he left Walker and sixty men in country for a year and in 1836 resumed his Army career at Fort Gibbons.

Fred Gowans neatly summarized other activities at the close of the 1833 rendezvous:[453] Robert Campbell and William Sublette were moving forward with their plan to compete with the American Fur Company on the Missouri River. Having traded for beaver at the rendezvous, Campbell asked Fitzpatrick to assist him in taking ten packs of beaver to the mouth of the Yellowstone, where he would meet his partner. William Sublette had spent the summer building Fort William on the upper Missouri, which was designed to provide competition with the AFC at nearby Fort Union. Campbell would then finish the post and remain there. Sublette would take the packs to St. Louis.

The 1832–33 trapping year had produced sixty-two packs of fur for the Rocky Mountain Fur Company, which they sold for $21,000 in St. Louis, leaving them still in debt to Sublette and Campbell for supplies. The increased competition, rising cost of supplies, and lower prices for their beaver made it imperative that supplies arrive on time and at a reasonable cost. As Fitzpatrick and Milton Sublette viewed the competitive activity on the Missouri River, they were also apprehensive about the demands on William Sublette and Campbell's time and feared that the partners would not be able to provide RMFC supplies for the next year.[454]

As a result, Fitzpatrick and Milton Sublette turned to Wyeth, who was determined to return to the Rockies in 1834. On August 14, 1833, Wyeth secretly contracted to supply them with not more than $3,000 worth of goods at the Ham's Fork rendezvous not later than July 1, for which he was to receive $3,521 above the original cost in beaver pelts that were to be valued at $4.00 a pound. If Wyeth could not perform, he would notify Milton Sublette, who would go east for the goods. Both put up a $500 bond.[455]

Near present-day Thermopolis, Wyoming, Campbell, Milton Sublette, Wyeth, Bonneville's Cerré, and other trappers built bullboats and floated down the Big Horn and Yellowstone rivers to the Missouri, arriving there in late August. The trip was trouble-free except for Campbell's upset. As his boat sank, he barely survived, but recovered all but four packs of furs and their arms. From Campbell's journal:

In the Big Horn the [Indian] skin [bull] boat in which I was sunk and I had like to have perished. Thrice I went under water and but for an all wise and all merciful God I should never have seen termination of this year. I got safe to shore and succeeded in recovering all but about 4 packs of Beaver and our arms. Besides I lost my saddle bags etc. I recovered again my boat and next day was joined by all the Crow Indians—and here again I must acknowledge my dependence on God who inclined those

Indians to treat me kindly and return most of my beaver when they had us completely in their power. And I may here observe that those same Indians 17 days after at the American Fur Company, robbed Mr. Fitzpatrick of all he had with him but of themselves afterwards returned animals for nearly all they had taken. I proceeded down to this place where I arrived on the 30th of August and found Mr. Sublette was taken sick. He had barely recovered when he left me on the 20th Sept for St. Louis with the return I had brought down."[456]

Campbell and Milton Sublette and their party started downriver with the furs, leaving Fitzpatrick with another visitor to the rendezvous, Sir William Drummond Stewart, and thirty men for the fall hunt on the Little Big Horn, Powder, and Tongue rivers. They also intended to show Stewart the Absaroka Range, the land of the Crow.

As Hafen reported when writing Fitzpatrick's story,[457] a nearby, apparently friendly camp of Crow robbed Fitzpatrick's camp, taking all the furs and stripping Fitzpatrick. He persuaded the Crow chief, apparently with the aid of Jim Beckwourth, then living with the Crow, to return his clothes, horses, and many traps, with rifles and ammunition. They kept the furs, which later appeared at the AFC's Fort Cass under trader Samuel Tulloch. Fitzpatrick was convinced that the robbery had been inspired by Kenneth McKenzie of the AFC, and the Crow verified it. When asked, McKenzie responded that he would sell the furs to Fitzpatrick for the same price he would ask from anyone else. Fitzpatrick appealed to the then congressman William Ashley, charging AFC agents with theft, and seeking some general government effort to police the competition.

Kenneth McKenzie later wrote Tulloch:

The 43 Beaver skins traded, marked R.M.F. CO., I would in the present instance give up; if Mr. Fitzpatrick wishes to have them, on his paying the price the articles traded for them were worth on their arrival in the

Crow village, and the expense of bringing the beaver in and securing it. My goods are brought into the country to trade and I would as willing dispose of them to Mr. Fitzpatrick as to any one else for beaver or beaver's worth if I get my price. I make the proposal as a favor, not as a matter of right, for I consider the Indians entitled to trade any beaver in their possession to me or to any other trader.[458]

Hafen wrote, "To such depths had the rivalry gone; had degenerated into open robbery and warfare."[459]

Fitzpatrick and his party left the Crows' land, recrossed South Pass, and joined a friendly band of Shoshone on Ham's Fork of the Green River. There in late October, they met Bonneville, who had suffered a similar robbery. Fitzpatrick wrote to Milton Sublette, reporting his current operations. He reported twenty-three packs of beaver, that Fraeb, with Bill Williams as a guide, had gone down the Green River with twenty men, and that he expected to see them March 1. He then wrote:

I have been uneasy ever Since we parted about our arrangements with Wyeth however it may terminate well but still I dread it...we will stand in need of a large supply of Madze [merchandise] at rendezvous as the Spanish companies will meet us there and there is now a party with Fraeb. I wish you to work with Wyeth....Studdy well the articles of profit. Liquor will be much wanted....Come as soon as possible to the rendezvous....I believe they [the Crows] will be hostile to all parties here after. They have good encouragement from the A.F.Co. Perhaps they may not Kill but they will certainly rob all they are able and perhaps Murder also.[460]

When Milton Sublette reached the Missouri with Wyeth, he found his brother, William, and Campbell building Fort William about three miles downriver from Fort Union. It was one of the posts with which they hoped to take control of the upper Missouri fur trade from the Upper

Missouri Outfit of Kenneth McKenzie. Milton Sublette remained with them because of his bad foot and later traveled downriver with William and the furs from the rendezvous in a keelboat. Wyeth traded his bullboats to Kenneth McKenzie at Fort Union for a twenty-foot sailing canoe and headed downriver.[461] It was on this trip that Wyeth, reaching Fort Leavenworth, revealed McKenzie's whiskey still.

Wyeth reached Boston in November. In Boston, his detractors, particularly his kinsman John B. Wyeth, had been busy decrying his 1832 accomplishments. Despite this, Wyeth organized the 1834 expedition in which Henry Hall and the firm of Tucker and Williams invested. Hall organized the Columbia River Fishing and Trading Company, capitalized at $40,000, with Wyeth providing $5,000 for one-quarter of the profit.

Milton Sublette, at Wyeth's urging, went east to help him buy the supplies he had agreed to provide the RMFC in 1834. Wyeth was also looking forward to supplying the RMFC in 1835 by supplies sent round Cape Horn. With Boston financial support, he supplied and sent a ship for that purpose. He believed also that he could ship furs back to New York cheaper by ship than they could be sent overland, figuring $.375 per pound, as opposed to Sublette's $.50. It is possible that Wyeth had underestimated RMFC's financial troubles and the resourcefulness of Sublette and Campbell.

William Sublette, though ill, had descended the Missouri safely with the furs. He then traveled to New York to the offices of the American Fur Company and began negotiations to sell them the Campbell/Sublette posts on the upper Missouri. The AFC was in "bad odor" with the federal government over liquor-law violations and knew that Sublette and Campbell had access to unlimited credit. On February 1, 1834, AFC agreed to retire from the mountain trade for one year, and Sublette and Campbell would relinquish their trade and posts on the upper Missouri. Campbell called this agreement "the partition of Poland."

Campbell at Fort William received word of the arrangement in the spring of 1834, and turned over his posts and trade goods to the UMO at Fort Union. He sent his trappers southwest to the headwaters of the Platte to the site of their new post, soon to be under construction and named Fort William, which became Fort Laramie. With the furs brought down from 1833, Campbell returned to St. Louis.[462] The American Fur Company now completely controlled the trade on the Missouri River.

Having acquired goods for overland travel and a ship to meet him at Astoria, Wyeth began his return to the Rockies. He reached Independence in April 1834, seeking to leave Independence with his supply train and seventy men ahead of William Sublette. With him were Milton Sublette, scientists Thomas Nutall and J. K. Townsend, and missionaries under Jason and Daniel Lee. Wyeth's caravan departed on April 28, 1834. Early on, Wyeth suffered the loss of the experienced leadership of Milton Sublette because of illness. More importantly, Wyeth did not know that William Sublette doubted the financial stability of the RMFC. Certainly he did not appreciate William Sublette's determination to not let an easterner beat him in the matter of wilderness travel and supply.[463]

Sublette and Campbell had to get supplies to the 1834 rendezvous before any other supplier, including Wyeth. Sublette was past Independence in early May, and traveling up the Platte, he passed Wyeth in the night. Wyeth soon discovered that Sublette's supply train had passed him. He then sent an express to advise Fitzpatrick that he would arrive with RMFC goods on July 1 as agreed.

Sublette reached the Laramie River on June 1 and joined the construction of a fort he and Campbell hoped would give them an ideal post for trade. He left a party there to build the fort, originally called Fort William,[464] and by June 11, had crossed South Pass. Three days later he was at the 1834 rendezvous site at Ham's Fork.

Wyeth suffered a bitter pill. Sublette had beaten him and he knew it. Arriving on June 20, he found that the RMFC would not accept his goods, "alleging that they were unable to continue business longer, and that they had dissolved, but offered to pay the advances made to M. G. Sublette and the forfeit [$500]."[465] Fitzpatrick had taken his goods from his old friend, Bill Sublette.

Determined to seek revenge, Wyeth moved to the Snake. About twelve miles north of present-day Pocatello, Idaho, he built Fort Hall. The log fort was enclosed by August 5, at which point Wyeth left a few men there and went to Walla Walla, where he rejoined the missionaries and W. D. Stewart. Trapping when possible, he descended the Columbia River on September 14 and met his ship, the *May Dacre*. It had been damaged by lightning and arrived too late for the salmon season. He built Fort William on Sauvies Island in the Columbia, established friendly relations with McLoughlin, and located a farm in the Willamette Valley. All failed. He returned to Fort Hall where he found about six thousand beaver skins that had been traded, but which, at present prices in New York, had little value.

Wyeth returned to Boston via Taos and Bent's Fort, twenty thousand dollars poorer and five years older. He provided the House Committee on Foreign Affairs a long memorandum on the physical and political facts of Oregon, a document that became important in gaining congressional support for the extension of the U.S. boundary along the forty-ninth parallel to the sea. Despite his difficulties, Wyeth was a respected and successful businessman. He died at Cambridge on August 31, 1856.

Historian William Sampson wrote of him: "Wyeth lived to see Oregon become a territory in the Union....Nathaniel Wyeth, engaged in a commercial enterprise that failed, was the unwitting precursor of a movement which was to help destroy the fur trade while gaining Oregon for the United States."[466]

The following sketch of AFC and RMFC movements leading to the 1833 rendezvous and into 1834 illustrates the AFC policy of following the RMFC, but neglects the experiences of the many Indian and independent trappers who also appeared at the rendezvous of 1832, 1833, and 1834.Trappers in the wilderness often sought congenial acquaintances regardless of the company they represented. After the 1832 rendezvous, Fitzpatrick began a long sweep of the Snake River area to find beaver, remaining longest with Andrew Drips of the AFC for the latest news. He spent Christmas at the mouth of the Blackfoot River with Joe Walker, and reached Bridger's camp on the upper Lemhi Valley, probably near present-day Leadore, Idaho, on about New Year's Day 1833.

All AFC trappers met on the Green River near Daniel, Wyoming, by June 8, waiting for Fontenelle to arrive with supplies from Fort Union. As spring came, RMFC parties had followed different routes from their winter camps to the July 1833 rendezvous on Green River. Bridger took a party north to today's Yellowstone Park, then south along the Hoback River to the Green.

Fitzpatrick sent Fraeb east to find Campbell and the supply train, which had left St. Louis early in May, carrying $15,000 of supplies that the RMFC needed. Fraeb met Campbell near the Black Hills of Wyoming, bringing part of the needed supplies. Campbell was moving more slowly, with Benjamin Harrison, son of President Harrison; the Scottish sportsman Sir W. D. Stewart; and Edmund Christy, a potential investor in the RMFC. They soon met Fitzpatrick with six mules loaded with beaver to trade. By the time Campbell reached the rendezvous site on July 5, most of his trade goods were gone. Fontenelle, who brought the AFC supply train from Fort Union, arrived on July 8 and found that Campbell had skimmed off the cream of the trading, benefiting by as much as five packs of beaver.

Drips and Fontenelle, as brigade leaders for the AFC Western Department, and as partners, had done well. Their credit with the

Western Department in June 1832 was $21,841.74, and in February 1833, was added to by $6,768.40. After the rendezvous of 1833, Drips sent Robert Newell to trade with the Flathead while he hunted in the Snake River country. As winter began at the Forks of the Snake, where Newell joined him, he "had many beaver and had lost neither men nor horses."[467]

Edmund Christy led twenty-five men to the Snake River. Fitzpatrick and Milton Sublette, accompanied by Wyeth, traveled with Campbell across South Pass to the Big Horn River. Michael Sylvestre Cerré, formerly of the AFC and one of Bonneville's stalwarts, was taking their meager furs to St. Louis and decided to go by bullboat with Campbell. Campbell had chosen this route because he was scheduled to meet William Sublette at the Missouri and because the Arikara were reported to be raiding on the Platte. However, the veteran man of the mountains, Etienne Provost, took the Platte route anyhow and successfully arrived at Fort Pierre to deliver the AFC furs with no trouble.[468]

William Sublette reached his farm near St. Louis by mid-November, after making business visits en route. There he put Milton in the care of his doctor, a prominent St. Louis physician. Meanwhile, during the winter at Fort William, Campbell confronted McKenzie's ability to draw Indian trade from him. McKenzie was friendly and hospitable, but outsold him at every turn. Illustrating the state of trade on the upper Missouri, McKenzie at Fort Union wrote to James Kipp at Fort Clark on December 17, in part:Our opponents are not idle, they have opened a house near Mr. Chardon [Fort Jackson, a few days' journey above Fort Union]....They are giving a blanket for a robe, and have already partially dressed several Indians. You know that I have hitherto abstained from this procedure but I suppose I shall be driven to it in my own defence and if I begin, I shall do it well...even with the utmost industry & exertion on our part our opponents contrive to get both beaver & robes that should come to us....A few days after my arrival [November 8] Mr. Campbell called upon me to ascertain if I was disposed to buy their Company out....I was somewhat indifferent to Mr. Campbell's proposition & after two interviews the negotiation broke off....Our opponents must get some robes but it is my wish that it should be on such terms as to leave them no profit.[469]

On December 15, he also wrote to Honoré Picotte of UMO, a former partner of his in the Columbia Fur Company, "If we are to be opposed on the river it will be more honorable to break up a formidable Company like our present opponents by dint of extra industry & long tried experience than for them to abandon the trade from other circumstances."[470]Though the AFC men knew of Ashley's and other eastern financiers' support of Sublette, they expected that Astor's resources and their hard work would win.

It is not clear how, where, or why Campbell left Fort William after that difficult winter and before or after the "partition." After a visit to his family in Philadelphia, Campbell made his last trip west. With three companions, he left St. Louis on April 9, 1834, and went to Fort Laramie to complete the sale of the fort and its supplies to a new company, Fontenelle, Fitzpatrick, and Company. He made a rare trip back by boat down the Platte with a load of buffalo robes. It is characteristic of the times that former opponents Fontenelle and Fitzpatrick were now partners.[471]

William Sublette had not given up. Traveling to New York, he benefited from John Jacob Astor's determination to retire, and in June 1834, he agreed for Sublette and Campbell "to give up their trade and posts on the Upper Missouri, in exchange for which the AFC agreed 'to retire from the mountain trade' for one year."[472] This agreement is known as the "partition of Poland." Also in 1834, Astor "sold his western and northern fur departments respectively to his managers, Pratte, Chouteau and Company, and to Ramsay Crooks, and associates."[473]

Though this agreement between Sublette and Campbell and the AFC was a remarkable Sublette accomplishment, it may have been caused, as Sunder believed, by the fact that the AFC was in bad political trouble because of their liquor violations, and because they believed Sublette and Campbell had adequate credit to continue. Sunder wrote, "Thus, Sublette and Campbell must have reached an agreement on strategy before Sublette left Fort William for St. Louis, and the strategy seems to have been that they would both, each in his own area, work for an agreement with the Astor men, cover up their own difficulties, and strike fear into the heart of the American Fur Company."[474]

Fontenelle reported that some of his men were going to Campbell for better pay. He wrote: "Drips has become very popular with the people in this country since last year, and I had hard work to retain him with me....I had to give him (and God knows how I will be able to pay him) fifteen hundred dollars a year to induce him to stay in the country."[475]

The Rocky Mountain Fur Company and Christy was dissolved on July 20, 1834, releasing Fitzpatrick, Milton Sublette, Gervais, and James Bridger from their mutual obligations, and settling, as much as possible, their debt to Sublette and Campbell.

William Sublette left the 1834 rendezvous in early July with seventy packs of beaver. He checked on the progress of the building at Fort William (Laramie), and was home in St. Louis by the end of August. Campbell, with news of the "partition," had settled his sale with McKenzie, and was in St. Louis by August 7.

At the rendezvous, a new company—Fitzpatrick, Sublette, and Bridger—was formed, but it soon expired. Fitzpatrick joined the AFC camp, and on August 1, another new company—Fontenelle and Fitzpatrick—was formed. Andrew Drips, Milton Sublette, and James Bridger were partners. Fontenelle wrote to his backer, Pierre Chouteau, on September 14, 1834:

The heretofore arrangements between him (William Sublette) and Messrs Fitzpatrick, Milton Sublette and others having expired last spring, they concluded not to have anything more to do with William Sublette and it will surprise me very much if he takes more than ten packs down next year. I have entered into a partnership with the others and the whole of the beaver caught by them is to be turned over to us by agreement made with them in concluding the arrangement.[476]

Mountain men remaining in the mountains now had to rely on Sublette and Campbell for at least a year, or to a lesser extent, Hudson's Bay Company, for supplies and for marketing furs and robes. Perhaps more important, the market for beaver, in 1834 and beyond, was fading fast.

The lasting contribution of the Rocky Mountain Fur Company and its contemporary trappers and traders was not in the heroic role of the mountain man, but in the geographic opening of the Rocky Mountain West. As Chittenden put it, "Perhaps the most important service which the company rendered its country was as a school for the education of those who were later to assist the government in the exploration of the West." [477] Albert Gallatin, using information specifically from Ashley and Jedediah Smith, and indirectly from a host of others, drew an 1836 map, which "was to settle many, and in fact nearly all, the important unknown and disputed questions in regard to the geography of the western portion of what is now the United States territory." Accompanying this map was Gallatin's "celebrated Synopsis of the Indian Tribes of North America, which formed the basis of all later work upon the ethnography and philology of the American Indians." The authors hasten to point out that by one means or another, these explorers learned of and followed trails made, perhaps hundreds of years before, by Indian people.

Who were the mountain men? Studies conducted by Richard J. Ferman and William R. Swagerty illustrate the diversity of the trappers and traders in North America. According to these studies, one out of every hundred trappers and traders was an Indian, except in Canada, where Indians were the predominant trappers. Of the mountain men surveyed, trappers and traders made up 63.4 percent of the total of 176, outnumbering factors, owners, and field partners. Most trappers had only one wife; 38.9 percent of 272 first marriages were to Indian women. In the Southwest, 67.7 percent of the 52 men who would settle in the Taos region married into Spanish-speaking cultures. "Among Indian cultures marriage yielded special trading and status privileges for a trader; among the Spanish-speaking cultures of New Mexico and California, material gains in the form of land acquisition accompanied many unions." In first marriages, there was a "noticeable concentration of Shoshoni, Sioux, Flathead, Arapaho, Nez Percé, and Blackfoot wives. Second wives were more geographically diverse." Some 60 percent of all French Americans took Indians as first wives; only 15 percent married Spanish American women.[478]

Gowans quotes Robert Newell in an epitaph for the mountain men:

Come, said Newell to Meek, We are done with this life in the mountains—done with wading the beaver dams, and freezing or starving alternately—done with Indian trading and Indian fighting. The fur trade is dead in the Rocky Mountains, and it is no place for us now, if ever it was. We are young yet, and have life before us. We cannot taste it here; we cannot or will not return to the States. Let us go down to the Wallamet and take farms....What do you say, Meek? Shall we turn American settlers?[479]

So important was the Indian role in the Rockies for trade and trapping that an accurate picture is needed. Indian life blossomed at Rocky Mountain rendezvous. The Scottish sportsman Sir William Drummond Stewart paid Robert Campbell five hundred dollars to "rough it" en route to the 1833 rendezvous. He became famous among trappers and traders in the Rockies. He had extensive British military experience at age thirty-eight, and the money to play with as he pleased. He attended the rendez-vous for eight years and was colorful, hardy, willing to take on all tasks of an expedition member, grasped Indian mores, and gained the wilderness qualifications and respect that enabled him to serve as captain of trapper groups. Stewart repeated and gloried in his mountain-man associations. He received from the trappers who had met him the supreme accolade: "Thar was old grit in him, too, and a hair of the black b'ar at that."[480]

Stewart wrote of his fur-trade life in a novel, *Edward Warren*. In the novel's introduction, Winfred Blevins wrote, "Modern Scholarship can know that it was indeed autobiography....The pictures he paints of his companions, the mountain men, and their trade...are drawn from life. Stewart saw that there were present 250 to 300 whites from five compa-nies and a great many free trappers. The Indian community was repre-sented by forty or fifty lodges of Snakes and Shoshonis." [481]

There had been a slight breeze during the day, which had sunk as the eve-ning fell; and now all was so still, I could hear the occasional howl of the wolf and the short low of the bull, as the herds were spreading abroad for pasture;...as musingly I tracked my course toward the scene of the rendez-vous. The camp of...the Indians on the edge of the river above Horse Creek, with its vast plain stretching to the west...and now that I had passed the close brushwood which had hitherto shut out the camp from my view, the whole glare of fires and tents and lodges blazed before me.

It was evening, and Indians and whites were flocking back from the excur-sions of the day...a war party had returned from the side of the Blackfeet country with scalps, the drum was beating and the squaws and some of the braves had already begun the dance to its slow and measured music. The Snake camp was full, and the games of the young, as well as the grown up, the shooting with the bow and arrow, as well as throwing an arrow like a javelin, diversified the scene; the bucks paraded in full paint....

Altogether, it was worth the journey, to wander unnoticed through the village of that noble nomad race, spread out on this plain, under the base of the great range which forms the backbone of half the world...wandering through the streets of lodges with their trophies and medicine hung out... alike for protection and display, among hieroglyphic paintings, captured arms and scalps...a cloud of dust was rising in a continuous line at the lower border of the plain...and those [of the Snake] who had their horses up, which it is the custom of the rich to have ever ready at their door, were mounting and galloping forth to meet what seemed to be a gay cavalcade... prancing over the sandy prairie.

There was one husband...young Philipson,...begirt with a sash of silk and decked in the holiday garb of a gumbo ball, and his wife followed him, unheeding the costly finery with which she was decked, and never leaving with her eye, for a moment, the form she loved. And that other, whose eye searched not for conquest, nor sought to retain, who rode simply on her folded saddle-cloths, and plaited rein guided her horse, a bow and quiver hung from her side, and whose seat was as firm, and hand as light and true as of the strongest man, and by whose side rode a noble-looking Spaniard, in his loose trowsers and sombrero,...

I stood upon a little mound of gravel by the riverside, and looked out upon a scene, the like of which is only to be beheld in that wild land of the hunter; the squaws had been already busy in taking in the meat, which hung in festoons on bars to dry, and which had been brought in from the morning's hunt, alike to rescue it from the dust and the chance of being overthrown by the gathering rush....Urged on by wild whoops, the dense charge came thundering on—the eye became bewildered, and the ear was stunned... it appeared as if the charge of five thousand horses must trample down every thing living in the camp, as well as its abodes—the dogs howled, and rushed into the lodges for shelter; and as I looked out from my height to see every thing overthrown and trampled under foot, as the headlong column tore onwards in mad career, the dust changed in its colour to a sober grey, had intervened to hide the general rout, and gradually thinning...I could see the squaws and the boys tying up their horses, panting and snorting from the race, and apparently each stable congregated at its owner's door... the lodges, which had appeared uselessly far part before, seemed now to leave but sufficient room for the tying up of the animals between them, whose cords encumbered the ground.

It is a moment in one of those villages, when every one is astir; [whose horses were tied ready at the door]...could now parade in all their bravery—a creek near supplies white and yellow clay, and the period is rich in vermillion; so the horses prance about smeared with the most brilliant hues, and toss their proud heads, as if glad in the sound of the human voice, while from the tail flies the falcon feather, the sign of speed, as from the only part visible when it is put forth, the distinction of the courser from the beast of burthen.

It was on a grassy bank...that I found myself, somewhat distant from the lodges of Bonneville and out of the way of those of the Snakes;...while hesitating whether to pass over the narrow branch which lay before me, I saw a figure, apparently of a squaw, almost directly opposite, who appeared to be carrying a load of wood, and making evidently for camp...I was met... in full face by a figure closely muffled in a robe; we both stopped for a moment, so sudden the meeting in the narrow buffalo-path through the thicket...one of those mystic instincts which communicate between certain persons, was before me, and I held out my arms to embrace my wild friend with the ardour of real joy. We had never been, while together, in any state of emotion; there had never occurred any thing to call forth any unusual demonstration of regard; but this meeting, so sudden and unlooked for, had destroyed all forms and reserve, and I strained my friend to my heart with unalloyed delight; neither us spoke—my heart was full.

CHAPTER 17:

SOUTHWEST TRAPPERS

T he Pueblo Indians of New Mexico welcomed the plains tribes to their trading fairs, where from ancient days, they traded their agricultural produce for buffalo meat and animal hides. The arrival of the Spanish in Mexico and the English and French on the East Coast of North America brought new and different trade items. Horses and sheep from the Spanish, and European-manufactured goods, such as iron tools and guns, finally led to the fur trade of the early nineteenth century, a new experience for the Southwest.

The large multistoried adobe pueblos were self-contained villages and had been present since the fourteenth century. The Hopi and Zuni, living in today's Arizona, and the Keresans, Tiwa, Tewa, and Towa, in the Rio Grande Valley, built pueblos to support their communal lifestyle. Their common culture included the development of irrigation systems permitting them to have a surplus of agricultural products. They wove fabrics from the cotton they grew. They made artistically designed baskets and pottery that reflected an advanced spiritual system. Through their widespread trading system, they had access to turquoise, copper, and shells for decorative purposes.[482] These pueblos, particularly at Taos, were the heart of the southwestern trading networks.

The Europeans moving inland from the Atlantic coastline and the French explorers and traders going up and down the Mississippi River were constantly pushing westward. The Spanish mercantile system, which controlled the trade in the Spanish colonies, limited the colonies to providing raw materials, silver, or gold to the mother country. The colonists were only allowed to buy Spanish-manufactured goods; no foreign traders were permitted. But there was no control of Indian-made products.

As plains middlemen, the Osage along the Mississippi and Missouri rivers passed manufactured trade goods, including guns and ammunition, from the Europeans to the Pawnee, Kiowa, Comanche, and others. Neither the Spanish settlers in the province of New Mexico nor the surrounding Indian nations trapped for furs. There was little market for furs in the warm climes of either Mexico or Spain; they were interested in leather goods, including shoes made from the skins of deer and elk.

The Siouan-speaking Osage had migrated to the Osage River Basin in the seventeenth century. They lived and hunted in the woodlands of that basin until the Osage Treaty of 1808 moved them south to the Arkansas River. They traveled annually to the central plains for buffalo hunting. The Osage resisted both white and Indian trespassers on their hunting territory.

Ferocious warriors, the Osage had allied with the French when the French and Spanish competed in the Mississippi River valley in the eighteenth century. The French provided gunpowder, guns, kettles, and blankets to the Indians along the Mississippi. The Osage made war on the Pawnee and Comanche, and they raided nearby Plains tribes: the Kaw, Kickapoo, Kiowa, Ponca, and Wichita west of the Mississippi River.[483]

The Osage territory marked the beginning of the Santa Fe Trail leading from Missouri to Spanish territory. There was no clear and agreed-upon description of the border of Spanish territories. Spain claimed it was the Mississippi River. In 1819 Spain and the United States agreed that the border would be the Red River, then north along the hundredth meridian to the Arkansas River and west along that waterway into the Rockies.[484]

It was here that the availability of the horse changed the life of Indians on the plains. Apparently the horses were first ridden by the Apache who lived on the borders of the Spanish settlements. They traded them to the Ute, who passed them north to the Shoshone. In less than a hundred years, the use of horses spread from the Rio Grande to the Saskatchewan River. Horses remained an important trade item for all tribes.

The intertwining of the fur trade and horses was strong. The Indians used them for hunting and warfare and as a symbol of wealth. The Osage, Comanche, Kiowa, and others used horses to expand their hunting areas and the extent of their trade. In the European fur trade, horses were extensively used for transport away from the river systems and for trading for necessities from the Indians. The fur-trade story in the Southwest is closely connected to the profitable trade carried out by the fur traders who sold not just furs, but also took horses from the Spanish lands, including California, to sell in Missouri.

South of the Arkansas River, the Comanche were dominant. They obtained horses as the Spanish fled the Pueblo Rebellion of 1680, and thereafter ranged widely across the plains and prairies between the Mississippi River and the Rocky Mountains. As horsemen, they hunted buffalo and developed cavalry tactics for warfare against other tribes.

The Comanche measured wealth and power by horses. Some Comanche had as many as fifteen hundred to three thousand horses, but as few as twelve were considered enough to provide a surplus to trade. Women owned horses and rode proficiently; children were lifted to a horse's back as babies. The Comanche, along with other Plains tribes, were innovative in their use of the horse in warfare and hunting, adapting their weapons, shields, and horsemanship into an incomparable native cavalry.

The Kiowa, who numbered about two thousand people, often joined the Comanche in raids and war parties. They roamed north of the Arkansas River. Among the Kiowa, twenty to fifty horses provided moderate wealth, but there, too, some people owned many more.[485] This wealth of horses allowed all the tribes to trade for guns, kettles, knives, swords, and personal finery.

The Comanche east of New Mexico and the Apache in the west hunted, robbed, and took slaves at will in the Spanish territories. In the late eighteenth century, the Spanish and Comanche came to a peace agreement. The Comanche agreed to help the Spanish defend their borders and control the Apache. The Comanche had driven the Apache out of their buffalo-hunting areas, which made the Apache dependent on the rancheros' sheep for food.

Wars for independence were springing up in Spanish America. In 1810, Miguel Hidalgo, a parish priest, led the first revolt in Mexico. From that time on, the Spanish were increasingly concerned about the defense of their borders. They captured and imprisoned those who crossed their borders without permits, whether it be Zebulon Pike and his expedition in 1806, which the Spanish perceived as a military threat, or trader Robert McKnight's party, which took trade goods there in 1812 and remained confined in jail until 1820, or trader August Chouteau and Jules De Munn, who spent six weeks in a Santa Fe jail in 1816.

Rumors of imminent Mexican independence sent several groups of traders to Santa Fe in 1821. From Superintendent Clark in St. Louis, they obtained licenses to trade with the Indians. En route they explored the streams along the Arkansas River for beaver. John McKnight, brother of Robert, joined Thomas James in leading a group of trappers along an alternate route to Santa Fe in 1821.[486] They went down the Mississippi to the mouth of the Arkansas, up to Fort Smith and beyond to the Cimarron River. Their route cross-country to the Canadian River took them to where they were caught on the prairie by Comanche bands and rescued by Spanish military scouts, who then acted as an escort to Santa Fe.[487] Thomas James then opened a store and sold their merchandise; the others trapped in area streams.

Osage trader Hugh Glenn, with a trading post on the Verdigris River, also had a license from Superintendent Clark to trade among the Indians in American territory. In the fall of 1821, he joined Jacob Fowler and formed a group that followed the Arkansas River into Colorado. His intention was to trap, but upon hearing of the open border, he took some trade goods into Santa Fe in the spring of 1822. Several from his party, including Jacob Fowler and Isaac Slover, remained trapping on the headwaters of the Arkansas, and some of the first furs to arrive in Missouri from New Mexico returned with Hugh Glenn. Ramsay Crooks of the American Fur Company bought the results of their trip: 1,100 pounds for $4,999.64.[488] To these men it was apparent that beaver were plentiful. Even to a beginner, the cut trees along the banks and the beaver dams were evidence that beaver were present. Beaver were visible in the Rio Grande, just outside of Santa Fe and Taos. The upper reaches of the Pecos River was full of them. The word spread rapidly among the trappers.

Although Santa Fe was the capital and commercial center for the province, the ancient trading center Taos became the home of fur traders and trappers who arrived over the Santa Fe Trail. It was a small village on the edge of the borderlands in a high mountain valley across Palo Flechado Pass from the Santa Fe Trail. The trail itself crossed Raton Pass, a high mesa that separates the valley of the Arkansas River and the valley of the upper Canadian River, descends down the east side of the Sangre De Cristo Mountains, and crosses the Gallines River at Las Vegas and the Pecos River at San Jose, before turning slightly northwest to Santa Fe. Taos and the other borderland villages were the homes of Indian, Spanish, and mixed-descent people who had often followed trails into Indian country to trade and could lead the trappers into the mountains.

None of the prominent St. Louis fur companies managed Southwest trapping locally as had occurred on the Missouri River and in the northern Rockies. Instead their role was that of suppliers and fur marketers. The Robidoux family illustrates the strong connection between the old "French" companies, as those that operated out of St. Louis were called, and the trading activity of the Southwest. The seven Robidoux brothers—Joseph III, Francois, Isidore, Antoine, Louis, Charles, and Michel—were sons of Joseph II and Catherine Rollet of Cahokia, Illinois. All were active in the fur trade.

In 1824, Joseph III privately equipped and launched an expedition to Santa Fe consisting of his brothers Francois, Isidore, Antoine, and Michel, accompanied by Manuel Alvarez and nine "traders to Mexico." On arriving in Taos, a local official, Juan Bautista Vigil, promptly confiscated Francois's goods because he was not a Mexican citizen and did not have a proper invoice. Alvarez and Francois went to Santa Fe to plead for release of the goods. They met with Vigil, and after paying him a hundred pesos, either as a bribe or a fee, recovered their goods.[489]

Three centuries of Spanish domination and trade had created a population that was strongly Spanish in language and culture, and the French American and other American traders who traveled in the Mexican Southwest had to learn to communicate in a profusion of combined Indian and Spanish terms. They also had to learn to maneuver within a different political system.

The Mexican culture substantially affected the activities and aspirations of American trappers and traders. Some of it was no doubt helpful. Much of Mexican lifestyle, as interpreted by the trappers, was illustrated by their celebration of independence, which James witnessed:

No Italian carnival ever exceeded this celebration in thoughtlessness, vice, and licentiousness of every description....I never saw any people so infatuated with the passion for gaming....I saw enough during this five days revelry to convince me that the republicans of New Mexico were unfit to govern themselves or anybody else."[490]

After independence in 1821, the Mexican economy moved from the Spanish-controlled mercantilism to a more entrepreneurial development of Mexican resources. Each Mexican province was to pay a quota to the central government, similar to the tithe or tax collected by the Spanish. But the people were poor. In New Mexico in the mid-1830s, the citizenry had a total tax quota of 5,000 pesos, but only 3,500 pesos were collected. They could not pay for a militia or for government employees, such as the governor, customs collector, and a local bureaucracy.

In the summer of 1824, eighty-three men came to Taos from Missouri with twenty-six wagons and eighty pack mules. This began the American traders experience with the restrictions with the new Mexican government. The Mexican governor levied an excise tax on foreign goods imported into the country. This, plus a tax on beaver pelts and license fees, was the only source of income for the province, and was bitterly denounced by the American traders. Obviously, without income, the country could no longer supply the Indians with food and goods as earlier Spanish treaties required, nor could the unpaid militia protect its citizens.

On caravans from Independence, Missouri, many merchants brought merchandise intended for the larger markets at Chihuahua, where specie, silver, horses, and mules were available for trade. But many of the men also came to trap.[491] The large number of newcomers seeking beaver was a problem for the newly formed Mexican government. The beaver were a product of their country, and they believed it should not be exploited by foreigners. Reacting quickly, the Mexican government required that only Mexican citizens could be licensed to trap. Foreigners could accompany them, but a crew must include Mexicans being taught to trap. A tax was levied and the license issued in the name of the crew's leader.

Stories of the trappers and traders in the Southwest during this period are many and varied. Joseph J. Hill carried out a scholarly analysis of the sources, bringing order to an otherwise confused history. Hill wrote of trapper Ewing Young, "For some twelve years…he was the central figure in the Far Southwest…he trapped the waters of the Rio del Norte, the Pecos, the San Juan, the Gila, the Colorado, and the Grand of the Rocky Mountain Southwest."[492] By 1822, according to Hill, Young had made two trips with Captain William Becknell from St. Louis to Santa Fe and back. In 1824, Young, William Wolfskill, and Isaac Stover led a large party of trappers north from Taos to trap on the San Juan and other Colorado River tributaries. Various trappers separated for each stream, finally leaving the three leaders to go where others had never been. Arriving back in Taos in June 1824, they brought in $10,000 worth of furs.

The trappers must have been aware of the Navajo who lived along the San Juan River, centered on Canyon de Chelly, and who in 1819 numbered about ten thousand. Athabaskan, they had migrated south along the east slopes of the Rockies in ancient times and were cousins of the Chiricahua Apache. Like the Apache, they were fierce fighters, cruel in revenge. The Navajo lived along the northwest border between today's New Mexico and Arizona. They had arrived from the north before the Spanish arrived from the south, and calling themselves the Dinetah, they hunted the mesas and canyons of northeastern Arizona. They established friendly trading relations with the pueblos, and traded for agricultural produce and intermarried with them.

The oval tepee-like structure called the "hoogan" in which the Navajo lived would have been apparent throughout the region. The hoogan consisted of arched poles, thatched with grass, brush, bark, rushes, mats, and cloth. The entrance was closed by a suspended hide. Pieces of hide provided waterproofing and could be removed in summer to enhance cooling. A smoke hole in the roof ventilated a central fire. The women constructed, maintained, and repaired the hoogan, and arranged everything in it. They were accorded high standing among the Navajo and could own livestock and jewelry, which their husbands could never appropriate.

Navajo chiefs, or headmen, were influential, wealthy men of good judgment and with ceremonial knowledge, particularly of the Blessing Way, a spiritual inner direction that brought good fortune through the supernatural. Throughout their recorded history, the Navajo were famous for weaving closely woven water-resistant blankets, today valued on a par with exquisite Oriental rugs. Before the nineteenth century, Spanish oppression had driven some Pueblo into Navajo lands, where they were made welcome. The Navajo fitted Pueblo customs into their lifestyle without becoming Pueblo. "The Navajo were neither peaceful nor sedentary. They were wild, unpredictable, and cruel. They wanted both the freedom of the wind and the rewards of the patient laborer."[493]

Ewing Young probably organized and led another, much larger party to the San Juan River in the autumn of 1824, and returned to Missouri in the summer of 1825, his seventh and last trip over the Santa Fe Trail. After the return of the Missouri resupply caravan in July 1825, several fur-trapping leaders sought licenses from Governor Antonio Narbona for "passports to Sonora." The licenses covered the trapping party, for which modern research places the numbers of trappers at well above 180 in and after 1826. Narbona soon realized the applicants' real intention was not to go south into Mexico, but was "hunting beaver on the San Francisco (Verde), Gila, and Colorado Rivers." He advised the governor of Sonora of the size and nature of the parties. However, to train Mexicans in trapping, Governor Narbona approved licenses to foreigners in the name of Mexican citizens.[494]

The opening of new trading and trapping frontiers needed someone who could record the story. Josiah Gregg, a merchant, was such a chronicler. Gregg made his first trip to Santa Fe in 1831 and successive trading trips back and forth from Independence, Missouri. His book *Commerce of the Prairies,* first published in 1844, illustrates the details of the trip; how the trade operated in a foreign country; and descriptions of the Indians, wildlife, and scenery, from his own experiences and that of others. Gregg estimated that about 120 men arrived in Santa Fe from Missouri in the first two years the border was open. That number was followed by 100 men in 1824 and 130 in 1825. In a country where foreigners had been rarely seen, this must have been almost overwhelming.[495]

Another trapper/trader with strong ties to the St. Louis fur trade was Sylvestre S. Pratte, eldest son of Bernard Pratte and Emilie Sauveru Labbadie. Sylvestre had served as a trader in one of his father's companies on the Missouri. In 1825, Jean Pierre Cabanné, a partner of Bernard Pratte and Company, outfitted an expedition to northern Mexico with Sylvestre as the leader.

Sylvestre Pratt, William Becknell, Francois Robidoux, and others received licenses to trap, although Governor Narbona, governing from isolated Santa Fe, had initially not enforced the Mexican federal decree prohibiting foreigners from trapping. However, when stricter instructions arrived from the government in Mexico City, Narbona changed his mind. When Francois Robidoux and Sylvestre Pratte returned from the mountains in May 1826, they were the first Americans to feel the result. The *alcalde* (mayor) of Taos announced that, in compliance with orders, he had confiscated the 630 pounds of beaver pelts belonging to Pratte and Robidoux. The two men went to Santa Fe and complained that they had supposed themselves to be licensed. Though Narbona agreed, a year later, after Manuel Armijo replaced Narbona as governor, the furs had still not yet been released.[496]

After the initial problem with importing trade goods, both Antoine and Louis Robidoux saw the advantage of trapping northward into what is now Colorado and avoiding Mexican customs, duties, and restraints. Later they became Mexican citizens, which was helpful to the trading business. Seeking an outlet for trade goods, in about 1825, Antoine established Fort Uncompahgre about a half mile southwest of present-day Delta, Colorado, at the junction of the Uncompahgre and Gunnison rivers. It lay on the north-south route to the Green River and Brown's Hole in extreme northwest Colorado. By 1830, Antoine had established Fort Uinta, near present-day Whiterocks, Utah.[497]

The Robidouxs established their fort for the Shoshone-speaking Ute, who had moved south through the Great Plains in previous centuries. At the Colorado Rockies, the twelve Ute bands had split into western and eastern factions. The western Ute and Paiute remained in the Great Basin, living in Colorado near the junction of the Taylor and Tamichi rivers. Various bands lived in northwestern Colorado. Closest to the southern fur trade were the Uinta who lived in southeastern Utah. While inclined to be friendly to whites, they fought with other Indians.

Not until the nineteenth century did the Western Ute and Paiute begin to see European trade items. European exploring expeditions began with the Spanish Franciscans, Dominguez and Escalante, who in 1776 surveyed part of what became the Old Spanish Trail northward from Santa Fe. They and Americans coming up the Arkansas River and down the Colorado ended Ute and Paiute isolation.[498] Their location made the Ute among the first to receive horses from Mexico and New Mexico, and they were active middlemen in the slaves-for-horses market.

Antoine Robidoux maintained Fort Uncompahgre for about twenty years, an indication that it was profitable. Antoine married Carmel

Venivides of Santa Fe in 1828, and with his brother Louis became a Mexican citizen in 1829. By 1830 Antoine was president of the town council of Santa Fe.

In 1826, Ewing Young organized an expedition to the Gila River with William Wolfskill as a leader. This expedition led the trappers into the heart of Apache country. An Apache attack forced the eleven men to return to Santa Fe. They had lost all their traps, but saved their scalps.

The Apache, having been pushed out of ancestral lands and having fought and stolen from the Spanish settlers, became militant warriors. The Apache, living on the borders of the Spanish settlements, raided for food and slaves to trade. They apparently were the first to ride horses and were the first southern-plains people to fight effectively on horseback. They used "a short bow and saber-tipped lances as well as leather shields and leather armor for horse and rider."[499]

The Apache first moved from the Chama valley out onto the Great Plains, but pushed by the incursions of other tribes from the north, they separated into eastern and western groups. The eastern Apache moved into southwestern Texas, becoming the Jicarilla and Mescalero bands. The western Apache became the Chiricahua, Coyotera, and Aravaipa bands in southern New Mexico and Arizona. The eastern Jicarilla band provided the Pueblos with bison meat and skins and traded for agricultural products. The western Apache, living in arid lands, relied on raiding the Pueblos and on the Spanish settlements for food.

"Each local group had a headman, who led by reason of prestige and good example, and a headwoman, whose function was to council her people in the ways of living, and especially to organize food gathering parties among the women."[500]The Apache had a splendid physique and were above average height. They had high regard for their women, who were respected, cherished, and protected. Chastity was rigidly enforced. Children in a family were generally four years apart. In war, women could accompany their husbands. Keeping promises was important, and liars were despised. "To their families they were kind and gentle, but they could be unbelievably cruel to their enemies—fierce and revengeful when they felt that they had been betrayed."[501]

During the fall, winter, and spring of 1826–27, Young organized another party of thirty-two and led it southwestward after a stop at the Santa Rita copper mine, which was owned by an American and at this time managed by Sylvester Pattie and his obstreperous son, James Ohio Pattie. Young's party had lost all of their goods on a trapping foray. The mine was located on the edge of the Gila River territory, which made it a convenient place at which to store goods and furs. Young's objective was to trap the Gila River and other tributaries of the lower Colorado. His party included George Yount, Hiram Allen, William Workman, Milton Sublette, and Peg-Leg Smith. James Ohio Pattie joined a party of Frenchmen led by Michel Robidoux. In his informative, but self-aggrandizing *Narrative*, Pattie described a massacre of their party by the Papago-Pima, which only three men survived.

On reaching the Gila River, the party had separated into smaller groups or teams for beaver trapping. According to Pattie,[502] the team led by Robidoux reached the Pima villages near the Gila River mouth of the Santa Cruz Wash, about twenty miles southwest of present-day Phoenix. The Pima, Papago, Hualapai, Havasupai, and Yavapai were agriculturalists living along the western Gila River. The Indians, displaying friendly intentions, seduced the Frenchmen into stacking their arms and camping with them. Pattie and one other man camped a distance away, fearing treachery.

In the night, the Indians attacked, killing all except Robidoux, who escaped to Pattie's camp. Soon after, Pattie and Robidoux, by chance, encountered Young's party. Young planned and executed a surprise reprisal on the Indian camp. As Holmes describes the event:

They quietly bivouacked not far from the Indian encampment, making no fires. The next morning, twenty-six of them started for the Indian village, making their way through a dry arroyo which came close to the objective. Suddenly two of the trappers showed themselves and drew the attention of the Indians, who sent a large body of warriors toward the two exposed men, who dropped down out of sight. The old "whites of their eyes" philosophy prevailed, as was usual among the trappers, and the Indians were allowed to approach to within about twenty yards when the Hawkins [Hawken] rifles spoke out with deadly results. A number of the braves fell, and the rest ran.[503]

Young's attack killed 110 and captured all the horses, supplies, and equipment the French had lost. Next morning, a party of Indians arrived, seeking peace. "Young did his best to convey a warning to the Indians that they were to leave American trapping parties alone."[504] He apparently believed that the word of a prompt and severe attack on one tribe would reach others. After this well-known skirmish, the party trapped downstream on the Gila River to the mouth of the Verde. There they parted, one team going to the headwaters of each river. Reuniting at the rivers' junction, they continued down the Gila to the Colorado River, meeting a tribe Pattie called the Yuma. From the lower Colorado, which Young reported rich in beaver, the parties trapped up the Colorado to the Mojave Valley.

The Mojave, Yuma, Cocopa, and Maricopa Indians hunted and fished along the Colorado River. They lived in small scattered farms called rancherías, and grew beans, corn, and pumpkin on small plots of rich bottomland watered only by the springtime flooding of the river.[505] The trappers found the Mojave fearful and agitated. After harsh words and a sleepless night, the Mojave attacked the next morning. Young's party killed sixteen. They moved on up the river, but were attacked again. This time, two of Young's party were killed and two wounded before they routed the Indians.[506]

After trapping north along the Colorado, probably until they reached the lower Grand Canyon, Young's party had all the beaver pelts they could carry, and headed for the Santa Rita mine, their staging point. They were hot and thirsty. Grizzly bears abounded and did not hibernate in winter. There were also herds of wild pigs, or peccaries, and rabid wolves and coyotes.

Thirst, starvation, and quarrelling among the trappers became critical. Finally reaching the Zuni villages, they found restoring food, water, and helpful assistance. The Zuni pueblo became one of the most important stops for trappers bound southwest from Taos and Santa Fe. Ewing Young, among others on this trip, and two years later in 1829, stopped at this "significant rendezvous point for trapping parties." There, trappers "obtained a supply of Pinole (roasted corn meal), and pinoche (sugar) and frijoles."[507]

In an account of his 1827 stop at the Hopi villages, George Yount gave this firsthand view of the Hopi (Hopituh Shi-nu-mu, meaning "the peaceful people"), according to a transcript of his dictation to his friend, Rev. Orange Clark:

> There is not to be found on the Continent another so remarkable people as the Moco… with them he cheerfully would have spent his life…these [Mocos] excel them all. In Yount's words… our horses, almost famished for water…ran until they reached the town. The people came out… unpacked our animals and gave them water with great prudence and precaution lest they might injure themselves in drinking to excess, gave them food, and invited us into their houses, and spread a sumptuous feast before us—Then allotted to us a fine spacious room; and mats spread for us…the families vied with each other in bringing into our apartment

food and luxuries....We found the people sober, civil, chaste and conscientious—During all our sojourn there we heard not one harsh or unkind or hasty word, even among children—Their food consists of meat well cooked, bread of parched corn, honey and dried fruits—Their houses are built of stone, a beautiful sandstone....The buildings are not so high as those of Taos, but generally more than two stories high. ... [Their high location is] strongly fortified by nature....Both sexes labor with great industry.

They spin, weave, make garments and blankets....They are masons, and familiar with the work—Their granaries and storehouses are immense and filled to overflowing...their laws are good and wholesome, evince great simplicity though by no means unwise—They never cultivate nor use horses....Their laws relative to marriage are rigid & rigidly enforced.... They dance very gracefully to music—Dancing makes a part of their religious worship;...

They never wage war....No spirit of revenge or retaliation [for an offense] was entertained....They say God may kill men, because he can make men live...they have learnt by experience, even without any divine revelation that "it is more blessed to give than to receive."...They maintain total abstinence from everything the least degree hurtful in food or drink.... All their athletic exercises are most salutary to health and longevity. When the time came for our departure...They all strove to bestow upon us the best possible expressions of respect and love....We were rough trappers of the desert streams...clad in the vestments of our occupation....We were young men and inconsiderate....Our beasts of burden were brought in sleek and well recruited.[508]

However, during their absence from Santa Fe, Antonio Armijo, whom Gregg called "an ambitious and turbulent demagogue" who "was notoriously corrupt in public affairs and dissolute in private life,"[509] had replaced Narbona as governor and promptly confiscated Yount's furs. The experience of Sylvestre Pratte, Francois Robidoux, Ewing Young, and Yount inspired caution in others. Once they grew wary, fur traders found smuggling goods in and fur out of the two ports of entry, Taos and San Miguel, not too difficult, since neither of them had customs houses. Yount managed to get his furs to market the next time without Mexican confiscation by hiding them, with the help of William Woodman, in "an underground passage, led to the grand subterranean cache, where goods to an enormous amount were being secretly deposited."[510]

Young and his party, fearing trouble because they had not obtained a license, deposited their twenty-nine fur packs at the home of Cabeza de Baca in Pena Blanca, a village on the Rio Grande southwest of Santa Fe. Governor Armijo sent a squad of soldiers to get the furs. They killed de Baca, who was defending the pelts. Soldiers took the furs to Santa Fe, where they were stored as contraband.

In March 1827, Francois Robidoux and Sylvestre Pratte, with Maurice Le Duc, still unlicensed, departed with fourteen men, telling the officials they were going to hunt for buried treasure in Ute country. Evidently the purpose, other than trapping, was to recover the furs previously cached in that country. With Bernard Pratte and Company funds, Pratte funded trapping trips for Peg-Leg Smith and another led by Ceran St. Vrain. The returns were poor, business was failing.

Though suffering from financial adversity, Sylvestre Pratte, in August 1827, organized and led a thirty-six man party north from Abiquiu with Ceran St. Vrain as his clerk. There was an array of trapping talent, including Thomas Smith, Alexander Branch, William "Old Bill" Williams, Milton Sublette, and Joseph Bissonette, famed for his knowledge of the Rockies. There were nineteen other Frenchmen and one Mexican. By late September, they were in North Park with three hundred pelts. After a brief illness, Sylvestre died on October 1. By acclamation, St. Vrain took command. Disaster continued. Ten days later, in a surprise Indian attack, a bullet struck Smith in the left leg, just above the ankle, shattering both bones. What followed was one of the most remarkable tales of hardihood in the fur trade. As Smith told it:

> [The bullet struck Smith] a few inches above the ancle [sic] shattering both bones; he attempted to step for his rifle, leaning against a tree hard by; the bones stuck in the ground, and he sat down, calling upon his friends to cut it off! No one had the hardihood to undertake the operation; in fact they were perfectly ignorant of what should be done. He then called upon Basin, the cook, for his butcher knife, who reluctantly, with tears in his eyes, handed him the knife, with which he severed the muscles at the fracture with his own hand; when Milton Sublette, compassionate at his condition, took the knife from his hand and completed the operation by severing the tendon achilles, and bound it up with an old dirty shirt.[511]

The wound was never cauterized, and his friends doubted he would last the night. He did, however, and outlived many of his companions. St. Vrain led the party to the Green River for the winter, Smith being carried on a stretcher by men and later between two mules. After the trappers made him an artificial leg, he became known as "Peg-Leg" Smith. In spring, short of ammunition in the face of Indian danger, St. Vrain took the party back to Abiquiu, arriving in mid-May 1828.

The party brought back about a thousand beaver pelts, which St. Vrain sold. There was no profit. As Weber reported, wages and expenses were $6,915.415; the gross sale was $5,780.50; Pratte's equipment and supplies brought $612.25; and St. Vrain paid the difference of $522.66.[512]

American trappers used various forms of deception, but they found that the most successful route was to convert to the Catholic faith and thus become qualified to seek Mexican citizenship. This could be difficult and time consuming, but worthwhile for those intending to stay in New Mexico. Marrying a senorita was an advantage.

Alexander Branch is an example of a trapper who used those means to become legal, though he also may have been ready to remain in one place. Formerly one of Ashley's trappers, he came to Taos and trapped on Gila River in 1826 and was a member of Sylvestre Pratte's ill-starred expedition to Colorado's South Park in 1827. In 1828, he was baptized at Taos, taking the name José de Jesús. In January 1829, he married Maria Paula de Luna, with whom he eventually produced seven children. By year's end he had become a Mexican citizen. Branch left his wife for a year and accompanied William Wolfskill to California in 1830, following the route that became famous as the Old Spanish Trail. When Wolfskill decided to stay in California to hunt sea otter, Branch and others brought his equipment back to Taos. Beginning in 1831, he apparently devoted his time to his Taos store.[513]

The merchants of Santa Fe and Taos who bought the furs and sold supplies were critical to the success of the fur trade. Manuel Alvarez was one of these. He was born in Spain and had lived in Mexico intermittently after 1818. Alvarez had traveled with the Robidoux brothers in the 1824 caravan carrying trade goods to open a store. He, too, had problems with government authorities, who confiscated his goods for a short time and prohibited him from trading guns to the Indians. His trapping experience began in the late 1820s on the Missouri with the P. D. Papin Company, later purchased by the American Fur Company's Upper Missouri Outfit. Alvarez was present with Drips and Fontenelle at Pierre's Hole during the 1832 rendezvous and wintered with them on the upper Snake River. In March 1833, he took forty men to trap Henry's Fork of the Snake and the Yellowstone country. All of this was in keen competition with the Rocky Mountain Fur Company.

The 1833 rendezvous marked Alvarez's shift from Rocky Mountain trapping to his life in Santa Fe.[514] After that time, Alvarez was primarily a successful Santa Fe merchant, establishing branch stores around the province. He several times traveled the Santa Fe Trail to buy goods and for various political reasons. He served effectively, if informally, as the American Consul in Santa Fe from 1839 to 1846.[515]

The enterprise that would become the largest fur-trading establishment in the Southwest was that of the Bent brothers, Charles and William. They grew up in St. Louis, members of a wealthy, educated, and distinguished family. In 1823, at age twenty-four, Charles joined the fur trade on the Missouri River. In the following adventurous, but difficult, six years he become an experienced western traveler and trapper. In 1825, he became a partner in the reorganized Missouri Fur Company with Fontenelle, Vanderburgh, Drips, and Pilcher. In 1827, the partnership made plans to go overland into the Rockies. Charles' brother William, age sixteen, may have been along. The Crow stole their herd of a hundred horses and mules, and they were forced to cache their trade goods. On foot they toiled through the snow, and fighting the north winds, they crossed South Pass to the Green River, where they spent a miserable winter. After trapping throughout the spring to get enough beaver to buy horses, they headed out of the mountains toward Council Bluff. There they learned the extent to which the American Fur Company had expanded on the upper Missouri and was gaining control in the mountains.

For the Bent brothers, the decision had been made; Charles and William Bent would try the Santa Fe Trail that spring of 1829. Their father had died, but somehow they managed to find backing for some trade goods, wagons, and mules. A trading caravan had gone to New Mexico yearly since 1822. It had evolved from a pack train loaded with goods, to long wagon trains that could more easily carry the furs, specie, and silver that returned to Missouri. The caravan formed in May, adding people, wagons, and horses as it moved along the Missouri River. Charles and William Bent met brothers David and William Waldo, who would become friends and business partners. David Waldo had gone to Mexico the previous year and after a successful trade, returned to Missouri for his brother and new trade goods.

There was not only a wagon train forming each spring and returning in the fall, but often additional caravans through the year. The trail to Santa Fe was over eight hundred miles long and the trip could take six weeks, more or less, depending on the makeup of the caravan. Caravans acted not just as carriers of cargo, but also as transportation for travelers and as protection for small groups on horseback.

Events on the Santa Fe Trail in the previous year had changed the nature of the travel. It was true that the Comanche, Kiowa, and Pawnee did not treat the white trading caravans any differently than they would have others who intruded into their hunting lands and camped at their springs. When attacked by anyone, their cultural response was revenge: stealing horses, counting coup, and taking slaves. They were also skilled at fighting from horseback.

In late summer of 1828, sixty to seventy traders were returning to Missouri from Santa Fe with profits from the year and a thousand horses for the Missouri markets. Two of the traders, Munroe and McNees, walked ahead of the caravan and stopped to take a nap beside a creek. When the caravan arrived, McNees was dead and Munroe near death from an Indian attack. In a panic, the caravan buried the dead and kept moving. When they saw a small group of Comanche, the men attacked, killing all but one. The Comanche came back in large numbers and took all of the horses and mules. A second, smaller caravan was also attacked, and their captain, John Means, was killed. The surviving traders left their wagons and carried their silver as far as they could, finally caching it on Chouteau's Island in the Arkansas River. They then walked on, four hundred miles, to Independence. These events led to the movement of U.S. soldiers to protect the Santa Fe Trail.

The Bent brothers missed the most profitable years of beaver trapping along the Gila, San Juan, and other rivers of the Southwest. After 1828, the number of beaver slowly diminished. The Mexican government was able to create and carry out consistent policies regarding trapping, and a number of trappers turned to other places and other things. But for the Bents, there was still profitable trade with the Ute, Cheyenne, and other tribes of the southern Rockies, which was rapidly changing into the buffalo-hide trade.

The U.S. government bowed to the demands of Missouri merchants to provide an Army escort for the trail. Charles Bent was elected the civilian captain of the wagon train, and on June 12, 1829, with an Army infantry escort commanded by Major Bennett Riley, they moved out of Round Grove. It was an adventurous trip. At Chouteau Island, the Army escort detail—two hundred men strong—recovered the thirty bags of silver cached by the wagon train in 1828. By July 9, the expedition was at the Arkansas River crossing, which led to Santa Fe. Here Major Riley's orders required him to stop and wait for a return caravan in the fall; Charles Bent expected to return to Missouri for trade goods and to meet them there in early October.

Shortly after taking the Cimarron cutoff south of the Arkansas, a band of perhaps five hundred Kiowa attacked. Charles asked nine volunteers to go back for Major Riley's troops. Charles and William created a diversion that would permit the teamsters to complete circling their wagons and organizing defenses. Riley arrived and constituted a threat, but as his orders precluded him from entering Mexican land, he retired back across the river as soon as possible. He agreed to continue on the north side of the Arkansas for a number of miles. The caravan moved on with one man dead and animals exhausted, but the trade goods were intact. Charles borrowed a team of oxen from Riley and demonstrated for the future their superiority in sure-footed endurance over mules.

Soon a mob of *ciboleros*—Mexican buffalo hunters—armed with bows, arrows, and lances, rode in, terrified. They brought news that two thousand Indians were on the warpath, and they wanted to travel with the caravan for protection. In Taos, Ewing Young, hearing (somehow!) of the caravan's distress, responded with about a hundred trappers. The caravan was saved; reunions with friends, such as Ceran St. Vrain and Kit Carson, brought rejoicing.[516] By October, Charles was back on the Arkansas with Riley. He was captain of a caravan of returning traders, loaded with specie and furs, and herding mules, reflecting a total value of $240,000—a considerable profit.[517]

Kiowa or Comanche attacks on caravans in 1829 brought U.S. Army military escort for subsequent caravans, but infantry proved ineffective. Lieutenant Philip St. George Cooke, West Point Class of 1827, accompanied Riley and wrote of the "humiliating experience" of trying to compete with Indian cavalry, stating, "much did we regret that we were not mounted, too."[518]

Later at Fort Atkinson, Cooke organized the first mounted troops; however, they were dragoons, who used horses not in combat, but for transportation only.

William Bent stayed in Taos when his brother returned to Missouri for more goods that fall. He, with other independent trappers, headed north, trapping and trading with the Cheyenne or Ute. They crossed the front range of the Rockies, probably to the present-day Fort Carson area, and made their winter camp apparently on the Arkansas River. A group of Cheyenne made a peaceful visit and left, though two remained. Their enemy, a Comanche horse-raiding party, suddenly arrived. The Comanche leader, Bull Hump, seeing the Cheyenne tracks, asked where they were. William had hidden them and told Bull Hump that they, with the others, had left. William's courageous action ensured the future friend-ship of the Cheyenne.[519]

A portion of the Cheyenne who remained in their old Black Hills haunts became known as the Northern Cheyenne, and another group descended to the Arkansas and became known as the Southern Chey-enne, remaining in the vicinity of Bent's Fort. According to George Bird Grinnell, who researched and wrote their history, Cheyenne chief Porcu-pine Bull said that "the Cheyennes…moved south of the Platte in 1826, or about that year, and began making [horse] raids on the Kiowas and Comanches, who lived south of the Arkansas." [520] Cheyenne chiefs, such as Big Foot, Elk River, and Yellow Wolf, were practiced in the acquisi-tion of horses. They were known for their ability to capture horses from the Kiowa and Comanche, as well as wild horses on the plains.[521]

The fur traders who had trapped to the Colorado River were soon look-ing westward, following generations of Indians and Spanish missionaries who had crossed the desert to California for trade and mission support. Richard Campbell led a group of men to San Diego in the fall of 1827 and learned he could sell his furs to ship captains on the coast.

In the same year, Sylvester Pattie and son James obtained a *guia*, or per-mission to travel, to Chihuahua and Sonora. Using this permission, they headed to California. Their horses were stolen en route and they floated down the Colorado River to Baja California. They were imprisoned in San Diego, where Sylvester died. The rest of the party later returned to New Mexico.

Peg-Leg Smith went to California for beaver, Ewing Young and Kit Carson for beaver and horses. Young applied for a passport from the U.S. government to allow his travel to California. This official document eased his way with the authorities in California, who were apprehensive of the arrival of so many Anglos. They returned in the spring of 1831, storing their furs in the Santa Rita mines until Young could get a license to trade.

William Wolfskill became a Mexican citizen and got a license to trap in California. George C. Yount went with him; the party disbanded while there, allowing Yount to become involved in otter hunting.

David Jackson and Ewing Young, with David Waldo as a third partner, went to buy mules and horses, as well as to trap in the fall of 1831. Jackson returned in the summer of 1832 with the horses and beaver. Ewing Young trapped the San Joaquin and Sacramento river valleys, where he met Chief Trader John Work, who was leading the Hudson's Bay Company brigades that were depleting the rivers of beaver.

This profitable trip encouraged others to cross the desert to California. Many were involved in the horse trade; George Nidever hunted otter skins; Isaac Slover settled in California. Louis Robidoux, after becoming a Mexican citizen, spent the rest of his life in California, becoming a rancher raising sheep and cattle and growing vineyards.

In May 1831, with about twenty wagons of trade goods and eighty men, business partners Jedediah Smith, William Sublette, and David Jackson, accompanied by Tom Fitzpatrick, started west on the Santa Fe Trail. They did not have a military escort. These experienced men were accustomed to traveling with open eyes. They had followed Indian trails across the Rocky Mountains, battling rain, wind, cold, and snow in search of beaver. Jedediah Smith had crossed the Mohave Desert from the Colorado River to California and discovered new paths through the Sierra Nevada Mountains and along the Pacific Coast. They had sold their business to the Rocky Mountain Fur Company and were ready to try something new. Investing in a wagon train of trade goods, they took the now well-worn Santa Fe Trail west from Council Grove.

The Smith, Sublette, and Jackson caravan had little trouble until well into the trip. Perhaps becoming complacent, a clerk, E. S. Minter, rode away from the caravan while hunting and was killed by Indians.[522] He was buried beside the trail and they kept moving. They crossed the

Arkansas and started across the sand hills. No clear wagon trail could be found. The herds of buffalo that came there for water had obliterated any clear path. After wandering fruitlessly for a couple of days, both men and animals were suffering from lack of water. Smith and Fitzpatrick volunteered to go ahead and scout for water. Reaching Sand Creek, Fitzpatrick attempted to dig a water hole, since his horse could go no further. Smith disappeared over a hill, and although his body was never found, word came into Santa Fe that he had been killed by the Comanche.

Later, in 1833, Lieutenant Colonel St. George Cooke organized the First Dragoon regiment at Fort Leavenworth. Dragoons were basically mounted infantry. In the early days, they carried a shortened musket, a weapon known as a musketoon. Later, they carried carbines. They used their horses basically for transport. But the military was still authorized to protect caravans only in U.S. territory.

In the 1830s, trouble with the Apache mounted throughout New Mexico. The now-famous Chiricahua Apache war chief Cochise was born in 1810 and came of age as the Apache went to war over the failure of the Mexicans to provide the rations promised in 1830. A three-day battle in 1832 near the Mogollon Mountains was the beginning of Apache raids and reprisals, often stimulated by mutual ignorance and misunderstanding. The Apache fought with Mexicans and Americans off and on until 1870.

In 1830, Charles Bent and Ceran St. Vrain, who had become a Mexican citizen, established Bent, St. Vrain, and Company, which eventually became the "largest and strongest merchandising and fur trading firm in the Southwest."[523] The company's location on the edge of the plains positioned it well for the buffalo-robe trade. Charles went to St. Louis in 1831 to arrange for Bernard Pratte and Company to be their supplier. In both 1832 and 1833, Charles Bent captained the principal westbound caravans over the Santa Fe Trail. In 1833, he and St. Vrain opened stores in both Taos and Santa Fe. The extensive inventories they built up allowed them to avoid the depressed prices that occurred during periods of merchandise glut when caravans arrived, and to restock their shelves from their inventory when shortages prevailed elsewhere.

As a result of William Bent's successful trading jaunts east of the Rockies among the Plains tribes, he was able to build a stockade at the mouth of Fountain Creek, near modern-day Pueblo. With Charles's help and using wagons, he stocked it with merchandise. Now the Indians could come to him to trade. Apparently in 1832, at the stockade, Charles saw that a stronger effort was needed to compete with other traders, such as Captain John Gantt and Jefferson Blackwell, who had trapped as far north as Laramie, and had built a fort on the confluence of the Fountain Creek and Arkansas River. Not only that, but Gantt was rebuilding it with adobe.

Faced with stiff competition that occasionally got violent, the Bent brothers, and no doubt St. Vrain as well, decided, probably in the summer of 1832, that a large fort along the upper Arkansas would be able to accommodate the St. Louis–Santa Fe trade, and would benefit from the beaver pelts and buffalo robes that various tribes, particularly the Cheyenne, could bring them. Legend or fact says that in 1831 on the Arkansas, Charles, William, and their younger brothers George, eighteen, and Robert, sixteen, met with the Cheyenne chiefs Yellow Wolf, Little Wolf, and Wolf Chief. Yellow Wolf advised them to build a trading post near Big Timbers, where the Cheyenne camped because of the shelter, wood, and water available. The Bents agreed on a location a dozen miles upstream from the mouth of the Purgatory Creek, on the north side of the Arkansas, about halfway between present-day La Junta and Las Animas, Colorado, but not as far as Big Timbers.[524]

Construction of the large, enclosed, two-story adobe fort was under way in 1833. On his trip to Missouri that year, Charles applied for and received a trading license to trade within the region. Possible trading partners would be the Cheyenne, Arapaho, Snake, Comanche, Kiowa, Sioux, and Arikara. The license was worded to include not only Fort William, which was under construction, but also such distant locations as near the Laramie Mountains and the Bear River in Colorado.

Trading in New Mexico between 1821 and 1831 had transitioned from pelts to buffalo robes, and from trappers to traders. In William Gordon's report to Congress in 1832, $50,000 worth of beaver came out of the Southwest the previous year. The beaver trade into Taos remained throughout the 1830s, but decreased as streams were depleted and the price of beaver remained low. By the end of 1833, the price of beaver pelts descended from $6 per pound to $3.50 in St. Louis.[525] Gantt and Blackwell, depending primarily on beaver, quit in 1835. William Bent bought their fort to serve as a minor trading post.

Charles Bent was appointed governor of the new Territory of New Mexico after the Mexican–American War. Discontent over the treatment of local prisoners resulted in a revolt in January 19, 1847. Governor Bent was murdered in his own house. A contemporary described him this way: "He was a noble man and was a great business man."[526]

William Bent's later life was lived much in Indian style, which he obviously loved. He married Owl Woman, daughter of Cheyenne chief Gray Thunder. Their first child, Mary, was born on January 12, 1838. While this may have been a beneficial marriage, it was also a successful one. The traditional tribal wars between the Comanche and Cheyenne and the Ute and Apache continued to affect the trade of the Southwest and caused the Bents to close down some of their forts. William continued to have good relationships with the various tribes. Beginning with the Cheyenne, he held a peace council of the Prairie Apache, Arapahoe, Cheyenne, and

Comanche. Peace was declared among the tribes, and the Bents promised to reopen trade, including the no-questions-asked purchase of Comanche surplus horses. Thus the Bent, St. Vrain, and Company influence spread east and south, lessening the fort's two-year fear of Comanche attack."[527]

It was estimated that the Comanche traded 30,000 buffalo robes yearly; an additional 130,000 buffalo would have been used for food, shelter, and other subsistence purposes for their population of 20,000 people. Twenty years after the construction of Bent's Fort, the Kiowa still brought in 20,000 robes and the Cheyenne, 40,000. The bison population of approximately six million on the southern plains was amazingly resilient until increased hunting of the females with softer robe hair began to affect their numbers.[528]

In the Southwest, the meteor shower of November 12, 1833, heralded at least two new changes in the life of fur trappers. At the new Bent's Fort, with the Cheyenne camped nearby, "a dazzling shower of meteors blazed across the night sky. All America saw them."[529] In California on the shores of Tulare Lake, where Ewing Young watched, he had decided to leave the beaver trapping and go to farm in Oregon, where he was instrumental in the formation of the territory.

CHAPTER 18:

FORT VANCOUVER TRADE

Marguerite Wadin McKay was the first lady of Fort Vancouver. The daughter of the Swiss independent fur trader Jean-Etienne Waddens by a Cree mother, she had been the country wife of Alexander McKay, who was lost in the *Tonquin* massacre in 1811. She and John McLoughlin were married in the fashion of the country in the Rainy Lake area in 1811. Before McLoughlin went to the HBC's Columbia District (which became the Columbia Department in 1827), they had two sons and two daughters. The family arrived on the lower Columbia in 1824.

Contemporaries noted Marguerite's "numerous charities and many excellent qualities of heart—one of the kindest women in the world."[530] She was much loved and greatly respected. So when the Reverend Herbert Beaver, arriving from England in 1836, called her only a "kept mistress…who should not be allowed to associate with Mrs. Beaver, who by marriage the parson had raised to his own level," he found himself being flogged by the cane of the very angry chief factor John McLoughlin. Catholic priests held that country marriages were a state of natural marriage, and that church marriage was renewing and ratifying their mutual consent of marriage. McLoughlin and Marguerite consented to such a marriage in 1842.[531]

McLoughlin lived in and managed the Columbia Department from Fort Vancouver, six miles above the mouth of the Willamette River. Governor Simpson had located it there in 1824 because it was more easily defensible than Fort George was and better for growing food crops. At sunrise on March 19, 1825, Simpson broke a bottle of rum on the fledgling post's flagstaff and portentously declared, "In behalf of the honorable Hudson's Bay Company, I hereby name this establishment Fort Vancouver. God save King George the Fourth!" In his journal he noted that he had chosen the name Vancouver after the distinguished British navigator "to identify our claim to the soil and trade with his discovery of the river and coast on behalf of Great Britain."[532]

Chief Factor John McLoughlin's twenty-two-year career as manager of the Columbia Department of the HBC began after his transcontinental trip with Governor Simpson in 1824. He remained a key figure until his retirement in January 1846. The remoteness of both the governor, located at York Factory on Hudson's Bay and Lachine near Montreal, and the Governor and Committee in London, as well as the integrity, loyalty, good judgment, and powerful presence of McLoughlin himself, resulted in his virtual autonomy in running the department.

The prime business of the Hudson's Bay Company, in competition with the American companies operating in the Columbia River drainage, was to exploit the Indian trade systems and develop them into profitable fur-trade channels. Under the royal charter, the Governor and Council had authority to make laws and act in a judicial capacity for and in the Columbia Department. The HBC was also responsible for advancing the territorial aspirations of the British government.

The department had wide responsibilities. It controlled Indian relations and trade in New Caledonia, the Snake River expeditions of Chief Trader Peter Skene Ogden, fur trade in the ancient flood-scoured inland plains—the Columbia Plateau of present-day Washington State—the

California expeditions, and American and Russian maritime competition on the Northwest Coast. In conjunction with these efforts, McLoughlin also developed other exportable products, such as timber and garden produce. McLoughlin's many letters reflect the incredible detail that demanded his action, interest, and response.

This chapter is concerned with Indian fur trade in the interior Columbia Plateau, as it is now known; it includes the Columbia River valley to the river's mouth, much of eastern Oregon, and in HBC expeditions, to California. The terrain involved is significant. Periodically in past, cataclysmic floods projected walls of water five hundred feet high, which carved the Columbia Plateau, the most recent about twelve thousand years ago. The immense dry canyons, the scab-like rock outcrops on the prairies, and the Columbia River Gorge are all marks of those cataclysms.[533] The scoured lands did not provide subsistence for the Indian tribes, although they hunted deer, elk, and bear; gathered berries, bulbs, and nuts from the prairie; and traded the flint, agate, and obsidian rocks they found there. The presence of the Columbia, Snake, and other rivers allowed them to develop a riparian culture. Riverine or linear settlement groups that relied on salmon, Pacific cutthroat trout, eulachon (smelt), and sturgeon defined the Indian network of the Columbia Plateau. As in New Caledonia, salmon was the key to subsistence.

George Simpson's view of the Columbia Plateau gained from his 1825 trip was grim: "The country...nothing but a Sandy desert....The face of the country we passed through to Day is Sand & Rock and the only symptom of Vegetation is a Solitary Wormwood bush [sagebrush] here and there of which we can barely collect sufficient to cook our Meals."[534] However, as he traveled westward, his opinion improved with the changing landscape. Simpson became enthusiastic about the climate west of The Dalles, and saw great natural beauty and resources. Of the site of Fort Vancouver, still under construction, he wrote, "It will in Two Years hence be the finest place in North America, indeed I have rarely seen a Gentleman's seat in England possessing so many natural advantages and where ornament and use are so agreeable combined."[535]

On this journey, Simpson expressed in his journal, and to the Governor and Committee in London, his plans for developing profitable operations in the Columbia Plateau. The principal items in the plan were:

- By every means possible, enforce a more economical, self-sustaining lifestyle at Columbia District posts. Emphasize farming as a prime element of provisioning.
- Establish high standards of Indian relations by managers of the Hudson's Bay Company.
- Close Fort Spokane and move its operations to a new Fort Colvile, near Kettle Falls on the Columbia. (Next to Fort Vancouver, Fort Colvile became the most successful agricultural source of foodstuffs in the Columbia District.)
- Place the principal depot at the mouth of the Fraser River.
- Whenever possible, prohibit the use of spirituous liquors.

Finally, Simpson estimated that Columbia District profits for the year would be £10,000; he expected it to yield double the profit of any other part of North America for the amount of capital employed, if New Caledonia and the coastal trade, as well as the interior, were carried on.[536]

Simpson was a keen observer of Indian life, aware of its importance to the company's trade profit. He observed that the banks of the Columbia had a denser population of Indians "than any other part of North America that I have seen." Natives of the river "appear to be well disposed, good humoured and inoffensive, the result of the firm judicious treatment" that he attributed to Donald McKenzie, who, in 1818, had built Fort Nez Perces.[537]

Four Chinookan groups comprised the Lower Chinook, or Chinook Proper: Chinook, Clatsop, Wahkiakum, and Kathlamet. The major Chinook-Clatsop occupation, distinct from inland tribes, was trade, not war. On the Columbia below The Dalles, trade was dominated by the Chinook culture, as a prominent part of the Chinookan, or Penutian, language family. "Chinooks proper" were those at and below The Dalles, but primarily, in the eyes of the white man, near the mouth of the river. Simpson singled out Concomly, the principal and most influential man of the Chinook tribe, and his son Casseno, both of whom contributed greatly to the operations of the Hudson's Bay Company. Concomly's great wealth was in slaves. Simpson commented that the furs they obtained came through the hands of three principal Indians: Concomly, king or chief of the Chinooks at Fort George; Casseno, Concomly's son and chief of a tribe; and Schannaway, the "Cowlitch Chief." Simpson considered Casseno the most intelligent chief he had ever seen.[538]

The Chinook trade was so important that Simpson commented on it in detail. He found the Chinook to have fair, pleasing looks, resembling whites more than any other he had seen. He believed them lazy and indolent because life was so easy, and considered them well-disposed and friendly. Their mode of warfare usually involved no one getting hurt and eventual negotiations between combatants. He described them "in general, exceedingly filthy in their habits, their persons and habitations swarming with loathsome vermin, which they convey to their mouths, but they are wonderfully healthy."[539]

Various other observers saw the Chinooks differently. Meriwether Lewis wrote: "They are generally cheerful but never gay. They speak without reserve in the presence of their women, of every part, and of the most familiar connection. Women were held inferior in every social and family way; maltreatment or lack of any care was normal, particularly of slave women."[540] The Chinook and Clatsop took as slaves mostly women and children; men were harder to take and keep. About the slaves, Simpson commented:

> Slaves form the principal article of traffic on the whole of this Coast and constitute the greater part of their Riches; they are made to Fish, hunt, draw Wood & Water in short all the drudgery falls on them; they feed in common with the family of their proprietors and intermarry with their own class, but lead a life of misery, indeed I conceive a Columbia slave to be the most unfortunate wretch in existence.[541]

Clark noted that "notwithstanding the servile manner in which they treat their women they pay more respect to their judgment than most Indian nations. Their women are permitted to speak freely before them, and sometimes command with a tone of authority. A few women were openly aggressive to the men of the party to the point of nuisance."[542]

Lewis and Clark observed the Chinookan haggling, and noted that time did not seem to matter. Often the women traded while the men gambled.

Historians Robert H. Ruby and John A. Brown described the adults as being thick-set, averaging five feet five inches tall, with light, coppery skin. Their faces were broad, eyes small and slanted; noses wide, flat at the tops, with fleshy tips and large nostrils. The septum and ears were perforated for decorations. Mouths were wide, lips thick, and teeth irregular and dirty. They were bow-legged, probably caused by continuous sitting and squatting; women's thick ankles and thighs were attributed to tight bindings. Their hair was course and black, and beards were plucked. Tattooing was customary. All observers noted their flattened heads, a mark of aristocracy. The heads of babies were placed between padded boards for an average of one year. They appeared not to suffer in intelligence from the deformed, flattened heads, Ruby and Brown said.[543]

The Chinook and Clatsop, living near the mouth of the Columbia, were first to encounter the whites, who found that these Indians traded with a surprising sophistication. Captain James Cook had encountered them in 1778. Coastal Indians and others upriver from the Pacific Ocean knew of iron, copper, brass, nails, coins with square holes, and iron tools before contact with the whites. The sea had washed these items ashore from Pacific-going ships, Spanish or even Japanese, which had foundered at sea or along the Pacific littoral.[544]

The most fundamental and political unit for both freemen and slaves was the village. The people lived in plank lodges in the villages, the center of their social and political life. Wealth alone determined rank, and was usually measured by number of slaves. The eldest son of high-ranking wives might succeed to the chieftainship, but in the absence of a son, a widow could assume the leadership. Women often traded with other women and could hold property independently of males.

Chinook Indians were skillful canoeists. Their canoes were swift, seaworthy craft, which they made for river use by hollowing out logs using a sharp-edged flint stone, and appeared to answer every purpose. For seagoing, they traded for the better Nootka canoes.

The Celilo falls and The Dalles rapids had restrained, if not blocked, trade from traversing the Columbia upstream or down. Lewis and Clark, in October 1805, described the "Great Falls" called Celilo and the "long and short narrows" below those falls that marked the upper end of the gorge. They observed a busy place, a principal fishery and trade center. Until The Dalles Dam was completed in 1957, Celilo Falls had been an important annual Indian fishery for literally thousands of years. Early traders noted that their dip nets were made from the stalk of a plant resembling hemp, which they preferred to use over HBC twine to fabricate nets.

William Clark described the "salmon trout"—steelhead—fried in bear oil as "I think the finest fish I ever tasted." He noted particularly "parcels of dried and pounded fish," the locally very popular fish pemmican. The

Chinookan-speaking tribes near The Dalles produced "salmon pemmican," a delicacy much in demand throughout the Columbia Plateau and beyond. They pulverized air-dried salmon and packed it in baskets lined with salmon skin for trade, with each basket weighing about a hundred pounds. Thus packed, and stored in packs of twelve, it would keep for two years. They consigned to trade a million pounds annually.[545]

On the lower Columbia, the medium of exchange, which only approximated a value, was the "dentalia fathom," a term describing the strings of dentalia with about forty shells to the string. Above The Dalles, dentalia were primarily adornment. As time passed, two dentalium fathoms equaled a beaver skin.

Farther up the Columbia River was another ancient trade center at Kettle Falls. There in 1825, the Hudson's Bay Company opened Fort Colvile in recognition of the site's strategic location. It was an important Indian fishery and trade site, and whites had been trading there since 1807. Another trade center beyond the Columbia Plateau, but involving the Columbia Plateau Indians, was the Shoshone rendezvous in southwestern Wyoming, attended by the Flathead, Nez Percé, Yakima, Walla Walla, and Cayuse. The Yakima trading route reached southward as far as the Spanish in California.

Unquestionably, the dominant feature of the Columbia Plateau from antiquity was the trade and communications role of the Columbia River and its tributaries. The most important change from that pattern was the arrival of the horse in about 1730. Until then, the articles carried had been of necessity light and of relatively high value, while trading parties had been small and their travels infrequent. With the horse, Indian middlemen and entrepreneurs could go overland, more frequently and with larger parties. The variety of goods increased, extending to raw and semi-processed materials. The horse itself became a source of wealth and was of great value in trade. However, the coastal traders were, to a substantial degree, as defined by Lewis and Clark, the soul of the trade. Their exciting and extensive source was American and British shippers.[546]

In the mid-eighteenth century, slaves were the most important item at The Dalles, even more important than its virtually unlimited fishery. Chinook, Clatsop, Wahkiakum, and Kathlamet traded for grass fibers of superior quality, pipes, and European-made battle-axes from beyond the Rockies. Spanish mules, horses, tack, and shells (dentalium or tooth shells of a mollusk) came up the Columbia from the south as far as Santa Fe. Buffalo robes, pipestone, and sweetgrass came from the plains east of the Continental Divide.

Simpson expressed the opinion that it was the duty of the HBC Indian trader to secure to himself the respect and esteem of the Indians. He commented, "It is a lamentable fact that almost every difficulty we have had with Indians throughout the Country may be traced to our interference with their Women…9 murders out of 10 Committed on Whites by Indians have arisen through Women."[547]

Simpson had no interest in civilizing the Indian: "I have always remarked that an enlightened Indian is good for nothing; there are several of them about the Bay side and totally useless, even the half Breeds of the Country who have been educated in Canada…not only pick up the vices of the whites upon which they improve but retain those of the Indian in their utmost extent."[548]

Burt Brown Barker, who edited an edition of McLoughlin's letters at Vancouver, explained that McLoughlin's Indian policy was to be so severe in the event an Indian murdered a Hudson's Bay Company man, that reports of his retaliatory action would spread and Indians would avoid repetition. When, in April 1832, Indians killed two trappers, McLoughlin sent Michel LaFramboise to punish the offenders. His instructions were, "Tis likely some innocent beings may in such cases become victims as well as the guilty, the severity necessary for our own safety and security may always be tempered with humanity and mercy."[549] Otherwise, McLoughlin was very strict about killing an Indian. LaFramboise attacked and killed six of the responsible tribe, expecting the word to be passed that another murder would result in the rest of the tribe being killed.

As chief factor, McLoughlin's immediate tasks were difficult because of Simpson's demand for immediate reduction in manpower and other costs. The border dispute between the United States and Great Britain was also a complicating factor: would the border between the two nations go through the Oregon country at the Columbia River, or be farther north along the forty-ninth parallel? In HBC trading, the rate of exchange of goods and pelts was specified, but McLoughlin could vary it to compete with the Americans.

He received an annual ship from London with goods, and returned furs by the same ship. The loss of a ship, such as the *William and Anne*, which wrecked at the Columbia bar, or damage to inadequately protected goods en route could cause him to be so short of goods as to be in extreme difficulty. He convinced the London headquarters that he needed a year's supply stored in advance. At times, Fort Nez Perces (later Fort Walla Walla) was used as a reserve supply fort.

McLoughlin had to worry constantly about the loss of men, goods, and furs in the violent Columbia River rapids. Furs required special care to avoid moths or mold in storage or transit. Disciplinary action was necessary to prevent thievery, not only by employees and ships' crews, but by Indians as well. Controlling the expressly forbidden trade in furs between Indians and individual whites was a constant problem.

McLoughlin was always concerned with balancing employee assignments with the individual post workload, and he moved them about as necessary. Wages were determined by the Council at York. Statements of account had to accompany any employee's move between posts. Clerks wrote his letters from his dictation or instruction. Letters were carried by company servants or Indian messengers. These letters enabled Governor Simpson and the Governor and Committee in London to maintain careful supervision of details. The chain of supervision was from London, to Governor Simpson at Lachine near Montreal, (where the headquarters had been moved from York Factory), to Chief Factor McLoughlin, thence to the various posts. All posts kept careful accounts and detailed journals. These were considered when the annual plan submitted by each post commander was evaluated. From the plans, requirements were consolidated at York and forwarded as requisitions to England.

As a matter of Columbia Department efficiency, and reflecting trust in McLoughlin, the Governor and Committee in London corresponded directly with both him and Governor Simpson. The London authorities saw trapping in the Columbia Department as a means of letting the fur sources of the Northern Department east of the Rockies rest and recoup. In 1827 they noted that even if the Snake River expeditions were unprofitable, they would still have the advantage of defeating the Americans.[550] Thus the early pattern of Columbia Department operations was established.

In the Columbia Department, the forts were: George, Vancouver, The Dalles, Nez Perces or Walla Walla, Okanagan, Colvile, Flathead, Kootenai, Nisqually, Victoria, Langley, Rupert, McLoughlin, Simpson, and Umpqua. In addition, there were the New Caledonia forts. Simpson had maintained that the Fraser River was a usable route for transport to the coast. But after he descended the Fraser in 1828, he abandoned the idea of making a depot at the river's mouth, and when the proposed depot, Fort Langley, was built in 1830, it became a stopping point for coastal shipping.

In the Oregon country, the HBC wanted to eliminate competition, especially the competition of American fur traders, whose presence supported American claims to land coveted by Great Britain. Simpson held Americans in contempt, saying they were "people of the worst character, outcasts of society and jail runaways, acknowledging no master, no discipline." He wrote to London: "The country is a rich preserve of beaver... which, for political reasons, we should endeavour to destroy as fast as possible."[551]

In all these considerations, the beaver were lost, except in the minds of those who trapped them. In 1827, Ogden wrote, "It is scarcely credible what a destruction of beaver by trapping this season. Within the last two days, upwards of fifty females have been taken and, on an average, each with four young, ready to litter. Did we not hold this country by so light a tenure it would be most to our interest to trap it only in the fall, any by this mode it would take many years to ruin it." Ogden later commented sadly, "Well may it be said beaver have many enemies, while they alone wage war with none." George Yount later put it, "No animal is more sly, cunning and sagacious than the beaver. His instinct almost amounts to reason and intelligence."[552]

Indians of the lower Columbia were few in number relative to the large area between the Cascade Mountains in the west and the Continental Divide in the east. On the lower Columbia, the Nez Percé appeared dominant. Simpson wrote:

The Nez Perce tribe is by far the most powerful and Warlike in the Columbia and may be said to hold the Key of the River as they possess and are Masters of the country from Okenagan down to the Chutes a distance little short of 300 miles by the course of the River....with the Snakes they are almost constantly at War. If a reconciliation is effected between those tribes...they then smoke a Pipe of Peace...but their treaties are no sooner ratified than broken as the moment the conference is over and we turn our backs they are ready to pillage each others' Women and Horses and cut each others throats....I therefore consider it an object of the first importance to keep on terms of friendship with the Nez Perces and not even venture the chance of a rupture with them which would involve such serious consequences....I therefore conceive that the less intercourse we have with the Nez Perce beyond what is absolutely necessary the better.[553]

It is significant that HBC traders were dependent upon the Nez Percé to supply them with literally hundreds of horses for a number years, and for all of their expeditions from New Caledonia to San Francisco Bay. As Alvin M. Josephy Jr. wrote in *The Nez Percé Indians and the Opening of the West,* Lewis and Clark revealed that in the valley of the Clearwater River, the Nez Percé village of the great chief Broken Arm was a building about 150 feet long, containing 24 fires down its center and housing about 48 families. Clark commented, "Those people has shown much grater acts of hospitality than we have witnessed from any nation or tribe since we have passed the Rocky Mountains."[554]

The explorers' regard for the Nez Percé grew with the time spent with them. They were industrious and able, somewhat reticent and reserved, with a dignified, proud bearing and high ethical standards. Sergeant Patrick Gass called them "the most friendly, honest, and ingenuous of all tribes." Clark, who may have left a Nez Percé woman with child, called them "much more cleanly in their persons and habitations than any nation we have seen since we left the Illinois."[555]

The Nez Percé, like all Northwest peoples, relied on gathering, rather than agriculture, for subsistence, and they suffered for it. They knew lean periods, though they were shrewd hunters and artful fishermen. They gathered a corn-like *krouse* and camas roots.

Their bitterest enemies were in southwestern Idaho and southwestern Oregon. These included the western Shoshone, Northern Paiute, and the

Bannock, an offshoot of the Northern Paiute who lived with the Shoshone.

Horses seemed to be their life. Josephy wrote, "Through the valley of the lower Snake, across the Palouse prairie, and on the broad Columbia plains, wherever conditions were favorable, the horses multiplied. At intertribal meetings, thousands of grazing horses covered the landscape."[556]

After about 1755, the Blackfoot Confederation traded for guns and began to strike savagely at all western tribes, pushing them west of the mountains. But in the early 1800s, as trade in guns came up the Columbia, the Nez Percé and their allies began to push back against the Blackfoot in their pursuit of buffalo. By the 1830s they hunted as far as the Bitterroot and into the Big Hole and Beaverhead river valleys. In 1855 the new governor of Washington Territory, Isaac Stevens, negotiated a treaty in which the tribes agreed to divide the buffalo country, the Nez Percé and allies would hunt south of the Missouri River and the Blackfoot on the north. After one hundred years of enmity with the Blackfoot, the Nez Percé could freely travel and hunt. It also brought them into closer contact with the Crow and Cheyenne.[557]

Extensive trading within the Columbia network and beyond created important social relationships among many tribes. Theodore Stern, an anthropologist, noted that Cayuse bands associated most intimately with those of the lower Nez Percé and with elements of the Shahaptin-speaking Walla Walla and Umatilla tribes. Some of these people visited and camped at Cayuse fishing stations. Joint war parties fought their common enemy, the southerly Shoshone tribes, and friendly bands from different tribes even traveled together to buffalo country along the Yellowstone. Stern further wrote:

In encampments of several thousands...they celebrated together the
thanksgiving ceremonies for first fruits, discussed political concerns and

gossiped, renewed friendships, and courted as well. They traded, raced horses, and gambled....Notwithstanding such fusing at the boundaries, the retention of distinctive dialects and characteristic local cultural traditions testify to the persistence of a sense of ethnic identity.[558]

The travels to the great plains brought the adoption of some of the plains tribes' complex skills in war and travel. These were reflected, primarily among the Cayuse and Nez Percé, by their forays, for example, into Chinook lands. As Stern described the development:

> Thus, in the first third of the nineteenth century, the tribes of the southwestern Plateau had reached what was to prove the zenith of their wealth and power, drawing on their own heritage, the influence of the Chinookians, their interactions with Plains tribes and the Plains experience, and the goods and ideas brought by the fur traders. Among the tribes of the district, Ross pronounced the Nez Percé and Cayuse "by far the most powerful and warlike," who "regulate all the movements of the others in peace and war, and as they stand well or ill disposed toward their traders, so do the others."[559]

Language differences were a critical problem. Carl Waldman, in his *Atlas of the North American Indian,* lists eight language families among thirty-eight inland tribes, of which two—Shahaptan and Salishan—were by far the most extensive. Chief Trader Samuel Black, writing of the central (inland) trade, described the language of the Nez Percé, Palouse, Walla Walla, and Yakima as being very different. He found Nez Percé the easiest, since it was the "smoothest and finest language & became the general language of the Nations in this quarter...[—]having only one name for one Article."[560] Among the solutions were bilingualism among tribes and various degrees of sign language, such as one based on the Crow language.

Evidently the Chinook Jargon, originating probably among shipborne trades and Indians at Nootka Sound, or possibly at Fort Vancouver, became the most valuable and widely used lingua franca throughout the Columbia Plateau. George Shaw, who studied the Chinook Jargon, found that it got its principal impetus at Astoria under the North West Company, whose personnel introduced both English and French Canadian words.[561]

Stern commented: "What is clear is that Chinook Jargon was late in coming to the Plateau, and among the Salishan tribes did not replace bilingualism in French as a medium of communication in the trading posts. Above The Dalles, signing, rather than the Jargon, facilitated trade."[562]

The HBC sent fur brigades up the Snake River valley, west of the Continental Divide, to create a "fur desert" (as discussed in chapter 14). Brigades also brought furs down the Columbia from New Caledonia, but the route south of Fort Vancouver and into California remained unknown.

Both Simpson and McLoughlin felt a sense of urgency about trading in California. On August 10, 1828, American mountain man Jedediah Smith and two companions reached Fort Vancouver after the disastrous attack on Smith's crew on the Umpqua River. Smith aroused McLoughlin's interest through his maps and his reports of beaver in California streams—quality furs in quantity. McLoughlin learned from Smith that "the Spanish" ignored their beaver, "an animal they hardly know by name, although some of the rivers within a few miles of their settlements abounded therewith."[563]

McLoughlin sent Alexander R. McLeod south to recover Smith's horses and goods, to punish the Indians, and to continue to California as the "Buena Ventura" expedition—to verify the existence of the Buenaventura River, which was believed to go from Salt Lake to the sea.

McLeod had joined the HBC with the 1821 merger as a chief trader. He was competent, but very indecisive. He and his thirty-eight men did not reach the attack scene until mid-October. He did recover much of Smith's goods and many of his horses. Mainly, he gained by Smith's maps of his route from California. He returned to Fort Vancouver on December 14, 1828. At Simpson's urging, McLoughlin ordered McLeod to go again, to hunt the "San Buenaventura."

McLeod left in January 1829, following Smith's trail southward, inland from the Pacific Ocean, with Arthur Turner, formerly of Smith's group, as guide. McLeod crossed the Rogue River near Grant's Pass, then crossed the Siskiyou Mountains, followed the Upper and Lower Klamath lakes, and reached the Pit River in late March. Following the Pit River, his party arrived at the Sacramento River on April 9. They camped on Cow Creek to rest horses and feed the men on local deer while they built canoes. They were pestered by local Indians, who periodically launched arrows at them. McLeod's brigade then descended the river by water and by land on the east side, trapping beaver as they went. They found the Sacramento valley heavily populated with Indians. They also regularly encountered Spanish patrols from the San Francisco Presidio chasing Indian horse thieves.

Trapping near San Francisco Bay was unprofitable because of the ebb and flow of the tides. As McLeod saw his ammunition depleting, he decided to winter in the highlands near Mount Shasta. In October he left Clear Lake for the Shasta Valley. He stopped in snow short of his destination, and spent part of a miserable winter on the McLeod River. He cached his five hundred pelts, which were destroyed by seeping snow. In January, he moved to the clear, warm Shasta Valley. In spring, after they had crossed the mountains and reached the Umpqua, McLeod left his men and returned to Fort Vancouver, arriving there on February 13, 1830. The Northern Council censured him for leaving his men, and Simpson sent him to Fort Simpson on the Mackenzie River.

The Hudson's Bay Company sent a total of thirteen expeditions to California from the 1820s into the early 1840s. Donald McKay led HBC's first expedition, Peter Skene Ogden led two others, Michel LaFramboise led six, and Alexander McLeod, John Work, Thomas McKay, and Francis Ermatinger each led one. All were supported or controlled from Fort Vancouver. Of these, an Ogden expedition—the sixth—was the most productive because of his descriptions of the area surrounding the lower Sacramento River and the debunking of the legends of the Buenaventura River from Salt Lake to the sea. Unfortunately, his journals were lost in the rapids at The Dalles on his return.

Both Simpson and McLoughlin were convinced that there was a coastal trail and that the coastal rivers would prove to be highly productive beaver streams. They emphasized this point in their instructions to expedition leaders. Ogden did not explore coastal rivers. John Work did, and found them bare of beaver. In the process, they developed an understanding of the geography of Northern California in the vicinity of Mount Shasta and the Sacramento River tributaries. Michel LaFramboise, in his expeditions, contributed to the understanding of the approaches to California west of Mount Shasta, which became the Siskiyou Trail. Because Work kept meticulous detail and Ogden's journals were lost in the Columbia River rapids at The Dalles, the authors rely on Work's journals for a summary of his effort and his understanding of the Indians, the beaver, and the geography of California north of the lower Sacramento River.

John Work joined the HBC as a "writer" in 1814 in the Orkney Islands. He was appointed clerk in the Severn District in 1822. In 1823, with Ogden, he came to the Columbia District, was assigned to Spokane House, and began his valuable journal, which he continued until 1835. He assisted John McLoughlin in building Fort Vancouver in 1824–25. He closed Spokane House in April 1826, took charge of Fort Colvile until 1829, and moved the Colvile District headquarters to Flathead Post. He commanded two Snake River expeditions after Ogden, successfully fighting off the Blackfeet. He led a California expedition to the lower Sacramento River in 1832, and with LaFramboise trapped the lower Sacramento with disappointing results. He was then assigned to the coastal trade, feeling forgotten, but was appointed chief trader in 1830 and chief factor in 1846.[564]

Work married a Spokane Métis woman, Josette Legace, in 1826, and had eleven children, all of whom he carefully educated. He was a devoted family man whose constant concern was the well-being and happiness of his wife and children. He was deeply religious, emphasizing "the genuine Religion of the heart which is practical" and objecting to "mere professional Religion," which he considered to be "too much show and parade." Work called Josette his "Little Rib."[565] She often accompanied him on his expeditions. Historian A. L. Bancroft, seeing Josette in 1884, wrote, "The Indian wife in body and mind was strong and elastic as steel." Josette died in 1896.[566]

Governor Simpson, in his famous "Character Book," described Work as a "very steady pains taking Man, regular, oeconomical [sic] and attentive in business, and bears a fair private character.…A queer looking fellow, of Clownish Manners and address, indeed there is a good deal of simplicity approaching to idiocy in his appearance, he is nevertheless a Shrewd Sensible Man, and not deficient in firmness when necessary." Work was known as "The Old Gentleman," and finally settled in Victoria, was prominent in the development of the government of Vancouver Island, where he died in 1861.[567]

Each of the HBC's thirteen expeditions to California contributed to understanding the geography, the many California Indian tribes, and the take of beaver en route and in California. Indian relations were, as elsewhere, very important. The expeditions encountered the Klamath in southwestern Oregon, the Modoc in northwestern California, and the numerous California tribes.[568]

Though the Klamath and Modoc were closely related in language, they were somewhat divergent in culture. The Klamath traded with the more southern Chinook and the Tillamook of the coast, as well as Sahaptan peoples of the southwestern Columbia Plateau. They acquired both Northwest Coast and Plateau characteristics, and demonstrated Plateau influences. Yet they manifested far stronger ties with their California neighbors—the eastern Shasta, Achumawi, and Mountain Maidu—than they did with the somewhat more remote tribes of the Columbia Plateau.[569]

The lifestyle of the Klamath and Modoc was aboriginal in arms and dress. They were expert horse thieves, and an unguarded camp usually lost horses. Though they lacked firearms, their unpredictable, hostile behavior with aboriginal weapons made them dangerous.

McLoughlin launched Work's expedition in two parts. First, trader Michel LaFramboise led a party from Vancouver in April 1832 headed down the coast. He took eighteen white men, seventeen Indian men, eighteen Indian women, and six children. En route to the beaver streams farther south, LaFramboise punished the Tillamook Indians for killing two Iroquois employed in the fur trade. They killed six Tillamook. They were then to follow the coast trail, but abandoned that route as impossible—actually, they later discovered that there was no coast "trail." LaFramboise moved inland and took the McLeod Track south. By summer, LaFramboise's party was encamped near present-day Stockton, California, in the California Central Valley, at "French Camp," which Chief Trader McLeod had established in about 1826.

Chief Trader John Work left Fort Vancouver for California on August 17, 1832, leading an expedition of about forty people, including Indian and mixed-descent women and children related to the white traders and trappers who had gone ahead. His wife, Josette, and his three small daughters traveled with him. The complete party included traders, trappers, clerks, and storekeepers. Work was no novice at leading an expedition, having led two Snake River expeditions and one into the Missouri headwaters, where three hundred Blackfeet had attacked his brigade; there they were repulsed, which reflects his defensive skill.

Work's California expedition was large and colorful. To get a sense of how such it might have looked, consider historian Alice Bay Maloney's generic description of fur brigades; her words are paraphrased here for brevity:

> Horses numbering as many as two hundred were assembled to carry the men, their families, and the stock of trade goods for barter. Hunters and trappers in deerskin garments gathered their Indian wives and half-breed children, and the sounds of laughter and song could be heard above the chatter of the women as they mounted for the long trek to the south.
>
> Behind the leader rode his Indian wife, gaily attired in the finest London broadcloth, with a wide-brimmed, feather-trimmed hat atop her wealth of long, shining, black hair. The bells on her leather leggings made a musical note as her pony jogged lazily along. At her saddle bow, in a basket of native weave, hung her youngest offspring. Older children on spotted cayuses rode at her side or close behind. Proud was the Indian girl chosen to be the consort of a "gentleman of the Company." Security and honor were hers.
>
> The French Canadian trappers wore bright red, knitted toques, but here and there among them might be seen the coonskin cap of an American free trapper who was welcomed to the party because of his Yankee ingenuity and his prowess with the rifle. All men were in deerskin. Each carried the long knife of the trapper and hunter.
>
> The leader of the fur brigade had to be a man of parts. Not only was he a dictator, the sole law and authority, but he was a military commander in case of attack by hostile Indians. He was physician in case of illness, linguist with knowledge of many native tongues, and diplomat to negotiate with the Spaniards, Russians, and Americans—his rivals for the harvest of fur. Above all he must be a highly competent trapper and trader, in

order that he might return to Headquarters with a highly satisfactory yield of beaver and land otter skins for shipment to the London market of his employers.[570]

Work left Fort Vancouver by boat in August 1832, and on reaching Fort Walla Walla, changed to the expedition's horses and left on September 2. Women performed important duties. They cared for the children. At each stop, they erected leather Indian lodges or brush shelters and prepared food. Hunters scouted daily for elk, deer, and bear meat to feed the company. To the Indian and mixed-descent women fell the task of dressing not only the meat but also the pelts trapped along the way. The women furthermore cared for the pelts until the brigade's return to Fort Vancouver. They tanned deerskins and made garments, including the moccasins that needed frequent replacement. The life of the women was ceaseless toil.

Members of the expedition soon came down with what Work diagnosed as fever and "ague" (now generally accepted to be malaria).[571] In the western medical practice of the day, Work treated the ill with both bloodletting and quinine. By the time he reached Fort Walla Walla, he had used up most of his supply of medicine. Malaria had been epidemic at Fort Vancouver and along the lower Columbia in 1830, and the disease still lingered in the population. Work's expedition was just one of several sources that may have carried the disease into California, where mosquitoes helped spread it widely (though the role of mosquitoes was not then understood) and where it devastated Indian populations.

The expedition route went to Malheur Lake, which they reached on September 30. By that time, their trapping had produced ninety-eight beaver and ten otter. They had also encountered Snake Indian horse thieves. From Malheur Lake they traveled southwest to Goose Lake, which they reached on October 22. This was Ogden's earlier route, going east of Mount Shasta. At each camp, Work sent out trappers, who took another sixty-two beaver and four otter. Their provision-hunting produced primarily waterfowl, though they did get one sheep and one deer.

The expedition descended the upper Pit River, crossed Adin Pass west of Grouse Mountain, and reached the Pit River again in Northern California on November 6, 1832. They continued south to the Sacramento River, arriving on November 18. It was the rainy season, and heavy rains had caused the river to rise, flood, and block their crossing. Work set men to hollowing out dugout canoes. He observed that the local Indians were mostly naked and carried only rods or staffs for protection. They were burning the dead after an attack by the Shasta Indians.[572] Work's trappers had trapped forty more beaver, for a total of two hundred, since leaving Fort Nez Perces. Game became more plentiful.

With the group divided into a water party and a land party, the expedition continued down the Sacramento and reached Sutter Buttes on November 29. Work camped on December 7 ten miles north of Butte Creek, which joined the Sacramento in a marsh (now known as Butte Sink). Rainfall was continuous.

At this campsite, two of LaFramboise's men, traveling as an express to Fort Vancouver, appeared. Work retained them long enough to get information. He learned that LaFramboise had abandoned the coastal trail at the sheer cliffs south of the Umpqua River and Winchester Bay, near the shifting and high sands of the Oregon dunes, and that LaFramboise had taken the McLeod Track[573] (later known as the Siskiyou Trail) west of Mount Shasta and had gone clear to Mission Dolores on San Francisco Bay. Evidently LaFramboise had trapped where Work had intended to trap. Work was displeased. He wrote in his journal: "They arr'd in August and have trapped it all from where we are here downward, as well as the Bay, so that after our long journey here there are no beaver remaining for our party....Thus...the coast...remains unhunted."[574] It was also disappointing to learn that LaFramboise had gained only 950 beaver pelts.

One tribe on the Feather River had lots of antelope meat, killing animals in a surround with bows and arrows and short lances. Work, seeing Indians bent down as animals, grazing, observed, "They are spread all over the plain and gathering and eating all kinds of herbs, like beasts."[575]

By March 3, 1833, when the rains ended, Work had collected 145 more beaver, for his party's total of 345. Flooding forced him to settle on the high ground near the Sutter Buttes, where there was elk and forage. Here, LaFramboise's party of 58 joined Work's party, making a camp of 163 people.

On March 3, Work's brigade left the dry land around the Sutter Buttes, and in five skin boats, men, women, children, horses, and baggage crossed the Sacramento River into the flat valley beyond. By the eighth, they were camped near today's town of Williams, still pestered by Indians stealing traps or robbing their traps for food. By March 11, they had moved southwest into the foothills, and camped on Cache Creek, west of Clear Lake.

Hearing that Ewing Young and his Americans had crossed the Sacramento and entered the Coast Range by an Indian trail along Putah Creek, Work began his exploration of coastal waters. He was absolutely convinced that in those short rivers, beaver must be plentiful. They moved down the Cache Creek valley to the Putah Creek at Winters, where they found the Americans' tracks. Work sent LaFramboise up Putah Creek to find Young's trail. He reported that Young's party had crossed the Coast Range by the Russian River to the sea south of the Russians' Fort Ross. By March 27, acting on this information, Work sent a second party of twenty trappers and eleven Indians, with two horses each, to follow Young to the coast. They were led by Astoria veteran Alexander Carson, who had been with Work on his first Snake expedition.

Work sent LaFramboise to Mission Dolores on San Francisco Bay for ammunition. LaFramboise went instead to another mission at Sonoma. There he got no ammunition and was advised to visit the Russians at Bodega (Fort Ross). Visiting them, he did get ten pounds of powder, thirty pounds of lead, and ten pounds of tobacco, all for a much higher price. The Russian manager at Fort Ross, Peter Kostromitinoff, told LaFramboise that he had explored the coast northward for thirty leagues—about ninety miles. He had found the route was bad, but passable. The rivers were small, the Indians hostile, and the beaver nonexistent.

During the early days of April, Work camped and trapped in the Suisan Bay area. He described it as "a swamp overgrown with bulrushes and intersected in almost every direction with channels of different sizes." LaFramboise returned to the Suisan Bay camp. An American from Young's party reported that LaFramboise had followed Young over the Coast Range but found no beaver. Work did not believe him, retaining his suspicions. With few beaver, recent horse purchases, and people beginning to get malaria, Work decided to move to the coast. By April 18, his brigade was camped at the mouth of the Russian River.

During the rest of April, Work's brigade followed the coast northward, despite difficult terrain in rain and cold. There were no beaver, and he lost horses and traps in river crossings. They encountered Indian camps but few Indians. By May 6, he had reached Shelter Cove at Point Delgado, after 125 miles of coast travel. The brigade had found the canyons deeper, the forest denser, and the Indians more warlike, though local Pomo Indians, wearing rabbit skins, helped him make rafts for river crossings. Work had twenty-seven white and six Indian trappers then. LaFramboise, who was ill, had seventeen whites and thirteen Indians. Scouts reported the road ahead was impassible, with long delays. Work was finally convinced that there were no beaver along the coast and that he had satisfied McLoughlin's and Simpson's instructions. He turned inland and sent LaFramboise, who was recovering, northward along the coast.

Work sent part of his trappers up the coast and part inland. By May 10, he reached his northernmost point, on the Mattole River. Heading southeast along the east slopes of the Coast Range, he reached Clear Lake on May 19, and on the twenty-fifth, camped in the lower Sacramento Valley, east of present-day Vacaville. The two parties rejoined, having lost both horses and traps. During this trip south, they had encountered friendly Pomo Indians, plenty of deer and bear, and mostly fine warm weather.

Now began again the travels, explorations, and dispatch of several canoe parties designed to get beaver from the Suisan Bay, San Joaquin, and Mokelumne river systems. The effort lasted from May 27 to July 24. Since mid-June, Work had gotten 249 beaver with indifferent fur, 850 land otter, and much game for provisions. His people were suffering from heat, mosquitoes, sand flies, and swampy camps. He decided to return to Fort Vancouver.

Work attacked an Indian camp on July 25 and recovered eighteen horses, but being low on ammunition, he could not attack all the Indian horse thieves. Illness from malaria was beginning to get serious. Work learned that the Indians had not suffered from the deadly Anopheles mosquitoes carrying the "malaria of the marshes" until 1830. Now whole villages died from infection, probably carried by whites who were not ill. Ogden and his men could have been such a source during Ogden's trip south in 1830, or LaFramboise in 1826.

By August 6, Work was again in the Sutter Butte Valley, having crossed the Feather River at Oroville. The weather was hot, the valley dry. By the tenth, more illness was cropping up. He crossed Pine Creek on the sixteenth and the next day counted forty-two ill. On the eighteenth, he headed northeast along modern California 299, and by August 24, he had seventy-two ill, with only two women clear of fever. Work wrote, "Our condition is really deplorable....I am afraid to stop lest we die like the Indians....I endeavor to keep up their spirits as well as I can, but it is become now of little effect."[576]

Work forced the brigade to continue, believing that their only salvation lay in reaching Fort Vancouver. With the higher elevation, a few were beginning to recover. Indians again were shooting at horses with arrows. Many horses were lame from the stony trail. Work commented, "This is the reward we meet for treating the barbarians kindly and endeavouring to conciliate them. Nothing but severe treatment is of any avail with such savages."[577]

Then Work himself became ill. The weather was cooling, but Indian harassment continued. He had only twelve men available for night guard. He took the old McLeod Track west of Mount Shasta northward. The sick could not take care of their horses, and eleven horses were lost on September 7. Some people recovered, then relapsed. The whole party seemed helpless. On the thirteenth, in fine cool weather, they crossed the Klamath River and found LaFramboise's track to Fort Vancouver. Work continued to be ill. Weather was turning frosty and cold. Horses were suffering from lack of forage where Indians had burned the grass. Some friendly Indians visited.

By September 17, they had crossed the Siskiyou Mountains and were on the south fork of the Rogue River. Indians killed a few horses. Illness continued to dominate Work and the brigade. By the thirtieth, they had crossed the Rogue River. Though the trail was often blocked by fallen trees, and the sick showed little improvement, they reached the South Fork of the Umpqua on October 4. On the eighth, they camped near Roseburg. The sick were getting better, but Work was very ill.

On October 13, Work wrote he was "very feeble" with fever. At that low point, LaFramboise and four men from Fort Vancouver arrived. They had reached Vancouver in early July. They brought with them three gallons of flour, three gallons of Indian corn, tea, and a half loaf of sugar, a great treat. The sick were beginning to recover.

On October 19, Work ferried his people across the Yamhill River to Champoeg, on canoes borrowed from HBC people settled there. Also at this company post, he got canoes to take himself to Fort Vancouver. He stopped at the Willamette Falls to bring people, baggage, and horses across, and to start men drying furs. Then he left and landed at Fort Vancouver on October 29, 1833. Two days later the whole party arrived.

The brigade had been out 483 days, spending only 59 days in trapping projects and canoe building. They had gotten 667 beaver and 123 otter, plus 580 deer, elk, bear, and antelope. From the start, July 23, 1832, until the end at Fort Vancouver, they were immobilized by illness, approximately 11 percent of the time. The rest was spent in travel, recovering horses, getting supplies, hunting, building boats, dressing skins, and caring for the sick. Work summarized their expedition accomplishments in California: "We had a great deal of trouble and some skirmishes with the natives on account of their stealing and killing some of our horses and attempting to kill some of the men....Our hunt only amounts to 1,023 beaver and otter skins. Indeed, the country is now so exhausted that little can be done in it."[578]

Work's report ended the HBC expeditions along the Snake River, among the Flatheads, the Missouri sources, and California. In its eagerness to defeat American efforts, HBC had truly despoiled the beaver population, as Ogden had noted with regret, and had reduced, but not ended, the fur trade in the Rocky Mountain areas and in California. Chief Trader John Work marked the shift of HBC efforts from the Columbia Plateau to the Northwest Coast marine trade.

CHAPTER 19:

THE NORTHWEST COAST

Indians of the Northwest Coast were in several ways different from the inland tribes. Their environment was a series of islands, inlets, tidal estuaries and bays, and coastal rivers draining from the interior. The generally cliff-like shoreline was penetrated by four great river systems: the Stikine, the Nass, the Skeena, and the Fraser. These rivers were the channels of ancient trade with the interior, and the routes of later Indian middlemen. The sea, warmed by the Japanese current, provided boundless varieties of food, obtainable with relative ease. The shore was steep, with narrow beaches, if any. Cool breezes in the summer changed to northwest winds with rain and moderate winters that rarely brought freezing.

Indian culture of the Northwest Coast was extremely complex and virtually determined the fur trade. Kinship groups formed the social tribal structure. They believed that they owned the area that provided food and materials. There was a distinct class hierarchy.

Northwest Coast Indians are better described as organized in villages, clans, and phratries, rather than tribes, though "tribe" is the term generally used to identify the main kinship groups: the Tlingit, the Haida, the Tsimshian, Bella Coola, Kwakuitl, and Nootka. Farther south were the Makah, Quinault, Chinook, Clatsop, Tillamook, Coos, and Umpqua. Other tribes south of the Columbia River had minor roles in the coastal fur trade, which flourished from the Columbia up to Russian America. Despite navigation skills and a broken coastline whose islands and inlets protected them from the ocean winds, thus permitting relatively free intertribal travel, northern coastal Indians remained isolated from people south of Puget Sound.

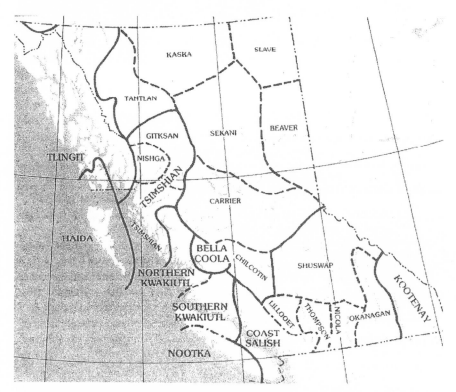

Fig. 19.1 Major ethnic divisions of British Columbia and Coastal Indians *Handbook of North American Indians*, vol. 7 Courtesy of Smithsonian Institution.

The rugged forested terrain provided meager arable land, so the land mammals, especially deer and elk, and the bounty of the sea made the people hunter-gatherers. Annual salmon runs, smelt (eulachon) runs, plus trout, sturgeon, and other fishes, and the maritime seals and whales provided a comfortable living in most years. The biannual cycle of teeming salmon life virtually regulated people's activities. Their culture suffered when the salmon did not run, the deer migrated elsewhere, or wildfires cleared the forests.

Northwest Coast Indian society was marked by two definite social classes: the freemen, made up of nobles and commoners, and the slaves.[579] Nobility could be determined by descent, but primarily by wealth, much of which could be in the form of slaves. Obtaining captives was a leading objective of raids, trade, and war.

Slaves were significant economic property. They might be treated kindly, might even live with the common people, but they could be traded or brutalized or killed to suit the fancy or passion or need for simple display of the master's wealth. They could be the objects of ceremonials, even cannibalism. As corpses, they were discarded, not buried. Descendants of the marriage of a free Indian and a slave inherited an inerasable measure of scorn. Slaves "scarcely need be considered in problems relating to the social structure....Their participation was purely passive, like that of a stage-prop carried on and off the boards by the real actors."[580]

The seagoing canoe enabled communication. The forest cedar, from which it was made, could be finely worked with primitive tools. Coastal Indians' skills in woodworking surpassed those of any other aboriginal people in America. All wood products displayed good workmanship. Symmetry of form and quality of finish governed within the limits of functional design.[581] Surfaces were always smoothed and corners squared. Superior woodworking skills extended to cedar-bark blankets, various waterproof containers, tools, crests, masks, armor, and totems large and small. The workmanship in canoes, especially by the Nootka, was matched nowhere else.

The canoes were designed to be useful in the coastal waters. They were made of large cedars so protected by close timber growth that they were devoid of knots. The Indians split them with adzes and hollowed them partly by fire. They spread gunwales by heating water with hot rocks in the canoe, and maintained the spread with thwarts. Without blueprints or try squares, levels, compasses, or curves, "the shapes of bow and stern were chopped out with the adz in well-nigh perfect symmetry."[582] The finished canoe, carefully smoothed, cut the water cleanly, and spread the rougher waves at sea. Canoes were carefully launched and recovered.

In the north, status and privilege was hereditary and was matrilineal; in the center, bilateral; and in the south, patrilineal. Wealth was important to establish or maintain status. The chief did not own; he was in effect an estate manager. He had heavy responsibilities, among them when to move to salmon-fishing camp, when it was time for berrying, the conduct of rituals, planning and conducting potlatches and feasts, and the conduct of effective warfare, as well as warlike confrontations.

Kwakiutl feasts and potlatches were important public occasions. When a chief and his group gave only food, to be eaten immediately and with portions to be taken home for others, it was a feast. When at a feast, if the giving or destruction of goods, even slaves, occurred, it was a potlatch. Potlatches were formal.

The potlatch, a celebration developed and presented by a chief, was an important event in Northwest Coast Indian culture. The Kwakiutl are, in many ways, typical. A potlatch could manifest rivalry between chiefs, celebrate marriage, or express mourning. It was basically a technique for resolving conflicting claims or presumptive heirs. It provided an emotional release for parties in conflict and permitted letting off steam, establishing an intergroup standard that opposed emotionally inspired physical violence. Invariably, the basic concept and purpose of the potlatch was to present claims to hereditary rights.

The potlatch required a great deal of preparation. Many people were involved. The host chief was the executive. Debtors must be notified, gifts defined for each guest, privileges selected to be granted, ceremonial equipment refurbished, dances rehearsed, songs made and taught, speeches planned, participation of other chiefs arranged, invitations sent, guest precedence established, and many other tasks. Dances of the secret societies were performed at every potlatch, but never at any other time.

Potlatch formality required that the status and rank of guests be observed carefully, not only in seating, but also in the sequence of recognition and serving. Potlatches were not to acquire hereditary status, but to confirm or validate it. This was key, along with "ego gratification" and the satisfaction that comes from proper and commendable entertaining. Wealth was a factor, and while extensive giving at the potlatch was a redistribution of wealth, it was not designed to offset chronic shortages due, for example, to weather. The giving and receiving of gifts was highly stylized. Potlatch giving was more of a loan, to be repaid in kind. Among the most important gifts were coppers, a gift that, with the successive giving, increased in value. These were copper plaques, usually rectangular with a raised section at one end and decorated with various designs.[583] The potlatch was a rich part of coastal Indian culture.

War and revenge also played a role in relationships. Alliances were formed when villages assembled at desirable winter and trade sites. For example, villages collected or assembled at Fort Simpson, Fort McLoughlin, and Fort Rupert to benefit from the trading available. Unallied tribes often went to war. They employed deception and stealth in attack, and defensive guards and other measures in defense, tactics common to all coastal tribes. Their lodges sided and roofed with planks often constituted effective defense works. Tactics involved personal combat using clubs, bludgeons, and heavy daggers. Tlingit, Haida, and Tsimshian combatants used wooden helmets and body armor. The helmets were elaborately carved, with separate wooden visors. Cuirasses were made of tough cedar roots woven together or of short flat rods sewn together with sinew or rawhide.[584]

In general Indians of the Northwest Coast followed many of the same routines as did the more eastern tribes. Noted differences included nakedness in men and small aprons for women, augmented by rain hats and robes, and no custom of smoking tobacco.

In 1774, a Spanish Navy ship named *Santiago,* under Juan Pérez, discovered that Indians had already traded, maybe three years earlier, with white men on a large ship, probably Spanish from the description. Pérez traded with Haida Indians at Nootka Sound, Vancouver Island, and Santa Margarita (later renamed Langara Island) just north of the Queen Charlotte Islands. He found the Indians "adept at trade and commerce." The trade was barter: Spanish ships traded abalone shells from California for furs, including sea otter, wolf, and bear pelts. The Spanish continued trading on the Northwest Coast and even established a post at Nootka Sound.[585]

The possibility of profits from the Orient also motivated Boston and London merchants to respond to Alexander Mackenzie's vision of trans-Pacific fur trade. When the sloop *Union*, out of Newport, Rhode Island, sailed the Northwest Coast in 1794, John Boit was a crew member and only nineteen years old. When the *Union* sailed for the Northwest Coast in 1795, it was Captain John Boit who commanded the sloop and a crew of twenty-two men. Before reaching home port again, in 1796, the *Union* had sailed all the way around the world. The primary destination of the cruise was the Northwest Coast of North America, where Boit was to trade for furs. Boit made many stops along the Northwest Coast and at many locations along Vancouver Island and in the Queen Charlotte Islands.

At Tatoosh Island, on the southern side of the entrance to the Strait of Juan de Fuca and named after the Makah Indian chief Tatoosh, Boit stopped to trade. The Makah of the Olympic Peninsula used Tatoosh Island for a summer village, living in long, cedar-plank buildings that housed communal homes. They were skilled at taking seals, salmon, halibut, whales, and sea otters. Boit wrote in the ship's log on June 29, 1795:

> Light winds & pleasant. At 3 Saw Tatooch's Isle bear'g EBS [east by south]
> 5 leagues. At 4 PM Many canoes with Natives came off and brought us a
> great plenty of Fish, & invited us strongly to stand in for the Village for
> they had great plenty of Skins. At 7 Clarclacko ye Chief came of & seem'd
> to be very glad to see me, he came on board, & sent his Canoe & people
> to ye Village to tell his people to fetch of ye furs. At 11 Above 20 Canoes
> came off & I purchased a handsome lot of Otter Skins.[586]

Boit left the Northwest Coast in September 1795, bound for Canton. He wrote in the ship's log: "Sold the cargo tolerable well so as to make a saving voyage for the owners, invested the return in nankeins [nankeen] & pelts which enabled me to take some freight & French passenger to the Isle de France [Mauritius] which helped the voyage very much."[587] Nankeen, a durable cloth from Nanking, China, was a desirable item in America.

Bolt's extensive trading along the Northwest Coast for furs taken, or at least traded, by various coastal tribes between Spanish America and Russian America was typical. Also typical was Boit's crossing the Pacific Ocean to get the best price possible at Canton, and to convert that return into Chinese trade goods for Boston merchants.

Captain James Cook of the Royal Navy in the *Resolution* led the British to the Northwest Coast, which he visited on his third exploring expedition in 1778. Cook traded with Indians, who offered furs (bear, wolf, fox, deer, raccoon, polecat, martin, and sea otter), clothing made of skins, clothing made of plant material, bows and arrows, fish hooks, wooden visors, blankets, red ochre, carvings, beads, and even brass and iron ornaments, as well as human skulls and hands. Cook, in turn, provided knives, chisels, nails, looking glasses, buttons, and any kind of metal, including pieces of iron and tin. Cook noted that Indian trade items came from inland people beyond the local Indians.[588]

The key to the Northwest Coast fur trade was the white trader's ability to control access to Indian hunters, fishermen, and middlemen. Coastal Indians early on found that it was easier to trade with inland Indians to obtain furs for trading than to hunt in the lands of those inland tribes. Some Haida and Nootka chiefs attempted monopolies, serving as middlemen between traders and other tribes. Kwakiutl middlemen traveling along the coast sold the furs to Yankee ships. Tsimshian and Tlingit chiefs even took control of all Skeena and Stikine River trade. This business was so profitable that they fought inland white traders to prevent their participation.[589]

British traders followed after Cook's expedition and the publication of his journal. In 1785, James Hanna traded iron bars for furs and sold the furs in China. Also in 1785, the Madras trader James Charles Stuart left a soldier, John Mackay, who was employed by the East India Company, at Nootka Sound. The next year, Captain George Dixon of the *Queen Charlotte* obtained three hundred sea-otter skins near Cloak Bay in the Queen Charlotte Islands. In 1787, Charles W. Barkley, a sea captain and trader with the British East India Company, rediscovered the Strait of Juan de Fuca. Barkley was commanding the trading ship *Imperial Eagle* on a voyage to Nootka Sound. Since the British captain James Cook had concluded the "Strait of Anian" did not exist, Barkley chose to name it after its original discoverer: Juan de Fuca. While at Nootka Sound, Barkley and his wife met John Mackay, who taught Barkley about trading with the Indians. Barkley sailed from the Northwest Coast to Canton, where he sold eight hundred furs on a glutted market, and took trade goods from Canton to Mauritius. Also in 1787, after wintering at the Sandwich (Hawaiian) Islands, Dixon returned to Nootka Sound. When he left this time, now sailing the *King George*, he took Mackay with him back to the Orient, where Mackay soon died.[590]

Another fur trader, English Captain John Meares, got frustrated trying to find the mouth of the Columbia River and in 1788, gave the name of Cape Disappointment to the northern cape hiding it from view.[591] Meares was aboard the Portuguese-flagged *Felice Adventurer*. The East India Company held the British monopoly on trade in the vast Pacific Ocean region, so a Meares partnership with a Portuguese merchant enabled him to sail under a Portuguese flag without sharing profits with the East India Company.

In 1787, two trading ships left Boston, both owned by a partnership of six Boston investors. Robert Gray, commanding the *Lady Washington*, traded along the west coast of South and North America, as far north as Russian America. In 1788, Gray stopped at Cloak Bay, northwest of the Queen Charlotte Islands, to barter with coastal Indians. He traded one iron chisel for each sea-otter skin and obtained two hundred skins.[592] Gray transferred the skins to the partnership's *Columbia Rediviva*, which he commanded on the trip back to Boston, via China, where he traded furs for tea. He left the *Lady Washington* on the Northwest Coast to continue trading under the command of John Kendrick of Wareham, Massachusetts. With a full load, the *Lady Washington* sailed for China and sold sea-otter skins for $18,000 in January 1790. By the time the *Columbia* reached Boston in 1790, it had circumnavigated the globe; this was the first circumnavigation by a ship flying the U.S. flag. Water damaged the tea on the *Columbia* en route to Boston, and as a result the venture failed the investors in Boston.

Gray joined some of the original Boston investors and two new investors in sponsoring another trading expedition to the Northwest Coast. He again commanded the *Columbia*. After eight months at sea, he reached the Northwest Coast in 1791. He traded that season and wintered at what he called Adventure Cove (Clayoquot Sound), Vancouver Island. The next season, while trading in May 1792, Gray sailed into the Great River of the West, thereafter called the Columbia River after his vessel.

George Vancouver of the British Royal Navy had sailed with two of Captain Cook's expeditions, including the last one, which went to the Northwest Coast. He further explored the Northwest Coast on expeditions under his command in 1792, 1793, and 1794. His expeditions charted the coast, islands, and islets. As needed to create the charts, he maintained friendly relations with the Indians in general, though there was an incident with the Tlingit in 1794. He was not a trader, but his maps helped the captains who sailed thereafter in coastal trade.

Journals of early British, French, and Spanish explorers arriving by ship report a friendly reception by the Nootka, Chinook, Coast Salish, and Kwakiutl. The relationships were helped by the fact that the white traders wanted only furs. They did not want land or to change Indian society. Chiefs such as Chinook Concomly and Nootka Maquinna competed with each other for trade precedence.

As the preceding few examples suggest, the Northwest Coast trade was international. Based on their "first discovery rights," the Spanish built a military post at Nootka Sound in 1789, but withdrew from the Northwest Coast the next year. Spain signed the Nootka Convention of 1790 with Great Britain, ceding Spanish claims in the Pacific Northwest to Britain.[593] The British dominated the trade, but American traders ventured into the waters between the United States and Russian America because there was trade to be had. In 1804–06, Lewis and Clark explored America's new Louisiana Purchase. Astor established Fort Astoria in 1811, and in 1818 the American flag was raised over Astoria, reinforcing Gray's discovery of the Columbia River as the basis for America's claim to the Oregon country.

After the departure in 1818 of the Russian-American Company trader Aleksandr Andreyevich Baranov, the difficult relations between the Tlingit and the Russians did not change. The Russians, unlike the Americans and British, moved into Tlingit territory. The Tlingit held the Russians responsible for depriving them of their wealth, the sea otter, fish, and other marine products. Until 1821, trade between the Russians and Tlingit was insignificant. By 1825, the Tlingit's traditional customers, the American shipmasters, were gradually beginning to quit the coast trade. Soon, the HBC was out-competing the Russian-American Company for Tlingit furs.[594]

In 1818, the North West Company on the Columbia Plateau and in New Caledonia was the controlling British company. With the acquisition of Fort George, they attempted to trade furs with Canton merchants. The British East India Company's tax policy prohibited their countrymen from returning to western markets with loads of China goods, as the Americans did, and between 1813 and 1821, the NWC suffered a net loss in Canton trade of £44,384.[595] When the HBC took over in 1821 by merging with NWC and acquiring New Caledonia, HBC made a stronger claim to the Oregon country, at least in British eyes. However, at Canton they suffered from the same tax restrictions the East India Company imposed on the North West Company captains.

Letters between Governor Simpson and the HBC Governor and Committee in London from 1822 onward confirm that the acquisition of the North West Company and the fur trade on the Columbia Plateau and along the Northwest Coast were primarily defenses against competition. The Governor and Committee wanted to advance the coastal trade so that others would not.

Hudson's Bay Company had reason to be concerned about the Americans, who could trade sea-otter pelts and other furs directly with the Chinese at Canton, and bring Chinese goods and huge profits directly back to Boston or other markets of their own choosing. The American cycle of trade included Boston, the Northwest Coast, Hawaii, Canton, and California.

The volume of American-Russian trade at Sitka was such that by the 1820s Russian America was experiencing a shortage of fur seals. Sitka residents, according to P. A. Tikhmenev, obtained necessary supplies of good quality at relatively moderate prices. In the late 1820s American imports accounted for 90 percent of the living expenses of Sitka officials and consumed two-thirds of the salaries of its workers. All of their rice, fine flour, sugar, molasses, tea, rum, and tobacco were provided by American traders....After trading with the Russians, the American captains dumped their remaining goods on the coast to the Indians at what the HBC termed an extravagant rate. This kept the Bostonians competitive in the face of mounting British and Russian pressure in the 1830s.[596]

American vessels usually "kept" the coast for two years. One or two of them remained on the coast in winter, when pelts were obtained more cheaply. They wintered at Kaigani and Tongass, where the Tlingit were on friendly terms with Boston men.[597] American traders visited most the areas between Dixon Entrance and Queen Charlotte Sound. Here they took sea and land furs, spars, and planks. Timber got a very high price in Hawaii.

John Work of the HBC noted that the Americans dumped their excess goods at such a low price that the Indians placed no value on them, particularly liquor and ammunition, and that the Americans probably made their profit in Hawaii, Sitka, and California. "The shipmasters also procured fresh water and firewood at Sitka, repaired their ships, and rested their crews."[598] McLoughlin also believed strongly that the HBC would have to carry on the coastal trade in conjunction with the inland business. In this, Governor Simpson and the G and C in London gave him full support.

In 1825, Governor Simpson and John McLoughlin arrived from York Factory. Historian Richard Mackie wrote that the HBC decided to develop the commercial and political potential of the Northwest Coast to protect New Caledonia fur trade, maintain a British mercantile presence on the northern Pacific Coast, keep the Russians well to the north, confront American coastal traders, and find new exports to Pacific markets.[599] The HBC could count on the skills of the interior fur trade, British expertise in maritime economy, and a century and a half of experience with native populations. At sea, however, Aleut baidarka teams and the coastal Indians were trading with American captains.

In the ten years after Cook's visit in 1786, there were 57 British ships and 40 American ones involved in the sea-otter trade. From 1797 until 1807, there were 109 American and only 17 British ships. This pattern continued until 1833, when British ships were dominant: 41 to 31, although HBC ships were never able to trade profitably at Canton because of the British East India Company tax restriction on return cargoes. HBC's expansion into beaver fur and other products explain this changing pattern. One other result was eventual HBC trading with Hawaii.[600]

McLoughlin associated posts with stable trade among Indians in the environs of the post, while Simpson preferred to develop shipborne trade. This was a continuing argument between Simpson and McLoughlin, who believed the posts essential. Land bases increased the white traders' dependence on Indians for provisions. Journals of coastal forts record the European needs met by local Indians. The Tsimshian forced the Gitskan to refrain from coming downriver to trade. The Haida, who raised potatoes, were forced to trade them to the post through the Tsimshian. The Tsimshian considered the benefits of being traders rather than hunters were so great, that Tsimshian chief Legaik, whose daughter married a Hudson's Bay Company physician, offered property for building Fort Simpson.

But ships were of course necessary for the trade, and Simpson was thinking in terms of expanded trade with Hawaii and other ports, and eventually of a steamer along the coast that could easily get into the small inlets, where sailing vessels could not enter or trade.

McLoughlin's experience was that British ship captains originally got their orders in London and were not responsive to successful coastal trading policies or needs. They had little experience with coastal Indian trade. Their ships were poorly arranged for trade, and the captains were too often heavy drinkers. Captain Henry Hanwell in the *William and Anne* was an example. He arrived at Fort George on April 16, 1825. Pleading repairs, he remained until June 2. Clerk Alexander McKenzie was aboard to apply his trading expertise, while Hanwell was to explore the coast between the Portland Canal and the Columbia. Hanwell's timidity prevailed. Trading amounted to thirty-seven beaver, five land otter, and no information on either geography or trade.

McLoughlin sent a scathing report to the G and C, noting that Hanwell didn't even take the opportunity to visit the American captain Kelly on the *Owyhee* to learn about trade and the essential facilities aboard a trading ship. Part of the problem was McLoughlin's lack of authority over visiting ships' captains. He had continuing problems with "gentlemen" traders or managers, ship captains, and servants, most of whom required long periods of time to grasp the essential trade tactics. In ships' cargoes, London never seemed to recognize which trade goods were best suited for the coastal trade. In 1826, Governor Simpson recommended that, in future, captains visiting the Columbia should be placed under the department chief factor.[601]

The Governor and Committee in London also had thoughts of expanding their empire. In 1824 they had written to Simpson: "We observe that your attention is directed…along the Coast to the Northward….We hope that the valuable part will be secured to this country but the actual occupation by traders will go far to establish the rights of the respective nations…upon the Coast as far north as may be practicable."[602] McLoughlin also agreed that the company's coast trade must destroy American and Russian competition so Hudson's Bay Company could acquire the interior furs sent down the coastal rivers by Indian middlemen.

Establishing a post on the Nass River was important. Simpson wrote to William Smith of the G and C that the salvation of the interior trade required a post at the mouth of the Nass River, which he considered the grand mart of the coast for both sea-otter and land skins. McLoughlin sent Lieutenant Aemilius Simpson northward in July 1830 with three ships; the *Eagle* and the *Vancouver*, with Simpson travelling in the accompanying *Cadboro*. After detaching the *Vancouver* to support Fort Langley, the *Eagle* and the *Cadboro* arrived at the mouth of the Nass River in August. But preceding him were the American ships *Louisa* and *Griffon*, both better equipped for the coastal trade than was the *Cadboro*. Simpson was forced to trade arms, ammunition, and spirits.

In 1826, McLoughlin wrote that more land furs were traded at Nass than at any other place along the coast. In 1827 he wrote, "To secure our Inland trade we must endeavor to destroy competition on the Coast, as these Coasters trade with Indians who in their turn trade with the Natives of the Interior some of these get Skins annually even from the vicinity of Babine Lake."[603]

There were shipwrecks and deficiencies. The *Cadboro* suffered dry rot. The *Vancouver's* deck seams would not hold caulk, and in 1834 she ran aground. The *William and Anne* sank with all aboard on the Columbia Bar in 1829. The *Isabella* also grounded on the Columbia Bar and sank in 1830, though most of her cargo was saved. The cargo of the *Gany-*

mede, improperly stowed, was spoiled. The *Dryad* arrived in 1830 late, her cargo damaged and her captain—Minors—drunken, incompetent, and independent. McLoughlin was able to relieve him. The loss of trade goods from shipping disasters prevented McLoughlin from trading effectively. He finally persuaded the G and C to build up a year's advance of trade goods at Fort Vancouver.

Despairing of the value of captains from England, in 1826 the company hired Royal Navy Lieutenant Aemelius Simpson to be superintendent of a new Marine Service. In 1829 he acquired authority over visiting captains, whether they came from England or were stationed on the coast.

The HBC Governor and Committee in London made an effort to shift emphasis to land-otter skins. In 1825, they planned the shipment of 20,000 beaver skins and 4,000 otter skins from England to Singapore. While some sea-otter skins were being taken, the trade had shifted to beaver and other skins, such as land otter. They were coming down the coastal rivers, and the Indians on those rivers and along the coast were Indian middlemen, jealous of their prerogatives.

Because he believed that American ships were getting £3,000 to £5,000 in Russian trade, Governor Simpson sent Lieutenant Simpson to New Archangel in 1829 to propose that the HBC supply the Russians in place of the Americans. They would observe the 1825 British–Russian agreement prohibiting the sale of liquor and war supplies, and would ship fifty to a hundred tons of goods from England, taking bills on St. Petersburg, regardless of profit. He also proposed to supply four thousand to five thousand bushels of grain and a supply of salt pork at minimum markup prices. Russian Governor Christiakoff was amenable to receiving provisions only, but had to refer a decision to St. Petersburg. Lieutenant Simpson was impressed with the number of Russian ships present and the orderly New Archangel organization. But they were dependent on

American ships bringing provisions from California. McLoughlin learned two years later that negotiations between governments had failed.

By the early 1830s, the fur-trade activity along the Northwest Coast of North America extended north to Russian America and in fact overlapped Russian claims. Vessels sailed and traded to the southern end of Sumner Strait, about latitude 56° 30,' off the mouth of the Stikine River and south to the Columbia River. There was little activity on the Oregon coast south of the Columbia. The trade had changed from sea otter to beaver and other furs brought by interior Indian middlemen to the coast along the New Caledonian rivers, and south along Puget Sound to the Columbia.

By the early 1830s, Hudson's Bay Company controlled the sea trade and had left Astoria to the American settlers, who resented the joint American-British occupation of the Oregon Territory. There were still independent traders and ships of various countries that dealt with coastal Indians.

Despite Governor Simpson's preference for ships over posts, it was Simpson who in 1827 ordered James McMillan, George Barnston, and Francis Annance to build Fort Langley at the mouth of the Fraser. After Simpson descended the Fraser in 1828, he was forced to agree with Fraser's report that the river was unnavigable. He reduced Fort Langley in size, but maintained it for fur trade and coastal transport. Seeing that there was much trade between the interior and American ships, in 1828 he ordered the building of Fort Simpson at the mouth of the Nass on Portland Inlet.

McLoughlin needed coastal trade expertise. The American, not the British, ship captains were expert in understanding the coastal natives. McLoughlin was at that time also trying to offset fur-trade losses to the competition by selling boards and salmon, primarily at Hawaii.

McLoughlin had planned to cross the mountains eastward in 1830, en route to England, but he delayed his departure. Further delay occasioned by his need to treat the "intermittent fever" (probably malaria) prevented him from sending Lieutenant Simpson, commanding the *Dryad* and *Cadboro*, northward to establish Fort Simpson on the Nass River until 1831. Peter Skene Ogden, destined to command Fort Simpson when built, accompanied Simpson to Nass. Simpson was to remain in the vicinity for trading but unfortunately, he died suddenly of an inflammation of the liver.

Ogden took over the Marine Service and, helped by Indian acceptance of the post, made a success of the Nass trade. For a better location that would improve ship access, permit gardening, and facilitate trade, Ogden moved the post in 1834 to a point close to the mouth of the nearby Stikine River, where it is today. Under Ogden, the Nass trade proved successful without reducing the production of New Caledonia posts. The move actually enhanced the exchange of rendered eulachon (smelt) oil, or "grease," for furs with Indians of the interior. The Indian middleman role was never more pronounced. Initially they objected to the post move, but their later acceptance made it clear that constant Indian access to European goods, not the satisfaction of plunder, had become important. As "home guards," the Tsimshian moved quickly to Fort Simpson to protect their trade interest.[604]

The G and C had provided two ships, *Dryad* and *Vancouver*, for permanent use on the coast. Ogden acted aggressively, to the consternation of the Russian-American Company governor, Baron Wrangell, who had replaced Christiakoff in September 1830. Wrangell observed Ogden's operations, and in a mixture of admiration, anxiety, and envy, noted that Ogden defeated the American ships by following them with his own ships and outbidding them. Nevertheless, Wrangell also observed that, while the British got two thousand beaver, the Americans got twelve thousand.[605]

In 1832, American Captain William Henry McNeill brought the *Lama* to Fort Vancouver after a successful coastal trade. McNeill wanted to sell his brig, but went to Hawaii. There Chief Factor Finlayson, who McLoughlin had sent to find a replacement for the *Vancouver*, which had been damaged in a storm, bought the *Lama* and hired McNeill. McLoughlin justified this to the G and C, citing McNeill's superior trade skills after fifteen years' experience. Initially, the Committee opposed hiring an American, but eventually approved the move. Both the *Lama* and her former captain, McNeill, became significant fur-trade assets to the HBC.

"In 1832, American traders paid more for beaver and land otter than the HBC offered in New Caledonia, resulting in a haemorrhage of pelts from the interior to the Coast via Native trade routes," reported Mackie. "In March, 1832, Duncan Finlayson was 'creditably informed that from 8 to 19 thousand Beaver Skins can be collected annually on the coast."[606] Hudson's Bay Company wanted to stop illegal American trade in arms and liquor because it was not possible to separate competition for furs from the trade in spirits. HBC used the same compromise in ethical tactics against the Russians as did the Americans, but without hedging, would not use liquor if others did not. Eventually, the Hudson's Bay Company and the Russian-American Company cooperated against the Americans; in 1832, for example, Wrangell proposed a joint organization or operation to oppose the Americans.[607] That did not happen formally, but informally it remained in the British and Russian interests to oppose and interfere with the American fur traders.

As Gibson summarized, the American captain William Smith, whom Lieutenant Simpson interviewed in 1827:

[Captain Smith] had plied the Northwest trade for many years, and trade was dying with him. But it had persisted for more than a half a century.

During that time it had enriched Boston ship owners and contributed to the formation of the capital that enabled New England to evolve from an agrarian to an industrial society. It had intensified the trading proclivities of the Northwest Coast Indians and stimulated their culture....It had exploited and publicized the natural advantages of the Hawaiian Islands and exposed the Hawaiians to overwhelming foreign influence. It had supplemented the Occident's commercial pressure on China at Canton, pressure that was to shutter its isolation and eventually topple its ruling dynasty.[608]

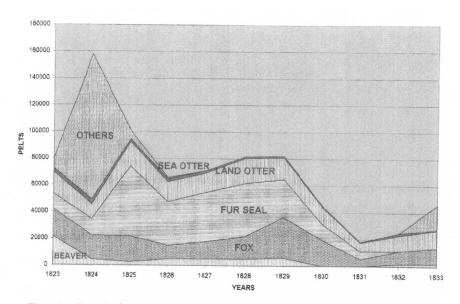

Fig. 19.2 Fur sales by American vessels in Canton, 1823-33. "Others" are muskrat, nutria, rabbit, and sable. Data by permission from James Gibson, *Otter Skins, Boston Ships, China Goods.*

American shipping began to decrease during the period, and British shipping increased somewhat. Russian shipping was negligible. American imports of furs at Canton were reduced by a factor of five. Americans sold much less beaver, attributable to British control of hunting in New Caledonia and trading with Indian middlemen along the coastal rivers.

Fur seal harvests had been reduced dramatically, attributable to over-hunting. The sea-otter fur trade became negligible.

McLoughlin and Ogden wanted another post on the Stikine River, in Russian territory. Ogden located a site beyond the Russian ten-league limit, believing this was allowable under the 1825 agreement. He proposed to build a post there in 1834. The Russians opposed him by establishing their own fort at the mouth of the Stikine. Furthermore, Governor Wrangell sent a ship to prevent Ogden's *Dryad* from proceeding into and up the river. Since McLoughlin believed that the Russians were acquiring furs that came downriver from British New Caledonia, the two monopolist fur companies faced off in an international dispute that became known as the Dryad Incident. The treaties of 1824–25 (see chapter 8) permitted ships to "frequent, without any hindrance whatever, the interior seas, gulfs, harbors, and creeks along the coast…for the purpose of fishing and trading with natives of the country."[609]

Ogden, in the *Dryad*, sailed to within fifteen miles of the Russian post and was intercepted by the Russian captain Sarembo in a ship with fourteen guns. Sarembo said that without orders from Governor Wrangell, he would use force to prevent Ogden from sailing up the Stikine. Language was a problem. Ogden sent Dr. Tolmie and Captain Duncan to visit Sitka, and wrote to Wrangell. Wrangell was absent, and Ogden had to abandon the Stikine. The problem was referred to the respective governments, though Wrangell realized that eventually the Russians and British would act together to eliminate American competition, since the Americans traded spirits and arms. Face was saved, and Ogden in 1835 went to command the New Caledonia District. There he built a post on the Stikine, moving downriver from Dease Lake.[610]

As the fur trade along the Northwest Coast and the beaver markets began to fade in the mid-1830s, the Hudson's Bay Company began to exploit other exportable resources, such as timber, salmon, and agricultural products. Similarly, the Russians began exporting coal and ice!

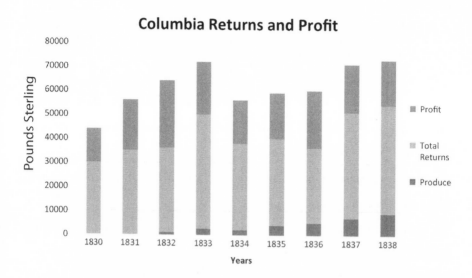

Fig. 19.3 Columbia Department Returns. Data by permission from Richard Mackie, *Trading Beyond the Mountains.*

McLoughlin still considered the use of posts rather than coastal ships a better way of taking trade from the Americans, who had monopolized it.[611] In 1833, there were four forts in the coastal trade: Forts Simpson and Langley and the newer Forts McLoughlin and Nisqually.

In 1833, Duncan Finlayson built Fort McLoughlin on Dowager Island in Milbank Sound. After Chief Trader Donald Manson fought off an Indian attack, a peaceful climate was established, both at the fort and in the Queen Charlotte Islands. The fort's presence substantiated McLoughlin's belief in the stabilizing influence of land bases.

Fort Nisqually was established in 1833 at the south end of Puget's Sound by Chief Factor Heron, and was designed to provide a base that would permit both Langley and Vancouver to work independently.

Nisqually became a grazing area and the headquarters of the Puget's Sound Agricultural Company, headed by the physician and trader, W. F. Tolmie. McLoughlin was a strong supporter, having observed the success of hide-and-tallow operations both in Red River and California.

As the coastal fur trade declined or changed, HBC diversified into other products. Its labor force included Indians and Hawaiians (Kanakas). The fur trade changed materially and increased only at Fort Simpson. Research in the Provincial Archives of British Columbia, "Fort Vancouver Returns," film MRD2, indicate that annual results at Fort Langley in 1833 were 13,604 pelts, with 20 percent beaver and 23 percent equal amounts of mink and muskrat. This pattern continued through 1839, when muskrat and mink predominated. At Fort McLoughlin in 1834, the total was 1,575, divided about equally among beaver, marten, mink, and land otter.

At Fort Nisqually, primarily an agricultural post, there were only 2,858 skins in 1834, 54 percent beaver and 24 percent muskrat. By 1844 there were only 1,708 total, with more muskrat and raccoon each than beaver.

Indian middlemen were impressive at Fort Simpson in 1832, which makes the conclusion reasonable that the increase was from Indian middlemen trading down the Nass and Stikine rivers, although New Caledonia returns at that time remained high. There were 6,683 skins, of them 54 percent beaver, and 42 percent marten, mink, and land otter. Ten years later, in 1842, there were 4,371 skins, 21 percent beaver and 66 percent marten, mink, and land otter. The highest year for Fort Vancouver returns recorded in the was in 1857, when there were 20,515 skins, of which 8 percent were beaver and 66 percent were marten, mink, and land otter. By this time, bear had increased gradually to 1,410, or 7 percent of the whole. In addition to these numbers, there was an increase in whales, whalebone, and seals.

Governor Simpson remained determined to acquire for Britain the lands lying west of the Continental Divide and north of the Columbia River. During this period, the competition continued, as far as Americans were concerned, with some continuing fur trade, until the Anglo-American treaty of 1846 established the east-west boundary line west of the Continental Divide between the northern Oregon country, now being called Washington Territory, and the southern edge of New Caledonia, now British Columbia.

Along the Northwest Coast, the two Anglo-Saxon powers had succeeded in eliminating Spain and Russia forever. The United States wanted to do the same to Great Britain but could not. British communications were too good, British interests were too substantial, and British diplomacy too able, to avoid being caught off guard. In consequence, the United States was forced into continuing its involuntary partnership with Britain in the Pacific Northwest, though the increasing flow of American settlers westward eventually determined the outcome below the forty-ninth parallel, and in 1867 the United States bought Alaska from Czar Alexander II. In effect, the Tlingit had finally discouraged the Russians.

NOTES

(ENDNOTES)

Chapter 1: Indian Culture

1. Mary Jane Schneider, *North Dakota Indians,* 242.
2. D. W. Moodie, "The Role of the Indian in Mapping and Exploration in Canada: A Preliminary Assessment," *Canadian Association of Geography* (June 1977), 2–4.
3. Dale L. Morgan, *Jedediah Smith and the Opening of the West,* 142.
4. Adrian G. Morice, *The History of the Northern Interior of British Columbia (formerly New Caledonia) 1660–1880,* 9–10.
5. David G. Mandelbaum, *The Plains Cree,* 36, 37.
6. Grant Forman, *Pioneer Days in the Early Southwest,* 26.
7. Bruce White, *Give Us a Little Milk,* 4.
8. Ibid.
9. Jack Nisbet, *Sources of the River: Tracking David Thompson across Western North America,* 227.
10. Edwin Thompson Denig, *The Assiniboine,* ed. J. N. B. Hewitt, 86.
11. Alvin M. Josephy, *The Nez Perce Indians and the Opening of the West,* 23.

Chapter 2: Beginnings on the St. Lawrence

12. Olive Patricia Dickason, *Canada's First Nations,* 70.
13. R. Douglas Francis, Richard Jones, Donald B. Smith, *Origins: Canadian History to Confederation.* 49.
14. R. G. Thwaites and Edna Kenton, *Jesuit Relations,* 189.
15. E. E. Rich, *The History of the Hudson's Bay Company, 1670–1870,* 2:18.
16. Paul C. Phillips, *The Fur Trade,* 1:223.
17. Ernest Voorhis, *Historic Forts and Trading Posts of the French Regime and of the English Fur Trading Companies,* 113.
18. Phillips, 1:521, and Rich, *Hudson's Bay Company,* 2:15.

19. Ibid.
20. Peter Newman, *Company of Adventurers*, 1:244.
21. Victor P. Lytwyn, *The Fur Trade of the Little North,* 29–30.
22. Rich, 2:61.
23. Phillips, 1:521.
24. Rich, *Fur Trade and the Northwest to 1857,* 200.
25. Rich, *Hudson's Bay Company*, 2:407.
26. Ibid.
27. Rich, *Northwest*, 215.
28. Glyndwr Williams, ed. *The Hudson's Bay Miscellany 1670–1870,* 153.
29. Rich, 2:415.
30. Ibid., 2:417.
31. Newman, *Caesars of the Wilderness,* 232.
32. Williams, 27, notes 108, 189, 237.
33. Richard S. Mackie, *Trading Beyond the Mountains,* 40.

Chapter 3: The Canoe and the Voyageurs

34. Timothy J. Kent, *Birchbark Canoes of the Fur Trade,* 1:105, and Grace Lee Nute, ed., "Journey for Frances," *The Beaver,* Dec. 1953, 50–54 and March 1954, 12–17.
35. Harold A. Innis, *The Fur Trade in Canada,* 292–293.
36. Thwaites and Kenton, *The Jesuit Relations and Allied Documents*, 21:251.
37. John Jennings, *The Canoe: A Living Tradition,* passim.
38. Kent, 1:99.
39. Father Pierre-François-Xavier de Charlevoix, Historie Nouvelle France, 1774, reprint of John Gilmay Shea's 1870 translation, 1870. 1:278.
40. "Minutes in Council," Northern Department, HBC, Moose Factory, 1832. Peel's River and back, the first woman tourist to go "down north" and was the first white woman to make this trip.
41. Kent, 1:109.
42. J. B. Tyrell, ed. *Journals of Samuel Hearne and Philip Turnor,* 222.
43. John McKay, *Lac La Pluie Journal,* 1797, HBCA, Winnipeg, Canada, B.105/a/4.
44. Kent,1:107, and James Parker, *Emporium of the North,* 62.
45. Kent, 1:111.
46. Kent, 1:256.
47. Thomas McKenney, *Sketches of a Tour to the Lakes.*
48. Jennings, 23.
49. W. A. Ferris, *Life in the Rocky Mountains,* 304.
50. Newman, *A Company of Adventurers,*30.

51. Eric W. Morse, *Fur Trade Canoe Routes of Canada: Then and Now*, 351.

52. Grace Lee Nute, "Down North in 1892," *The Beaver* (June 1948) 45. Elizabeth Taylor was the daughter of the American consul in Winnipeg. She traveled from Edmonton to Peel's River and back, the first woman tourist to go "down north," and was the first white woman to make this trip.

Chapter 4: The Old Northwest

53. This location, at the confluence of the St. Peter's River, (now the Minnesota) and the Mississippi River, developed into the twin cities of St. Paul and Minneapolis, Minnesota. The importance of the location was based on the ease of water transportation into the forests of the region, which lead to the Indian tribes west of Lake Michigan and south of Lake Superior. As early as 1803, President Thomas Jefferson sent Zebulon Pike up the Mississippi River from St. Louis to meet the Indians. There he purchased land from the Dakota for a fort.

54. www.galafilm.com/1812/e/people/Dickson. Robert Dickson (Mascotapah or "Red-Hair Man"): born about 1768, Dumfires, Scotland; employed by British Indian Department at Mackinac Island; in 1780s married Helen or Totwin, daughter of Chief Wanote and sister of Nakota chief Red Thunder, and had four children. He became one of the most influential fur traders by the War of 1812, and an adopted leader of the Sioux nation. Because of his influence in the Great Lakes area and westward, he was placed in charge of British Indian Department for Western Tribes. He brought and led four hundred warriors in successful attack on Mackinac. Appointed lieutenant colonel during the War of 1812, he resigned the military and Indian affairs after the War of 1812 and moved to Red River to assist Selkirk.

55. Olive Patricia Dickason, *Canada's First Nations*, 223.

56. Royal B. Hassrick, *The Sioux,* 7.

57. Gary C. Anderson, *Little Crow: Spokesman for the Sioux,* 21.

58. General William Clark had been appointed brigadier general of the militia of the Louisiana Territory and Indian agent for the territory in 1807. From 1822 until near his death in 1838 he was superintendent of Indian affairs for the territory.

59. Henry R. Schoolcraft, "Report of the Expedition to the North West Indians," War Department Report, Doc. No 323, 1832, 48ff.

60. "Competition on the Bow and the Great Lakes," *HBC Miscellany* 2:525, Hudson's Bay Company Record Society.

61. Clark Wissler, *Indians of the United States,* 116.

62. Schoolcraft, "Report."

63. James A. Clifton, *Prairie People,* 33.

64. Richard White, *The Middle Ground, Indians, Empires, and Republics in the Great Lakes Region, 1650–1815,* 35.

65. Helen Hornbeck Tanner, ed., *Atlas of Great Lakes Indian History,* 47,123.

66. Clifton, 119.

67. Ibid.

68. White, 37.

69. Ibid.

70. Clifton, 135.

71. Ibid., 143.

72. Ibid., 235.

73. Lawrence Taliaferro, *Lawrence Taliaferro Journals,* Minnesota Historical Society, St. Paul.

74. *New American State Papers, Military and Indian* Affairs *1:174.* 1832–1861. (Reprinted, Buffalo: W.S. Hein, 1998).

75. William Clark Whitford, "History of Education," *Collections of the State Historical Society of Wisconsin* (Madison: State Historical Society of Wisconsin), 5:332.

76. Ibid.

77. Taliaferro to Bailly, May 26, 1830, in *Lawrence Taliaferro Papers.* (Manuscript Collection Microfilm, Minnesota Historical Society, St. Paul).

78. Clark to Elbert Herring, Oct. 25, 1833, William Clark, Papers 1812–1840 (Manuscript Collection Microfilm, Minnesota Historical Society, St. Paul).

79. *Taliaferro Papers.*

80. Joseph Shafer, "The Wisconsin Lead Region," *Wisconsin Domesday Book,* 36.

81. Carl Waldman, *Atlas of the North American Indian,* 118ff.

82. Ibid.,120.

83. Charles J. Kappler, ed., "Treaty with the Sac and Foxes, 1832 and Treaty with the Potawatomi, 1828, *Indian Affairs: Laws and Treaties,* 2, also: http://.digital.Library.Okstate.edu/kappler/Vol12/treaties/win0292.htm, (accessed Feb. 25, 2007).

84. Novak, et al., *Furbearer Harvests in North America, 1600–1909, Ontario Ministry of Natural Resources* (1967), 150.

85. Schoolcraft, *Thirty Years with the Indian Tribes,* 451.

Chapter 5: Indian Trade with John Jacob Astor

86. John Upton Terrell, *Furs by Astor*, 140.

87. Ibid., 263.

88. Ibid.

89. Ibid., 165.

90. Ibid., 166.

91. Ibid.

92. Gabriel Franchère, *Journal of a Voyage on the North West Coast of North American During the Years 1811,1812, 1813, and 1814.* W. Kaye Lamb, ed., 123n2.

93. Gabriel Franchère and Hoyt C. Franchère. *Adventure at Astoria, 1810–1814*, 76.

94. Ibid., 88.

95. Harvey L. Carter, "Robert Stuart," in *Mountain Men and the Fur Trade of the Far West*, ed. LeRoy Hafen, 9:362.

96. Franchère, *The Journal*, 20.

97. Ibid., 25.

98. David Lavender, *The Fist in the Wilderness*, 223.

99. Harvey L. Carter, "Ramsay Crooks," in *Mountain Men and the Fur Trade of the Far West*, 9:129.

100. In the Northern Department, "outfit" came to mean two different but related things. As used by the American Fur Company (AFC), Hudson's Bay Company (HBC) and others, "outfit" with a small o was a year's supply of trade goods. An "Outfit" with a capital O, was a subsidiary organization that took and "outfit" and used it to trade within its assigned region at its central location and subordinate posts. Under American Fur Company, the Outfit had a principal trader, under contract to the Northern Department, who employed other traders, clerks, boatmen, laborers, and interpreters as needed, and who were paid under the account of that Outfit. Individuals could also be termed an Outfit.

101. James A. Lockwood, "Early Times in Wisconsin," *Collections, State Historical Society of Wisconsin,* ed. Lyman C. Draper (Wisconsin State Historical Society 1856), 2:130.

102. Thomas Forsyth, U.S. Congress, Sen. Document 90, 22nd Congress, 1st Session, Report No 6. Also in *Messages from the President on the State of the Fur Trade 1824–1832*, 113.

103. Alexis Bailly, "Indian Credit Book for Bailly Outfit 1833,"Alexis Bailly Papers, 1821–1898,69. Manuscript Collection Microfilm A/m Bi58, Minnesota Historical Society (St. Paul).

104. Phillips, *The Fur Trade* 1:415; and Richard White, *The Middle Ground*, ed., 151.

105. Grace Lee Nute, "The Papers of the American Fur Company, A Brief Estimate of Their Significance." *American Historical Review,* vol. 22, no. 3 (April 1927), 45.

106. American Fur Company Ledger, April 1817 to September 1834, AFC papers, Ottawa, Public Archives of Canada, Microfilm Canadian Library Association, Reel 35:524.

107. Franchère, *Journal,* 29.

108. Ibid., 109–112.

109. Terrell, 261.

110. Lockwood, 109.

111. Lavender, 418.

Chapter 6: Across the Methye Portage .

112   June Helm, ed., "The Dene" *Handbook of North American Indians* (hereafter referred to as HNAI), *Subarctic,* 6:1.

113. Daniel Williams Harmon, *Sixteen Years in Indian Country: The Journal of Daniel W. Harmon, 1800–1816*.ed. W. Kaye Lamb, 225.

114. P. Gillespie. "Athabascans of the Shield and the Mackenzie Drainage," *HNAI, Subarctic,* ed. June Helm, 6:164.

115. Helm, other authors, i.e., J. B. Munro, *Language, Legends, and Lore of the Carrier Indians*, (Ottawa: University of Ottawa, 1945), specifically the Thaltan Nahannis, those along the Taku River, and those near Dease Lake, "so-called Kaska." HBC explorations of 1823 and 1824 found them on the upper Liard River.

116. Harmon, *Journal.*

117. Diamond Jenness, *The Indians of Canada,* 378 ff.

118. Cornelius Osgood, "The Distribution of the Northern Athapascan Indians," *Yale University Publications in Anthropology, No 7* (1936).

119. James C. Yerbury, *The Subarctic Indians and the Fur Trade, 1680–1860,* 11.

120. Ibid.

121. Ibid.

122. Pierre Dufour, "Laurent Leroux," *Canadian Biography Online,* vol. 8. www.biographi.ca/index-e.html (accessed October 2010).

123. Barry Gough, *First Across the Continent,* 86ff.

124. Ernest Voorhis, *Historic Forts and Trading Posts of the French Regime, and of the English Fur Trading Companies,* 53.

125. James Parker, *Emporium of the North*, 141.

126. W. S. Wallace, *John McLean's Notes of a Twenty-Five Year's Service in The Hudson's Bay Territory,* 136–137.

127. Theodore Karamanski, *Fur Trade and Exploration*, 88ff.

128. Ibid., 11.

129. Shepard Krech III, ed., "The Trade of the Slavey and Dogrib at Fort Simpson," *The Subarctic Fur Trade*, 138.

130. Shirley Anne Smith, "John Stuart," *Dictionary of Canadian Biography,* 7:837.

131. Daniel Francis and Michael Payne, *A Narrative History of Fort Dunvegan*, 49n26.

132. Fort Simpson Post Journals, 1833–34, HBCA b. 200/a/15.

133. Elizabeth Vibert, *Traders Tales*, 33.

134. This was possibly Bernard Brisbois (1808–1865), son of French Canadian voyageur Michel Brisbois and his wife Domitelle (Madelaine) Gautier de Verville. Bernard Brisbois was born at Prairie du Chien, Wisconsin. He spent his career in the fur trade and built the Brisbois Store in Prairie du Chien in 1851–52.

135. Part French and part Indian, Pierre St. Germain (1790–1843) accompanied British Arctic explorer John Franklin on a land expedition in the far north of North America. He worked in the North West Company's Athabascan District from 1812 to 1818. The next year he joined the Hudson's Bay Company. He worked for the company as an interpreter in the Mackenzie River District well into 1834. He retired with his family to the Red River community.

136. George Back (1796–1878), British explorer, who had been on three Arctic expeditions with John Franklin by this time, including the expedition that Stuart had gone on. In 1833–35 Back was searching for the missing John Ross. The Back River (formerly the Great Fish River) is named in his honor. Explorers depended on fur traders for provisions, direction, and general assistance.

137. Emile Petitot, "Notes on the Métis People of the North," extracted from the *Writings of Emile Petitot,* compiled by Donat Savoi.

138. C. D. La Nauze, "Mackenzie Memories," *The Beaver,* September 1948, 24.

139. Rosemary Allerston, "Where the Beaulieus Began," *Up Here,* (Jan/Feb. 1999, Yellowknife, NWT).

140. There were many men with the last name St. Germain in the fur trade, many apparently descended from Jean Francois St. Germaine, a French soldier who had deserted in North America to settle with his wife's tribe.

Two examples: Antoine St. Germain was a free trader, and Leon St. Germaine worked as a translator for the North West Fur Company. Big St. Germain Lake and St. Germain, Wisconsin, both got their names from this French Indian family.

141. HBC 1M140 HBC b 200/a/15 *Fort Simpson Journal* 1833–34.

142. *Fort Simpson Journal*

143. Governor Simpson's Correspondence to London, 1834, HBCA D. 14/19.

144. James Parker, *Emporium of the North*, 138–139.

Chapter 7: New Caledonia

145. Adrian G. Morice, *The History of the Northern Interior of British Columbia (formerly New Caledonia) 1660–1880*, 9–10. Rev. Morice was a Catholic Oblate missionary who arrived in British Columbia in 1862. He learned the languages, translated the Bible, and recorded oral histories. He was given an honorary doctorate from the University of Saskatchewan in 1933 for his work in anthropology, history, and Indian linguistics. His descriptions of the various tribes and bands reflect the knowledge gained from intimate familiarity.

146. Barry Gough, *First Across the Continent: Sir Alexander Mackenzie*, 137ff.

147. Ibid., 184.

148. Jack Nisbet, *Sources of the River*, 178.

149. Encyclopedia Britannica, "British Columbia," www.encyclopediabritannica.com (accessed February 20, 2009).

150. Rich, Hudson's Bay Company 1670–1870, 2:267.

151. HBCA, D.4/99, Official Reports to the Governor and Committee.

152. James R. Gibson, *The Lifeline of the Oregon Country: The Fraser-Columbia Brigade System*, 51.

153. Glenda Denniston, "Sekani," *HNAI*, 6:433.

154. Robin Riddington in David V. Burley, J. Scott Hamilton, and Knut R. Fladmark, *Prophecy of the Swan: The Upper Peace River Fur Trade, 1794–1823*, 17.

155. Ibid.

156. Mackie, 15, 17.

157. Denniston, 439.

158. Frieda E. Klippenstein, *The Role of the Carrier Indians at Fort James, 1806–1915* (Historical Services, Parks Canada, Western Regional Office, 1992), 51.

159. Theodore J. Karamanski, *Fur Trade and Exploration* (UBC Press), 76.

160. Catharine McClellan, "Intercultural Relations and Cultural Change in the Cordillera," *HNAI*, 6:388.

161. Diamond Jenness, *Indians of Canada*, 365.

162. Charles A. Bishop, "Kwah, a Carrier Chief," Judd and Ray, *Old Trails and New Directions, 3rd North American Fur Trade Conference*, Winnipeg, 1978, 202; and Morice, *History of the Northern Interior of British Columbia*.

163. Klippenstein, 38.

164. Bishop, 202.

165. Newman, *Caesars of the Wilderness*, 305.

166. Morice, 4ff.

167. Jenness, 363.

168. Jenness, 351.

169. James A. Teit, *The Shuswap*, 470.

170. Jenness, 351.

171. Ibid., 455.

172. Daniel Francis and Michael Payne, *A Narrative History of Fort Dunvegan*, 14.

173. James R. Gibson, *The Lifeline of the Oregon Country*, 73.

174. Gibson, 79.

175. Ibid., 99.

176. Arthur Ray, Elizabeth Bedard, Alan McMillan, *The Land Based Fur Trade Project*, "First Project Report."

177. Jean Murray Cole, *Exile In The Wilderness: The Biography of Chief Factor Archibald McDonald*, 196.

Chapter 8: Russians in Alaskan Waters

178. "Peter the Great," as translated and quoted in Derek Hayes, *Historical Atlas of the North Pacific, Maps of Discovery and Scientific Exploration, 1500–2000*, 63.

179. Evgenii G. Kushnaev, *Bering's Search for the Strait: the First Kamchatka Expedition, 1725–1730*, ed. and trans. E. A. P. Crownhart-Vaughan.

180. "February 28, 1744, An Eyewitness Account of Hardships Suffered by Natives in Northeastern Siberia during Bering's Great Kamchatka Expedition, 1735–1744, as Reported by Heinrich von Füc, Former Vice President of the Commerce College, Now a Political Exile," in Basil Dmytryshyn, E. A. P. Crownhart-Vaughan, and Thomas Vaughan, eds. and trans., *To Siberia and Russian America: Three Centuries of Russian Eastward Expansion, a Documentary Record*, Volume 2, *Russian Penetration of the North Pacific Ocean* (Portland: Oregon Historical Society Press, 1988); hereafter cited *Russian Penetration*, 168–189.

181. Ibid.

182. P. A. Tikhmenev, *A History of the Russian American Company*, 470 N22.

183. Henry W. Elliott, *An Arctic Province, Alaska and the Seal Islands* (London: Sampson Low, Marston, Searle & Rivington, 1886), 131–32.

184. James R. Gibson, *Imperial Russia in Frontier America*, 34.

185. "Sea Otter Facts," The Alaska Sea Otter and Steller Sea Lion Commission, TASSC, Old Harbor, AK, http://www.seaotter-seals.org (accessed June10, 2009).

186. Stepan Cherepanov, "August 3, 1762, the Account of the Totma Merchant, Stepan Cherepanov, Concerning His Stay in the Aleutian Islands, 1759–1762," in Dmytryshyn et al., *Russian Penetration*, 210.

187. *Encyclopedia of North American Indians*.

188. Edward J. Vajda, *Asian Studies*, 210, "Notes: Eskimo/Aleut.," http://pandora.cii.wwu.edu/vajda/ea215/aleut (accessed March 20, 2010).

189. Hector Chevigny, *Lord of Alaska: The Story of Baranov and the Russian Adventure* (New York: Viking Press, 1942), 18.

190. Ibid., 111.

191. C. L. Andrews, "Alaska Under the Russians, Baranov the Builder," *Washington Quarterly*, vol. 7 (1916–1917), 203.

192. Dmytryshyn et al., *The Russian American Colonies*, xxxiv ff.

193. Ibid., 164.

194. Ibid., 3:xxix,1ff.

195. *Encyclopedia of North American Indians,* and Drucker, Philip, *Cultures of the North Pacific Coast* (Chandler Publishing, Scranton, PA, 1965), passim.

196. Ibid., 199, and Gibson, 14.

197. Andrews, 210.

198. Dmytryshyn, *Russian American Colonies.*

199. Rezanov as quoted in G. I. Davydov, *Two Voyages to America, 1802–1807*.

200. Ibid., 224.

201. Howard J. Kushner, "Conflict on the Northwest Coast," *Contributions to American History*, 41.

202. Kyrill T. Khlebnikova, *Colonial Russian America: Kyrill T. Khlebnikov's Reports, 1817–1832,* trans. by Basil Dmytryshyn, and E.A. P. Crownhart-Vaughan.

203. Tikhmenev, 153 ff.

204. Ibid.

205. Chevigny, 301.

206. R. H. Pierce, *The Russian Governors, 1818–1867*, 200.

207. Chevigny, 304.

208. Kushner, 41.

209. Tikhmenev,3, Gibson, 33.

210. Ferdinand P. Wrangell, *Russian America, Statistical and Ethnographic Information, 1839.* 5.

211. Gibson 11.

212. Tikhmenev, 425 n. 25.

213. Ibid., 153ff.

Chapter 9: Horses in Indian Life

214. John C. Ewers, "The Horse in Blackfoot Indian Culture," *Smithsonian Bureau of Ethnology Bulletin* 159, 3.

215. Francis Haines, *The Nez Perce Tribesmen of the Northern Plateau*, 22ff.

216. Ewers, 32.

217. Régis de Trobriand, *Journal of Phillip St. Regis: Military Life in Dakota*, 64.

218. Ewers, 112.

219. Ewers, 73ff.

220. Bertha P. Dutton, *American Indians of the Southwest*, 108.

221. Ibid., xi.

222. Gilbert L. Wilson, "The Horse and the Dog in Hidatsa Culture 1924," *Anthropological Papers,* American Museum of Natural History, 15 ff.

223. Ibid., 129.

224. Ibid.

225. Ibid., 130.

226. Ibid., 142.

Chapter 10: The Saskatchewan

227. E. E. Rich, *Hudson's Bay Company, 1670–1870,* 2:299.

228. David O. Mandelbaum, *The Plains Cree,* 44ff.

229. Edward Anenakew, *Voices of the Plains Cree,* ed. Ruth M. Buck, 84.

230. Ibid.

231. Philip Drucker, *Indians of the Plains,* 93, and Barry M. Pritzker, *A Native American Encyclopedia*, 313.

232. Mandelbaum, 161ff.

233. Pritzker, 311.

234. Mandelbaum, ibid.

235. George Catlin, *Letters and Notes on the Manners, Customs and Conditions of the North American Indians,* 1:57, fig. Plat 30.

236. Hudson's Bay Miscellany, 1670–1870, 3:183 N1.

237 J. G. MacGregor, *John Rowand: Czar of the Prairies,* 102.

238. Ernest Voorhis, *Historic Forts and Trading Posts of the French Regime and of English Fur Trading Companies,* 35.

239. Ibid., *Hudson's Bay Miscellany, 1670–1870.*

240. List of Chief Factors, 1821–1860, MG 19, D3-01. 2 Nipissing House, 00-09027, National Archives of Canada.

241. Susan Hartmann, "Women's Work Among the Plains Indians," *Gateway Heritage*, 3, iss. (1983) 4:2–9.

242. Ibid.

243. H. M. Robinson, *The Great Fur Land,* 163; and Merk, *Fur Trade and Empire,* 117.

244. HBCA B. 239/k/a.

245. HBCA D. 4/90.

246. Harold A. Innis, *The Fur Trade in Canada,* 326.

247. Ibid.

248. Paul C. Thistle, "Indian European Trade Relations in the Lower Saskatchewan River Region to 1840," *Manitoba Studies in Native History,* (1986), 2.

249. Innis, 288.

250. HBCA A. 6/23 fo 12.

251. Ibid.

252. HBCA D4/98.

253. HBCA D4/90.

254. David Smyth, "James Bird" *Dictionary of Canadian Biography,* 12:110. and Denise Fuchs, *Native Sons of Rupert's Land, 1760 to the 1850s.*

255. J. G. MacGregor, *John Rowand,* 102.

256. Simpson, HBCA D.r/99 fo 22a.

257. Ibid.

258. Ibid.

259. Ibid.

260. Fort Edmonton Journal, HBCA B. 60/a/27

261. Ibid.

262. HBCA B. 60/a/32.

263. HBCA D. 4/102,fo 39a.

264. James Parker, *Emporium of the North, Alberta Culture and Multiculturalism,* 139ff.

265. Sir George Simpson, "Rowand" in "Character Book," *Hudson's Bay Miscellany, 1670–1870.*

Chapter 11: The Missouri from St. Louis to Fort Union

266. Hiram Chittenden, *The American Fur Trade of the Far West,* 1:884.
267. Ibid.
268. John Upton Terrell, *Furs by Astor,* 345.
269. Chittenden, 1:100, and Terrell, 384.
270. Janet Lecompte, "August Chouteau," ed. Leroy R. Hafen, *The Mountain Men and the Fur Trade of the Far West,* 9:63–90.
271. David Lavender, *The Fist in the Wilderness,* 377 n15.
272. Clark Wissler, *Indians of the United States,* 103.
273. James Mooney, *The Aboriginal Population of America North of Mexico,* 80:7.
274. Lavender, 383.
275. John E. Sunder, *The Fur Trade on the Upper Missouri, 1840–186,* 106.
276. John Jacob Astor, "Astor to Chouteau," Chouteau Collection, Papers of the St. Louis Fur Trade, Part 1, Missouri Historical Society, St. Louis.
277. Alexander Maximilian, Prince of Wied, "Field Journal, August 1833," in *Travels in the Interior of North America, 1748–1846,* ed. Reuben Thwaites, 22:32.
278. John C. Ewers, *Plains Indians History and Culture,* 28.
279. Edward T. Denig, *Five Indian Tribes of the Upper Missouri,* 49.
280. Maximilian, 32.
281. Ibid., 34.
282. Ibid., 244.
283. Denig, 53.
284. Maximilian, 242.
285. Ibid., 36.
286. Ibid., 37.
287. Ibid., 148.
288. Ibid., 39.
289. Ibid.
290. Ibid., 51.
291. Ibid., 50.

Chapter 12: Fort Union and Beyond

292. Edwin T. Denig, *Five Indian Tribes of the Upper Missouri,* ed. John C. Ewers, 72ff.
293. Maximilian, "Field Journal, August 1833," eds. Davis Thomas, Darin Ronnefeldt, *People of the First Man,* 109.
294. Ibid.
295. Ibid., 109–110.

296. Alexander Maximilian, Prince of Wied, *People of the First Man: Life Among the Plains Indians in Their Final Days of Glory: The Firsthand Account of Prince Maximilian's Expedition Up the Missouri River, 1833–34,* eds. Davis Thomas and Karin Ronnefeldt, 55.

297. Ibid., 330.

298. David Smyth, "The Struggle for the Piegan Trade: The Saskatchewan versus the Missouri," *Montana, the Magazine of Western History,* 34 no. 2 (Spring 1984), 8–9.

299. Denig,72.

300. Ibid., 114.

301. Shepard Krech III, *The Ecological Indian,* 131ff.

302. Maximilian, 55.

303. Ibid., 330, John C. Ewers, *The Blackfeet: Raiders on the Northwestern Plains,* 39.

304. Oscar Lewis, "Effects of White Contact upon Blackfoot Culture, with Special Reference to the Role of the Fur Trade," 31 Centennial Anniversary Publications, ed. A. I. Hallowell (American Ethnographic Society).

305. Ewers, *Indian Life on the Upper Missouri,* 53.

306. Bernard DeVoto, *Across the Wide Missouri,* 7, 18.

307. Warren Ferris, *Life in the Rocky Mountains,* 193.

308. Terrell, 411.

309. Chittenden, *The American Fur Trade of the Far West,* 1:344.

310. Ibid., 334.

311. Ewers, *The Blackfeet Raiders,* 58.

312. Phillips, *The Fur Trade,* 2:420.

313. DeVoto, 139.

314. William R. Swagerty, "Indian Trade in the Trans Mississippi West to 1870, *HNAI,* 4:370.

315. J. G. MacGregor, *Czar of the Prairies,* 94–95, and Eugene Arima, *Blackfeet and Palefaces,* 147.

316. Swagerty, 367.

317. Papers of the St. Louis fur Trade, Par 2 Fur Company Ledgers and Account Books, 1802–1871. Reels 5 & 6 (University Publications of Americas, Bethesda, MD), courtesy of W. R. Swagerty.

318. W. R. Swagerty and D. A. Wilson, "Faithful Service under Different Flags: A Socioeconomic Profile of the Columbia District, Hudson's Bay Company and the Upper Missouri Outfit, American Fur Company, 1825–1835," in *Proceedings The Fur Trade Revisited, Sixth North American Fur Trade Conference, Mackinac Island, MI, 1991,* 243–267.

319. Chittenden, 1:350, and Terrell, 444.

320. Astor to Pierre Chouteau, Jan. 31, 1833, Chouteau Papers, Missouri Historical Society.

321. Chittenden, 1:350, and Terrell, 444.

Chapter 13: Indians and Ashley's Rendezvous System

322. Dale L. Morgan, *The West of William H. Ashley*, 1, 2. Morgan has compiled many primary sources, including journals and letters from the men involved in this journey.

323. Chittenden, *The American Fur Trade of the Far West*, vol 1 & 2; James Clyman, "A Short Detail of Life and Incidents of My Trip in and through the Rockey Mountains," *Journal of a Mountain Man;* Maurice Sullivan, *The Travels of Jedediah Smith*; Hafen, biographies of Andrew Henry, and Milton and William Sublette; Hafen, *Broken Hand;* Morgan, *Ashley*.

324. Louis J. Clements, "Andrew Henry," *The Mountain Men and the Fur Trade of the Far West*, ed. LeRoy R. Hafen, 6:173ff.

325. Morgan, *Smith*, 33, and Morgan, *Ashby*, 12.

326. Morgan, *Ashley*, 14.

327. Don Berry, *a Majority of Scoundrels*, 22ff.

328. Morgan, *Ashley*, "Joshua Pilcher, Acting Partner on the Missouri River, Missouri Fur Company to Thomas Hempstead, Acting Partner at Lt. Louis," 50.

329. Morgan, *Ashley*, 63.

330. Ibid., 59.

331. Chittenden, 1:151, Note 18.

332. Clyman, *Journal of a Mountain Man*, 27.

333. Ibid.

334. Morgan, *Smith*, 87, and Hafen, *Mountain Men and the Fur Trade in the Far West*, 9:380.

335. Theodore Binneman, *Common and Contested Ground*, 17.

336. Morgan, *Smith*, The following notes are from pp. 88, n18, 388.

337. Ibid., 695, 88, 89.

338. Morgan, *Smith*, 88.

339. Ibid., 89.

340. Clyman.

341. Morgan, *Smith*, 93–94.

342. William Swagerty, "Plains Indians With in the Present United States to 1850." *HNAI*, Vol.13, *Plains*.

343. O. Russell, *HNAI*, 2:309.

344. Virginia Cole Trentholm and Maurine Carley, *The Shoshoni: Sentinels of the Rockies*, 292.

345. Chittenden, 389.

346. Ibid., 44, 77.

347. Morgan, *Ashley*, "William H. Ashley to William Carr Lane, Fort Atkinson, October 29, 1824" (Ashley Papers, Missouri Historical Society), 98.

348. *Encyclopedia Britannica,* vol. 17 (1969), 491.

349. Joseph Jablow, *The Cheyenne in Plains Indian Trade Relations 1795–1840,* 30.

350. Wissler, 153ff.

351. Morgan, *Smith,* 156.

352. Ibid., 271 n118.

353. Ibid., 275 n133.

354. Ibid., 277 n151.

355. Provost, a legendary character in his own time, was known as "The Man of the Mountains." When thirty, he first entered the mountains with De Mun in 1815; in 1817, De Mun's party landed in a Spanish jail in Santa Fe, and the Spanish confiscated furs and all other property. After Mexican independence in 1821, Provost and LeClerc, as partners, trapped up the Old Spanish Trail country to White River and met Ashley on the Duchene River. Returning to St. Louis, he worked independently and for the AFC, was highly paid and respected in a variety of fur-trade activities, by whites and Indians alike. At the 1833 rendezvous, Stewart met Provost and described him later in his book, "Edward Warren," as "Old Provost, the burly Bacchus...a large heavy man with a round face, bearing more the appearance of a mate of a French merchantman than the scourer of the dusty plains." He quit trapping himself in 1830, but led many expeditions and caravans westward after that. His last trip up the Missouri was in 1849. He died in St. Louis on July 3, his sixty-fifth year, survived by his wife and grown daughter. From Jack B. Tykal, *Etienne Provost: Man of the Mountains*, and Hafen, *Mountain Men and Fur Traders of the Far West,* 6:371–385.

356. Gowans, *Rocky Mountain Rendezvous*, 18, 19.

357. Ibid., 18.

358. Ibid., 21.

359. Morgan, *Smith,* 173.

360. Morgan, *Ashley,* 129.

361. Ibid., 137 n275.

362. Ibid.

363. Gowans, 24.

364. Morgan, *Ashley*, 150.

365. Ibid., 153.

366. Morgan, *Smith*, 190.
367. Morgan, *Ashley*, 152.
368. DeVoto, *Across the Wide Missouri*, 41–44.
369. Rachel Kelley, practicing pharmacist, provided the following on the medical uses of gunpowder: gunpowder is 10 percent sulfur, 15 percent charcoal, and 75 percent potassium nitrate. Sulfur must be converted to pentathionic acid H2S506 in order to exert germicidal action. Epidermal cells oxidize sulfur to pentathionic acid. Sulfur is used as a fungicide or parasiticide, and in the treatment of psoriasis, seborrhea, and eczema topically. I would imagine it would have these same effects internally (i.e., fungicide, parasiticide).

Chapter 14: The "Fur Desert"

370. Alexander Ross, *Fur Hunters of the Far West*, 69. Ross's presence allowed him to record the trip in his journal.
371. Ibid., 69, 70.
372. Ibid., 71.
373. Ibid., 90.
374. Kent Nerburn and Louise Mengelkock, eds. *Native American Wisdom*, 11.
375. Theodore Stern, *Chiefs and Chief Traders*, 55.
376. Gary E. Moulton, *The Journals of the Lewis and Clark Expedition*, 5:166.
377. Ibid., 188.
378. Morgan, *Smith*, 8.
379. Ibid., 117–118.
380. Ibid., 125.
381. Ibid.
382. Ross, 209.
383. Glyndrw Williams, "Peter Skene Ogden," *Canadian Biography Online*, University of Toronto, http://www.biographi.ca (accessed May 3, 2009).
384. Morgan, *Smith*, 100.
385. Ted J. Warner, "Peter Skene Ogden," *Mountain Men and the Fur Trade of the Far West*, ed. LeRoy Hafen, 3:213.
386. Binns, 124.
387. Binns. 141.
388. K. A. Spaulding, "Introduction," Alexander Ross, *Fur Hunters of the Far West*, xvii.
389. L. B. Shippee, "Federal Relations in Oregon," in *Oregon Historical Quarterly*, 19:200.
390. Ross, 193.
391. Morgan, *Smith,* 142.

392.   Merk, 274.

393.   Binns, 210.

394.   O. Russell, *HNAI*, 2:309.

395.   Merk, 284.

396.   Ibid., 286.

397.   Ibid.

398.   Ibid., 20.

Chapter 15: Rocky Mountain Fur Company

399.   Carl D.W. Hayes, "David E. Jackson," *The Mountain Men and the Fur Trade of the Far West*, ed. Leroy Hafen, 9: 221.

400.   John E. Sunder, "William Lewis Sublette," ed. Hafen, 5: 347ff.

401.   Fred R. Gowans, *Rocky Mountain Rendezvous,* 135.

402.   Morgan, *Smith*, 193ff.

403.   Harvey L. Carter, "Jedediah Smith," ed. Hafen, 8:332.

404.   Morgan, *Smith*, 313.

405.   Morgan, *Smith*, 235.

406.   Ibid., 254.

407.   Ray H. Mattison, "Joshua Pilcher," ed. Hafen, 4:257.

408.   Frances Fuller Victor, *The River of the West*, 49.

409.   Ibid., 38.

410.   Gowans, 49.

411.   Sunder, "Bill Sublette," 86.

412.   Gowans, 56.

413.   Hafen, 1:82.

414.   Gowans., 86.

415.   Leroy R. Hafen and Ann W. Hafen, "Thomas Fitzpatrick," 7:87ff.

416.   Message from the President of the United States to the Senate of the United States, January 25, 1831, 21st Congress, 2d Session (Missouri Historical Society).

417.   Chittenden, *The American Fur Trade of the Far West*, 1:295.

418.   Letter, W. Sublette to Ashley, Sept 24, 1831 (Campbell Papers, Missouri Historical Society).

419.   Victor, 103–104.

420.   J. Cecil Alter, *Jim Bridger: A Historical Narrative*, 118.

421.   Fred R. Gowans, *Rocky Mountain Rendezvous,* 65– 66.

422.   Gowans, 67.

423.   Gowans, 71.

424.   Victor, 1:112ff.

425.   Hafen, *Broken Hand*, 119–120.

426. "Sublette-Campbell Agreement, December 20, 1832" (Missouri Historical Society).

427. Chittenden, 301.

428. Alter, 126ff.

429. Ibid., 127.

430. Ferris, *Life in the Rocky Mountains,* 235.

431. Alter, 128.

432. Ibid., 243.

433. Ibid., 248.

434. Victor, 107.

435. Washington Irving, *The Adventures of Captain Bonneville, USA: In the Rocky Mountains and the Far West,* 154–156.

436. Alter, 135.

437. Ibid., Irving.

438. Sublette Papers (Missouri Historical Society, St. Louis).

439. Ibid.

440. Chittenden, 305–306.

Chapter 16: American Rockies Competition

441. Nathaniel Wyeth, *The Journals of Captain Nathaniel J. Wyeth's Expedition to the Oregon Country, 1831–1836,* ed. Donald R. Johnson, 44ff.

442. Chittenden, 1:440.

443. Ibid., 397.

444. Wyeth, *Journal,* 15.

445. Ibid., 42.

446. Ibid., 45ff.

447. Ibid., 55.

448. Chittenden, 1:402.

449. Wyeth, 103 n29.

450. Ibid., 111.

451. Edgeley W. Todd, "Captain Eulalie de Bonneville," *Mountain Men of the Far West,* ed. Hafen, 5:53.

452. Zenas Leonard, *The Adventures of Zenas Leonard,* 44.

453. Gowans, *Rocky Mountain Rendezvous,* 97.

454. John E. Sunder, *Bill Sublette, Mountain Man, 1840–1860,* 129.

455. Gowans, 137.

456. "Campbell's Journal," *Campbell Papers* (Missouri Historical Society).

457. Hafen, *Broken Hand,* 134ff.

458. Chittenden, 303, and Hafen, *Mountain Men of the Far West,* 1:140.

459. Hafen, *Broken Hand,* 135.

460. Ibid., 137.

461. Sunder, 129.

462. Ibid., 135.

463. Wyeth, *Journals,* 109.

464. William Marshall Anderson, *The Rocky Mountain Journals of William Marshall Anderson: The West in 1834,* eds. Morgan and Harris, 35, 130. Alfred Jacob Miller described Fort Laramie in 1837 as "of a quadrangular form, with bastions at the diagonal corners to sweep the fronts in case of attack; over the ground entrance is a large block house, or tower, in which is placed a cannon. The interior is possibly 150 feet square, a range of houses built against the palisades overlooking the interior court. Tribes of Indians encamp here three or four times a year, bringing with them peltries to be traded or exchanged for dry-goods, tobacco, vermillion, brass, and diluted alcohol."

465. Wyeth, *Journals,* 111.

466. William R. Sampson, "Nathaniel Jarvis Wyeth," ed. Hafen, 5:381ff.

467. Harvey L. Carter, "Andrew Drips," ed. Hafen, 8:149.

468. Gowans, 97.

469. Annie Heloise Abel, ed., "McKenzie to Kipp, December 17, 1833," Chardon's Journal at Fort Clark, 1834–1839.

470. Ibid., "McKenzie to Picotte, Dec. 15, 1833," 539.

471. Harvey L. Carter, "Robert Campbell," ed. Hafen, 8:56.

472. Cabanne to Fontenelle, April 9, 1834, Drips Papers, Missouri Historical Society.

473. Sunder, 134.

474. Ibid., 135.

475. Fontenelle to Llaidlaw, July 31, 1833, Chouteau-Walsh Collection (Missouri Historical Society).

476. Gowans, 119, quoting from Chittenden, *The American Fur Trade of the Far West,* 1:305.

477. Chittenden, 1:306, 309 n15.

478. Richard J. Fehrman, "The Mountain Men—A Statistical Review": in ed. Hafen, vol. 10, and William R. Swagerty, in *Western Historical Quarterly,* vol. 2 (Jan. 1980 Western History Association, Utah State University).

479. Gowans, *Rocky Mountain Rendezvous,* citing Victor, *River of the West,* 264–65.

480. Bil Gilbert, *Westering Man, The Life of Joseph Walker,* 120.

481. William Drummond Stewart, Winfred Blevins, eds. "Introduction, " *Edward Warren.*

Chapter 17: Southwest Trappers

482. Donald Cutter and Iris Engstrand, *Quest For Empire*, 20.
483. Barry M. Pritzker, *A Native American Encyclopedia*, passim.
484. Stephen G. Hyslop, *Bound for Santa Fe*, 22.
485. James F. Brooks, *Captives and Cousins*, 178.
486. Thomas James, *Three Years Among the Indians and Mexicans*, 172.
487. Hyslop, 35.
488. Lavender, *The Fist in the Wilderness*, 334.
489. David J. Weber, *The Mexican Frontier*, 95.
490. James, 95.
491. Josiah Gregg, *Commerce of the Prairies*, 332.
492. J. J. Hill, *Ewing Young and the Fur Trade of the Southwest: 1822–1834*, 4.
493. John Upton Terrell, *The Navajos*, 18.
494. Kenneth L. Holmes, *Ewing Young, Master Trapper*, 47.
495. Gregg, passim.
496. David J. Weber, "Sylvestre S. Pratte," *Fur Trappers and Traders of the Far Southwest*, ed. Hafen, 181.
497. William S. Wallace, "Antoine Robidoux," ed. Hafen, 5:269.
498. Virginia McConnell Simmons, *The Ute Indians of Utah*, 37ff.
499. William R. Swagerty, "Plains Indians Within the Present United States to 1850," *HNAI*, 13:32.
500. Bertha P. Dutton, *American Indians of the Southwest*, 106ff.
501. Ibid., 70.
502. Richard Batman, *James Pattie's West: the Dream and the Reality*, 162.
503. Holmes, 34.
504. Ibid., 35.
505. Waldman, *Atlas of the North American Indian*, 35.
506. Harvey L. Carter, "Ewing Young," *Fur Trappers and Traders of the Far Southwest*, ed. Hafen, 56.
507. Holmes, 45.
508. Charles L. Camp, ed., *George C. Yount, and His Chronicles of the West*, 55–59.
509. Gregg, 79, 95.
510. Weber, 157, 175.
511. Weber, *The Taos Trappers*, 170.
512. Ibid., 171.
513. Janet Lecompte, "Alexander K. Branch," ed. Hafen, 4:61ff.
514. Harold A. Dunham, "Manuel Alvarez," ed. Hafen, 1:181ff.
515. Thomas E. Chávez, *Conflict and Acculturation*, 5.

516. Lavender, *Bent's Fort,* 105.
517. Harold H. Dunham, "Charles Bent," ed. Hafen, 2:27ff.
518. Hyslop, 52.
519. Samuel P. Arnold, "William W. Bent," ed. Hafen, 6:66–67.
520. Joseph Jablow, *The Cheyenne Indians in Plains Indian Trade Relations,* 47. Quote from George Bird Grinnell, *The Cheyenne Indians: Their History and Ways of Life.*
521. Ibid., 84.
522. David Dary, *The Santa Fe Trail, Its History, Legends, and Lore,* 128.
523. Dunham, Hafen, 2:37, 38.
524. Lavender, *Bent's Fort,* 142.
525. Gordon, *Messages from the President on the State of the Fur Trade, 1824–1832,* 93.
526. Dunham, *Bent,* Hafen, 2:48.
527. Ibid., 73.
528. Weber, *Taos Trappers,* 141ff.
529. Gregg, 150.

Chapter 18: Fort Vancouver Trade

530. Sylvia Van Kirk, *Many Tender Ties,* 155.
531. W. Kaye Lamb, "John McLoughlin," *Dictionary of Canadian Biography Online.* http://www.biographi.ca (accessed March 15, 2007).
532. Peter C. Newman, *Caesars of the Wilderness,* 278.
533. John Logan, Allen, Burns, Sargent, *Cataclysms on the Columbia,* passim.
534. Merk, *Fur Trade and Empire,* 126.
535. Ibid., 124.
536. Ibid., 72.
537. Samuel Black, "Faithful to their Tribe and Friends," *Samuel Black's 1829 Fort Nez Perces Report.*
538. Merk, 86.
539. Ibid., 99.
540. Moulton, ed., *The Definitive Journals of Lewis and Clark Expeditions,* 6:190.
541. Merk, 101.
542. Moulton, 6:190, and Vernon K. Ray, "The Chinook Indians in the Early 1800s," in *The Western Shore: Oregon Country Essays Honoring the American Revolution,* ed. Thomas Vaughan, 141.
543. Robert H. Ruby and John A. Brown, *The Chinook Indians,* 46.
544. Ibid.
545. Theodore Stern, "Columbia River Trade Network," *HNAI,* 7:641ff.

546. Ibid.
547. Merk, 127.
548. Ibid., 181.
549. John McLoughlin, *Letters of John McLoughlin: Written at Fort Vancouver, 1829–1832*, ed. Burt Brown Barker, 269.
550. Merk, 286.
551. Richard Dillon, *Siskiyou Trail,* 24, 33.
552. Ibid., 37.
553. Merk, 55, 56.
554. Alvin Josephy, *The Nez Perce Indians and the Opening of the West,* 11ff.
555. Ibid.
556. Ibid., 29.
557. Francis Haines, *The Nez Perce, Tribesmen of the Columbia Plateau,* 137ff.
558. Stern, 1:27–28.
559. Ibid.
560. Black, "Faithful to their Tribe and Friends."
561. George C. Shaw, *Chinook Jargon and How to Use It,* ix.
562. Stern, 2:26.
563. Morgan, *Smith,* 287.
564. William R. Sampson, "John Work," Canadian Biographical Dictionary Online, http://www.biographi.ca (accessed March 5, 2007).
565. Ibid.
566. Ibid.
567. Ibid.
568. Clark Wissler, *Indians of the United States,* 64ff.
569. Theodore Stern, "Klamath and Modoc," *HNAI,* 12:446.
570. Alice Bay Maloney, ed., "Fur brigade to the Bonaventura," *John Work's California Expedition, 1832–1833.*
571. Linda Nash, "Inescapable Ecologies," *A History of Environment, Disease, and Knowledge,* 22–23.
572. Dillon, 184.
573. Ibid., 181.
574. Ibid.
575. Ibid., 208.
576. Ibid., 208.
577. Ibid., 210.
578. Ibid., 212.

Chapter 19: The Northwest Coast

579. Philip Drucker, "Rank, Wealth, and Kinship in Northwest Coast Society," Tom McFeat ed. *Indians of the North Pacific Coast,* 135.

580. Drucker, "Rank and Wealth," 130, 135.

581. Drucker, *Cultures of the North Pacific Coast,* 24.

582. Ibid., 27.

583. Ibid., 57ff.

584. Drucker, *Indians,* 97.

585. Herbert K. Beals tran., *Juan Pérez on the Northwest Coast, Six documents of His Expedition in 1774,* 77. See also W. J. Langlois ed., "Captain Cook and the Spanish Explorers on the Coast," *Sound Heritage,* 7:1.

586. Edmund Hayes ed., *Log of the Union, John Boit's Remarkable Voyage to the Northwest Coast and Around the World, 1704–1796,* North Pacific Studies, 6:62.

587. Ibid., 88.

588. Glyndwr Williams ed., *Captain Cook's Voyages, 1768–1779,* 406–425.

589. Wilson Duff, "The Impact of the White Man," *The Indian History of British Columbia,* Anthropology in British Columbia, Memoir No. t. 58.

590. Derek Pethick, *The Nootka Connection: Europe and the Northwest Coast 1790–1795,* 13; Barry M. Gough, "Dixon, George," *Dictionary of Canadian Biography Online, (DCBO)* at http://www.biographi.ca (accessed April 28, 2009); Frederic W. Howay ed., *Voyages of the "Columbia" in the Northwest Coast,* vol. 7; Barry M. Gough, "Barkley, Charles William," DCBO, April 28, 2009; J. M. Bumsted, "Mackay, John," DCBO, April 29, 2009.

591. E. E. Rich, *The Fur Trade and the Northwest to 1857,* 162.

592. Howay ed., *Voyages of the "Columbia,"* vols. 6 & 9.

593. Wallace Olson, *Search for the Northwest Passage,* Bicentennial Exhibition catalog, and Rich, 163.

594. James R. Gibson, *Otter Skins, Boston Ships, and China Goods,* 16.

595. Richard S. Mackie, *Trading Beyond the Mountains,* 23.

596. P. A. Tikhmenenev, *History of the Russian American Company,* trans. Pierce and Donnelly, passim.

597. Gibson, 266.

598. Ibid., 264, 265.

599. Mackie, 39.

600. Gibson, 299–310.

601. Duff, 58.

602. John McLoughlin, "Vancouver Letters, First Series, 1825–1838", ed. E.E. Rich. vol 4.

603. Ibid., 208.
604. Drucker, 638.
605. McLoughlin, "Vancouver Letters," 87 (lcccviii).
606. Mackie, 125.
607. Rich, *Fur Trade,* 632.
608. Gibson, 296.
609. Richard W. Van Alstyne, "International Rivalries," Oregon Historical Society, vol 46, no 3, 202.
610. Rich, *Fur Trade*, 640–641.
611. McLoughlin, "Letters," 89.

BIBLIOGRAPHY

Manuscript Collections

Hudson's Bay Company Archives (HBCA), Winnipeg.

Section A: Headquarters Records

HBCA A. 16/35 fo 75d-76
HBCA A. 16/35, fo 12
HBCA A. 6/23 fo 12

Section B: Post Records

HBCA B. 60/a/27, 28 fo 15, 32, Fort Edmonton Journal
HBCA B. 60/a/6/23; fo 12
HBCA B. 1051a/1-4 McKay, John. *Lac La Pluie Journal, 1793–1797*
HBCA B. 200/a/15 Fort Simpson Journal 1833–34
HBCA B. 223/b/41. Chief Factor Donald MacTavish to Sir George Simpson, Vancouver, Washington Territory, January 3, 1855
HBCA B. 239/k/a

Section D: Governors' Papers

HBCA D. 4/5 fo 25d. "Sir George Simpson to J. McLoughlin," Forks, Spokane River, April 10, 1825
HBCA D. 4/90
HBCA D. 4/98
HBCA D. 4/102, fo 39
HBCA D. 4/99 fo 22a "Official Reports to the Governor and Committee"
HBCA D. 14/19."Governor Simpson's Correspondence to London, 1834"
Hudson's Bay Record Society (HBRS)

Section E: Provincial Archives of British Columbia,Fort Vancouver Returns, film MRD2

Davis, K. G., and A. M. Johnson, eds. *North Quebec and Labrador: Journals and Correspondence*. Vol. 24. London: HBRS, 1963.

Rich, E. E., and Harvey Fleming, eds. *Minutes of Council, Northern Department of Rupert Land*, 1821–1831. Vol. 3. London: HBRS, 1832.

Rich, E. E. Hudson's Bay Company 1670–1870. 2 vols. London: HBRS, 1958.

Simpson, Sir George. "Character Book." In *Hudson's Bay Miscellany,* 1670–1870, Vol. 30. London: HBRS. 1975.

Williams, Glyndwyr, ed. *Hudson's Bay Miscellany, 1670–1870,* Vol. 30. Winnipeg: HBRS, 1975.

Williams, Glyndwyr. "Introduction." In *North Quebec and Labrador Journals and Correspondence, 1819–1835*, edited by K. G. Davis. Vol. 24. London: HBRS, 1963.

The Champlain Society

Franchère, Gabriel. *Journal of a Voyage on the North West Coast of North American During the Years 1811, 1812, 1813 and 1814*. Edited by W. Kaye Lamb. Translated by W. Kaye Lamb. Publications of the Champlain Society. Toronto: Champlain Society, 1969.

Lamb, W. Kaye. "Introduction." In *The Letters of John McLoughlin from Fort Vancouver to the Governor and Council Series, 1825–1838*, edited by E. E. Rich, Vol. 4. Toronto: Champlain Society, 1940.

McLoughlin, John. The Letters of John McLoughlin from Fort Vancouver to the Governor and Council Series, 1825–1838, edited by E. E. Rich, Vol. 4. Toronto: Champlain Society, 1940.

Thompson, David. *David Thompson Narrative of his Explorations in Western America, 1784–1812*, edited by J.W. Tyrrell. Toronto, Champlain Society, 1916.

Hearne, Samuel, and Philip Turner. *Journals of Samuel Hearne and Philip Turner.* edited by J.W. Tyrrell. Vol. 21. Toronto: Champlain Society, 1934.

Oliver, E. H., editor. "The Canadian North-West." In *Minutes of the Councils of the Red River Colony and the Northern Department of Rupert's Land*, Vol. 1. Ottawa: Government Printing Bureau, 1914.

American Manuscript Sources

American Fur Company Papers. Public Archives of Canada. Ottawa.

Cabanné, Charles J. to L. Fontenelle. April 9, 1834. Drips Papers. Missouri Historical Society, St. Louis.

Campbell Papers. Capt. Marcy [Randolph B.], 1859. Missouri Historical Society, St. Louis.

Fontenelle to Llaidlaw, July 31, 1833, Chouteau-Walsh Collection, Missouri Historical Society, St. Louis.

Gardner, Johnson. UMO Fort Union to American Fur Company, Chouteau Papers. Missouri Historical Society, St. Louis.

Letter of Agreement with Wyeth, Aug 14, 1833, Sublette Papers. Missouri Historical Society.

Chouteau Collection, Papers of the St. Louis Fur Trade, Part 1. Missouri Historical Society, St. Louis.

Bailly, Alexis. Papers, 1821–1898. Manuscript Collection. Minnesota Historical Society, St. Paul.

Clark, William. Papers 1812–1840. Manuscript Collection Microfilm, Minnesota Historical Society, St. Paul.

Taliaferro, Lawrence. *Lawrence Taliaferro Journals.* Minnesota Historical Society, St. Paul.

Papers of the St. Louis Fur Trade. Part 2: Fur Company Ledgers and Account Books. 1802–1871. Reels 5 and 6. University Publications of Americas, Bethesda, MD. Courtesy of W. R. Swagerty.

Kappler, Charles J., ed. *Indian Affairs: Laws and Treaties.* Sen. Doc. 58th Congress, 2nd Sess. Doc. N. 319. http://.digital.Library.Okstate.edu/kappler/Vol12/treaties/win0292.htm. Accessed July 2009.

"Robert H. Gore, Jr. Numismatic Endowment." University of Notre Dame, Special Collections.

Schoolcraft, Henry. "Report of the Expedition to the North West Indians." Senate Document, War Department 22nd Congress 2nd Session, Doc. No. 323, 1832.

Schoolcraft, Henry. U.S. Doc. 90, 22nd Congress, 1st Session, Report No. 6:43, and Thomas Forsyth, Report No. 19:80 Policy on Trapping: (Act approved May 6, 1822), United States at Large, Vol. 3, pp. 682–683.

Secondary Sources

Ahenakew, Edward. *Voices of the Plains Cree,* edited by Ruth M. Buck. Toronto: McClelland and Stewart, 1973.

Alaska Sea Otter and Steller Sea Lion Commission, Sea Otter Facts, Old Harbor, AK. http://www.seaotter-seals.org. (accessed June10, 2009).

Alter, J. Cecil. *Jim Bridger: A Historical Narrative.* Norman: University of Oklahoma Press, 1986.

Allen, John Logan, Marjorie Burns, and Sam Sargent. *Cataclysms on the Columbia.* Portland, OR: Timber Press, 1991.

Allerston, Rosemary. "Where the Beaulieus Began." *Up Here* (Yellowknife, NWT), Jan/Feb.1999.

American State Papers, Military Affairs, Vol. 7, and Indian Affairs, Vol. 2. 1832–1861. Reprinted Buffalo, NY: W .S. Hein, 1998.

Anderson, William Marshall. *The Rocky Mountain Journals of William Marshall Anderson: The West in 1834,* edited by Dale L. Morgan and Eleanor Towles Harris. Lincoln: University of Nebraska Press, Bison Books Division, 1967.

Anderson, Gary C. *Little Crow: Spokesman for the Sioux.* St. Paul: Minnesota Historical Society, 1986.

Andrews, C. L. "Alaska Under The Russians, Baranov the Builder," *Washington Historical Quarterly*, vol. 7. (1916–1917): 203.

Arima, Eugene. *Blackfeet and Palefaces: The Pekani and Rocky Mountain House.* Ottawa: Golden Dog Press, 1995.

Arnold, Samuel P., "William W. Bent." *The Mountain Men and The Fur Traders of The Far West*, Vol. 6, edited by LeRoy Hafen. Glendale: Arthur H. Clark Co., 1968.

Athearn, Robert G. *Forts of the Upper Missouri.* Lincoln: University of Nebraska Press, 1967.

Baird, Elizabeth Thérèse. "Reminiscences of Life in Territorial Wisconsin." In *Collections of the Wisconsin Historical Society of Wisconsin, Vol. 15,* edited by Reuben Gold Thwaites. Madison: Wisconsin Historical Society. 1900. 15:225–233.

Baird, Henry. "Recollections of the Early History of Northern Wisconsin." In *Collections of the Wisconsin Historical Society of Wisconsin,* Vol. 4, edited by Reuben Gold Thwaites. Madison: Wisconsin Historical Society, 1859.

Bancroft, Hubert Howe. *Works,* 39 Volumes. San Francisco: A. L. Bancroft & Co., 1886.

Bancroft, Hubert Howe. *History of Alaska, 1730–1885.* Vol. 38 of *Works.* San Francisco: A. L. Bancroft & Co., 1886.

Batman, Richard. *James Pattie's West: The Dream and the Reality.* Norman: University of Oklahoma Press, 1984.

Bauer, John E. "Richard Campbell." In *The Mountain Men and The Fur Traders of The Far West,* Vol. 3, edited by LeRoy Hafen. Glendale: Arthur H. Clark Co., 1965–1972.

Bauer, John E. "Zachariah Ham." In *The Mountain Men and The Fur Traders of The Far West,* Vol. 9, edited by LeRoy Hafen. Glendale: Arthur H. Clark Co., 1965–1972.

Beals, Herbert K., trans., *Juan Pérez on the Northwest Coast: Six Documents of His Expedition in 177.* Portland: Oregon Historical Society Press, 1989. See also

W. J. Langlois, ed., *Captain Cook and the Spanish Explorers on the Coast, Sound Heritage*. Vol. 7, no.1 Province of British Columbia, 1978.

Beckman, Margaret E., and William H. Ellison, "George Nidever." In *The Mountain Men and The Fur Traders of The Far West*, Vol. 1, edited by LeRoy Hafen. Glendale: Arthur H. Clark Co., 1965–1972.

Bell, Major Horace "Reminiscences of a Ranger," 1927, in Iris H. Wilson, "William Wolfskill." In *The Mountain Men and The Fur Traders of The Far West*, Vol. 2, edited by LeRoy Hafen. Glendale: Arthur H. Clark Co., 1965–1972.

Benedict, Ruth. *Patterns of Culture*. Boston: Houghton Mifflin,1934.

Berry, Don. *A Majority of Scoundrels*. New York: Ballantine Books, 1961.

Binns, Archie. *Peter Skene Ogden: Fur Trader*. Portland: Binsford and Mort, 1967.

Binneman, Theodore. *Common and Contested Ground: A Human and Environmental History of the North West Plains*. Norman: University of Oklahoma Press, 2001.

Birchfield, D. L., ed. *Encyclopedia of North American Indians*. New York: Marshall Cavendish, 1997.

Bishop, Charles A. "Kwah, A Carrier Chief." In *Old Trails and New Directions, 3ʳᵈ North American Fur Trade Conference*, edited by Carol M. Judd and Arthur J. Ray. Winnipeg, 1978.

Black, Lydia T. *Russians in Alaska 1732–1867*. Fairbanks: University of Alaska Press, 2004.

Black, Samuel. "Faithful to their Tribe and Friends." In *Samuel Black's 1829 Fort Nez Perces Report*, edited by Dennis Baird. Moscow: University of Idaho Press, 2000.

Blair, Emma H., ed. *The Indian Tribes of the Upper Mississippi Valley and Region of the Great Lakes*, Vol. 1. Los Angeles: A. H. Clark, 1911.

Brooks, James F. *Captives and Cousins*. Chapel Hill: University of North Carolina Press, 2002.

Boorstin, Daniel J. *The Americans: The National Experience*, New York: Random House, 1965.

Brown, Jennifer S. H., and Elizabeth Vibert, eds. *Reading Beyond Words: Contexts for Native History*. Peterborough, Ontario: Broadview Press, 1996.

Brown, Jennifer S. H., and Robert Brightman, eds. *The Orders of the Dreamed: George Nelson on Cree and Northern Ojibwa Religion and Myth, 1823*. Manitoba Studies in Native History Series #3. Winnipeg: University of Manitoba Press, reprinted St. Paul: Minnesota Historical Society, 1988.

Brown, Jennifer S. H., *Strangers in Blood*. Vancouver: University of British Columbia Press, 1980.

J. M. Bumsted, "John Mackay," Dictionary of Canadian Biography Online, at http://www.biographi.ca/009004-119.01-e.phj, accessed April 29, 2009.

Burley, David V., J. Scott Hamilton, and Knut R. Fladmark. *Prophecy of the Swan: The Upper Peace River Fur Trade, 1794–1823.* British Columbia Studies. Vancouver: University of British Columbia Press, 1996.

Camp, Charles L., ed. "George C. Yount, and His Chronicles of the West." *California Historical Society Quarterly*, Vol. 2, April, 1923.

Carpenter, Cecelia Svinth. *Fort Nisqually, A Documented History of Indian and British Interaction.* Tacoma, WA: Tahoma Research Publication, 1986.

Carter, Harvey L. "William H. Ashley." *The Mountain Men and the Fur Trade of the Far West,* vol. 7, edited by LeRoy R. Hafen. Glendale, CA: Arthur H. Clark Co., 1969.

Carter, Harvey L. "Jedediah Strong Smith," *The Mountain Men and the Fur Trade of the Far West,* vol. 8, edited by LeRoy R. Hafen. Glendale, CA: Arthur H. Clark Co., 1971.

Carter, Harvey L. "Kit Carson." *The Mountain Men and the Fur Trade of the Far West,* vol.6, edited by LeRoy R. Hafen. Glendale, CA: Arthur H. Clark Co., 1968.

Carter, Harvey L. "Moses Carson." *The Mountain Men and the Fur Trade of the Far West,* vol. 2, edited by LeRoy R. Hafen. Glendale, CA: Arthur H. Clark Co., 1965.

Carter, Harvey L. "Ramsay Crooks," *Mountain Men and the Fur Trade in the Far West,* vol. 9, edited by LeRoy R. Hafen. Glendale, CA: Arthur H. Clark Co. 1972.

Harvey L. Carter, "Robert Campbell," *Mountain Men and the Fur Trade in the Far West,* vol. 8, edited by LeRoy R. Hafen. Glendale, CA: Arthur H. Clark Co., 1971.

Carter, Harvey L. "Andrew Drips," *The Mountain Men and the Fur Trade of the Far West,* edited by LeRoy R. Hafen. Glendale, CA: Arthur H. Clark Co., vol. 8, 1971.

Carter, Harvey L. "Robert Stuart," *The Mountain Men and the Fur Trade of the Far West,* vol. 9, edited by LeRoy R. Hafen. Glendale, CA: Arthur H. Clark Co., 1972.

Chardon, Francis A. *Chardon's Journal at Fort Clark 1834–1839. Descriptive of Life on the Upper Missouri, of a Fur Trader's Experiences Among the Mandans, Gros Ventres, and Their Neighbors, of the Ravages of the Small-Pox Epidemic of 1837,* edited by Annie Heloise Abel. Lincoln: University of Nebraska Press, 1997.

Chávez, Thomas E., *Conflict and Acculturation :Manuel Alvarez's 1842 Memorial.* Santa Fe: Museum of New Mexico Press, 1989.

Charlevois, Father Pierre-François-Xavier de. *Historie Nouvelle France, 1774,* 6 vols, translated by John Gilmary Shea, and Noah Farnham Morrison. Chicago: American Historical Association, 1962.

Cherepanov, Stepan. "August 3, 1762, the Account of the Totma Merchant, Stepan Cherepanov, Concerning His Stay in the Aleutian Islands, 1759–1762," in Dmytryshyn et al., *To Siberia and Russian America, Three Centuries of Russian Eastward Expansion, a Documentary Record,* Vol. 2, *Russian Penetration of the North Pacific Ocean.* Portland: Oregon Historical Society Press, 1988; hereafter cited *Russian Penetration.*

Catlin, George. *Letters and Notes on the Manners, Customs and Condition of North American Indians.* New York: Dover Publishing, Inc. 1973. Fig. Plat 30 1:57.

Chatters, James C., "Culture Pattern." *Handbook Of North American Indians*, Vol. 12, *Plateau,* edited by Deward E. Walker, Jr. Washington: Smithsonian Institution, 1998.

Chevigny, Hector. *Lord of Alaska: The Story of Baranov and the Russian Adventure.* New York: Viking Press, 1942.

Chevigny, Hector. *Russian America: The Great Alaskan Venture, 1741–1867.* New York: Viking Press, 1943._

Chittenden, Hiram. *The American Fur Trade of the Far West,* 2 vols. New York: Press of the Pioneers, 1935.

Clements, Louis J., "Andrew Henry," *The Mountain Men and the Fur Trade of the Far West,* Vol. 6, edited by LeRoy R. Hafen Glendale, CA: Arthur H. Clark Co., 1965–1972.

Clifton, James A. *The Prairie People: Continuity and Change in Potawatomi Indian Culture, 1665–1965.* 1977; new edition, Iowa City: University of Iowa Press, 1998.

Clyman, James. "A Short Detail of Life and Incidents of my trip in and through the Rockey Mountains." *Journey of a Mountain Man,* edited by Linda M. Hasselstrom. Missoula, MT: Mountain Press Publishing Company, 1985.

Coues, Elliott, ed. *New Light on the Early History of the Greater Northwest: The Manuscript Journals of Alexander Henry and of David Thompson.* New York: Francis P. Harper, 1897.

Coues, Elliot, ed. *The History of the Expedition under the Command of Lewis and Clark.* 1893; reprinted, 3 vol. New York: Dover Publications, 1965.

Crooks, Drew W. *Past Reflections: Essays in the Hudson's Bay Company in the Southern Puget Sound Region.* Tacoma, WA: Fort Nisqually Foundation, 2001.

Davidson, J.N. "Missions on Chequamegon Bay." *Collections of State Historical Society of Wisconsin,* Vol. 12, edited by Reuben Gold Thwaites. Madison: Wisconsin Historical Society, 1892.

Dary, David, *The Santa Fe Trail,* New York: Penguin Books, 2000.

Davydov, Gavriil Ivanovich. *Two Voyages to America, 1802–1807,* translated by Colin Bearne and edited by Richard A. Pierce. Kingston, Ont.: Limestone Press, 1977.

Denig, Edward T. *The Assiniboine,* edited by J. N. B. Hewitt. Norman: University of Oklahoma Press, 2000.

Denig, Edward T. *Five Indian Tribes of the Upper Missouri,* edited by J. C. Ewers. Norman: University of Oklahoma, 1961.

Denniston, Glenda. "Sekani." In *Handbook of North American Indians Series.* Vol. 6, *Subarctic,* edited by June Helm. Washington: Smithsonian Institution, 1981.

DeVoto, Bernard. *Across the Wide Missouri.* Boston: Houghton Mifflin Co., 1947.

Dickason, Olive Patricia. *Canada's First Nations.* Norman: University of Oklahoma Press. 1992

Dillon, Richard. *Siskiyou Trail.* New York: McGraw Hill, 1975.

Dmytryshyn, Basil, E. A. P. Crownhart-Vaughan, and Thomas Vaughan, eds., trans. *The Russian American Colonies, 1798–1867,* 3 Vols. Portland: Oregon Historical Society Press, Vol.1, 1985, Vol. 2, 1988, Vol. 3, 1989.

Dmytryshyn, Basil, and E. A. P. Crownhart-Vaughan. "Khlebnikov's Reports." *Oregon Historical Society Journal,* 1976

Dmytryshyn, Basil, E. A. P. Crownhart-Vaughan, and Thomas Vaughan, eds. and trans., *To Siberia and Russian America, Three Centuries of Russian Eastward Expansion, a Documentary Record,* Vol. 2, *Russian Penetration of the North Pacific Ocean.* Portland: Oregon Historical Society Press, 1988.

Driver, Harold E. *Indians of North America.* Chicago: University of Chicago Press, 1969.

Drucker, Phillip. *Cultures of the North Pacific Coast.* San Francisco: Chandler Publishing Co., 1965.

Drucker, Phillip. *Indians of the Northwest Coast.* Garden City: Natural History Press, 1955.

Drucker, Phillip. *Indians of the Plains.*

Drucker, Phillip. "Rank, Wealth, and Kinship in Northwest Coast." *Indians of the North Pacific Coast,* edited by Tom McFeat. Seattle: University of Washington Press, 1967.

Drucker, Phillip, and Robert F. Heizer. *To Make My Name Good.* Berkeley: University of California Press, 1967.

Duff, Wilson. *The Indian History of British Columbia.* "The Impact of the White Man." Anthropology in British Columbia, Memoir No. t, 1964 Provincial Museum of British Columbia, Victoria, B.C 1:58. New edition., Victoria, BC: Royal British Columbia Museum, 1992.

Dufour, Pierre "Laurent Leroux," *Canadian Biography Online,* **Vol, 8. Toronto: University of Toronto. http://www.biographi.ca/index-e. html, (accessed October 2010).**

Dutton, Bertha P. *American Indians of the Southwest.* Albuquerque: University of New Mexico Press, 1983.

Dunham, Harold A. "Manuel Alvarez." *The Mountain Men and The Fur Traders of The Far West,* Vol. 1, edited by LeRoy Hafen. Glendale, CA: Arthur H. Clark Co., 1965.

Dunham, Harold A. "Charles Bent." *The Mountain Men and The Fur Traders of The Far West,* Vol. 2, edited by LeRoy Hafen. Glendale, CA: Arthur H. Clark Co., 1965.

Dunham, Harold A. "Ceran St. Vrain." *The Mountain Men and The Fur Traders of The Far West,* Vol. 2, edited by LeRoy Hafen. Glendale, CA: Arthur H. Clark Co., 1965.

Elliott, Henry W. *An Arctic Province, Alaska and the Seal Islands.* London: Sampson, Low, Marston, Searle & Rivington, 1886.

Elliott, T. C., ed. "A Hudson's Bay Company Marriage Certificate." *The Quarterly of the Oregon Historical Society* 10, no 3 (Sept. 1909).

Elliott, T.C., ed. "The Journal of John Work, July 5 – September 15, 1826." *The Washington Historical Quarterly* 6 (1915).

Ewers, John C. *The Horse in Blackfoot Indian Culture.* Washington: Smithsonian Institution Press, 1969

Ewers, John C. *Indian Life on the Upper Missouri.* Norman: University of Oklahoma Press, 1988.

Ewers, John C. *Plains Indian History and Culture.* Norman: University of Oklahoma Press, 1988.

Faulkner, Harold Underwood. *American Economic History.* New York: Harper & Bros., 1954.

Favour, Alpheus H. *Old Bill Williams, Mountain Man,* Norman: University of Oklahoma Press, 1987.

Fehrman, Richard J. "The Mountain Men—A Statistical Review" *Mountain Men and the Fur Trade in the Far West,* vol. 10, edited by LeRoy R. Hafen. Glendale, CA: Arthur H. Clark Co. 1972 .

Ferris, W. A. *Life in the Rocky Mountains,* edited by Paul C. Phillips. Denver: Old West Publishing Company, 1940.

Fisher, Robin. *Contact and Conflict: Indian European Relations in British Columbia, 1774–1890.* 1977; 2nd ed., Vancouver: University of British Columbia Press, 1992.

Forsyth Thomas, U.S. Congress, Sen. Document 90, 22nd Congress, 1st Session, Report No 6. March 1832. Also in *Messages from the President on the State of the Fur Trade 1824–1832,* Fairfield, WA: Ye Galleon Press, 1985.111–119.

Franchère, Gabriel, and Hoyt C. Franchère. *Adventure at Astoria,1810–1814.* Edited and translated by Hoyt C. Franchère. American Exploration and Travel Series. Norman: University of Oklahoma Press, 1967.

Francis, R. Douglas, Richard Jones, Donald B. Smith. *Origins: Canadian History to Confederation.* Toronto: Holt, Rinehart, and Winston of Canada, 1988.

Francis, Daniel and Michael Payne. *A Narrative History of Fort Dunvegan*. Winnipeg: Watson & Dwyer Publishing, 1993.

Franklin, Sir John. *Narrative of a Journey to the Shores of the Polar Sea, in the Years 1819–20–21–22*. 1828; Edmonton: M.G. Hurtig, 1969.

Frazer, Esther. *The Canadian Rockies, Early Travel and Explorations*. Edmonton: M.G. Hurtig, 1969.

Fuchs, Denise. *Native Sons of Rupert's Land, 1760 to the 1860's*. Ph.D. diss., University of Manitoba, 2002.

Galbraith, John S. *The Hudson's Bay Company as an Imperial Factor, 1821–1869*. New York: Octagon Books, 1977. Originally printed 1957.

Galbraith, John S. *The Little Emperor: Governor Simpson of the Hudson's Bay Company*. Toronto: Macmillan of Canada, 1976.

Gianettino, Susan. "The Middleman Role in the Fur Trade" *Western Canadian Journal of Anthropology* 7 (1977): 4.

Gibbon, Edward. *The Decline and Fall of the Roman Empire. 6 vols., 1776–1788;* reprint edited by Hugh Trevor-Roper. New York: Everyman's Library, Alfred A Knopf, 1993.

Gibson, James R. *Imperial Russia in Frontier America*. New York: Oxford University Press, 1976.

Gibson, James R. *The Lifeline of the Oregon Country: The Fraser-Columbia Brigade System*. Vancouver: University of British Columbia Press, 1997.

Gibson, James R. *Otter Skins, Boston Ships, and China Goods*. Seattle: University of Washington Press, 1992.

Gilbert, Bil. *Westering Man, The Life of Joseph Walker*. Norman: University of Oklahoma Press, 1983.

Gillespie, P. "Athabascans of the Shield and the Mackenzie Drainage," *Handbook of North American Indians*, Vol 6. *Subarctic* edited by June Helm, General Editor, William C. Sturtevant. Washington: Smithsonian Institution, 1982.

Gilman, Carolyn. *Where Two Worlds Meet: The Great Lakes Fur Trade*. St. Paul: Minnesota Historical Society, 1982.

Gordon, William. "Questions Answered by William Gordon." *Messages from the President on the State of the Fur Trade 1824–1832*. Fairfield, WA: Ye Galleon Press, 1985.

Gough, Barry M. "Dixon, George," *Dictionary of Canadian Biography Online*, at http://www.biographi.ca/009004-119.01-e.phj (accessed April 28, 2009).

Gough, Barry. *First Across the Continent, Sir Alexander Mackenzie*. Oklahoma Western Biographies, Vol. 14. Norman: University of Oklahoma Press, 1997.

Gough, Barry, M. Barkley, Charles William," Dictionary of Canadian Biography Online, , at http://www.biographi.ca/009004-119.01-e.phpj: (accessed April 28, 2009).

Gowans, Fred. *Rocky Mountain Rendezvous.* Layton, Utah: Peregrine Smith Books, 1985.

Gregg, Josiah. *Commerce of the Prairies,* edited by Max L. Moorhead. Norman: University of Oklahoma Press, 1954.

Hafen, LeRoy R. *Broken Hand.* Lincoln: University of Nebraska Press, 1973.

Hafen, LeRoy R., editor, *The Mountain Men and the Fur Trade of the Far West,* 10 Vols. Glendale, CA: Arthur H. Clark Co., 1965–1972.

Hafen, Leroy R., and Ann W. Hafen, " Thomas Fitzpatrick," Vol. 1, *Mountain Men of the Fur Trade.* Glendale, CA: Arthur H. Clark Co., 1969.

Haines, Francis. *The Nez Perce: Tribesmen of the Northern Plateau.* Norman: University of Oklahoma Press, 1955.

Harmon, Daniel W. *Sixteen Years in Indian Country: The Journal of Daniel W. Harmon, 1800–1816,* edited by W. Kaye Lamb. Toronto: Macmillan, 1957.

Hartman, Susan. "Women's Work Among the Plains Indians." *Gateway Heritage,* 3, iss. 4:209, 1983.

Hassrick, Royal B. *The Sioux.* Norman: University of Oklahoma Press, 1989.

Hays, Carl D.W. "David E. Jackson." *The Mountain Men and The Fur Traders of The Far West,* Vol. 9, edited by LeRoy Hafen. Glendale, CA: Arthur H. Clark Co., 1972.

Hayes, Edmund, editor. *Log of the Union: John Boit's Remarkable Voyage to the Northwest Coast and Around the World, 1704–1796,* North Pacific Studies No. 6. Portland: Oregon Historical Society Press, 1981.

Helm, June. *The People of the Denendeh.* Montreal & Kingston: McGill-Queen's University Press, 2000.

Helm, June "The Dene." In *Handbook of North American Indians, Subarctic* Vol. 6 edited by William C. Sturtevent. Washington: Smithsonian Institution, 1982.

Hickling, William. "Reminiscences of Wisconsin in 1833." In *Wisconsin Collections,* Vol. 7, edited by L.C. Draper. Madison: State Historical Society. 1876.

Hill, J.J. "Ewing Young and the Fur Trade of the Southwest, 1822–1834," *Quarterly of the Oregon Historical Society,* Vol. 24, no.1, March 1923: 4.

Holloway, Drew Alan, ed. *A Narrative of Colonel Robert Campbell's Experiences in the Rocky Mountain Fur Trade from 1825 to 1835.* Fairfield, WA: Ye Galleon Press, 1991.

Holmes, Kenneth L. *Ewing Young, Master Trapper.* Portland: Binfords and Mort, 1967.

Holmes, Kenneth L. "Joseph Gervais," In *The Mountain Men and the Fur Trade of the Far West,* Vol. 7, edited by LeRoy Hafen. Glendale, CA: Arthur H. Clark Co., 1969.

Howay, Frederic W. ed. *Voyages of the Columbia in the Northwest Coast, 1787–1790 and 1790–1793*, Portland: Oregon Historical Society in cooperation with the Massachusetts Historical Society, 1990, Vol. 6, 7, 9.

Hyslop, Stephen G. *Bound for Santa Fe*. Norman: University of Oklahoma Press, 1950.

Innis, Harold A. *The Fur Trade in Canada: An Introduction to Canadian Economic History*. Toronto: University of Toronto, 1970.

Irving, Washington. *Astoria*. Lincoln: University of Nebraska Press, 1982.

Irving, Washington. *The Adventures of Captain Bonneville, USA: In the Rocky Mountains and the Far West*, edited by Edgeley W. Todd. 1961; Norman: University of Oklahoma Press, 1986 reprint.

Jablow, Joseph. *The Cheyenne Indians in Plains Indian Trade Relations 1795–1840*. Lincoln: University of Nebraska Press, 1994.

Jarvenpa, Robert and Hetty Jo Brumbach. "Socio-spatial organization and Decision-making Processes: Observations from the Chipewyan." *American Anthropologist,* March 1998, 90:3.

James, Thomas. *Three Years Among the Indians and Mexicans*. Crabtree, OR: Narrative Press, 2002.

Jenness, Diamond. *The Indians of Canada*. 1932; 7th ed., Ottawa, Ontario: University of Toronto, 1977.

Jenness, Diamond. *The Sekani Indians of British Columbia*. National Museum of Canada, Bulletin # 84. Government Printing Bureau, Anthropological Series II, No. 20, 1937. Reprinted, Ottawa: J.O. Patenaude.

Jennings, John. *The Canoe: A Living Tradition*. Toronto: Firefly Books, 2002.

Josephy, Alvin M. *The Nez Perce Indians and the Opening of the West*. New York: Houghton Mifflin, 1971.

Kamenskii, Fr. Anatolii. *Tlingit Indians of Alaska,* translated by Sergei Kan. Fairbanks: University of Alaska Press, 1985.

Karamanski, Theodore J. *Fur Trade and Exploration: Opening the Far Northwest, 1821–1852*. Vancouver: University of British Columbia Press, 1983.

Keithahan, R. C. *Trading Posts in the Upper Mississippi Valley.* M.A. thesis. University of Minnesota, 1929.

Kelsey, Vera. *Young Men So Daring*. Indianapolis: Bobbs-Merrill. 1956.

Kent, Timothy J. *Birchbark Canoes of the Fur Trade*, 2 Vols. Detroit: Silver Fox Enterprises, 1997.

Khlebnikova, Kyrill T. *Colonial Russian America: Kyrill T. Khlebnikov's Reports, 1817–1832,* translated and edited by Basil Dmytryshyn and A. E. P. Crownhart-Vaughan. Portland: Oregon Historical Society, 1976.

Klippenstein, Frieda E. "The Role of the Carrier Indians at Fort St. James, 1806–1915." Report from Historical and Anthropological Sources. Western Regional Office.

Canadian Parks Service, March 1992.

Krech, Shepard III. *The Ecological Indian.* New York: W. W. Norton, 2003.

Krech, Shepard III. "The Trade of the Slavey and Dogrib at Fort Simpson." In *The Subarctic Fur Trade: Native Social and Economic Adaptions,* edited by Shepard Krech III. Vancouver: University of British Columbia Press, 1990.

Kushnaev, Evgenii G. *Bering's Search for the Strait, the First Kamchatka Expedition, 1725–1730.* 1976 Russian edition. Edited and trans. by E. A. P. Crownhart-Vaughan. Portland: Oregon Historical Society Press, 1990.

Kushner, Howard I. *Conflict on the Northwest Coast*: American-Russian Rivalry in the Pacific Northwest, 1790–1867." *Contributions to American History Series.* Westport, CT: Greenwood Press, 1975.

Lamb, W. Kaye. "John McLoughlin." In *Dictionary of Canadian Biography Online.* Toronto: University of Toronto, 2000, at www.biographi.ca./EN/index.html, (accessed June 10, 2009).

La Nauze, C.D. "Mackenzie Memories." *The Beaver,* vol. 28 no. 2, September, 1948. (outfit 279), 22–28.

Larocque, Francois-Antoine. "Missouri Journal" and "Yellowstone Journal." In *Early Fur Trade on Northern Plains: Canadian Traders Among the Mandan and Hidatsa Indians, 1738–1818,* by W. Raymond Wood and Thomas D. Thiessen. Norman: University of Oklahoma Press, 1985.

Lavender, David. *Bent's Fort.* Lincoln: University of Nebraska Press, 1972.

Lavender, David. *The Fist in the Wilderness.* Garden City: Doubleday, 1964.

La Verendrye, P. G. V. *Journals and Letters of Pierre Gaultier de Varennes de la Verendrye and his sons,* Ed. Lawrence J. Burpee. Champlain Society. Publication 16. Toronto, 1927.

Lecompte, Janet. "Alexander K. Branch." *The Mountain Men and the Fur Trade of the Far West,* edited by Leroy R. Hafen, Glendale, CA: Arthur H. Clark Co., 1966. 4:61ff.

Lecompte, Janet. "August Chouteau," *The Mountain Men and the Fur Trade of the Far West,* edited by Leroy R. Hafen, Glendale, CA: Arthur H. Clark Co.,1968. 9:63–90.

Lecompte, Janet. *Pueblo: Hardscrabble Greenhorn.* Norman: University of Oklahoma Press,1978.

Leonard, Zenas. *Narrative of the Adventures of Zenas Leonard,* New York: Readex Microprint Corp,1966.

Lewis, Oscar. "Effects of White Contact Upon Blackfoot Culture, with Special Reference to the Role of the Fur Trade." In *Centennial Anniversary Publications,* edited by A. I. Hallowell. American Ethnographic Society. Seattle: University of Washington Press. 1942, 6:73.

Lockwood, James H. "Early Times in Wisconsin." In *Collections, State Historical Society of Wisconsin,* edited by Lyman C. Draper. Vol. 2. Madison: Wisconsin State Historical Society, 1856. 2:130.

Lytwyn, Victor P. *The Fur Trade of the Little North: Indians, Pedlars, and Englishmen East of Lake Winnipeg, 1760–1821.* Rupert's Land Research Center. Winnipeg: University of Winnipeg. 1986.

MacGregor J.G. *John Rowand: Czar of the Prairies.* Saskatoon: Western Producer Prairie Books, 1978.

Mackenzie, Alexander. *Voyages from Montreal, on the River St. Laurence, through the Continent of North America, to the Frozen and Pacific Oceans; in the Years 1789 and 1793.* Edmonton: M.G.Hurtig, 1971.

Mackie, Richard S. *Trading Beyond the Mountains.* Vancouver: University of British Columbia Press, 1998.

Maclachlan, Morag. *The Fort Langley Journals, 1827–30.* Vancouver: University of British Columbia Press, 1998.

Maloney, Alice. *Fur Brigade to the Bonaventura.* San Francisco: California Historical Society, 1945.

Mandelbaum, David G. *The Plains Cree.* Canadian Plains Research Center. Regina: University of Regina Press, 1979.

Matson, Nehemiah "Sketch of Shaubena." In *Collections of the State Historical Society of Wisconsin,* Vol. 7, edited by L.C. Draper. Madison: State Historical Society, 1908.

Matttes, Merrill J. "Joseph Robidoux," In *The Mountain Men and The Fur Traders of The Far West,* Vol. 8, edited by LeRoy Hafen. Glendale, CA: Arthur H. Clark Co., 1971.

Mattison, Ray H. "Joshua Pilcher," In *The Mountain Men and The Fur Traders of The Far West,* Vol. 4, edited by LeRoy Hafen. Glendale, CA: Arthur H. Clark Co., 1966.

Maximilian, Alexander, Prince of Wied. "Field Journal, August 1833." Vol.22. In *Travels in the Interior of North America, 1748–1846,* 32 vols., edited by Reuben Thwaites. Reprinted New York: EP Dutton & Co., 1976.

Maximilian, Alexander, Prince of Wied. *People of the First Man: Life Among the Plains Indians in Their Final Days of Glory: The Firsthand Account of Prince Maximilian's Expedition Up the Missouri River, 1833–34,* edited by Davis Thomas and Karin Ronnefeldt, illustrated by Karl Bodmer. New York: Dutton, 1976.

McClellan, Catharine. "Intercultural Relations and Cultural Change in the Cordillera." In *Handbook of North American Indians,* Vol. 6, *Subarctic,* edited by June Helm. Washington: Smithsonian Institution, 1981.

McClellan, Catherine *My Old People Say, An Ethnographic Survey of Southern Yukon Territory*. National Museums of Canada Publications in Ethnology 6. Ottawa: National Museums of Canada, 1975.

McKenney, Thomas. *Sketches of a Tour to the Lakes,* 3 vols. Philadelphia: American Philosophical Society, 1826.

McLean, John. *John McLean's Notes of a Twenty-Five Years' Service in the Hudson's Bay Territory*, edited by W.S. Wallace. Reprinted, Toronto: Champlain Society, 1949.

McLean, Thomas Wesley. *National Archives of Canada: Exploring the Fur Trade, Routes of North America*. 1976; Winnipeg: Heartland Publications, 2000.

McLoughlin, John. *Letters of John McLoughlin: Written at Fort Vancouver, 1829–1832. Edited* by Burt Brown Barker. Whitefish, MT: Kessinger Publishing, June 2008.

Menzies, Gaven. *1434*, Harper and Collins, New York, 2008.

Menzies, Gaven. *1434, The Year a Magnificent Chinese Fleet Sailed to Italy and Ignited the Renaissance*. New York: Wm. Morrow, 2008.

Merk, Frederick, ed. *Fur Trade and Empire, George Simpson's Journal: Remarks Connected with the Fur Trade in the Course of a Voyage from York Factory to Fort George and Back to York Factory, 1824–1825, together with Accompanying Documents*. Revised ed., Cambridge: Harvard University Press, 1931.

Miller, Harry B. "These Too Were Pioneers," 1984, Seniors Consultant Service, Melville, Saskatchewan.

Mooney, James. *The Aboriginal Population of America North of Mexico*. Smithsonian Miscellaneous Collections, Vol. 80, No. 7. Washington: Smithsonian Institution, 1928.

Morantz, Toby. "The Fur Trade and the Cree of James Bay." In *Old Trails and New Directions,3ʳᵈ North American Fur Trade Conference*, 1980, edited by Carol M. Judd, Arthur J. Ray. Toronto: University of Toronto Press,1980.

Morgan, Dale L. *Jedediah Smith and the Opening of the West*. Lincoln: University of Nebraska Press, 1969.

Morgan, Dale L. "License granted to William H. Ashley to Trade With Indians of the Missouri River, 11 April, 1822, J.C. Calhoun, Secretary of War." In *The West of William H. Ashley: 1822–1838*. Denver: Mountain Press Publishing Co.

Morgan, Dale L., ed. *The West of William H. Ashley: Recorded in the Diaries and Letters... 1822–1838*. Denver: Mountain Press Publishing, 1964.

Morice, Adrian G. *The History of the Northern Interior of British Columbia (formerly New Caledonia) (1660–1880)*. Toronto: Wm. Briggs, 1904.

Morse, Eric W. *Fur Trade Canoe Routes of Canada: Then and Now*. Toronto: University of Toronto, 1979.

Moulton, Gary R., ed. *The Journals of Lewis and Clark*, 7 vols. Lincoln: University of Nebraska Press, 1988.

Nash, Linda. "Inescapable Ecologies," *A History of Environment, Disease, and Knowledge,* Berkeley: University of California Press, 2007, online at http://books.google.com/books? (accessed June 15, 2009).

Neihardt, John G. "The Song of Hugh Glass." In *A Cycle of the West,* by John G. Neihardt. New York: Macmillan, 1949.

Nerburn, Kent and Louise Mengelkoch, eds. *Native American Wisdom.* Novato, CA,: New World Library, 1991.

Nisbet, Jack. *Sources of the River: Tracking David Thompson Across Western North America.* Sasquatch Books: Seattle, 1994.

Newell, Robert. *Memorandum of Robert Newell's Travels in the Territory of Missourie,* edited by Dorothy O. Johansen. Portland: Champoeg Press, 1959.

Newman, Peter C. *Company of Adventurers,*Vol.1. Ontario: Penguin Books Canada, 1985.

Newman, Peter C. *Caesars of the Wilderness,* Vol. 2, New York: Penguin Books, 1987.

Nicks, Trudy. "The Iroquois and the Fur Trade in Western Canada." In *Old Trails and New Directions: Papers of the Third North American Fur Trade Conference,* edited by Carol M. Judd and Arthur J. Ray. Toronto: University of Toronto Press, 1980.

Novak, M., J.A. Baker, M.E. Obbard & B. Mallock, *Furbearer Harvests in North America, 1600–1909.* Ontario Ministry of Natural Resources, 1967.

Nute, Grace. "Calendar of the American Fur Company's Papers, Part 1. 1831–1840." In *Annual Report of the American Historical Association.* 1,2. Washington: U.S. Government Printing Office, 1944 & 1945.

Nute, Grace Lee. "Down North in 1982." *The Beaver,* vol 28, no.1 (Outfit 279, June 1948). 42–46.

Nute, Grace Lee. "Journey for Frances." *The Beaver,* Dec.(1953) 50–54 and March (1954) 12–17.

Nute, Grace Lee. "The Papers of the American Fur Company, A Brief Estimate of Their Significance." *American Historical Review,* Vol. 22, No. 3, (April, 1927) 45.

Ogden, Peter Skene. *Traits of American Indian Life.* Fairfied, WA: Ye Galleon Press, 1998.

Oglesby, Richard Edward. *Manuel Lisa and the Opening of the Missouri Fur Trade.* Norman: University of Oklahoma Press, 1963.

O'Meara, Walter. *Daughters of the Country: The Women of the Fur Traders and Mountain Men.* New York: Harcourt, Brace & World, 1968.

Osgood, Cornelius. *The Distribution of the Northern Athapaskan Indians.* Yale University Publications in Anthropology. New Haven: Yale University Press, 1936.

Parker, James. *Emporium of the North: Fort Chipewyan and the Fur Trade to 1835.* Alberta Culture and Multiculturalism, Regina, Saskatchewan: Canadian Plains Research Center, 1987.

Peters, Virginia B. *Women of the Earth Lodges: Tribal Life on the Plains.* Norman: University of Oklahoma Press, 1995.

Peterson, Jacqueline and Jennifer S. H Brown, eds. *The New Peoples: Being and Becoming Métis in North America.* Winnipeg: University of Manitoba Press, 1985.

Pethick, Derek *The Nootka Connection: Europe and the Northwest Coast 1790–1795.* Vancouver: Douglas & McIntyre, 1980.

Petitot, Emile. "Notes on the Métis People of the North" In *The Amerindians of the Canadian Northwest in the 19th Century, as seen by Émile Petitot,* compiled by Donat Savoi. Ottawa : Canadian Dept. of Indian Affairs and Northern Development, Northern Science Research Group, 1970.

Phillips, Paul C. *The Fur Trade.* 2 Vols. Norman: University of Oklahoma Press, 1961.

Pierce, R. H. *Builders of Alaska: The Russian Governors, 1818–1867.* Kingston, Ont.: Limestone Press, 1986.

Porter, Kenneth Wiggins. *John Jacob Astor, Business Man,* 2 vols. Cambridge: Harvard University Press, 1931.

Pritzker, Barry M. *A Native American Encyclopedia,* New York: Oxford University Press, 2000.

Pullar, Gordon L. "Kodiak Island Alutiiq," Encyclopedia of North American Indians. (Boston: Houghton Mifflin) http://Encyclopedia of North American Indians/college/hmco.com   /history/readerscomp/naind/na-001300-aleut. htm. Page 2 of 3. (accessed July 10, 2009).

Ray, Arthur J. *I Have Lived Here Since the World Began: An Illustrated History of Canada's Native Peoples.* Toronto: Lester Publishing, 1996.

Ray, Arthur J. *Indians in the Fur Trade: Their Role as Trappers, Hunters, and Middlemen in the lands Southwest of Hudson Bay 1660–1870.* Toronto: University of Toronto, 1974.

Ray, Arthur, Elizabeth Bedard, Alan McMillan, *First Project Report.* The Land Based Fur Trade Project, Department of Archeology. Simon Fraser University, April, 1986.

Ray, Vernon K. "The Chinook Indians in the Early 1800s." *The Western Shore: Oregon Country Essays Honoring the American Revolution,* edited by Thomas Vaughan. Portland: Oregon Historical Society, 1976. 141.

Reeder, Ray M. "John Work," In *The Mountain Men and the Fur Traders of the Far West,* Vol. 2, edited by LeRoy Hafen. Glendale, CA: Arthur H. Clark Co., 1965.

Rich, E.E. *The Fur Trade and the Northwest to 1857.* Canadian Centenary Series. Toronto: McClelland and Stewart, 1968.

Rich, E. E. *The History of the Hudson's Bay Company,1670–1870.* London: Hudson's Bay Record Society, 2 vols.,1958.

Rich, E. E. "The Indian Traders," *Beaver* 5 (Winter 1970).

Rich, E. E. "Trade Habits and Economic Motivations Among the Indians of North America." *Sweet Promises : A Reader of Indian-White Relations in Canada.* Edited by J. R. Miller. Toronto: University of Toronto Press, 1992.

Rittenhouse, Jack D. *The Literature of the Santa Fe Trail.* Essays and Monographs in Colorado History, No. 6. Denver: Colorado Historical Society, 1987.

Robinson, H. M. *The Great Fur Land or Sketches of Life in Hudson's Bay Territory,* London & New York: G.P. Putman's Sons, 1987.

Rogers, E. S. "The Naskapi." *The Beaver.* Vol. 49, No. 3, Outfit 300 (Winter 1969) Winnipeg: Hudson Bay Company.

Ross, Alexander. *The Fur Hunters of the Far West,* edited by Kenneth A. Spaulding. Norman: University of Oklahoma Press, 1961.

Ruby, Robert H. and John A. Brown. "Lower Chinook Lands." In *The Chinook Indians, Traders of the Lower Columbia River,* Civilization of the American Indian Series. Norman: University of Oklahoma Press, 1976. 21.

Russell, O. *Handbook of North American Indians,* General Editor William C. Sturtevant, Smithsonian Institution: Washington, D.C. 2008.

Russell, Terry, ed. *Messages from the President on the State of the Fur Trade, 1824–1832.* Fairfield, WA: Ye Galleon Press, 1985.

Sage, Rufus. *Rocky Mountain Life.* Originally published as *Scenes of the Rocky Mountains.* Carey & Hart, 1846; reprinted Boston: Wentworth, 1857

Saum, Lewis O. "The Fur Trade and the Noble Savage." *American Quarterly.* Journal of the American Studies Association. Boston: Johns Hopkins University. 2:15, 1963: 554–71.

Saum, Lewis. *The Fur Trader and the Indian.* Seattle: University of Washington Press, 1965.

Sampson, William R. "John Work" Canadian Biographical Dictionary Online. Toronto: University of Toronto, 2000. www.biographi.ca./EN/index.html (accessed March 5, 2007).

Sampson, William R. "Nathaniel Jarvis Wyeth." In *The Mountain Men and The Fur Traders of The Far West,* Vol. 5. edited by LeRoy Hafen. Glendale, CA: Arthur H. Clark Co., 1968.

Schafer, Joseph. "The Wisconsin Lead Region." In *Wisconsin Domesday Book,* by State Historical Society of Wisconsin. Wisconsin Studies Series. Madison: State Historical Society of Wisconsin, 1932.

Schneider, Mary Jane. *North Dakota Indians*. Dubuque, IA: Kendall/Hunt Publishing Co., 1986.

Schoolcraft, Henry. *Personal Memoirs of Residence of Thirty Years with the Indian Tribes of the American Frontier.* Philadelphia: Lippincott, Grambo & Co., 1851.

Schoolcraft, Henry. *Expedition to the North West Indians, 1832,* House Doc.323. United States House of Representatives.

Shaw, George C. *The Chinook Jargon and How to Use It.* Seattle: Rainier Printing Co., 1909.

Shippee, L.B. "Federal Relations in Oregon, II" *Oregon Historical Quarterly* 19, no. 3 (Sept. 1918):200.

Simmons, Virginia McConnell. *The Ute Indians of Utah: Colorado and New Mexico.* Boulder: University Press of Colorado, 2000.

Sladen, J. A. *Making Peace With Cochise: The 1872 Journal of Captain Joseph Alton Sladen,* edited by Edwin R. Sweeney. Norman: University of Oklahoma Press, 1997.

Slotkin, Richard. *Regeneration Through Violence, the Mythology of the American Frontier, 1600–1860.* Norman: University of Oklahoma Press, 2000.

Smith, Shirlee Anne. "John Stuart." In *Dictionary of Canadian Biography. 1851– 1860, Vol. 7.* Toronto: University of Toronto Press, 1966.

Smyth, David. "James Bird." In *Dictionary of Canadian Biography.* Toronto: University of Toronto Press, 1990.

Smyth, David. "The Struggle for the Piegan Trade: The Saskatchewan versus the Missouri." *Montana, the Magazine of Western History,* 34 no.2 (Spring 1984).2–15.

Smythe, Terry. *Thematic Study of the Fur Trade in the Canadian West, 1670–1870,* Agenda Paper, at *Historic Sites and Monuments Board Meeting.* 1968.

Spry, Irene M. *The Palliser Expedition.* 1963; 2d ed., Calgary: Fifth House, 1995.

Stager, John. *Fur Trading Posts in the Mackenzie Region up to 1850.*Canadian Association of Geographers, B.C. Division. Occasional Paper no. 3.

Steer, Donald N. *Report on Archeological Survey of Methye Portage.* Regina, Saskatchewan: Archaeological Resource Management Program, Heritage Resources Unit. 1971.

Stern, Theodore. *Chiefs and Chief Traders.* Corvallis: Oregon State University Press, 1993.

Stern, Theodore. "Klamath and Modoc." In *Handbook of North American Indians.* Vol. 12 *Plateau,* edited by Deward E. Walker, Jr. Washington: Smithsonian Institution, 1998.

Stewart, William Drummond. *Edward Warren.* Missoula: Mountain Press Publishing Company, 1986.

Sullivan, Maurice S. *The Travels of Jedediah Smith, a Documentary Outline, Including His Journal.* Lincoln: University of Nebraska Press, 1992.

Sunder, John E. *Bill Sublette, Mountain Man, 1840–1865*. Norman: University of Oklahoma Press, 1959.

Sunder, John E. *The Fur Trade on the Upper Missouri, 1840–1865*. Norman: University of Oklahoma Press, 1965.

Sunder, John E. "William Lewis Sublette," *Mountain Men of the Fur Trade*, Vol. 5, edited by LeRoy Hafen, Glendale, CA: Arthur H. Clark Co., 1968.

Swagerty, W. R. "Indian Trade in the Trans-Mississippi West to 1870." In *Handbook of North American Indians*, Vol. 4, *History of Indian-White Relations*, edited by Wilcomb E. Washburn. Washington: Smithsonian Institution, 1988.

Swagerty, W. R. "Marriage and Settlement Patterns of Rocky Mountain Trappers and Traders," Western Historical Quarterly 11, no.2 (April 1980). Western Historical Association :Utah State University. 159–180.

Swagerty, W. R. "Plains Indians Within the Present United States to 1850." In *Handbook of North American Indians Series*, Vol. 13, *Plains*, edited by Raymond J. DeMallie. Washington: Smithsonian Institution, 2001.

Swagerty, W. R. and D. A. Wilson, "Faithful Service under Different Flags: A Socioeconomic Profile of the Columbia District, Hudson's Bay Company and the Upper Missouri Outfit, American Fur Company, 1825–1835." *The Fur Trade Revisited: Sixth North American Fur Trade Conference, Mackinac Island, MI, 1991,* edited by Jennifer S. H. Brown, W. J. Eccles, and Donald P. Heldman. East Lansing/Mackinac Island: Michigan State University Press, 1994, 243–67.

Tabeau, P. A. *Tabeau's Narrative of Loisel's Expedition to the Upper Missouri,* edited by Annie Heloise Abel. Norman: University of Oklahoma Press, 1939.

Talbot, Vivian Linford. *David E. Jackson, Field Captain of the Rocky Mountain Fur Trade.* Center Books Series. Jackson Hole, WY: Jackson Hole Historical Society and Museum, 1996.

Tanner, Helen Hornbeck, ed. *Atlas of Great Lakes Indian History.* Norman: University of Oklahoma Press, 1987.

Tanner, John. *A Narrative of the Captivity and Adventures of John Tanner,* edited by James Edwin. New York: G & C & H Carili, 1830. Reprinted as *Falcon: A Narrative of the Captivity and Adventures of John Tanner.* New York: Penguin, 2003.

Teit James A., "Mythology of the Thompson Indians," The Jessup North Pacific Expedition, *American Museum of Natural History Memoirs,* 1912, 8, part 2: 156.

Teit, James A. *The Shuswap.* Memoir No.4, Part 7. New York: American Museum of Natural History, 1909.

Terrell, John Upton. *Furs by Astor.* New York: Wm. Morrow, 1963.

Terrell, John Upton. *The Navajo, The Past and Present of a Great People.* New York: Harper Perennial, 1970.

Terrell, John Upton, and Donna Terrell. *Indian Women of the Western Morning: Their Life in Early America.* New York: Doubleday, 1974.

Thistle, Paul C. "Indian European Trade Relations in the Lower Saskatchewan River Region to 1840," *Manitoba Studies in Native History, 2* (1986).

Thistle, Paul C. *Indian Trader Relations.* M.A. thesis. University of Manitoba, 1983.

Thompson, Erwin N. *Fort Union Trading Post: Fur Trade Empire on the Upper Missouri.* Williston, ND: Fort Union Association, 1994.

Thwaites, Reuben Gold, ed. *Jesuit Relations and Allied Documents.* 71 vols. Cleveland: Burrows Bros, 1896–1901.

Thwaites, R. G. and Edna Kenton, *Jesuit Relations.* New York: Albert and Charles Boni, 1925.

Thwaites, R. G. ed. *Original Journals of Lewis and Clark Expedition.*

Tikhmenev, P. A. *A History of the Russian American Company,* edited by Richard A. Pierce and Alton S. Donneley. Seattle: University of Washington Press, 1978.

Tobey, Margaret L. "Carrier." In *Handbook of North American Indians Series,* Vol. 6, *Subarctic,* edited by June Helm. Washington: Smithsonian Institution, 1981.

Tolmie, William Fraser. *Physician and Fur Trader.* Vancouver: Mitchell Press Ltd., 1963.

Trentholm, Virginia Cole and Maurine Carley. *The Shoshonie: Sentinels of the Rockies.* Norman: University of Oklahoma Press, 1964.

de Trobriand, Régis. *Journal of Phillip St. Regis: Military Life in Dakota.* Translated and edited by Lucille M. Kane. Lincoln: University of Nebraska, 1982.

Turnbaugh, William A. "Wide-Area Connections in Native North America." *American Indian Culture and Research Journal.* Los Angeles: University of California. vol 1, no.4 (1976).

Turner, Frederick Jackson. "The Significance of the Frontier in American History." In *History, Frontier, and Section: Three Essays,* by Frederick Jackson Turner. Albuquerque: University of New Mexico Press, 1993.

Turner-High, Harry H. *Flathead Indians of Montana.* Menasha, WI: American Anthropological Association, 1937.

Tykal, Jack B. *Etienne Provost: Man of the Mountains.* Liberty, Utah: Eagle's View Publishing Company, 1989.

Vajda, Edward J. "Notes: Eskimo/Aleut." *Asian Studies,* 210. http://pandor.ciiwwwu.edu/vojda/ea215/aleu (accessed March 20, 2008).

Van Alstyne, Richard. "International Rivalries." *Oregon Historical Society,* 46, No.3 (Sept.1945), 202.

Van Kirk, Sylvia. "Thanadelthur." *The Beaver,* (Winter 1973 Outfit 304) 3.

Van Kirk, Sylvia. *Many Tender Ties: Women in Fur-Trade Society, 1670–1870.* Winnipeg: Watson & Dwyer, 1980.

Vajda, Edward J., "Notes: Eskimo/Aleut." *Asian Studies,* 210, http//pandor. ciiwwwu.edu/vojda/ea215/aleu (accessed March 20, 2018).

Vibert, Elizabeth. *Traders Tales.* Norman: University of Oklahoma Press, 1997.

Victor, Frances Fuller. *River of the West.* Missoula, MT: Mountain Press Publishing Company, 2 vols, Classics of the Fur Trade Series, Winfred Blevins, General Editor,1983.

Voelker, Frederick E. "Thomas Eddie." In *The Mountain Men and the Fur Traders of the Far West.* Vol. 1. edited by LeRoy Hafen. Glendale, CA: Arthur H. Clark Co., 1965.

Voget, Fred W. "The Crows." In *Handbook of North American Indians Series,* Vol.13, *Plains,* edited by Raymond J. DeMallie. Washington: Smithsonian Institution, 2001.

Voorhis, Ernest. *Historic Forts and Trading Posts of the French Regime, and of the English Fur Trading Companies.* Ottawa: Department of the Interior, 1930.

Waldman, Carl. *Atlas of the North American Indians.* New York: Facts On File Publication, 1988.

Wallace, William S. "Antoine Robidoux," In *The Mountain Men and The Fur Traders of The Far Wes.,* Vol. 4. edited by LeRoy Hafen. Glendale, CA: Arthur H. Clark Co., 1966.

Walker, Deward E. Jr., and Roderick Sprague. "History until 1846." In *Handbook of North American Indians,* Vol. 12, *Plateau,* edited by Deward Walker. Washington: Smithsonian Institution Press, 1998.

Walker, Deward. "Introduction." In *Handbook of North American Indians.* Vol. 12, *Plateau,* edited by Deward E. Walker, Jr. Washington: Gales & Seaton, 1998.

Warner, Ted J. "Peter Skene Ogden." In *The Mountain Men and The Fur Traders of The Far West,* Vol. 3, edited by LeRoy Hafen. Glendale, CA: Arthur H. Clark Co., 1966.

Weber, David J. "Louis Robidoux." In *The Mountain Men and the Fur Traders of the Far West,* Vol. 8, edited by LeRoy Hafen. Glendale, CA: Arthur H. Clark Co., 1971.

Weber, David J. *The Mexican Frontier: The American Southwest under Mexico,1821-1846.* Albuquerque: University of New Mexico Press, 1982.

Weber, David J. "Sylvestre S. Pratte" In *The Mountain Men and the Fur Traders of the Far West,* Vol. 6. edited by LeRoy Hafen. Glendale, CA: Arthur H. Clark Co. 1968.

Weber, David J. *The Taos Trappers: The Fur Trade in the Far Southwest, 1540–1846.* Norman: University of Oklahoma Press, 1982.

Wells, Merle. "Finan McDonald." In *The Mountain Men and The Fur Traders of The Far West,* Vol. 5, edited by LeRoy Hafen. Glendale, CA: Arthur H. Clark Co., 1968.

White, Bruce M. *Give Us a Little Milk: Economics and Ceremony in the Ojibway Fur Trade.* M.A. thesis, McGill University, 1985.

White, Richard. *The Middle Ground, Indians, Empires, and Republics in the Great Lakes Region, 1650–1815.* Cambridge: Cambridge University Press Whitford, William Clark. "History of Education." In *Collections of the State Historical Society of Wisconsin,* Vol. 5. 1868; reprinted Madison: State Historical Society of Wisconsin 1907.

Williams, Glyndwr, ed. *Captain Cook's Voyages, 1768–1779,* London: Folio Society, 1997, 406–425.

Wilson, Gilbert L. "The Horse and Dog in Hidatsa Culture, 1924." In *Anthropological Papers, American Museum of Natural History.* 15:125–311,

Wishart, David J. *The Fur Trade of the American West, 1807–1840: a Geographical Synthesis.* Lincoln, University of Nebraska Press, 1979.

Wissler, Clark. *Indians of the United States.* New York: Doubleday and Company, 1966.

Wood, W. Raymond; and Thomas D. Thiessen, eds. *Early Fur Trade on the Northern Plains: Canadian Traders Among the Mandan and Hidatsa Indians, 1738–1818.* Norman: University of Oklahoma Press, 1985.

Wrangell, Ferdinand P. *Russian America, Statistical and Ethnographic Information,* translated from the German edition of 1839 by Mary Sadouski. Kingston, Ontario: The Limestone Press, 1980.

Wyatt, David. "Thompson." In *Handbook of North American Indians Series. Plateau,* Vol. 12, edited by Deward E. Walker Jr. Washington: Smithsonian Institution, 1998.

Wyeth, Nathaniel J., *The Journals of Captain Nathaniel J. Wyeth's Expedition to the Oregon Country, 1831–1836,* edited by Don Johnson. Fairfield, WA: Ye Olde Galleon Press, 1984.

Yerbury, J. C. *The Subarctic Indians and the Fur Trade, 1680–1860.* Vancouver: University of British Columbia Press, 1986.

INDEX